Christian dualist heresies in the Byzantine world *c.* 650–*c.* 1450

MANCHESTER
UNIVERSITY PRESS

Manchester Medieval Sources Series

series advisers Rosemary Horrox and Janet L. Nelson

This series aims to meet a growing need amongst students and teachers of medieval history for translations of key sources that are directly usable in students' own work. It provides texts central to medieval studies courses and focuses upon the diverse cultural and social as well as political conditions that affected the functioning of all levels of medieval society. The basic premise of the new series is that translations must be accompanied by sufficient introductory and explanatory material and each volume therefore includes a comprehensive guide to the sources' interpretation, including discussion of critical linguistic problems and an assessment of the most recent research on the topics being covered.

already published in the series

J.A. Boyle *Genghis Khan: history of the world conqueror*

John Edwards *The Jews in Western Europe, 1400–1600*

Paul Fouracre and Richard A. Gerberding *Late Merovingian France*

Chris Given-Wilson *Chronicles of the Revolution, 1397–1400: the reign of Richard II*

P.J.P. Goldberg *Women in England, c. 1275–1525*

Rosemary Horrox *The Black Death*

Janet L. Nelson *The Annals of St-Bertin: ninth-century histories, volume I*

Timothy Reuter *The Annals of Fulda: ninth-century histories, volume II*

R.N. Swanson *Catholic England: faith, religion and observance before the Reformation*

Jennifer Ward *Women of the English nobility and gentry, 1066–1500*

forthcoming titles in the series will include

Mark Bailey *English manorial records, c. 1180–1520*

Ross Balzaretti *North Italian histories, AD 800–1100*

Brenda Bolton *Innocent III*

Richard Fletcher and Simon Barton *El Cid and the Spanish Conquest*

Judith Jesch and Bridget Morris *The Viking Age*

Graham A. Loud and Themas Wiedemann *The history of the tyrants of Sicily by 'Hugo Falcandus', 1153–69*

Simon Lloyd *The impact of the crusades: the experience of England, 1095–1274*

Alison McHardy *The early reign of Richard II*

Edward Powell *Crime, law and society in late medieval England*

Ian Robinson *The Pontificate of Gregory VII*

Richard Smith *Sources for the population history of England, 1000–1540*

Elisabeth van Houts *The Normans in Europe*

CHRISTIAN DUALIST HERESIES IN THE BYZANTINE WORLD
c. 650–*c.* 1450

selected sources translated and annotated
by Janet Hamilton *and* Bernard Hamilton

assistance with the translation of Old Slavonic texts
by Yuri Stoyanov

Manchester University Press
Manchester and New York

distributed exclusively in the USA by St. Martin's Press

Copyright © Janet Hamilton and Bernard Hamilton 1998
Translation of Old Slavonic texts © Yuri Stoyanov 1998

Published by Manchester University Press
Oxford Road, Manchester M13 9NR, UK
and Room 400, 175 Fifth Avenue, New York, NY 10010, USA

Distributed exclusively in the USA by
St. Martin's Press, Inc., 175 Fifth Avenue, New York, NY 10010, USA

Distributed exclusively in Canada by
UBC Press, University of British Columbia, 6344 Memorial Road, Vancouver, BC, Canada V6T 1Z2

British Library Cataloguing-in-Publication Data
A catalogue record for this book is available from the British Library

Library of Congress Cataloging-in-Publication Data

Christian dualist heresies in the Byzantine world, *c.* 650–*c.* 1450; selected sources / translated and annotated by Janet Hamilton and Bernard Hamilton; assistance with the translation of Old Slavonic texts by Yuri Stoyanov.
    p.   cm. – (Manchester medieval sources series)
Includes index.
    ISBN 0-7190-4764-1, – ISBN 0-7190-4765-X (pbk.)
    1. Dualism (Religion) – Christianity – History of doctrines – Sources. 2. Heresies, Christian – History – Middle Ages, 600–1500 – Sources. 3. Heresies, Christian – Byzantine Empire – History – Sources. I. Hamilton, Janet. II. Hamilton, Bernard, 1962. III. Stoyanov, Yuri, 1961– . IV. Series.
BT 1318.C48   1998
273'.6 – dc21   97-25001

ISBN 0 7190 4764 1 *hardback*
      0 7190 4765 X *paperback*

First published 1998

02 01 00 99 98   10 9 8 7 6 5 4 3 2 1

Typeset in Baskerville MT
by Best-set Typesetter Ltd., Hong Kong
Printed in Great Britain
by Biddles Ltd, Guildford and King's Lynn

CONTENTS

Foreword   *page* vii
Preface   ix
List of abbreviations   xiii
Maps   xiv
Gazeteer   xvi

Historical introduction   1

1. Paulician population transfers under Constantine V (741–75)   57
2. The empress Irene (780–802) and the Paulicians   58
3. Alleged Paulicians in Constantinople in the early ninth century   59
4. Theodore of Studium (d. 826) opposes the death penalty for heresy   60
5. St Macarius of Pelecete converts a Paulician in prison   61
6. Renewed persecution of the Paulicians in Asia Minor and the matyrs of Amorium   62
7. Peter of Sicily's *History of the Paulicians* (870)   65
8. Peter the Higoumenos: an abridgement of Peter of Sicily   92
9. The death of the Paulician leader Chrysocheir (*c.* 878)   96
10. Theophylact Lecapenus (933–56) writes to Tsar Peter of Bulgaria about Bogomils   98
11. Abjuration formulae (tenth century) for Paulician converts to orthodoxy   102
12. Theodore, metropolitan of Nicaea (956–), writes about Paulicians in Euchaita   110
13. St Paul of Latrus (d. 955/6) converts Paulicians near Miletus   113
14. John I Tzimisces (969–76) settles Paulicians at Philippopolis   114
15. The discourse of the priest Cosmas against Bogomils (after 972)   114
16. The *Synodikon of Orthodoxy*: clauses about Bogomils   134
17. Paulicians in eleventh-century southern Italy   139
18. St Lazarus the wonder-worker converts Paulicians near Ephesus (before 1054)   141
19. Euthymius of the Periblepton condemns Bogomils (*c.* 1045)   142
20. The Paulicians of Philippopolis ally with the Patzinaks (*c.* 1050)   164
21. A letter of the patriarch Cosmas (1075–81) against the Bogomils   165
22. Alexius Comnenus (1081–1118) and the Paulicians   166
23. Extracts from Euthymius Zigabenus' *Dogmatic Panoply* against the Paulicians and the Messalians   171
24. Anna Comnena's account of the trial of the Bogomil Basil (*c.* 1098)   175
25. Extracts from Euthymius Zigabenus' *Dogmatic Panoply* against the Bogomils   180

CONTENTS

26. Abjuration formula and form of reception into the Church for Bogomil converts — 207
27. A sermon against the Bogomils for the Sunday of All Saints (*c.* 1107) — 210
28. The posthumous trial of Constantine Chrysomallus for heresy (1140) — 212
29. The Patriarch Michael II (1143–46) orders the burning of Bogomils — 215
30. Two Cappadocian bishops are condemned for Bogomilism (1143) — 215
31. The monk Niphon is condemned for Bogomilism (1144) — 219
32. The Patriarch Cosmas (1146–47) is deposed for favouring Bogomils — 222
33. St Hilarion of Moglena (1136–64) converts Bogomils in his diocese — 225
34. An Anti-Bogomil work, possibly by Nicholas of Methone — 227
35. Popular beliefs about Bogomilism recounted by George Tornices (1154) — 233
36. Hugh Eteriano (a Pisan) writes a treatise against the Bogomils of Constantinople (*c.* 1165–80) — 234
37. The mission of *papa* Nicetas of Constantinople to the West (*c.* 1170) — 250
38. The *Secret Book* brought from Bulgaria (*c.* 1190) — 253
39. Pope Innocent III and the Bogomils of Bosnia (1198–1203) — 254
40. The Fourth Crusade and the Paulicians of Philippopolis (1205) — 259
41. The *Synodikon* of Tsar Boril against the Bogomils (1211) — 260
42. Pope Honorius III and the Balkan pope of the heretics (1221–23) — 263
43. Pope Gregory IX (1227–41) urges the king of Hungary to crusade against the Bogomils — 265
44. The Patriarch Germanus II (1222–40) writes and preaches against Bogomils — 267
45. An Italian inquisitor's view of Bogomilism (*c.* 1250) — 275
46. Evidence of Bogomilism in a liturgical commentary (date unknown) — 276
47. Pope John XXII alleges that Cathars are fleeing to Bosnia (1325) — 276
48. St Gregory Palamas (1296–1359) and the Bogomils — 278
49. St Theodosius of Trnovo (*c.* 1350) legislates against Bogomils — 282
50. Symeon, archbishop of Thessalonica, preaches against Bogomils (before 1429) — 286

Appendix 1. The *Ritual* of Radoslav the Christian — 289
Appendix 2. Armenian sources and the Paulicians — 292

Glossary — 298
Bibliography — 304
Index — 319

FOREWORD

Religious dualism, founded on belief in two cosmic principles, has a more venerable, varied and influential history than adherents of the major world religions have usually acknowledged. In recent decades, dualist belief and organization in the Byzantine world has attracted growing interest from historians and theologians alike. Documented by rich but difficult and diverse materials, it has generally been studied piecemeal; and very little has been available in English. Janet and Bernard Hamilton in this path-breaking work present a goodly selection of this evidence, some of it never previously published. The introduction supplies the historical context, and a comprehensive commentary is supplied for each text. In line with the goals of the Manchester Medieval Sources series, the Hamiltons thus make important material accessible to a wider audience than ever before. They allow English-speaking students to grasp for the first time the scale and significance of dualism in the eastern Mediterranean and the Balkans: for some eight hundred years, varieties of dualist religion existed and flourished, some not too far from orthodoxy, others quite distant, mostly within the lands ruled from Constantinople but sometimes beyond Byzantine frontiers. Eastern dualism thus amply deserves study in itself. Equally, it deserves attention from all those interested in western medieval heresy; for the Hamiltons also show that contacts between eastern and western dualists were close, and that western Catharism was strongly influenced from the Balkans. This book transforms our understanding of religious traditions throughout the medieval Christian world, showing their interconnectedness as well as their differences.

Janet L. Nelson, King's College London

To Sarah and Alice

PREFACE

This book is about the rise of Christian dualism and its influence in the Byzantine world. Before the seventh century there had been dualist religions like Gnosticism and Manichaeism which contained Christian elements, but they were theosophical movements, based on myths which were not Christian, although they could be interpreted in a Christian sense. The Christian dualism preached by Constantine of Mananalis in the mid-seventh century was truly Christian because it was based on the authority of the New Testament alone. This way of understanding Christianity later took various forms, and proved attractive to large numbers of people for some 800 years. In the central Middle Ages it spread to Western Europe, where its adherents were known as Cathars (or in Italy as Patarenes).

Ever since the publication of Sir Steven Runciman's *The Medieval Manichee* in 1947 and Sir Dmitri Obolensky's *The Bogomils* in 1948 coherent accounts of eastern Christian dualism have been available in English. Indeed, we trace our own initial interest in this field to the work of these two scholars to whom we should like to express our thanks. But very few of the sources for the history of the Paulicians and Bogomils have been translated into English. Although rather more have been translated into French, thanks to the efforts of scholars at the Centre de Recherche d'Histoire et Civilisation de Byzance in Paris, this work is found in journals which are not widely available in British academic libraries, while it is a sad truth that few students reading history degrees in British universities have a good enough knowledge of French to be willing to read these texts.

So the situation has arisen that many students become interested in the history of Catharism, the most important sources for which are available in English translation in W.L. Wakefield and A.P. Evans, *Heresies of the High Middle Ages*, but when they wish to learn more about its origins in the Byzantine world they are frustrated by their inability to read the sources. This has certainly been our experience. Bernard Hamilton has been teaching a course on Cathar History to third-year undergraduates for more than twenty-five years, and in order to cope with this problem Janet Hamilton has translated some of the key texts about Bogomilism for the use of his students. It was the success of this experiment which has led us to undertake the present work in the hope that colleagues throughout the English-speaking world, faced with similar problems, may find this collection of translated sources helpful.

The chronological limits of this book have been determined by the material. Christian dualism began with Constantine of Mananalis who lived in the reign of Constans II (641–68), and the Byzantine Empire ended with the conquest of Constantinople by the Sultan Mehmet II in 1453. Although it is possible and

PREFACE

indeed likely that Christian dualist movements persisted after that date, not enough work has yet been done on the early Ottoman records to make it possible to reach any firm conclusions about this. The geographical limits of the work have been less easy to determine. We have defined them as those of the Byzantine world rather than of the Byzantine Empire, because the political frontiers of that Empire fluctuated a great deal in the 800 years with which we are concerned, whereas the area affected by Byzantine civilization remained relatively constant. The Byzantine world comprised those lands which were influenced by the religion and culture of Orthodox Byzantium, and included the whole of Greece and of the Balkans south of the Danube, and extended eastwards through Anatolia to the Christian states of the Caucasus and Caspian regions. In addition, we have included a brief section on the Bogomil missions to Western Europe which influenced the way in which the Cathar churches there developed, but otherwise we have only used Western sources when they provide direct information about Byzantine dualism.

There are two areas of Christian dualism which we have decided not to deal with in any detail. The first is the Tondrakian movement in Armenia, which appears to us to be cognate with, but not identical to, Paulicianism. The Tondrakians need to be interpreted in the context of Armenian history of the ninth to twelfth centuries but we lack the linguistic expertise to make such a study. We have therefore merely pointed out in an Appendix what we consider to be the main problems relating to this movement. The second area which we have only dealt with in a limited way is Bosnia, which though on the frontiers of the Byzantine world was not part of it. Ecclesiastically it was a diocese of the Western Church, and politically the kings of Hungary claimed suzerainty over it. But Bosnia was infiltrated by Bogomil missions in the twelfth century and developed links with the Cathar churches of Italy, and so we have included a selection of sources dealing with the early history of dualism there. We have not attempted to include the later history of Bosnian dualism because the sources are too prolific: the papal archives from the thirteenth century onwards contain a great deal of material relating to Bosnia which would need to be reviewed if this highly controversial subject were to be satisfactorily discussed, and such treatment would not be compatible with our word limit.

All but one of the texts we have translated are already in print. The exception is the Treatise against the Patarenes of Constantinople by Hugh Eteriano [36]. Our translation is based on a collation of the two manuscripts known to us, one in the Biblioteca Colombina at Seville, and the other in the Bodleian Library at Oxford. We wish to thank both libraries for supplying us with photocopies of these manuscripts and allowing us to use them, and we are preparing an edition of the Latin text for publication in the near future.

It would not have been possible for us to produce satisfactory translations of the Old Slavonic texts without the help of Yuri Stoyanov, who has collated our translations with the most recent editions of the texts and has amended them where necessary. We are very grateful to him for the time and assistance which he has so readily given to us.

PREFACE

A special word of thanks is due to Janet Nelson who encouraged us to write this book and has made many valuable suggestions about the ways in which the text might be improved. Our thanks also to Rosemary Horrox who read the final draft and gave us useful advice about it. In the years which we have spent collecting and writing this material we have received help about specific points from a number of friends and we should particularly like to mention George Every, Bob Moore, Graham Loud and Mary Cunningham-Curran. Bernard Hamilton would like to express his special thanks to Professor J.M. Hussey who, although she has not been directly involved in this work, may nevertheless in his case be regarded as its ultimate inspirer, as he first introduced him to the Byzantine world when he was an undergraduate.

Our work has been made possible by the cooperation of the staff of those libraries in which we have worked, and we should therefore like to express our thanks to the following institutions: the British Library, the Warburg Institute of the University of London, the London Library and Dr Williams's Library. But our thanks are specially due to the staff of the Library of the University of Nottingham, where most of our work has been done, and particularly to those who have dealt with our many requests for inter-library loans.

We should like to say a special word of thanks to the efficient and genial staff of Manchester University Press who have given us every encouragement and support, in particular to Vanessa Graham, Carolyn Hand and Gemma Marren; and also to Richard Wilson who did a remarkable job in standardizing a manuscript which contained many unintended variant readings. We of course take full responsibility for any inconsistencies which remain.

The writing of books is an activity which impinges, seldom benevolently, on one's family and friends. We are grateful to all our friends and kin for their support, but we would particularly like to thank our daughters, Sarah and Alice, for all their practical help and good humour. We have dedicated this book affectionately to them.

Bernard and Janet Hamilton, Nottingham

ABBREVIATIONS

AC	Anna Comnena
AFP	*Archivum Fratrum Praedicatorum*
CICO III	Pontificia Commissio ad redigendum codicem iuris canonici Orientalis, *Fontes. Series III*
CMH	*Cambridge Medieval History*
CSHB	*Corpus scriptorum historiae byzantinae*
DOP	*Dumbarton Oaks Papers*
DTC	*Dictionnaire de Théologie Catholique*
EP	Euthymius of the Periblepton
EZ	Euthymius Zigabenus
Mansi	G.D. Mansi, *Sacrorum Conciliorum nova et amplissima Collectio*
MGH SS	*Monumenta Germaniae Historica Scriptores*
NTA	W. Schneemelcher, ed. and R.McL. Wilson, tr., *New Testament Apocrypha* (Lutterworth Press, London, 1965), 2 vols.
OCP	*Orientalia Christiana Periodica*
PG	J.P. Migne, ed., *Patrologia Graeca*
PH	Peter Higoumenos
PL	J.P. Migne, ed., *Patrologia Latina*
PS	Peter of Sicily
REB	*Revue des études byzantines*
RP	*Les régestes des Actes du Patriarcat de Constantinople*, ed. V. Grumel, V. Laurent, J. Darrouzès
T & M	*Travaux et Mémoires*

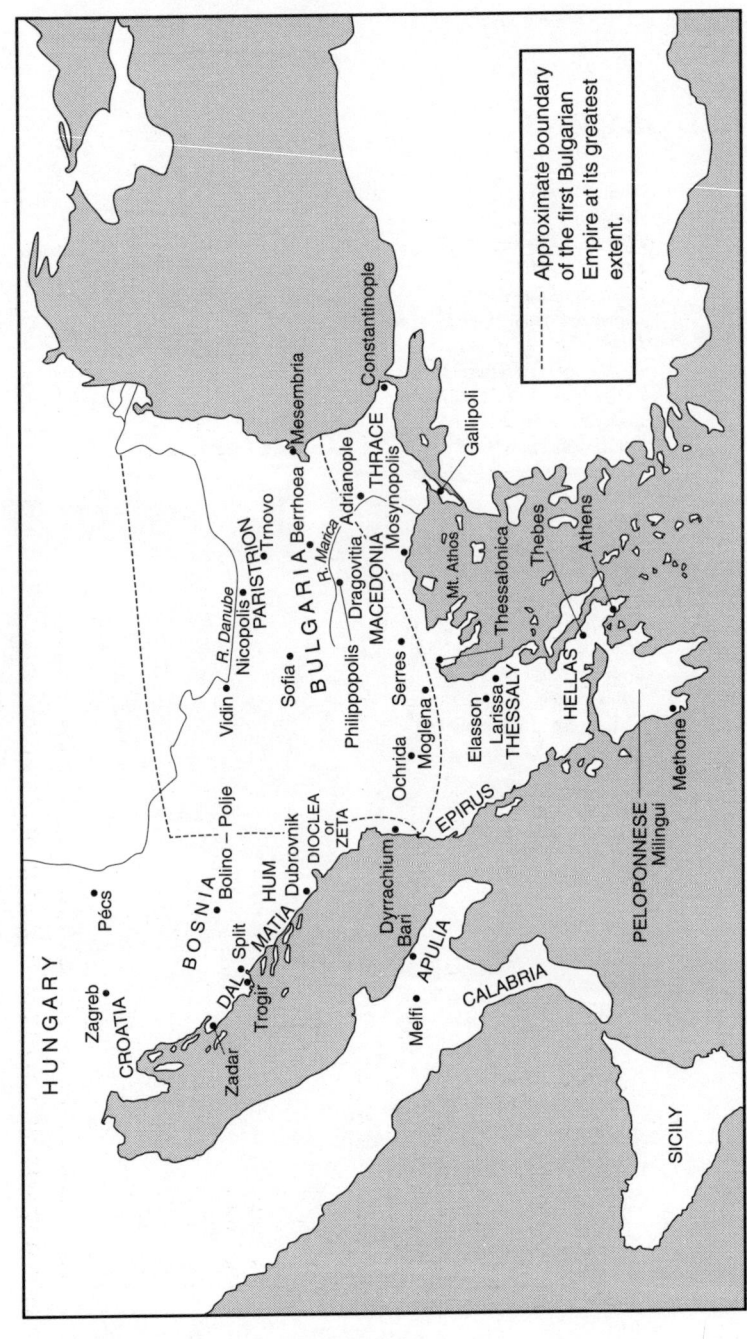

THE BYZANTINE LANDS 1: EUROPE

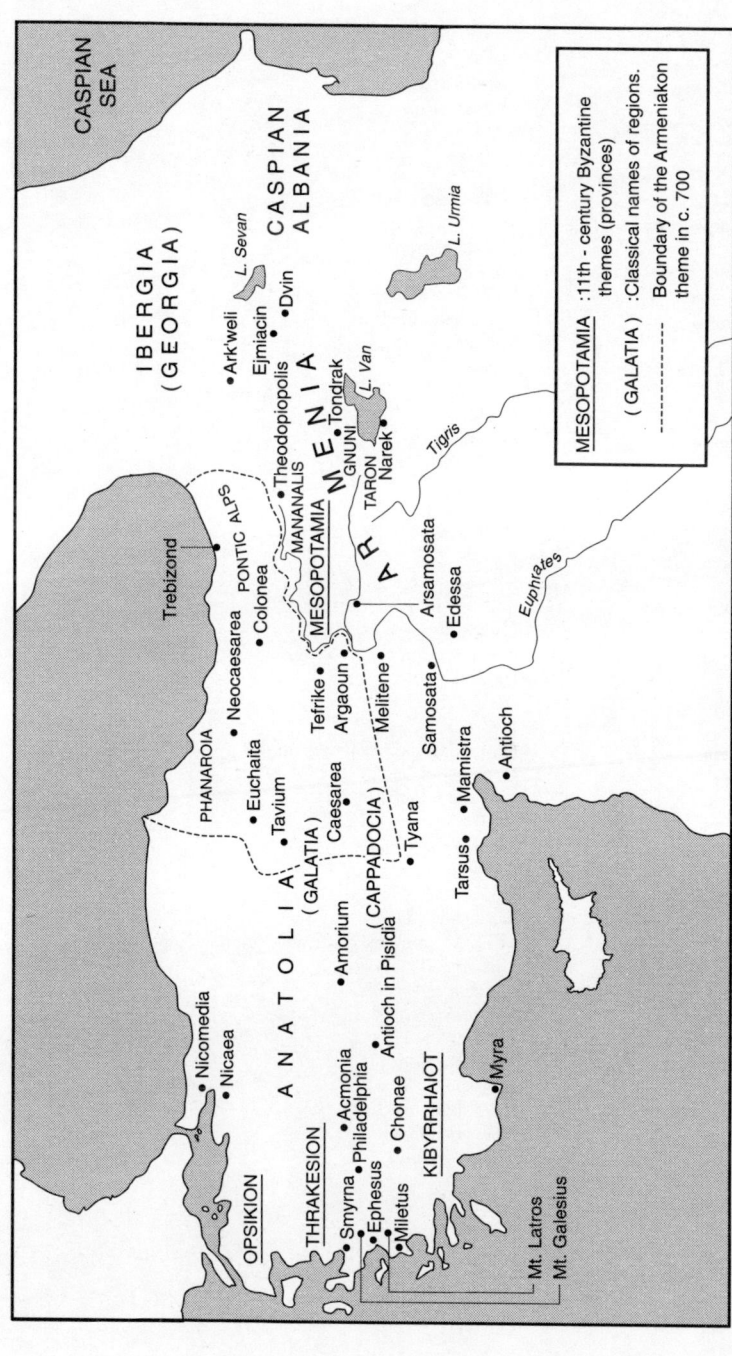

THE BYZANTINE LANDS 2: THE ASIATIC LANDS

GAZETEER

Medieval name
(as it appears on the map)

Modern name

Acmonia	Ahat Keui
Adrianople	Edirne
Amorium	Now abandoned
Antioch	Antakya
Antioch in Pisidia	Yalvach
Argaoun	Argovan
Ark'weli	Unchanged
Arsamosata	Shimshat
Athens	Unchanged
Bari	Unchanged
Berrhoea	Stara Zagora
Bolino-Polje	Unchanged
Caesarea	Kayseri
Chonae	Khonaz
Colonea	Šebin Karahisar
Constantinople	Istanbul
Dubrovnik	Unchanged (formerly Ragusa)
Dvin	Dabil
Dyrrachium	Durrës
Edessa	Urfa
Ejmiacin	Sometimes spelt Echmiadzin
Elasson	Unchanged
Ephesus	Now abandoned
Euchaita	Avkhat
Mt. Galesios	Alaman Dağ
Gallipoli	Gelibolu
Larissa	Larisa
Mt. Latros	Beş Parmak Dağ
Mamistra	Misis (Mopsuestia: classical)
Melfi	Unchanged
Melitene	Malatya
Methone	Methoni
Mesembria	Nesebar
Miletus	Now abandoned
Moglena	Meglena
Mosynopolis	Now abandoned
Myra	Now abandoned
Neocaesarea	Niksar
Nicaea	Iznik
Nicomedia	Izmit
Nicopolis	Nikopol
Ochrida	Ohrid
Pécs	Unchanged
Philadelphia	Alashehir
Philippopolis	Plovdiv

GAZETEER

Samosata	Samsat
Serres	Serrai
Smyrna	Izmir
Sofia	Unchanged (Sardica, classical)
Split	Unchanged
Tarsus	Unchanged
Tavium	Precise location uncertain
Tefrice	Divrigi
Thessalonica	Salonika
Thebes	Thevai
Theodosiopolis	Erzerum
Tondrak	Near Malazgirt
Trebizond	Trabzon
Trnovo	Unchanged
Trogir	Unchanged
Tyana	Now abandoned
Vidin	Unchanged
Zadar	Unchanged
Zagreb	Unchanged

HISTORICAL INTRODUCTION

THE ORIGINS OF CHRISTIAN DUALISM

Constantine of Mananalis, who was born in the reign of Constans II (641–68), was considered by Byzantine theologians to be the founder of Christian dualism in the sense that, while teaching that the material universe was not the creation of the Good God but of an autonomous evil principle, he would only accept the canonical Christian scriptures, or some part of them, as authoritative.[1] Christian dualism was to form a very important dissenting tradition in the Orthodox world of Byzantium for the next 800 years, and in the twelfth and thirteenth centuries was to spread to western Europe, where its adherents were known as Cathars.

But the Byzantine scholars who wrote about heresy thought that Constantine of Mananalis was only pretending to teach a new form of belief. For the most part they agreed with the author of Ecclesiastes that 'there is no new thing under the sun' (Eccles 1.9). When confronted with some new heretical movement their instinctive response was to equate it with some more ancient sect with which it shared certain characteristics. This can cause problems for the modern student, because the Orthodox theologians sometimes wrongly assumed that the new heretics shared all the beliefs and practices of the old sectarians with whom they had often arbitrarily identified them. Byzantine writers working in this tradition were convinced that all Christian dualists were Manichaeans in disguise, and so persuasive have their arguments proved that to this day those Christian dualists are sometimes referred to as neo-Manichaeans.

Nevertheless, the comparison is misleading, for although the Manichaeans had been dualist, they had not been Christian. Mani (216–77) was a Persian nobleman who founded a new, syncretistic mystery religion: his dualist cosmology was Zoroastrian; his belief in the reincarnation of beings in the ceaseless wheel of existence was Mahayana Buddhist; while his teaching about salvation through knowledge was derived from Gnostic Christianity. He taught that the entire physical creation was evil in its nature, apart from spiritual elements which were trapped in it, notably the souls of living creatures which were subject to

---

1 See below, p. 8.

transmigration. He offered his followers deliverance at death from reincarnation in this material world, provided that they were initiated into his faith and led lives of great austerity. Though his religion proved attractive to some Christians, and was designed to be so, Mani did not regard the Christian scriptures as authoritative, but wrote a number of books himself which were treated by his followers as the sacred texts of their faith.[2]

Manichaeism spread into the Roman Empire in the late third century and persisted there until it was extirpated by the persecution of the Emperor Justinian (527–65).[3] In Iraq and Persia the movement survived until the tenth century and also spread into central Asia and China.[4] But although Manichaeism survived as a living faith in the period with which we are concerned in this book and may even on occasion indirectly have influenced the movements we are describing, the Christian dualists were not 'new Manichaeans' in any but a typological sense, and they were always willing to anathematize Mani and his followers.

It is also sometimes claimed that some Christian dualists, notably the Bogomils, were really Gnostics.[5] Gnosticism, which developed at about the same time as Christianity, encompassed a wide variety of schools of thought, all of which shared a common cosmology: belief in the existence of a perfect spiritual world, coupled with a conviction that the universe in which we live is imperfect because it has come into being as the result of a cosmic accident. All Gnostics believed that the deliverance of the spiritual part of man from this flawed world was dependent on *gnosis*, the knowledge of the truth about the human condition.[6] Christian Gnostics interpreted the Old and New Testaments in accordance with their cosmological premises, and claimed that they had received the esoteric teaching of Christ which unlocked the mysteries of the sacred writings, but which was concealed from ordinary Christians belonging to the Great Church.[7]

There is no evidence known to us of organized Gnostic groups surviving in the Byzantine world after the sixth century, so they are unlikely to have had any direct influence on the Christian dualists, but they had left

---

2 For further reading about the Manichaeans see Lieu, *Manichaeism in the later Roman empire and medieval China*; Puech, *Le Manichaeism*; Widengren, *Mani and Manichaeism*.
3 Lieu *Manichaeism in the later Roman empire and medieval China*, pp. 168–75.
4 *Ibid.*, pp. 78–85, 178–219.
5 E.g. Söderberg, *La religion des Cathares*.
6 For further reading about the Gnostics see Filoramo, *A history of Gnosticism*; Rudolph, *Gnosis*.
7 *The Nag Hammadi library in English*.

many writings, often attributed to Old and New Testament figures to enhance their authority. Many of these works were preserved in Byzantine libraries, and some of them did later became known to those dualist groups.

The only Gnostics who may have survived into the age of Christian dualism were the Marcionites. Marcion (d. *c.* 160) was concerned with the problem, which has troubled many Christians through the ages, of the contrast between the God of the Old Testament and the God revealed by Jesus Christ. He taught that the creator of this universe was the God of the Old Testament and a God of Justice who treated his creation harshly. The God of the New Testament, who is the God of Love, was extraneous to this creation, but, having become aware of the plight of men living here, sent his Son Jesus Christ to rescue them.[8] Marcion founded an episcopal church which may have survived in Asia Minor into the seventh century,[9] but there is no evidence that it influenced the Christian dualists. Indeed, the differences between Marcionism and later dualist movements like Paulicianism and Bogomilism are greater than the rather superficial similarities between them.

The Christian dualists of the Middle Ages were not the spiritual descendants of the Gnostics, even though they read some Gnostic books, for Christian Gnosticism was not so much an alternative version of Christianity as a theosophical movement presenting a quite different view of the universe, while using a largely Christian vocabulary. Nor were they new Manichaeans as the Orthodox claimed, for Manichaeism was a religion in which Jesus did not have a unique role, while to the Christian dualists he was the only saviour, just as he was to the Orthodox. The Christian dualists were not an alien graft on a Christian stock, but dissenters who had broken away from the Orthodox Church and interpreted the Christian faith in an exceptionally radical way.

This new heresy came into being in the second half of the seventh century, which was a time of great change throughout the Near East. The Arab followers of the prophet Muhammad in the century following his death in 632 absorbed the Persian Empire, conquered the Byzantine provinces on the southern shores of the Mediterranean from Cilicia to Mauretania, and established a new Islamic state which stretched from

---

8 For a brief study of Marcion see the introduction to Evans, ed. and tr., *Tertulliani adversus Marcionem*, I, pp. ix–xxiii.
9 Jarry, 'Hérésies et factions à Constantinople du Ve au VIe siècle', pp. 348–71.

CHRISTIAN DUALIST HERESIES

the foothills of the Pyrenees to the Indus valley. Thereafter the eastern frontier of the Byzantine Empire ran from the Mediterranean coast west of the Taurus Mountains to the Black Sea coast east of Trebizond. As a result of these huge territorial losses, the Byzantine Empire became almost coterminous with the Patriarchate of Constantinople, and consequently the fortunes of the Byzantine state became more closely identified with those of the Orthodox Church.[10] Until the eleventh century the Byzantine Church and the Catholic Church of the West formed a single communion: the differences between them were largely cultural.[11]

The Orthodox Church claimed the right to define heresy and to excommunicate those heretics who would not be reconciled, and the Byzantine emperor claimed the right to punish those whom the Church labelled heretics.[12] When Justinian I (527–65) systematized the Roman law code he equated heresy with treason, and made both capital offences. His legislation against the Manichaeans was particularly harsh: 'We decree that those who profess the pernicious error of the Manichaeans shall have no legal right or official permission to live in any place in our republic [*sic*] and that if they shall have come there or been found there they shall undergo capital punishment.'[13] This law was later invoked against Christian dualists whom the Orthodox authorities believed to be Manichaeans. They viewed them with particular detestation because they really did suppose that they were not Christian at all, but only claimed to be so in order to infiltrate and ultimately destroy the Orthodox Church.

Christian dualism is first found in Armenia. Armenians are justifiably proud that theirs was the first state to accept Christianity under Tiridates III (d. 314). In the fifth century the Bible and the service books were translated into Armenian, and the Armenian Church became autonomous under a Catholicus. In 451 a rift developed between the Armenian and Byzantine Churches because the Armenians refused to recognize the Fourth general Council of Chalcedon at which they had not been represented.[14] Nevertheless, a schism was averted for many centuries. Armenians who migrated to the Byzantine Empire accepted the canonical authority of Greek bishops, while conversely the Byzantines did not

---

10 Whittow, *The making of Orthodox Byzantium*, pp. 38–95.
11 Every, *The Byzantine patriarchate*.
12 On the principles underlying Byzantine canon law see A. Schmink in the *Oxford Dictionary of Byzantium*, ed. A. Kazhdan, I, pp. 372–4.
13 *Cod.Iur. Civ.* I, 5, 12, 2–3, ed. P. Kreuger, *Corpus Iuris Civilis* II, p. 53.
14 Tournebize, *Histoire politique et religieuse de l'Arménie*, pp. 86–93.

HISTORICAL INTRODUCTION

attempt to appoint a rival Greek hierarchy in Armenian lands when they established political control there.[15] Despite this appearance of good will considerable tensions existed between the two confessions. The Council *in Trullo* of 691–92, which carried out a wide-reaching review of Byzantine canon law, was critical of certain Armenian practices,[16] and Byzantine churchmen in general clearly regarded Armenians with some misgivings, as though their orthodoxy was suspect.

Since the late fourth century Armenia had been partitioned between the empires of Rome and Persia, but the Arabs began raiding Byzantine Armenia in 640, and despite a spirited opposition had conquered it by 661.[17] Even before the Arab invasions there had been some Armenian immigration into the Greek lands of Byzantium, but after 640 this became much greater. Many of the refugees settled in an arc of territory stretching from Trebizond to Caesarea, which came to be called the Armeniakon theme.[18] Attempts to enforce religious conformity on these immigrants caused some of them to return to Armenia, where the new Islamic rulers were more tolerant of their traditional faith.[19] This was the context in which the Paulician movement evolved.

THE PAULICIANS

Sources and beliefs

All the sources for the study of Paulicianism were written by their religious opponents, apart from some extracts from the letters of their leader Sergius, which are quoted by Peter of Sicily, and some statements made by Paulicians which are recorded in other Orthodox sources. This is a familiar problem to medieval historians dealing with dissenting movements. Most of what we know about the Paulicians comes from Greek sources. Arab writers have little to say about them except in the ninth century when they were briefly a political force, while the Armenian sources are not very helpful about the early history of the movement.[20]

---

15 This system only ended in the reign of the Catholicus Khatchik I (971–92); Every, *Byzantine Patriarchate*, p. 72, n. 3.
16 *Canones Trullani sive Quinisextae Synodi*, nos. xxxii, xxxiii, lvi, xcix, in Mansi, XI, 955–9, 969–70, 985–6.
17 Laurent, *L'Arménie entre Byzance et l'Islam*, p. 90, n. 1.
18 Theme (from *thema*, 'army') was the Byzantine name for a province. See map.
19 Laurent, *L'Arménie entre Byzance et l'Islam*, p. 198, note.
20 See Appendix 2.

CHRISTIAN DUALIST HERESIES

The Greek sources have been edited by a group of scholars at the Centre de Recherche d'Histoire et Civilisation Byzantines at Paris, on whose editions of the Greek texts our translations are based. There are three principal texts: the *History of the Manichaeans who are also called Paulicians* of Peter of Sicily; the *Epitome about the Paulicians who are also the Manichaeans* of Peter the Abbot; and *The Abridged Account of the recent reappearance of Manichaeans* by Photius, Patriarch of Constantinople (d. *c.* 893). Peter of Sicily's work survives only in a single eleventh-century copy [7], in which he is also identified as Peter the Abbot, the author of the *Epitome*. That is a precis of the *History* and is more clearly arranged, though it contains little extra information [8]. Photius' *Account* exists in ten manuscripts, but is entirely derived from Peter of Sicily's *History*, although on a few points it does help to clarify obscurities in Peter's text. We have therefore not translated it, but have noted the relevant points in our commentary on Peter's work. Photius, although a controversial figure in his lifetime, was justly considered one of the great scholar-churchmen of Byzantium after his death,[21] and this accounts for the popularity of his work, but Peter is the prime source for the history and faith of the Paulicians. Some additional information can be found in a set of Abjuration Formulae drawn up by the Orthodox Church for the reception of Paulician converts [11]. There are also some references to Paulicians in contemporary chronicles and in other Byzantine sources.

Nothing is known about Peter of Sicily beyond what he tells us. He was an abbot, and presumably one of that group of Sicilians who assumed a high profile in the Byzantine Church during the post-Iconoclast period of whom the Patriarch Methodius I (843–47) is the most eminent example.[22] In 869–70 Peter was sent as ambassador by the Emperor Basil I to the Paulician ruler Chrysocheir, who had established an independent state on the Arab-Byzantine frontier. The choice of a churchman to lead a mission of this kind may reflect the desire of the Byzantine government to obtain accurate information about the beliefs of the Paulicians, about whom they had received conflicting reports, as only an envoy with a theological training would have been competent to evaluate such evidence.

The Paulicians were absolute dualists:

They say: 'There is only one thing which separates us from the Romans [i.e. the Orthodox], that we say that the heavenly father is one God who has no power in this world, but who has power in the world to come, and that there is another

21 Dvornik *The Photian Schism*.
22 Another was Gregory Asbestas, Archbishop of Syracuse (*ibid.*, pp. 13–19).

God who made the world and who has power over the present world. The Romans confess that the heavenly father and the creator of all the world are one and the same God.' **[8]**

In Peter's view this meant that they were Manichaeans: 'There are not two separate groups, but the Paulicians are also Manichaeans, who have added the foul heresy they discovered to the heresy of their predecessors and have sunk in the same gulf of perdition' **[7]**. Peter relates a legend which purports to explain the link between Mani and the Paulicians. There once lived in Arsamosata a Manichaean woman named Callinice who had two sons called John and Paul. She raised them in her faith and sent them out to preach. They conducted a mission in Phanaroia using Episparis as their base: 'the heresy took its name from its preachers', Peter concludes: 'From that time instead of Manichaeans they were called Paulicians' **[7]**. This story carries little conviction. Callinice is not historically credible, for although women could become Manichaean elect, that involved a life of continence and they never held any position of authority in the hierarchy. Callinice, the Manichaean mother and organizer, is therefore literally unbelievable.

Peter of Sicily's explanation of the name Paulician is not acceptable either, because there is no evidence that John and Paul, the sons of Callinice, ever existed. Paulician was a name which other people gave to the sect whose members simply called themselves Christians.[23] Paulician is a Graecized form of the Armenian word *Paylikeank*, formed from a derogatory diminutive of the name Paul. It means 'the followers of the wretched little Paul'.[24] Who was this Paulnik? Such a term would not have been used of the Apostle Paul; nor does it refer to Paul of Samosata, the most famous heretical Paul, whose followers were called Paulinians by the Armenians, and whose teachings have nothing in common with those of the Paulicians.[25] The most likely origin of the name is that suggested by Lemerle: that it comes from the Paulician leader Paul, who took his followers back to Armenia in the early eighth century and refounded the sect.[26]

Lemerle has argued that the first ninety-three chapters of Peter of Sicily's work, which include the material about John and Paul, were based on what he had learned about the Paulicians from hearsay in Constantinople, but that from about chapter ninety-four onwards he was reporting

---

23 **[7]**.
24 Obolensky, *The Bogomils*, p. 55.
25 Appendix 2.
26 Lemerle, 'L'Histoire des Pauliciens d'Asie Mineure', *T & M* 5 (1973), p. 52. **[7]**.

what he had learned from the Paulicians themselves at Tefrice.[27] They traced their origins to Constantine of Mananalis, who had lived in the reign of Constans II (641–68) and had sheltered a deacon, returning home from prison in Syria, who had given him a Gospel Book and a book of the Epistles of St Paul, on which he had based his teaching. Peter made the gratuitous assumption that Constantine was a Manichaean, who traced his spiritual descent from the sons of Callinice, and that fearing the Byzantine heresy laws he had decided to abandon the Manichaean books on which he had hitherto based his teaching, together with the Gnostic works of Valentinus and Basilides, and base his Manichaean teaching instead entirely on the Christian scriptures. There is no evidence of any Gnostic or Manichaean influence in the Paulician tradition, so this appears to be pure fantasy.

It is not necessary to link Constantine with the Manichaeans to explain how he became familiar with the concept of dualism, since that was a central tenet of Zoroastrianism, the established religion of the Persian Empire, which had ruled half of Armenia until 640. The dualism of Constantine was different from that of the Zoroastrians, for whereas they believed that the material world was the creation of the Good God, Constantine considered it the work of the evil principle. But the two faiths had much in common, for they both shared a view of cosmic history as a duel between the forces of good and evil in which man has a key role to play, and neither of them had any tradition of asceticism.[28]

Constantine identified himself as a Christian and based his teaching on the Bible, but only accepted a part of it. He rejected the entire Old Testament, but accepted as canonical the four Gospels and the fourteen Epistles of St Paul. Peter of Sicily says that in his day the Paulicians also accepted the Acts of the Apostles, and the Catholic Epistles of St James, St John and St Jude, but the status of those books seems to have been a matter of debate among them.[29] Lemerle points out that there is no evidence that the Paulicians considered the Revelation of St John as canonical, and it is known that they excluded the Epistles of St Peter from their New Testament, although it is not known why.[30]

---

27 Lemerle, *T & M* 5, pp. 17–26. The *History* is clearly a composite document, and this is the most convincing explanation of that fact. N.G. Garsoian seeks to explain it in a complicated way, which is based on the false assumption that Peter of Sicily wrote in the reign of Constantine VII (944–59) (*The Paulician heresy*, pp. 27–79).
28 Zaehner, *The dawn and twilight of Zoroastrianism*.
29 Photius, *Récit*, c. 28, *T & M* 4 (1970), p. 129.
30 Lemerle, *T & M* 5 (1973), p. 131. Peter of Sicily offers his own polemical explanation of the omission of the Epistles of St Peter from the Paulician canon [7].

Their faith centred round Jesus Christ, but they believed that he was a spiritual being who had come into this world but had not shared our humanity. This meant that Mary was not in any meaningful sense his Mother, a view graphically condemned in the oldest of the Abjuration Formulae: 'Anathema to him who ... believes ... that the Lord brought his body from above and made use of the womb of the Mother of God like a bag' **[11(a)]**. It followed from this that Christ could not have given his Church material sacraments, since the material world had not been created by the Good God and was not under his control. The Paulicians understood Christ Himself to be the sacrament of baptism, because he had said: 'I am the living water'; and they understood the institution of the Eucharist to refer to his teaching.[31] They refused to venerate the cross, saying that Christ was himself the living cross, and they rejected the cults of the saints and of the icons. They claimed that theirs was the true church and rejected the Orthodox Church and its hierarchy. Their Orthodox critics were as scandalized by the devotional habits of the Paulicians as they were by their doctrinal assertions, in particular by their refusal to venerate the cross or to give cult to the Blessed Virgin Mary and the saints and angels.

The central teaching of the New Testament is that 'the Word was made flesh and dwelt among us' (John 1.14), and these writings do not lend themselves very readily to a purely spiritual interpretation of the kind which the Paulicians envisaged. So like every other Christian denomination they interpreted allegorically those New Testament texts whose literal meaning did not accord with their understanding of the faith.[32]

The supreme authority in the Paulician Church during the first two centuries was a series of religious teachers called *didaskaloi*, the first of whom was Constantine of Mananalis. Peter of Sicily says that the Paulicians regarded them 'as apostles of Christ'. Each *didaskalos* seems to have been considered the authoritative teacher of the Christian revelation in his own generation: there could be only one legitimate *didaskalos* at a time, although there were quarrels about who should fill this office. In one passage Peter suggests that the *didaskalos* was chosen by his subordinate clergy, the *synekdemoi*, but if this was so, their function would seem to have been to authenticate a leader who had a divine charisma:

---

31 The Paulician quotation about living water was not exact, cf. John 4.10; their interpretation of the Eucharist is based on the saying of Christ, the Word of God, 'I am the living bread which came down from heaven', (John 6.51).
32 A practice sanctioned by Christ, who invoked the sign of Jonah as an allegory of his death and resurrection (Matt. 12.39–41).

there is no indication that there was any ceremony of ordination, and there were periods in Paulician history when there was no *didaskalos*.

The *synekdemoi* are Christian ministers mentioned in the New Testament on two occasions as assistants of St Paul. The word means 'travelling companions'.[33] Peter of Sicily tells us that they held positions of religious authority among the Paulicians, and were assisted by a subordinate group known as notaries, who 'are not distinguished from all the others by dress or diet or the rest of their manner of life' **[7]**.

There is no indication in any of our sources that the Paulicians in Peter of Sicily's day had any initiation ceremony: 'They say that baptism is the words of the Gospel, as the Lord says, "I am the living water"' **[8]**. Nor is there any indication that at any time in their history the Paulicians had a class of initiates, like the Manichaean elect or the Cathar perfect. They are unique among dualist groups who attribute the creation of the phenomenal world to a malign god in not enjoining on their followers an ascetic way of life. They do not seem to have fasted or to have observed any food taboos. Their enemies accused them of sexual licence, homosexuality and incest, but these are commonplaces of orthodox polemic, tiresomely familiar to anyone who works on medieval heresy, and do not warrant serious attention.[34] But the Paulicians were unlike all other Christian dualists in that they had no tradition at all of sexual abstinence.[35] They married and procreated children, and this was true even of the *didaskaloi*. Finally, they were not in any sense world-renouncing: all of them had ordinary occupations. The Paulicians saw nothing incompatible with their faith in exercising temporal dominion or in being involved in power politics, and they had no inhibitions about taking life: on the contrary, they were universally admitted to be excellent fighting men. It appears to us that Constantine of Mananalis really did found a new type of Christianity, a world-affirming dualism based on his understanding of the New Testament.

The early history of the Paulicians

In the days of the Emperor Constantine, grandson of Heraclius, there was born in the territory of Samosata in Armenia an Armenian named Constantine, in a village called Mananalis, a village which even now rears Manichaeans. **[7]**

---

33 Acts 19.29; 2 Cor. 8, 18–19.
34 **[8]**, *c.* 24; **[1]**, *c.* 7.
35 In this they were like the Zoroastians (Zaehner, *The dawn and twilight of Zoroastrianism*, pp. 265–83).

This passage is based on the account of their own origins which the Paulicians gave to Peter of Sicily. The emperor to whom it refers is Constans II (641–68).[36] Peter's account suggests that Constantine was a layman, while his name implies that he had grown up as a member of the Armenian Church. The story which Peter was told, of how Constantine sheltered a refugee deacon who gave him a Gospel Book and a Book of St Paul's Epistles, was presumably intended to symbolize how the first Paulician *didaskalos* learned the faith from studying the scriptures. This is a commonplace in the historiography of Christian sects which claim to have rediscovered the true apostolic tradition, but that Constantine's teaching was based on the New Testament alone, and that he only accepted certain parts of it, is evident from the way in which his Paulicianism developed.

Peter of Sicily quotes a passage from a letter in which the *didaskalos* Sergius (d. 835) lists seven Paulician churches. He attributes the foundation of six of them to himself and his predecessors, but writes of the seventh: 'Again I say that Paul established the Church in Corinth' **[7]**. Corinth, unlike the others, may be a symbolic Church, representing the Pauline tradition which Constantine claimed to have revitalized, or it may represent some earlier dissenting movement which the Paulicians considered formed the link between the Apostles and themselves. Certainly some early Christian sects survived in eastern Anatolia in the seventh century, with which Constantine could have had contact. I once suggested that the Church of Corinth referred to the Novatians, a doctrinally orthodox and deeply conservative group who had split from the Great Church in the mid-third century, but I made this point merely as a speculation, and neither I nor anybody else has yet found any firm evidence to support it.[37]

Although Peter of Sicily's *History* is largely uncorroborated, it seems to be a substantially true version of what he was told, because it correlates very well with the known history of what was happening on a military and political level in the eastern provinces of the empire in the period he was describing. He tells us that when Constantine had worked out his version of the Christian faith he went to live in Cibossa near Colonea.[38] Lemerle has tentatively dated the beginning of Constantine's ministry

---

36 This emperor, the son of the short-lived Constantine III, was crowned as Constantine, and the name Constantine appears on his coins. He was called Constans by the chronicler Theophanes, and is now normally called Constans II.
37 Gouillard, 'L'Hérésie dans l'empire byzantin', *T & M* 1 (1965), pp. 299–312; B. Hamilton, 'The Cathars and the Seven Churches of Asia', pp. 269–95.
38 Colonea was the see of an Orthodox bishop and later became a provincial capital.

to *c.* 655, and this would fit quite well with Constans II's restoration of Byzantine control in Armenia in 654–55, because there would have been no frontier to cross between Mananalis and Colonea.[39] Constantine appears to have thought that he was reviving the true church which had been founded by St Paul: 'He used to show his disciples the book of the Apostle, which he had got from the deacon . . . saying: "You are the Macedonians and I am Silvanus sent to you by Paul"' **[7]**. This refers to St Paul's vision of a man saying 'Come over into Macedonia and help us' (Acts 16.9). Peter of Sicily thought this comparison absurd, but he was looking at Colonea from the viewpoint of Constantinople, perhaps even Syracuse, and saw it as somewhere in the distant East, near to Armenia. But if viewed from Armenia, as it was by Constantine, Colonea was in the land of the Greeks, a western region which might fittingly be referred to as Macedonia. In calling himself Silvanus, Constantine was following the monastic custom of taking a new name at profession to signify conversion of life. Silvanus was associated with St Paul in his first Epistle to the Thessalonians, and it was no doubt this which suggested Constantine's choice of a name, for Thessalonica was the chief city of Macedonia.[40] Later *didaskaloi* followed Constantine's example and took the names of Paul's disciples, and also called their churches after places visited by Paul. The implication was that they were restoring the true apostolic Church.

Constantine–Silvanus ministered in the area round Colonea for twenty-seven years. He was then denounced to the Emperor Constantine IV (668–85), who sent an official named Symeon with orders to execute Constantine and to reconcile his followers to the Orthodox Church. This implies that Constantine had been accused of Manichaeism and that the emperor treated this very seriously, because there had been no outbreaks of that heresy in the empire for more than a century. Peter of Sicily reports that Constantine was stoned to death, but it is difficult to accept this, because stoning was not a normal punishment in Byzantine law and was not the penalty prescribed for Manichaeism. We would suggest that Constantine was executed in a conventional way and that

39 Lemerle, *T & M* 5 (1973), p. 84. An alternative date for Constantine's journey to Episparis is 657–58, when the Byzantines regained control of Armenia (Laurent, *L'Arménie entre Byzance et l'Islam*, p. 90, n. 1).
40 Silvanus is mentioned in 2 Cor. 1.19, 1 Thess.1.1 and also 1 Pet. 5.12, which the Paulicians did not read. Had they done so, Constantine might have been less anxious to adopt that name, because St Peter calls Silvanus his secretary. Although Paul was assisted in his mission at Thessalonica by St Silas (Acts 16), he should not be confused with Silvanus; they are different names.

the story of death by stoning was told by the Paulicians in order to draw a parallel between their first martyr and the first Christian martyr, Stephen.[41]

Constantine's followers were handed over to Orthodox churchmen to be converted from their error. Symeon returned to Constantinople, but had been so impressed by the faith of the Paulicians that he resigned his office and three years later returned to Cibossa and placed himself at the head of their community. His conversion, no doubt intentionally, parallels that of St Paul, who had been present at the stoning of Stephen. Symeon was recognized as the new *didaskalos*, and took the name of Titus, perhaps because of Paul's words: 'But God, who comforts the downcast, comforted us by the coming of Titus' (2 Cor. 7.6). Under his guidance the Paulician Church in Cibossa flourished once more until three years later, when Justus, the adoptive son of Constantine of Mananalis, developed doubts about whether Christian dualism was consonant with St Paul's teaching, and asked the Orthodox Bishop of Colonea to adjudicate between him and Titus in this dispute. The bishop denounced Titus to the Emperor Justinian II, and Titus and those loyal to him were condemned to death and burnt alive. No doubt the severity of this punishment was dictated by the fact that Symeon had once been an imperial official, and was therefore considered to have offended the emperor as well as Almighty God. These events are likely to have happened during Justinian II's first reign (685–95), for in 686–87 imperial forces with the help of the Khazars succeeded in regaining control of Armenia, which they held until 693, and the emperor was therefore in a position to intervene decisively in the eastern provinces.[42]

Since Justus and his supporters had already been reconciled to the Orthodox Church, the Paulician Church of Macedonia at Cibossa was left in a fragile condition. One of its members, an Armenian named Paul who had escaped the persecution, fled with his sons, Genesius[43] and Theodore, to Episparis in Phanaroia, a region to the west of Colonea. Paul rallied the Paulicians, but did not exercise any religious authority over them. Nevertheless, it seems to have been from him that the

---

41 Cf. Acts 7.57–60.
42 Head *Justinian II of Byzantium*, pp. 33–4, 45–50, 63–4. The use of burning at the stake as a punishment for dualist heresy was a seventh-century innovation. The laws of Justinian I had decreed the execution of impenitent Manichaeans but had not specified what form this should take. See p. 4, n. 13 above.
43 Whom Peter of Sicily calls Gegnesius.

followers of Constantine of Mananalis took their name.[44] Both Paul's sons claimed to have received the charismata of a *didaskalos*, but he supported Genesius, who took the name in religion of Timothy, who had been one of the most trusted companions of St Paul, and had helped Paul and Silvanus in their missionary work.[45] Peter of Sicily relates that Timothy held office for thirty years, and as he probably died in 748, he must have become leader in *c.* 718.

The 'official' history of the Paulician movement which was told to Peter of Sicily was clearly not the whole story, any more than the Book of Acts gives a complete picture of the early spread of Christianity. There were Paulician congregations in places other than Cibossa and Episparis by the early eighth century. In *c.* 719 John of Ojun, Catholicus of Armenia (717–28), presided at a church council at Dvin at which the Paulicians (*Payl-i-keank*) were condemned. John also wrote a tract against them, in which he relates that they had been admonished by the Catholicus Nerses, but after his death 'had gone into hiding in certain other parts of our country'. That must have been Nerses III (641–61), for as Runciman points out, his reign coincided with the first preaching by Constantine of Mananalis.[46] John of Ojun added that the Paulicians had been joined by some iconoclasts from Caspian Albania who had been expelled from the Orthodox Church there.[47] This is confirmed by the twelfth-century Armenian historian, Samuel of Ani, who has preserved the text of the canons of a Council of the Albanian Church, held in the reign of the Armenian Catholicus Elias (703–17), outlawing the *Payl-i-keank*.[48] That Constantine of Mananalis had made converts in Armenia before moving to Greek territory, and that the movement had persisted there and spread into the distant lands of Caspian Albania, is clear from these Armenian records, and helps to explain the policies of some of the later *didaskaloi*.

---

44 These seem to be the true facts behind the story of John and Paul, the sons of Callinice, preaching the faith at Episparis, reported by Peter of Sicily. I am not convinced by Lemerle's suggestion that Episparis was on the Armenian frontier, not in Phanaroia *T & M* 5 (1973), pp. 77–8.
45 Acts 16.1; Rom.16.21; 1 Cor.16.10; 2 Cor. 1.1; 1 Thess.1.1; 3.2; Heb. 13.23; 1 and 2 Tim.
46 Runciman, *The medieval Manichee*, p. 34.
47 Canon 32 of the Council of Dvin and extracts from John of Ojun's Tract are reproduced in the Latin translation of the Venice edition of 1834 in Conybeare, *The Key of Truth*, Appendix IV, pp. 152–4.
48 Translated in Garsoian, *Paulician heresy*, pp. 92–4, who argues for an earlier date for this Council. See Appendix 2 for a discussion of Dr Garsoian's views about the nature of Armenian Paulicianism.

HISTORICAL INTRODUCTION

The toleration of the Paulicians (c. 740–813)

Timothy was *didaskalos* in the reign of Leo III (717–41), when Byzantium was divided by the Iconoclast Controversy. In the Byzantine world during the sixth and seventh centuries a popular cult of religious devotion to images of Christ, of Mary his Mother and of the angels and saints had developed. Initially the term icon was applied to religious representations of all kinds, although later it became reserved chiefly for painted wooden panels. Those who found this form of religious activity congenial were known as iconodules. They argued that as God the Son had shared our humanity, it was legitimate to represent Him in material form, and if this was so, there could be no impropriety in representing the angels and saints, and that all reverence which was paid to a likeness was in fact paid to its prototype. Those who opposed the practice were known as iconoclasts, and they cited God's prohibition of graven images in the Second Commandment.

The iconoclasts found a champion in the Emperor Leo III (717–41), who became convinced that the excessive veneration paid to images rather than to God alone was the reason why for almost a hundred years Byzantium had been defeated by the Muslims, who, whatever their other errors, prohibited religious representational art.[49] In *c.* 730 he issued an edict ordering the destruction of all religious images throughout the empire, and although this led to the resignation of the Patriarch of Constantinople and provoked some strong opposition, it remained imperial policy.[50]

Peter of Sicily relates that Leo III ordered the *didaskalos* Timothy to come to Constantinople, where he was examined by the patriarch, who is not named. This is likely to have happened after 726, when Leo's new law code, *The Eclogues*, came into force, enacting severe penalties against heretics, particularly Manichaeans.[51] It was unusual for the patriarch to examine a provincial heretic in person, and I would suggest that Timothy's trial took place after the publication of the Iconoclast decree in 730. The Paulicians were strongly opposed to all religious images just as the emperor himself was, and the imperial officials in Constantinople who received the complaint against Timothy may have supposed that he was an Iconoclast who was being victimized by local officials with

---

49 Representational art is not prohibited in the Koran, but in a *hadith*, part of the oral tradition of the Prophet's teachings.
50 Hussey, *The Orthodox church in the Byzantine empire*, pp. 30–43; Bryer and Herrin, eds *Iconoclasm*.
51 *Ecloga*, pp. 129–32.

iconodule sympathies, and may therefore have convoked the case to the capital. If this hypothesis is correct, then Timothy would have been examined by the iconoclast Patriarch Anastasius (730–54).

Peter of Sicily relates how the patriarch required Timothy to anathematize those who denied the Orthodox faith, refused to show reverence to the Cross or reverence the Mother of God, and refused to receive Holy Communion. Timothy had no difficulty about condemning all these errors, the Paulicians told Peter of Sicily, because he understood these doctrines in an allegorical sense: by the Orthodox faith he understood the Paulician faith; by the Holy Cross he understood Christ with his arms outstretched; by the Mother of God he understood the heavenly Jerusalem; by receiving Holy Communion he understood receiving the sayings of Our Lord. The patriarch then asked him whether he believed in the 'holy, catholic and apostolic Church' and in baptism; the juxtaposition of these two questions suggests that Timothy was required to give his assent to the Nicene Creed, the standard profession of Orthodox belief, in which two consecutive clauses are: 'I believe in one, holy, catholic and apostolic Church; I acknowledge one baptism for the remission of sins.' Timothy willingly assented, understanding the apostolic Church to be the Paulician Church, and baptism to be Christ himself, the living water. There is no reason to doubt the truth of Peter of Sicily's account, even though there is no surviving patriarchal record of the trial, for the acts of the iconoclast patriarchs were mostly not preserved by their Orthodox successors.[52]

The trial must have taken place between 730, when Anastasius became patriarch, and Leo III's death in 741, and it had important consequences, for Timothy was declared Orthodox by the patriarch, and returned to Phanaroia with an imperial safe-conduct. In view of this, it is surprising to be told by Peter of Sicily that Timothy then took his followers back to Armenia, to Mananalis, the home of the Paulician founder Constantine, which was in Arab hands. But if the trial was held towards the end of Leo's reign, then Timothy's flight may have been occasioned by the revolt of Artavasdus, son-in-law of Leo III, who in 742–3 seized Constantinople and restored the icons.[53] Timothy may have judged that the new government would be unfavourable to a group

---

52 No other acts of the Patriarch Anastasius have been preserved. Grumel assigns the trial of Timothy to the Patriarchate of Germanus I, but admits that it might equally well have taken place in the reign of Anastasius (RP, no. 336, p. 6).
53 Theophanes Continuatus, ed. Bekker, pp. 413–21.

HISTORICAL INTRODUCTION

which had enjoyed the support of the Iconoclast Leo III and therefore have sought refuge with his followers in Arab territory.

Sergius, the last *didaskalos*, credited Timothy with founding the third Paulician church, that of Achaia, at Mananalis. Timothy died at Mananalis from the plague, it is generally assumed in the great epidemic of 748, though that is not certain. During his ministry the Paulicians had been transformed from a small, persecuted community into a respectable movement which enjoyed imperial protection and was able to spread in the Byzantine world as well as in the Christian Caucasus. That movement became even more widely diffused during the reign of Constantine V (741–75).

Timothy's death occurred just before the Abbasid revolution of 749 which overthrew the Umayyad Caliphate and convulsed the Islamic world.[54] The Emperor Constantine V (741–75) profited from this by invading Armenia and capturing Theodosiopolis in 751.[55] He took back to the empire all those Christians who wished to follow him, and later resettled some of them in Thrace to repopulate regions devastated by the plague of 748 and to defend them against the Bulgars. Among the immigrants were Paulicians, who were not treated as heretics because the Patriarch of Constantinople had declared them to be orthodox [1].

Constantine V was a convinced Iconoclast, and in 754 convoked what he held to be the Seventh Oecumenical Council, with power to define doctrine binding on the Catholic Church throughout the world. The Council declared that Iconoclast teaching was orthodox. But as only Byzantine representatives were present at it, it lacked oecumenical status in the eyes of the rest of Christendom.[56]

In the wake of the Byzantine invasion there was a revolt in Armenia against Arab rule, and large parts of the country remained independent for more than twenty years. The Paulicians there were divided about the succession to Timothy, some following his son Zacharias and others his adopted son Joseph, each of whom claimed to be the new *didaskalos*. But some years later both leaders agreed to migrate into Byzantine territory with their followers at the same time. The catalyst which led to this *rapprochement* was probably the restoration of Islamic rule in Armenia by the Abbasid Caliphate in 772. Many Armenians sought refuge in Byzantine territory at that time, and the Paulicians seem to have been part of

---

54 Shaban, *The Abbasid revolution*; H. Kennedy, *The early Abbasid Caliphate*, pp. 35–56.
55 Laurent, *L'Arménie, entre Byzance et l'Islam*, p. 208.
56 Hussey, *The Orthodox Church*, pp. 38–41.

this general movement.[57] But the Arab frontier patrols challenged them, and many of Zacharias' followers were killed trying to cross into the Byzantine lands. Because Zacharias deserted them and fled in the face of danger, he lost his claim to be a *didaskalos*, and nothing more is known about him.

Joseph told the frontier patrols that his people, travelling in a convoy of wagons, were seeking new grazing lands in Syria, and they were allowed to proceed to the south; but later turned west and went to the centre of Paulicianism in Byzantine Anatolia, Episparis in Phanaroia. This episode is illuminating because it suggests that many of the Armenian Paulicians were transhumant herdsmen, and this would certainly explain the willingness of members of the movement to travel long distances at short notice.

Joseph, now the undisputed *didaskalos*, took the name in religion of Epaphroditus, described by St Paul as 'my brother and fellow-worker, and fellow-soldier' (Phil. 2.25). He was warmly welcomed by the Paulicians of Episparis, where his father had once lived, but later a local official arrested the Paulicians while they were meeting for prayer. As Paulicianism was a licit religion at that time, Lemerle's suggestion that they were arrested for political reasons is plausible.[58] The arrival from across the Arab frontier of Armenians, whose leader was regarded as an authority figure by some of the local community, and who held large assemblies in private houses, might well have appeared suspicious to the imperial authorities.

Epaphroditus escaped arrest and went to Antioch in Pisidia in central Anatolia, which had been evangelized by St Paul.[59] There he founded the Paulician Church of Philippi, the name presumably being chosen because the first Epaphroditus had been a prominent member of the Pauline church of Philippi. After a ministry of almost thirty years Epaphroditus died some time before 800.

His successor, Baanes (Vahan in Armenian),[60] was born in Armenia and according to Photius had a Jewish father.[61] He later joined Epaphroditus in Antioch in Pisidia and eventually succeeded him as *didaskalos*, but his leadership was challenged by a certain Sergius, whose followers

57 Laurent, *L'Arménie, entre Byzance et l'Islam*, p. 192.
58 Lemerle, *T & M* 5 (1973), p. 68.
59 Acts 13.13–43.
60 Garsoian, *The Paulician Heresy*, p. 119.
61 *Récit*, c. 94, *T & M* 4 (1970), p. 152.

always referred to Baanes as 'the Foul', and they were Peter of Sicily's informants.

Sergius was a Greek. He had been brought up as an Orthodox Christian in a village near Tavium in Galatia, and he was literate. Peter of Sicily relates that he became the lover of a Paulician woman who converted him to her faith, but a different tradition was known to later Byzantine writers, who claimed that Sergius' teacher had been a magician called Lycopetrus, or Peter the Wolf **[16, 19]**. Sergius was accepted by some Paulicians as *didaskalos* and took the name in religion of Tychicus, whom St Paul described as 'a beloved brother and faithful minister in the Lord' (Eph. 6.21). It is not known what happened to Baanes, except that some Paulicians remained faithful to him throughout Sergius' lifetime.

Sergius began his ministry in the reign of the Empress Irene (797–802), who, while regent for Constantine VI, had in 787 convoked the Second Council of Nicaea, which repealed the Iconoclast decrees and defined orthodox doctrine about the cult of images, pronouncements accepted as authoritative by the Churches of East and West.[62] In Irene's reign and that of Nicephorus I (802–11) the Paulicians continued to enjoy legal toleration. Like St Paul, Sergius wrote pastoral letters to the Paulician churches, some of which Peter of Sicily cites, and he was later credited with writing a commentary on St Matthew's Gospel **[16(d)]**. He moved his headquarters to Cynochorion near Neocaesarea (Niksar), where he founded the Church of Laodicea, another Pauline name (Col. 4.15–16).

The Paulicians at Tefrice

The Patriarch Nicephorus (806–15) believed that the Paulicians were dualists, but they were also politically suspect, because units in the imperial army which had been disbanded by Irene for opposing her religious policies had joined the Paulicians, since they too rejected the cult of icons **[2]**. Moreover, in the reigns of Nicephorus I and Michael I the Paulicians were associated with anti-government demonstrations in Constantinople **[3]**. The Patriarch therefore persuaded the new emperor, Michael I (811–13), to declare the Paulicians heretical and to restore the death penalty for those who professed that faith.[63]

Michael I's successor, Leo V (813–20), rescinded the edicts of the Second Council of Nicaea and restored Iconoclasm,[64] but he did not revoke the legislation against the Paulicians. This may have been because he

---

62 Hussey, *The Orthodox Church*, pp. 44–50.
63 Alexander, *The Patriarch Nicephorus of Constantinople*, p. 99.
64 *Ibid.*, pp. 111–40.

CHRISTIAN DUALIST HERESIES

was an Armenian, perhaps a member of the princely family of Gnuni, and therefore connected to the Bagratid house, which was emerging as the dominant power in Armenia at that time.[65] He would therefore have been aware of the Paulicians' true beliefs. The heresy laws were certainly enforced, for St Theodore of Studium, the chief critic of the new Iconoclasm, protested vigorously, though unavailingly, against the endorsement by the Orthodox Church of the death penalty for Paulicians **[4]**, while St Macarius of Pelecete, a staunch iconodule, once found himself imprisoned with a group of Paulicians awaiting execution **[5]**.

The prosecution of the Paulicians in Anatolia was spearheaded by Thomas, Archbishop of Neocaesarea, aided by the exarch Paracondacus, who arrested and executed a number of them. But then the members of the Paulician Church of Laodicea struck back and murdered Archbishop Thomas, while followers of Sergius called the *Astatoi* assassinated the exarch. Lemerle has suggested that the name *Astatoi* was derived from St Paul's description of the apostles as 'we who wander without a home'.[66] It would appear from later references to them that they formed the military wing of the Paulician movement. The *Astatoi* took refuge with the Emir of Melitene, who gave them the fortress of Argaoun.[67] Peter of Sicily does not date this event, but the unusual grant of a border fortress to a group of Christian warriors, albeit heretical ones, would fit most naturally into the context of Thomas the Slav's rebellion. He was an iconodule pretender to the Byzantine throne, who, with the support of the Caliph al-Mamun, invaded Anatolia in 820 and was not defeated until 823.[68]

Sergius–Tychicus and many of his other followers later joined the *Astatoi* at Argaoun, where he founded the Paulician Church of the Colossians. He also travelled to Cilicia, where, presumably with the permission of the Emir of Tarsus, he conducted a mission and founded the Church of the Ephesians, based at Mamistra. Colossae and Ephesus were both Pauline churches with which the original Tychicus had had close links.[69] The converts must have come from the local Christian communities, since the conversion of Muslims to other faiths was an offence in Islamic law punishable by death. Meanwhile the *Astatoi* joined the Muslims of

---

65 Toumanoff, *Studies in Christian Caucasian history*, pp. 200–1, n. 228.
66 *astatoumen*, 1 Cor. 4.11; Lemerle, *T & M* 5 (1973), p. 72.
67 The identity of this emir is uncertain; see the plausible suggestion of Cl. Cahen cited by Lemerle, *T & M* 5 (1973), p. 73, n. 64.
68 P. Lemerle, 'Thomas le Slave', *T & M* 1 (1965), pp. 255–97.
69 Col. 4.7; Eph. 6.21.

HISTORICAL INTRODUCTION

Melitene in raiding Byzantine Anatolia, perhaps in the reign of Michael II (820–30) and certainly in that of Theophilus (830–42).[70]

Sergius did not take any part in the fighting, but earned his living, like the Church's Founder, as a carpenter. It was while at work that he met his death: 'For Tzanios, who came from the *kastellon* of Nicopolis, found [Sergius] in the mountain above Argaoun cutting planks, seized the axe from his hands, struck him and killed him' **[7]**. This happened in 834–35, but nothing is known about the reason for it. Nicopolis is to the south of Colonea, and Tzanios may have been an Orthodox fanatic, but it is also possible that he was a member of the rival Paulician Church, the followers of the *didaskalos* Baanes, for after Sergius' death his followers began to kill those of Baanes until peace was mediated by Sergius' *synekdemos*, Theodotus. Photius relates that in the late ninth century the schism between the followers of Sergius and those of Baanes had still not been healed.[71]

For reasons which are not known, no new *didaskalos* was ever recognized, and after Sergius' death the leadership of his followers passed to the six *synekdemoi* whom he had trained. They lived at Argaoun, but many Paulicians continued to live in Byzantine territory.

When the Emperor Theophilus died in 842, his widow Theodora became regent for Michael III. She was an iconodule, and in 843 convoked a council which repealed all the iconoclast legislation and reinstated the canons of the Second Council of Nicaea as a true statement of the faith of the Orthodox Church.[72] The Patriarch Methodius drew up the Synodikon of Orthodoxy, a list of heresies condemned by the Byzantine Church, which was to be publicly recited on the first Sunday of Lent each year, probably with effect from 844 **[16]**. The empress was anxious to enforce the new Orthodoxy, and the heresy laws against Paulicians were enforced with great vigour in the provinces **[6(a)]**. Among those executed was the father of the *protomandator* Carbeas, an important official on the staff of the governor of the Anatolikon theme. This caused Carbeas to revolt, and with a band of Paulicians said to number about 5,000, he fled to Argaoun and placed his services at the command of the Emir of Melitene. Lemerle argues cogently that this happened in 843–4, since a contemporary source relates that Carbeas was already in command of Argaoun in 844 when the Paulicians of Colonea

70 Lemerle, *T & M* 5 (1973), pp. 82–3.
71 *Récit*, c. 11, *T & M* 4 (1970), pp. 122–5.
72 Hussey, *The Orthodox Church*, pp. 62–5.

kidnapped the governor Callistus and handed him over to Carbeas **[6(b)]**.[73]

By 856 Carbeas and his followers had moved to Tefrice, a new fortress on the Byzantine frontier, where they were effectively independent of the Emir of Melitene.[74] Tefrice became a refuge for Paulicians who were persecuted in the Byzantine Empire, and Carbeas is said also to have offered attractive terms to non-Paulician Byzantines who would come and settle in this dangerous frontier zone. He continued to co-operate with the Muslims of Melitene in their raids on Byzantine territory until his death in 863.[75]

He was succeeded as secular head of state by his nephew Chrysocheir, who was also his son-in-law, but Basileius and Zosimus, the two surviving *synekdemoi* of Sergius, were the religious leaders.[76] In 867 there was a palace revolution in Constantinople when Basil the Macedonian masterminded the assassination of Michael III and became the Emperor Basil I. Chrysocheir took advantage of the disruption which this caused, and raided Nicaea, Nicomedia and Ephesus in the extreme west of Anatolia.[77] This led Basil I to send Peter of Sicily to Tefrice to try to negotiate peace in 869–70, but he was only able to arrange the exchange of prisoners. The war continued; Chrysocheir was killed in action in 872, and his head was cut off and sent to the emperor as a trophy **[9(a)]**. But Tefrice remained independent until 878, when, having recently been damaged in an earthquake, it surrendered to the Byzantines.[78] The imperial authorities enlisted some of their defeated opponents in their own armies. A Paulician regiment commanded by Chrysocheir's trusted groom Diaconitzes served under Nicephorus Phocas the Elder on his Apulian campaign in 885, and Diaconitzes was later converted to Orthodoxy by the Emperor Leo VI (886–912) **[9(b)]**.

The later Paulicians

Nothing is known about the organization of the Paulician Church after the fall of Tefrice, but the scattered congregations seem to have pre-

---

73 Lemerle, *T & M* 5 (1973), pp. 88–9.
74 Peter of Sicily says that this was done to escape the tyranny of the Muslims, and it is possible that the Emir of Melitene had restricted the full practice of the Paulician faith.
75 Lemerle, *T & M* 5 (1973), p. 93 and n. 19.
76 It is not known whether Chrysocheir the Paulician leader was the same as John Chrysocheir, with whom Photius at one time corresponded (Lemerle, *T & M* 5 (1973), pp. 40–2).
77 *Ibid.*, p. 98; Grégoire, 'The Amorians and Macedonians', pp. 115–17.
78 Lemerle, *T & M* 5 (1973), pp. 104–8.

HISTORICAL INTRODUCTION

served a common sense of identity and belief, even though their communion lacked any organized structure. After the capture of Tefrice the systematic persecution of Paulicians living in imperial territory seems to have come to an end, although the Church authorities tried to persuade them by peaceful means to accept Orthodox baptism [11]. During the tenth and early eleventh centuries they spread more widely throughout Anatolia and are reported at Euchaita [12], Miletus [13], and in villages near Ephesus [18].

By the 970s the Byzantines had extended their eastern frontiers to the upper Euphrates and northern Syria, and groups of Paulicians living in those areas came under their rule.[79] Theodore II, Orthodox Patriarch of Antioch (970–76), persuaded John I Tzimisces (969–76) to remove these heretics from the eastern provinces, and the emperor settled a large number of Paulicians at Philippopolis in c. 975, thus strengthening the Paulician presence in the Balkans [14]. But despite the Byzantine conquests, some Paulicians continued to live under Muslim rule until at least the early twelfth century, because a wide range of western writers name them as forming contingents in the Muslim armies that the First Crusade encountered.[80]

After 975 the Balkan Paulicians are mentioned in Byzantine sources principally as good fighting men who were employed in the imperial armies despite their heretical beliefs. They seem to have lost their missionary zeal and to have been content with practising their faith within their own community. Even Euthymius of the Periblepton, normally so shrill in his reaction to heresy of any kind, merely says of the Paulicians: 'their heresy is obvious and cannot harm anyone except those who hold it as an inherited tradition: no one is grieved or upset on their account' [19]. George Maniaces took a Paulician detachment on his Sicilian campaign of 1038–41, and they were later redeployed in Apulia against the Normans [17]. In 1081 Alexius I (1081–1118) enlisted a regiment of some 2,800 Paulicians to repel the Norman attack on Dyrrachium [22(a)].

But the Paulicians considered themselves allies rather than subjects of Byzantium. Constantine IX (1042–55) had settled the Patzinaks, a warlike people from the south Russian steppes, in northern Bulgaria to defend the Danube frontier, but their loyalty was always uncertain,[81]

---

79 Whittow, *The making of Orthodox Byzantium*, pp. 310–27.
80 They are listed in Garsoian, *The Paulician Heresy*, pp. 15–16.
81 M. Angold *The Byzantine empire*, pp. 14–17.

and the Paulicians sometimes supported them [20]. In a similar spirit of independence the Paulicians under Alexius' command returned home before the Norman campaign had ended, so in 1083, having beaten off the Norman threat, Alexius sought to reduce the Paulicians to obedience by requiring them all to receive Orthodox baptism. Reprisals were taken on those who refused: their leaders were imprisoned and the rest were evicted from their homes. This caused a revolt, led by Traulus, a trusted member of the imperial staff, who was a Paulician convert to Orthodoxy, but who objected to his sisters being made homeless. He allied with the Patzinaks and seized the hill fortress of Belyatovo near Philippopolis, from which Alexius found it impossible to dislodge them [22(b)]. The emperor's attempt to discipline the Paulicians had been premature, and he left them alone for the next thirty years. But in 1114 he made another personal attempt to convert the Paulicians of Philippopolis to the Orthodox faith. Although according to Anna Comnena so many Paulicians were baptised that her father had to build a new town for them to live in, many in fact remained firm in their belief, and two of their leaders were sentenced to life imprisonment [22(d)].

After Alexius' death the Paulicians attracted much less comment from Orthodox writers than the new heresy of Bogomilism. Some Paulicians, it seems reasonable to infer, were converted to Bogomilism,[82] but this was probably true only of a minority. St Hilarion of Moglena found Paulicians in his diocese in the reign of the Emperor Manuel I (1143–80) [33], and when armies of the the Fourth Crusade captured Philippopolis in 1204–05 the Paulicians still occupied a quarter in the town and led the opposition to them [40].

The Paulicians are not known to have been persecuted by the Orthodox authorities in the later Middle Ages, and consequently nothing is known about them except that they survived as an independent religious communion after the Ottoman conquest. Pietro Cedolini, Pope Gregory XIII's Apostolic Visitor to the western provinces of the Ottoman Empire from 1580, and his successors in that office, discovered seventeen villages between Nicopolis on the Danube and Philippopolis inhabited by self-styled 'Paulians'. They were Paulicians: they venerated the Apostle Paul, had a horror of the cross of Christ, rejected all religious images and icons, refused baptism with water, dissociated themselves from the Orthodox Church, and used the Paulician canon of scripture.[83] In the end they were converted to Catholicism. Any detailed consideration of these

82 See below, pp. 35, 38.
83 See above, pp. 6–10.

HISTORICAL INTRODUCTION

late Paulician communities is beyond the scope of this book, and we cite them simply as evidence of the resilience of the religious movement started by Constantine of Mananalis.[84]

THE BOGOMILS

The Rise of Bogomilism

Peter of Sicily dedicated his *History of the Paulicians* to the Archbishop of Bulgaria.[85] In his introduction he explains that while visiting Tefrice in 869-70: 'I had heard these blasphemers babbling that they intended to send some of their number to the country of Bulgaria to detach some from the Orthodox faith and to bring them over to their own foul heresy' [7]. This report reads persuasively. Paulicians had been living in Thrace for more than a century, and the religious situation across the frontier in Bulgaria made it particularly susceptible to their influence. Peter's report implies that the Paulician leaders in Tefrice were in regular contact with the Thracian Paulicians, from whom the missionaries to Bulgaria were presumably chosen.

The Balkans south of the Danube had been Christian in the sixth century, but had subsequently been intensively settled by pagan Slavs and church organization there had broken down, although the 'Roman' inhabitants may have remained Christian. The Bulgars, who first settled south of the Danube in 681, had built up a huge kingdom by the mid-ninth century.[86] Most of them were still pagan at that time, but Khan Boris (852-89) wished to establish Christianity as the religion of his state, and invited both Orthodox and western Catholic missions to evangelize his people before finally acknowledging the authority of the Patriarch of Constantinople in 870.[87]

In Bulgaria during the 870s well-instructed Christians must have been comparatively few, because it took a long time to establish a network of Orthodox parish clergy in the villages. Christian and pagan mythologies must therefore have coexisted in the minds of most people, and many of

---

84 For further details see Loos, *Dualist heresy*, pp. 336-9. Yuri Stoyanov has drawn our attention to an important new work, Yovkov, *The Pavlikians and the Pavlikian towns and villages*, pp. 190 ff. (in Bulgarian with an English summary).
85 He does not name him, which suggests that he wrote his account between February 870, when the Archbishopric of Bulgaria was set up by the Council of Constantinople, and the appointment of the first incumbent before 5 October 870 (Dvornik, *The Photian schism*, p. 157, n. 1).
86 See map.
87 Fine, *The early medieval Balkans*. pp. 94-131.

25

them must have been aware that there were various ways of practising the Christian faith, because they had seen both Orthodox and Catholic missionaries at work. In such a society Paulician preachers would not have seemed at all out of place.

That the Paulicians did make converts in Bulgaria in the late ninth century is confirmed by John the Exarch, a scholar-priest writing in the reign of Boris's son, Symeon (893–927), who denounced Manichaeans and pagan Slavs 'who are not ashamed to call the devil the eldest son of God'.[88] The term Manichaean when used by Orthodox clergy in the ninth century invariably refers to Paulicians. But the belief attributed to the pagan Slavs, that the devil is the eldest son of God, had not been learned from the Paulicians, although it was later developed by the Bogomils.

Symeon's son Peter (927–69) was recognized as Tsar by the Byzantine Emperor Romanus I Lecapenus (920–44) and married Romanus' granddaughter Maria. During his reign Byzantine influence was strong in Bulgaria,[89] and when a new heretical movement appeared there Peter sought the advice of his wife's uncle, Theophylact Lecapenus, Patriarch of Constantinople. He was not noted for his theological acumen,[90] and his reply, presumably drafted by his advisers, is not very clearly expressed **[10]**. He describes the heresy as 'a mixture of Manichaeism and Paulianism'. Although Byzantines sometimes wrongly used the term Paulians to refer to Paulicians, it was normally reserved by them for the followers of Paul of Samosata,[91] and Theophylact was undoubtedly using it in that sense, because he ordered that these new heretics should be reconciled to the Church in accordance with the forms used for the followers of Paul of Samosata.[92] But the new heretics had nothing in common with the 'Paulians', who are an irrelevance in this context. Manichaeism was invariably equated by the Byzantines with Paulicianism, and Theophylact certainly supposed that the new heretics were in part Paulician, since he anathematized their teaching under fourteen heads, all but two of which are taken from Peter of Sicily's report. The two doctrines distinctive to the new heretics were these: anathema no. 2 shows them to be moderate dualists, who attribute the

---

88 Obolensky, *The Bogomils*, p. 89, n. 3, p. 95.
89 Browning, *Byzantium and Bulgaria*, pp. 67–9.
90 Only one other letter issued by his chancery has been preserved (*RP* I (II), no. 789, pp. 222–4).
91 See Appendix 2.
92 Obolensky, *The Bogomils*, p. 115.

making of the material universe to the devil, and not absolute dualists like the Paulicians; and anathema no. 4 shows that, unlike the Paulicians, they have an ascetic lifestyle. Indeed, later in his letter the patriarch speaks of those who associated with these heretics supposing that 'they were ascetics and good and religious men'. The patriarch advised the tsar to impose the death penalty on any heretics who would not recant.

The first reliable account of the rise of Bogomilism is the *Sermon* of Cosmas the Priest. The earliest manuscript comes from the fifteenth century, and the only indication in the text about when it was written is that Tsar Peter (d. 969) is referred to as dead **[15]**. But although some scholars have argued that Cosmas wrote in the early thirteenth century, we find the arguments for a late tenth-century date more convincing.[93] The type of Bogomilism which he describes is more primitive than that recorded in later sources: for example, by the thirteenth century the Bogomils had a liturgy and a hierarchy of which there is no trace in Cosmas' account.[94] Moreover, there is no information in this text which is inappropriate to a work written in the last quarter of the tenth century. Nothing is known about the author except that he was an Orthodox priest writing in Old Slavonic. He is highly critical of the Bulgarian Orthodox Church, which he holds responsible for allowing heresy to spread because of the corrupt lives of the clergy and their preoccupation with wealth, but that may be simply a rhetorical device designed to detract from the heretics' success by implying that they faced little opposition. For reasons of space we have not translated that part of Cosmas' work, because it adds nothing to our knowledge of the heresy.

Cosmas begins his account: 'In the reign of the good Christian Tsar Peter there was a priest called Bogomil . . . who started for the first time to preach heresy in the country of Bulgaria' **[15]**.

The Bogomils whom Cosmas describes were moderate dualists: they believed in one God who had two sons: the elder was Christ, the younger the devil; and the devil had fashioned the phenomenal universe. They rejected the Old Testament and based their teaching on the New Testament alone. They understood Christ's institution of the Eucharist allegorically, believing that at the Last Supper he had given his disciples the four Gospels (his Body) and the Acts of the Apostles (his Blood).

---

93 See the review of literature about this supported by the author's own comments: M. Dando 'Peut-on avancer de 240 ans la date de composition du Traité de Cosmas le prêtre contre les Bogomiles?', pp. 3–25.
94 See below, pp. 33, 34.

Although Cosmas ridicules this opinion as evidence of Bogomil ignorance, since the New Testament had not been written at the time of Christ's Passion, it is possible that the Bogomils, like their spiritual descendants the Cathars, believed that Christ brought down to earth these sacred books which had been written in Heaven and entrusted them to his Church.[95] They identified themselves as Christians, and although Cosmas does not directly say that they held a docetic Christology, that is implied by the rest of his account. The Bogomils totally rejected the hierarchy of the Orthodox Church. They lived an ascetic life, rejecting sexual intercourse, the eating of meat and the drinking of wine. They prayed frequently, using the Lord's Prayer, and did not observe any special religious feast days, treating Sundays like any other day. They made regular confession of their faults to each other, and Cosmas implies that they practised sex equality in that ministry.

Cosmas admits that the Bogomils seemed to lead good Christian lives, which made it difficult to distinguish them from the Orthodox. Some Bogomils were imprisoned for their faith, and consequently all of them had begun to adopt forms of passive resistance to evade conviction: they would reverence crosses and icons in churches if they wished to pass as Orthodox, and were prepared, when put on oath, to deny their heretical practices. Cosmas also accuses the Bogomils of wishing to overthrow the government: 'They teach their followers not to obey their masters; they scorn the rich, they hate the Tsar, they ridicule their superiors, they reproach the boyars, they believe that God looks in horror on those who labour for the Tsar and advise every serf not to work for his master' **[15]**. Perhaps the early Bogomils really were social radicals, although, if so, they soon lost their fervour, for there is no trace of such sentiments in any of the later evidence about them or about their western descendants, the Cathars. But it is possible that in this passage Cosmas is misrepresenting Bogomil teaching about the evils of all aspects of this world for polemical reasons.

Finally, Cosmas sees in the lifestyle of the Bogomils the fulfilment of St Paul's prophecy about the coming of Antichrist: 'Now the Spirit expressly says that in later times some will depart from the faith by giving heed to deceitful spirits and doctrines of demons, through the pretensions of liars whose consciences are seared, who forbid marriage and enjoin abstinence from foods which God created to be received with

---

95 Raynerius Sacconi, *Summa de Catharis*, ed. F. Sanjek (*AFP* 44 (1974), pp. 51–2).

thanksgiving by those who believe and know the truth' (1 Tim. 4.1–4) **[15]**.

Cosmas was writing at a time when there was a strong current of popular eschatological fervour in the Byzantine world: viewed in that context, the new heresy indeed appeared portentous.[96]

Superficially Bogomilism seemed to have a good deal in common with Paulicianism. Both were Christian dualist movements whose adherents denied that the Good God had made the visible universe; both rejected the belief that Christ had taken our humanity upon him; both rejected the Jewish dispensation and its sacred books as diabolically inspired; both rejected the Orthodox Church, its hierarchy and its sacraments. Although this appears to be a very broad area of consensus, the view of spiritual reality which lay at the centre of Bogomil belief was quite different from that of the Paulicians.

The Bogomils believed in one God, the source of all being, whose sons were Christ and the devil; and they believed that the devil was the maker of the phenomenal universe. This view of God did not derive from the Paulicians or from the ancient Manichaeans: its nearest parallel in Near Eastern thought was in Zurvanism, a form of Zoroastrianism which had been strong in the Sassanian Empire, and which postulates the existence of a High God, Zurvan, who is the father both of Ohrmazd, the God of Light, and of Ahriman, the God of Darkness.[97] As John the Exarch proves, this belief was present in Bulgaria before the rise of Bogomilism, and may date from a period when the Bulgars had lived on the Russian steppes and had more opportunities of direct contact with Sassanian Persia.[98]

The Bogomils did not derive their asceticism from the Paulicians, nor from the Zurvanites, neither of whom had any tradition of that kind. But the Manichaeans had required their elect to observe an ascetic rule of life, and their reasons for doing so were identical with those of the Bogomils, springing from a conviction that the material creation was evil. Although Manichaeism had died out in the Byzantine Empire by about 600, it still survived in the Islamic world when Bogomilism first appeared. The Caliph al-Muqtadir (908–32), a near contemporary of *pop* Bogomil, persecuted the Manichaeans of Baghdad, who took refuge

---

96 Alexander, 'Historiens byzantins et croyances eschatologiques', 2, pp. 1–8a.
97 Zaehner, *Zurvan: a Zoroastrian dilemma*, Appendix.
98 See the evidence of pagan Bulgarian temples in Stoyanov, *The hidden tradition in Europe*, p. 113.

in Samarkand, while the Uighurs of Turfan professed Manichaeism, and there were Manichaeans in China. Theoretically, travellers might have introduced Manichaean beliefs into tenth-century Bulgaria from these distant communities, but this seems unlikely. The linguistic problems involved in such transmission would have been considerable, nor would it be easy to explain why the Bogomils had only adopted the Manichaeans' lifestyle, while rejecting their belief system.[99]

Byzantine theologians labelled Bogomil asceticism Messalianism. The Messalians, also known as Euchites, 'those who pray', were a Christian sect of the mid-fourth century who taught that original sin caused each human being to have an individual demon which was resistant to baptism and could only be driven out by a life of constant prayer and extreme mortification. When this process had been successfully completed, the Christian would receive an immediate vision of the Holy Trinity. Their opponents claimed that enlightened Messalians considered themselves above the moral law and committed all kinds of excesses. There is no evidence that organized Messalianism survived beyond the seventh century,[100] even though the label continued to be used by Byzantine heresiologists to describe excesses in Orthodox monastic practice **[23(b)]**. There can therefore have been no possibility of contact between the Bogomils and a living Messalian tradition.

But there is no need to postulate an exotic origin for Bogomil asceticism. *Pop* Bogomil taught his followers to live like Orthodox monks: they should meet together for prayer at regular times each day and night, remain celibate, and abstain from eating meat or drinking wine. The monastic way of life was believed by the Churches of East and West in the central Middle Ages to approximate most closely to the life of Christian perfection, and the Bogomils were criticized not because the way in which they lived was in itself wrong, but because their motives for embracing asceticism were different from those recognized by the Orthodox tradition. Monastic *ascesis* involved giving up things which were of their nature God-given, in order the better to respond to Christ's invitation to self-denial,[101] whereas the Bogomils gave these things up because they believed them to be inherently evil and therefore incompatible with the practice of the Christian life.

99 *Ibid.*, pp. 125, 279, n. 22; Lieu, *Manichaeism in the later Roman Empire and medieval China*, pp. 84–5.
100 For a brief survey of Messalianism, see Bareille 'Euchites', 1454–65. For a Byzantine understanding of this heresy see **[23(b)]**.
101 Luke 9.23.

The tentative conclusion which these considerations suggest is that *pop* Bogomil's movement was deeply indebted to the Orthodox Church, from which he derived the monastic concept of holiness which he sought to cultivate among his followers. His moderate dualism, while it may have owed its initial stimulus to Paulician preachers who were certainly active in Bulgaria in his lifetime, nevertheless had a close resemblance to the beliefs of the Zurvanite Zoroastrians with which some Bulgarians seem to have been familiar before his day.

Bogomil was also indebted to the Orthodox Church in another way. Khan Boris had patronised Sts Clement and Nahum, who introduced the Old Slavonic translations of the Bible and the Orthodox liturgy in the Bulgarian Church and founded a flourishing school at Ochrida in western Macedonia for the translation of Greek texts into Old Slavonic.[102] It was the Old Slavonic text of the New Testament which *pop* Bogomil used as the foundation of his teaching.

The simple religion described by Cosmas soon became far more sophisticated. As Yuri Stoyanov has rightly observed, the materials for this development were to hand because of the school of translation founded by Sts Nahum and Clement: 'What remains undisputed is the link between the crystallization of Bogomil doctrine and the influx of a rich and diverse apocryphal literature in tenth-century Bulgaria, some of which came to be adopted for the purpose of Bogomil propaganda.'[103]

Byzantine Bogomilism

The fifty years following the death of Tsar Peter in 969 were a troubled time in Bulgarian history. First the country was occupied by the army of Prince Sviatoslav of Kiev, then in 972 John I Tzimisces, arguably the greatest general to occupy the Byzantine throne, turned out the Russians and brought Bulgaria under direct Byzantine rule. But in Basil II's reign (976–1025) the Bulgarian Empire was restored under Tsar Samuel (after 987–1014), and Basil only finally reconquered it in 1018 after a lengthy series of campaigns.[104] During that period Bogomilism was able to grow virtually unchecked, and by the early eleventh century it had spread into the Greek-speaking lands of Byzantium. The Byzantine annexation of Bulgaria must have made this easier, and the presence of large numbers

---

102 Soulis, 'The legacy of Cyril and Methodius to the Southern Slavs', pp. 21–43; Vlasto, *The entry of the Slavs into Christendom*, pp. 78, 163–72; Fine, *The early medieval Balkans*, pp. 134–7; Obolensky, 'Clement of Ohrid', in *Six Byzantine portraits*, pp. 8–33.
103 Stoyanov, *The hidden tradition in Europe*, pp. 132–3; Ivanov, *Livres et légendes bogomiles*.
104 Fine, *The early medieval Balkans*, pp. 181–99.

of Slavs who had been settled in the Asiatic provinces since the mid-seventh century may also have helped the Bogomil missions.[105]

The earliest account we have of Byzantine Bogomilism is the letter written in *c*. 1045 by Euthymius of the Periblepton monastery in Constantinople **[19]**. Unfortunately, he is not distinguished for his clarity of exposition – indeed, the text of his letter might justly be described as rambling – but it does contain a good deal of information about the way in which Bogomilism was spreading and evolving as a faith in the first half of the eleventh century.

Euthymius did not know the *Sermon* of Cosmas the Priest, written in Old Slavonic, and did not associate the heretics he describes with Bulgaria, but his evidence broadly corroborates that of Cosmas, although there are some significant differences between the two accounts. One merit of Euthymius' work is that he did not suppose that the Bogomils were the votaries of an older heresy, and therefore did not attempt to ascribe to them inappropriate beliefs and practices. But the chief problem in handling this text is that of trying to separate factual information from the excessive anxieties which these heretics inspired in the writer. In that regard it is, no doubt, an advantage that Euthymius did not have a very subtle mind.

He tells us that the Bogomils called themselves true Christians, but were known by various names among the Orthodox: 'the people of the Opsikion [theme] call ... [those] who are members of this most evil blasphemy Phundagiagitae, but towards the Kibbyrhaiot [theme] they call them Bogomils' **[19]**. The name Phundagiagitae has never been satisfactorily explained: it may be cognate with *phunda*, 'a bag', and relate to scrips which these heretics carried. Euthymius discovered a Bogomil 'cell' in his own monastery, but he also gives details of other Bogomils, including John Tzurillas, a heretical minister at Acmonia. Michael Angold has argued that Tzurillas was not a Bogomil at all, but a follower of Eleutherius of Paphlagonia (d. 950), who had practised a kind of mystical Messalianism. We do not find this view convincing, because although the two movements had certain negative features in common, they differed in one very central way: the followers of Eleutherius were each allowed two wives to show how superior they were to carnal temptations, whereas John Tzurillas and his followers considered it

---

105 Under Constans II, *ibid.*, p. 66; Justinian II, Head, *Justinian II of Byzantium*, pp. 41–4; Constantine V, Anastos, 'Iconoclasm and imperial rule, p. 74.

essential to salvation to separate from their wives, which is a distinctive Bogomil trait.[106]

The chief difference between the Byzantine Bogomils described by Euthymius and the Bulgarian Bogomils described by Cosmas is that the former had adopted an initiation rite which enabled them to make a distinction between fully professed members of their church and sympathizers. There is no clear evidence that this had been the case with the primitive Bogomils described by Cosmas. Euthymius describes how candidates were required to undergo a long and rigorous period of ascetic training which culminated in a ceremony at which the Gospel book was placed on the candidate's head and a hymn was sung. He believed that this ceremony involved the washing off, or renunciation, of Orthodox baptism, although there is no evidence for this in any other source. Perhaps he inferred that this took place because he could not otherwise explain how it was possible for Orthodox believers to apostatize.

He also cites part of the Bogomils' daily liturgy: 'The leader . . . takes his stand and begins by saying: "Let us adore the Father, the Son and the Holy Spirit." Those who pray with him answer: "It is right and fitting." He begins the Our Father . . . making a genuflection; they bob their heads up and down like those who are possessed' **[19]**. Euthymius is the earliest witness to the use by the Bogomils of a *Ritual*, closely related to the Cathar *Rituals* and the Bosnian *Ritual* of Radoslav (Appendix I).

He admits that the Bogomils' way of life was very austere. All the initiated were required to live as celibates. John Tzurillas and his wife lived apart and styled themselves abbot and abbess, and these titles suggest that they had formed their followers into single-sex communities of the kind which later became common in the Bogomil Church of Bosnia **[39]** and among the Cathars of the West, but it is not clear how generally this pattern of life was adopted by eleventh-century Bogomils elsewhere. Euthymius also implies that the initiates renounced all property, for he describes them as being left with only one tunic apiece, and he adds that they devoted themselves to a life of liturgical prayer built round the Lord's Prayer. He says nothing about a Bogomil hierarchy apart from reporting that Tzurillas was called *papa* by the people of Acmonia, not just by his own followers. This may simply have been a courtesy title which local people gave to a respected religious leader. But

---

106 Angold *Church and society in Byzantium*, pp. 472–6.

as Bogomil had been called *pop*, and as Nicetas, the leader of the Bogomils of Constantinople in the twelfth century, was known as *papa* [37(a)], it is possible that Tzurillas had this title because he held an office in the Bogomil Church.

The movement caused Euthymius grave anxieties because it was spreading very rapidly: he reports outbreaks in the Opsikion, Thrakesion and Kibyrrhaiot themes[107] and in the 'regions towards the West', as well as in Constantinople and its environs. Moreover, the Bogomils were indistinguishable in appearance from the Orthodox. They were prepared at need to conform to Orthodox practices, to take part in Orthodox worship and even to receive the Orthodox sacraments, while attaching no importance to them. If challenged about their faith, Euthymius adds, they will say that they believe 'all that we do'.

But Euthymius did not believe what the Bogomils told him about themselves. Although they claimed to be continuing the evangelical work of Sts Peter and Paul, he was certain that they were in fact spreading the teachings of heretics with the same names: thus not Simon Peter, but Simon Magus was their spiritual father, and, more recently, Peter the Wolf (Lycopetrus), who, transported to the Caucasus by art magic, claimed that he would rise bodily from the dead, and did so in the form of a wolf. Euthymius accused the Bogomils of worshipping Satan. The purpose of their initiation rite was, in his view, to make candidates subject to the power of the devil, and he asserted that the Bogomils had told him that they had received from Peter Lycopetrus 'a satanic spell which we call the Revelation of St Peter'. Euthymius was sure that it was this, not the text of the Gospel, which they recited over the candidate at his initiation, although he was unaware of it. If the Bogomils really did tell Euthymius that they read the Revelation of St Peter (even though there is no evidence that it played any part in their initiation rite), this would show that they were already beginning to use apocryphal writings, as well as the New Testament. That work, which was Gnostic in origin, would have appealed to them because of its cosmology, which assumes that the phenomenal world is the work of an imperfect demiurge.[108]

Given these premises, which are totally unsupported in any other source and which appear to be the product of Euthymius' own spiritual insecurity, it is difficult not to feel sceptical about other information of a similar

107 See map.
108 Ch. Maurer, text tr. H. Duensing, 'The Apocalypse of Peter', in *NTA* II, pp. 663–83.

kind which he gives: for example, that if Bogomils have their children baptized in the Orthodox Church they go home and wash off the baptismal water with urine; or that those who make their communion in the Orthodox Church secretly spit out the consecrated Host and trample it under foot.[109] Because the Bogomils tended to be considered saintly people, since their way of life approximated closely to the Orthodox ideal of holiness, Euthymius feared that they were deliberately seeking to infiltrate the Orthodox hierarchy: that they not merely dressed and behaved like monks and priests, but that they also exercised monastic and priestly functions in order to undermine the Church's saving work. He claimed that one Bogomil had gone so far as to build, and serve as priest in, an Orthodox church in order to profane the sacred mysteries.

Euthymius' work affords evidence that some groups of Bogomils had been influenced by Paulicians. When writing of the heresiarchs whom the Bogomils truly revere, he tells the story of Sergius, the disciple of Lycopetrus, and his dog Arzeberius. This tale has nothing to do either with the Bogomils or with the Paulicians, but is a folkloristic attempt to explain why the Armenian Church keeps the Fast of Nineveh.[110] Yet the Sergius who figures in it is Sergius–Tychicus, the last *didaskalos* of the Paulicians.[111] This suggests that some Paulicians, probably from western Anatolia, where Bogomil missions operated, were converted to the new teaching, and that their own folklore had become part of the general Bogomil tradition by the 1040s.

Yet although Bogomilism was clearly spreading in many parts of the Byzantine Empire in the first half of the eleventh century, the imperial authorities did not take any special measures to combat it.[112] The Bogomils found in the Periblepton monastery seem to have been disciplined by their own superiors, but no action was taken against John Tzurillas, for example: he had earlier been put on trial for rape, not heresy.

---

109 Almost contemporaneous with Euthymius is the assertion of Cardinal Humbert in 1054 that Nicephorus, the *sacellarius* of the patriarch Michael, had 'trodden the sacrifice of the Latins under his feet in the sight of everyone' (Michael Cerularius, *Edictum Synodale* (*PG* 120, 743–4)).
110 This is a two-week pre-Lenten fast kept by the Armenian Church.
111 Gouillard, 'L'Hérésie dans l'empire byzantin', pp. 316–18.
112 A set of anti-dualist anathemas found in some manuscripts of the Synodikon of Orthodoxy probably date from the tenth century, but relate to beliefs which Bogomils and Paulicians held in common, and may well have been formulated against the Paulicians. ([**16(c)**]) J. Gouillard, 'Le Synodikon de l'orthodoxie: édition et commentaire', *T & M* 2 (1967), pp. 230–2.

The reason for this inaction should probably be sought in the political circumstances of the empire during the years following Basil II's death in 1025. Thirteen emperors held power in the next fifty-six years, which produced a lack of continuity in central government policies, while the empire was threatened by Normans in the west, Patzinaks to the north, and Turks in Anatolia.[113] It is not surprising that the imperial government did not accord high priority to checking the spread of a quietist dissident movement.

All the patriarchs who presided over the Byzantine Church in this troubled period, Alexius the Studite (1025–43), Michael Cerularius (1043–58), Constantine III Lichudes (1059–63) and John Xiphilinus (1064–75), were concerned to combat heresy, but their energies were directed against the non-Chalcedonian Christians of the eastern provinces, whose leaders they sought to bring into full dogmatic union with the Orthodox Church. Cerularius varied this policy only by quarrelling with the Roman pontiff as well about differences in faith, usage and jurisdiction.[114] Cosmas I of Jerusalem (1075–81) was the first patriarch of Constantinople since Theophylact Lecapenus to take any action against the Bogomils.

His letter to the metropolitan of Larissa in Thessaly, although it contains very little new information, casts an interesting light on the popular perception of Bogomilism: 'To those who say that Satan is the creator of the visible creation and call him the steward of thunder, hail and all that is provided by the earth, anathema' **[41]**. If lay people were beginning to attribute such powers to the evil Archon, this might help to explain why Bogomilism was popular in rural areas. The patriarch also anathematizes '*pop* Bogomil who welcomed the Manichaean heresy in the time of King Peter of Bulgaria and spread it throughout Bulgaria . . .' **[41]**. This is the earliest mention of Bogomil in a Greek source, and shows that the Byzantine Church in the eleventh century considered that he was indeed the founder of the new heresy.[115]

The Patriarch Cosmas abdicated for political reasons in 1081, so his anti-Bogomil measures were not followed through. Most members of the Orthodox establishment do not seem to have considered that the Bogomils were particularly dangerous. Theophylact of Ochrida, Archbishop of Bulgaria (*c.* 1090–*c.* 1118), for example, makes few clear

---

113 Angold, *The Byzantine empire*, pp. 12–58.
114 Hussey, *The Orthodox Church*, pp. 127–40.
115 Cosmas' condemnation of him may have been incorporated in a provincial recension of the Synodikon of Orthodoxy dating from Alexius I's reign **[16 (a)]**.

references to them in his writings,[116] even though the cradle of Bogomilism lay in his own province.

Alexius I (1081–1118) was very strongly opposed to heresy, but was too occupied with defending his state from attack by the South Italian Normans, the Patzinaks and the Seljuk Turks, to have leisure to act against the Bogomils in the early years of his reign.[117] His daughter Anna in her history of his reign **[24]** and his theologian, Euthymius Zigabenus **[25]**, who are the chief sources for the history of Bogomilism at this time, both agree that the heresy was well concealed, probably because the Bogomils looked like Orthodox monks. Anna writes: 'You would never see a lay hair-style on a Bogomil; the evil is hidden under a cloak or a cowl. A Bogomil has a grave expression; he is muffled to the nose, walks bent forward and speaks softly, but inwardly he is an untamed wolf' **[24]**.

Alexius may have become alarmed about this sect because some of the great families in the capital patronised its members.[118] Yuri Stoyanov has suggested that this was in part a consequence of the marriages which Basil II had arranged between Bulgarian princesses and Byzantine noblemen, because some of the women in Tsar Samuel's family were known to have had Bogomil sympathies.[119] Certainly the Bulgarian imperial family did marry into the greatest families of Byzantium: the Emperor Alexius' mother-in-law was Maria of Bulgaria.[120]

Alexius arrested a Bogomil named Diblatius and tortured him in order to discover details of the movement's organization. He found that it was led by a certain Basil, who dressed as a monk, and who, Zigabenus tells us, was a doctor who had 'studied erroneous doctrine for fifteen years and taught it for more than forty'. **[25]** If true, this would mean that he was in his seventies when he was brought to trial, and was a link with the first known Bogomil cell in Constantinople reported by Euthymius of the Periblepton. Anna says that his closest advisers were a group of twelve apostles, together with some women disciples. The number may not be exact, and perhaps is intended to imply that he was a counterfeit Christ,

---

116 Most of these references might equally well relate to the Paulicians (Obolensky, 'Theophylact of Ochrid', in *Six Byzantine portraits*, pp. 34–82).
117 Angold, *The Byzantine empire*, pp. 102–13.
118 'The evil had weighed heavily even on the greatest houses'. See **[24]**. On the role of the monk as spiritual director see Morris, *Monks and laymen in Byzantium, 843–1118*, pp. 90–102.
119 Stoyanov, *The hidden tradition in Europe*, pp. 135–6; Anguélov, *Le Bogomilisme en Bulgarie*, p. 104.
120 Anna Comnena, *Alexiad* 2.6 (ed. B. Leib, vol. 1 pp. 80, 173 n.).

but her comment suggests that he had what western Cathars would call a 'council', made up of members of both sexes.[121] The historian Zonaras, who was a contemporary, places these events immediately after the passage of the First Crusade through the capital in 1097, and they certainly took place before 1104, the latest date for the death of the Sebastocrator Isaac, who was involved in the proceedings.[122]

According to Anna, Alexius and his brother Isaac invited Basil to the Great Palace and asked him to enlighten them about the Christian faith. It was a clever but credible approach, since the Comneni brothers appeared to be treating Basil as an Orthodox monk who was a respected spiritual director; and this provided him with an opportunity of converting the emperor, which, had he succeeded, would have turned his sect into an imperially protected movement. No doubt a number of meetings took place, for the emperor was able to learn about the organization and membership of the Bogomil movement in Constantinople, as well as about its faith.

Alexius then had Basil and his associates arrested, and Basil was examined by Euthymius Zigabenus, who provides the only systematic description of Bogomil theology that we have. It agrees in the main with the accounts of Euthymius of the Periblepton and Cosmas the Priest, and amplifies them, as a comparison of these texts will show the diligent reader. Bogomilism was clearly still evolving in the late eleventh century: for example, Basil and his followers accepted the non-historical books of the Old Testament as divinely inspired, as well as the whole of the New Testament.

Zigabenus provides further evidence about Paulician influence on the Bogomils: 'they banish all the pious emperors from the fold of Christians, and say that only the Iconoclasts are orthodox and faithful, especially [Constantine V] Copronymus' **[25]**. Since Iconoclasm ended about a century before the birth of Bogomilism, this opinion must reflect Paulician influence, for the Paulicians had every reason to honour the memory of the Iconoclast emperors.[123] Basil claimed to have a text of the Bible which had not been edited by St John Chrysostom, which is another way of saying that it was a different text from that which the Orthodox used. There is no easy way of verifying whether this was so, since no copy of the Bible used by the Bogomils has ever been found, but

---

121 There is no evidence that women were ever members of Cathar councils.
122 Zonaras *Epitome historiarum*, XVIII, 23, ed. Buttner-Wobst, pp. 742–4; Angold. *Church and society in Byzantium*, pp. 485–6.
123 See above, pp. 15–19.

HISTORICAL INTRODUCTION

it is possible that they may have used a text which, like the Cathar New Testament of Lyons, contained a number of significant variant readings, while in general conforming to the Vulgate.[124] Zigabenus also obtained a Bogomil commentary on St Matthew's Gospel, from which he cites extracts from chapters 1–9 in order to put his readers on their guard against the ways in which Bogomils allegorize the text of holy scripture. This is the only exegetical work which has come down to us from any eastern Christian dualist sect, and so it forms a particularly valuable piece of evidence.[125]

Zigabenus relates that the Bogomils at first instructed their followers in those beliefs and practices which they shared with the Orthodox, and only later expounded the beliefs which were particular to themselves, and in his *Narratio* he gives a description of the kind of instruction that Bogomil converts received. This is the only known example of Bogomil methods of catechizing, and for that reason we have translated it in full **[25, 'Origin myth']**.

Efforts were made to convert the Bogomils; Alexius, as guardian of Orthodoxy, reasoned in person with the Bogomil 'apostles'. All those who recanted were released,[126] but a hard core remained, led by Basil, who was burnt alive in the Hippodrome of Constantinople. His was the only death: the other unrepentant Bogomils were imprisoned for life.

In 1107 Alexius ordered a special group of preachers to be attached to the Church of the Holy Wisdom, partly to instruct the population of the capital about the dangers of heresy. We have included a sermon of this kind to give some indication of the form which this instruction took **[27]**.[127]

Gouillard suggests that the Bogomil anathemas found in the Synodikon of Orthodoxy used in the province of Athens are based on the canons of the synod which condemned Basil. The only new information which they give is that the Bogomils read the *Vision of Isaiah*[128] and recited the

---

124 Clédat, *Le Nouveau Testament traduit au xiiie siecle en langue provençale*; Hamilton, 'Wisdom from the East', pp. 49–52.
125 A commentary on St Matthew is ascribed to the Paulician leader Sergius–Tychicus in an anti-Bogomil section of a text of the Synodikon of Orthodoxy **[16 (d)]**. If this relates to the work cited by Zigabenus, then that must have been a Paulician commentary adapted for Bogomil use. See *T & M* 4 (1970), p. 191.
126 See the forms for the reception of Bogomil converts, **[26]**.
127 Angold, *Church and society in Byzantium*, p. 487.
128 Gouillard, *T & M* 2 (1965), pp. 232–3. The text of *The Vision of Isaiah*, is in Ivanov, *Livres et légendes bogomiles*, pp. 133–60; an English translation is in Wakefield and Evans, *Heresies of the High Middle Ages*, no. 56A, pp. 447–58.

Lord's Prayer without the doxology which was customarily used in the Byzantine Church **[16(d)]**.

There is no mention of dualist heresy in Byzantine sources for some forty years after Basil's trial. Then in the 1140s a series of heresy trials, allegedly involving Bogomils, were held in Constantinople. In May 1140 a synod convoked by the Patriarch Leo Stypes (1134–43) found evidence of Bogomilism in the writings of Constantine Chrysomallus, who had recently died in the monastery of St Nicholas at Hieron **[28]**. These writings were withdrawn from circulation and burned. Chrysomallus allegedly insisted on the need to 'have been catechized and receive regeneration and the formation of the discipline of their souls through the mediation and laying on of hands of the expert stewards of this great mystery, who are skilled in holy knowledge', **[28]**. This could be construed as evidence of the Bogomil rite of initiation by baptism in the Holy Spirit, and was so construed by the synod, but most scholars now consider that he was not a Bogomil, but a follower of the great Orthodox mystic, St Symeon the New Theologian (d. 1022), who emphasised the importance of the union of the individual soul with God.[129]

The trial is important chiefly because it alerted the authorities to the possibility that Bogomilism was still at work among church leaders. Soon after the Emperor Manuel I was enthroned in 1143, the new Patriarch Michael II of Oxeia (1143–46) presided at a synod, at which imperial judges were also present, to try two Cappadocian bishops accused of heresy. They were found guilty of Bogomilism and condemned to solitary confinement, although nothing in the charges made against them bears any relation to that heresy **[30]**. Their trial was to have important repercussions.

A monk called Niphon, who was widely regarded as a holy man and who had been held in esteem by the late emperor John II (1118–43),[130] protested against this judgment, and he too was condemned as a Bogomil and imprisoned in the Periblepton monastery at Constantinople **[31]**. The Patriarch Michael reacted violently to this evidence of the growth of heresy, and during his reign the synod took the unusual step of commanding that unrepentant Bogomils should be burnt without reference to the civil courts, a ruling which later embarrassed the great canon lawyer, Theodore Balsamon **[29]**.

---

129 Magdalino, *The empire of Manuel I Komnenos*, p. 276; Angold, *Church and society in Byzantium*, pp. 489–90.
130 Angold, *Church and society in Byzantium*, p. 78.

But in 1146 the Patriarch Michael retired and was succeeded by Cosmas II Atticus, who immediately released the monk Niphon from prison and allowed him to teach freely. The content of his teaching is not known in any detail, though he is said to have rejected the God of the Jews, which might be evidence that he shared a Bogomil view of the Old Testament, but which might mean nothing more than that he pointed out that the Jews did not believe in the Holy Trinity **[31]**. The patriarch defended Niphon's orthodoxy, but by doing so gave a handle to his own enemies: on 20 February 1147 at an assembly of bishops and lay officials over which the Emperor Manuel presided he was found guilty of favouring Bogomils solely because he had released the monk Niphon, whom the Holy Synod had convicted of that heresy, and he was deposed **[32(a)]**. The patriarch was not himself convicted of holding or teaching Bogomil doctrines. He certainly had many enemies, who used his friendship with Niphon to conduct a campaign of vilification against him, as John Tzetzes, a member of his household, had the courage to warn the emperor **[32(c)]**. But it seems unlikely that Manuel would have agreed to Cosmas' deposition on such flimsy grounds unless he had had other reasons for wishing to be rid of him, and it is possible that he believed that Cosmas was siding with his elder brother, the Sebastocrator Isaac, in a plot to seize the throne **[32(b)]**.

In the 1140s Constantinople seems to have been in the grip of Bogomil fever: the accusation of being a covert Bogomil then became a very useful weapon against opponents of all kinds, because it touched on a general fear, that Bogomils were masters of disguise who were in league with the powers of darkness and were intent on overthrowing the divinely ordained society of Orthodox Byzantium. In fact they occupied much the same place in the public imagination as Communists did in that of the USA during the 1950s (see also **[35]**).

There were, of course, still a large number of real Bogomils in the provinces; there is evidence of them at Philippopolis[131] and at Moglena, west of Thessalonica **[33]**. There is also evidence which suggests that Manuel ordered the arrest of Bogomil provincial leaders, but it is difficult to interpret. This is the work usually called *The Dialogue concerning Demons* **[34]**, which used to be attributed to Michael Psellus (d. 1078), but which Gautier has argued dates from the mid-twelfth century and may have been written by Nicholas of Methone. Gautier's dating is

---

131 Browning, 'Unpublished correspondence between Michael Italos, archbishop of Philippopolis, and Theodore Prodromos', *Byzantinobulgarica* 1, pp. 279–97; reprinted in his *Studies on Byzantine history, literature and education*, no. VI.

more convincing than the traditional one, which would mean that the treatise was written at a time when no action was being taken against the Bogomils by the imperial authorities.[132]

The treatise is cast in the form of a dialogue between Timothy and Thrax, the man from Thrace. There is no doubt that it is about Bogomils. Thrax describes the heretics as those who believe in a threefold God: a Father who is supreme, his younger Son who rules the heavens and his elder Son, Satanael, who rules the earth and is 'the creator of plants and animals and everything that is composite' **[34]**. This is the Bogomil cosmology described by all earlier writers. The narrative is discursive: Thrax tells us that he had visited the city of Elasson in Thessaly and tried to arrest the local Bogomil leader and his followers and take them back to Constantinople to stand trial, but had been prevented from doing so, presumably by the strength of local opposition. His chief informant about the heretics was a monk called Mark Mesopotamites. A scholion in an early manuscript states: 'This Mark came from Thebes. At first he was a teacher of the Bogomils, later he became Orthodox. He encountered Thrax who had been sent against the Bogomils' (**[34]**, note 6).

Michael Angold points to independent evidence that the Mesopotamites family had a connection with Thebes in the early twelfth century.[133] It would seem, therefore, that Thrax's mission was directed to Thessaly and Hellas, and the presence of Bogomils in those provinces during the twelfth century is confirmed by the fact that special anti-Bogomil anathemas were added to the Synodikon of Orthodoxy by the church of Hellas at that time **[16(d)]**.

The quality of information which the *Dialogue* contains about the Bogomils is poor. They are accused, as heretics so often were, of disgusting and orgiastic practices, far removed from the asceticism of the Bogomil elect; and of worshipping Satanael and his minions. Angold is certainly correct in saying that because Orthodox observers could not accept that the Bogomil initiation rite was a true vehicle of grace, they had to suppose that it was diabolically inspired.[134] One consequence of this was that Bogomils were believed to be particularly well informed about the operation of demons. The chief interest of this text is that it reveals that there was a great deal of overlap between the Bogomil and

132 Angold, *Church and society in Byzantium*, p. 496.
133 *Ibid.*, p. 498, n. 125.
134 *Ibid.*, p. 499.

Orthodox views of the place of demons in the natural order. Thrax explains to Timothy that there are six different kinds of demons who have varying powers, all of whom can harm people in a variety of ways, including making them ill.

The author of this *Dialogue* was no more credulous in his view of demons than most Orthodox believers whom we know about in this period. The demon-haunted universe of Euthymius of the Periblepton has already been described **[19]**. Anna Comnena, a well-educated laywoman, interpreted the hailstorm and the earthquake which occurred on the night of Basil the Bogomil's arrest as 'an expression of anger on the part of the enraged demons of Satanael' **[24]**; while even Zigabenus, a learned theologian with a logical mind, took the presence of demons in the natural world completely for granted.

In a universe in which demons were so powerful and walked abroad so openly, Bogomils, who claimed to be able to free men from their dominion, could compete on terms of parity with the Orthodox clergy who claimed identical powers. Given that it was popularly believed that demons were responsible for many kinds of illness, the profession of doctor exercised by Basil the Bogomil may well have helped him in gaining an entrée to the great houses of Constantinople.[135]

The Bogomils and the West

After Alexius I's reign Greek and Slav sources provide very little information about the internal history of Bogomilism, but this lack can in some measure be supplied from western sources. There is now a virtual consensus among scholars that Catharism was in origin a western form of Bogomilism. Although there is still considerable disagreement about when Catharism first appeared in the West, it is certain that it was securely rooted there by the 1140s.[136] At first all the Cathars were moderate dualists, and described themselves as members of the *ordo Bulgariae*. This term might best be rendered 'the Bulgarian succession', meaning the succession of spiritual baptisms (which the Cathars called consolings) which linked them to the Church of the Apostles.

But in *c.* 1170 *papa* Nicetas, Bogomil bishop of Constantinople, visited the West, claiming that consolings performed within the Bulgarian *ordo* were invalid **[37(b)]**. He represented the *ordo Drugonthiae*, and he presided over a Cathar Council at Saint-Félix near Toulouse attended by

---

135 Greenfield, *Traditions of belief in late Byzantine demonology*.
136 Lambert, *Medieval heresy*, pp. 55–61.

the Cathar bishops of Northern and Southern France and Lombardy. He reconsoled all the Cathar perfect present, reconsecrated the bishops, and consecrated three additional bishops for the southern French communities. He recommended that the churches should define their diocesan boundaries in the interests of future harmony, claiming that that was the practice of the churches of the East **[37(a)]**.

All western sources show that the Cathars who traced their descent from Nicetas and the *ordo* of Drugonthia were absolute dualists, like the Paulicians, but they were not Paulicians because they shared with the members of the Bulgarian *ordo* an ascetic way of life and a common form of worship and of organization, which indicates that both groups had a common origin.[137] Drugonthia and its many variations are western attempts to render the name Dragovitia, which as Dujčev has shown designates 'the region of the Rhodope mountains to the south of Philippopolis'.[138] There was a strong Paulician presence in twelfth-century Philippopolis, and it is possible that Paulician converts to Bogomilism may have been responsible for the adoption of absolute dualist beliefs by the Church of Dragovitia/Drugonthia.[139] Zigabenus and earlier Byzantine sources knew nothing of this schism, which must have developed between *c.* 1100 and *c.* 1170 when Nicetas came to the West, by which time the Dragovitian *ordo* had been adopted by the Bogomil church of Constantinople.

Before the schism occurred, but after Zigabenus wrote his account of them, the Bogomils adopted a distinctive form of episcopal government, in which each diocesan bishop was assisted by two coadjutors, known as his elder and younger sons, who had rights of succession. This system closely resembles the Bogomil teaching about God and his two sons. The first known Cathar bishop was tried at Cologne in 1143,[140] but the first known Bogomil bishop is Simon, or Symeon, of Drugonthia, the consecrator of Nicetas **[37(b)]**. Whether this form of government first developed among the Cathars or the Bogomils, it antedated the schism, because both moderate and absolute dualist Bogomils practised it.

The Saint-Félix document preserves a list of five Bogomil Churches which it attributes to Nicetas: Rome, Dragometia (that is Dragovitia),

137 Hamilton, 'The origins of the dualist church of Drugunthia', pp. 115–24; Nelli, *La Philosophie du catharisme*. See also Nelson, 'Religion in "histoire totale"', pp. 67–70; Angold, *Church and society in Byzantium*, pp. 490–5.
138 Dujčev, 'Dragvitsa–Dragovitia', pp. 218–19.
139 Hamilton, 'The Cathars and the Seven churches of Asia', pp. 282–3; Obolensky, 'Papa Nicetas'.
140 Appendix to the Letters of St Bernard, no. CDXXXII (*PL* 182, 679).

HISTORICAL INTRODUCTION

Melenguia, Bulgaria and Dalmatia [37(a)]. Any Byzantine Greek, and Nicetas, to judge from his name, was a Greek and not a Slav, would have understood the word Roman to mean Byzantine, and the *Ecclesia Romana* of which he spoke must be the Bogomil Church of the Byzantine Empire, ruled from Constantinople, over which he himself presided. The Church of Dragovitia was the Bogomil Church of the Philippopolis region. The Church of Bulgaria was the mother-church founded by *pop* Bogomil. The Church of Melenguia can only, as Dossat pointed out, relate to the Slav tribe of the Milingui, who lived on the Taygetus range in the southern Peloponnese.[141] This people, who remained Slav-speaking and effectively self-governing into the thirteenth century,[142] would have formed a sympathetic audience for Bogomil preachers, and Bogomilism was already established in Thessaly and Hellas. The Church of Dalmatia is the earliest mention of what later became known as the Church of Bosnia [39]. There seem to be gaps in Nicetas' list: no mention is made of Anatolia or of Thessaly and central Greece, although there are known to have been Bogomil communities in both those areas, which were too distant from the capital to have come under Nicetas' jurisdiction.

Some years after Nicetas' visit the Bogomil Church of Bulgaria sent an envoy named Petracius to the Cathars of Lombardy, who reported that Bishop Symeon of Dragovitia, who had consecrated Nicetas, had fallen into mortal sin, and that all the consolings which derived from him were therefore invalid. This news produced a schism among the Cathars of northern and central Italy which was never subsequently healed. The Cathars of Desenzano remained true to the absolute dualism of Nicetas (as did those of southern France) and sent their bishop-elect to Dragovitia to be consecrated; but the other Cathars reverted to moderate dualism and turned for guidance either to the Church of Bulgaria or to that of Bosnia [37(b)]. During this period apocryphal writings used by the Bogomils were translated into Latin and circulated among the Cathars [38].

---

141 Dossat, 'À propos du concile cathare de Saint-Félix', pp. 209–14; he argued that this supported his view that the document was a seventeenth-century forgery. For counter-arguments that have been generally accepted see Hamilton, 'The Cathar council of Saint-Félix reconsidered', pp. 23–53. Nelson, 'Religion in "histoire totale"', pp. 67–70; Moore, *The origins on European dissent*, pp. 212–15; Lambert, *Medieval heresy*, pp. 126–8.
142 Lurier, tr., *Crusaders as conquerors*, pp. 159–60. Cf. Constantine Porphyrogenitus, *De administrando imperio*, c. 50, pp. 232–5.

CHRISTIAN DUALIST HERESIES

The success of the western missions and the close links which the Italian Cathars maintained with the Balkan Bogomils are sure signs of how vigorous Bogomilism was in the second half of the twelfth century. This is borne out by Theodore Balsamon, who remarked how whole towns and villages in the provinces were given over to Bogomilism, and no attempt was made to stamp it out.[143] Moreover, Bogomils were still to be found in the capital in the later years of Manuel's reign.

This is known from the *Adversus Patherenos*, a tract against the Bogomils written by Hugh Eteriano, a Pisan living in Constantinople, who was one of Manuel I's advisers on western Church affairs **[36]**. He was well established in Constantinople by 1166, and so this tract must have been written between *c*. 1160 and Manuel's death in 1180, most probably in the 1170s. It has not been published before.[144] Hugh was writing about Byzantine Bogomils, not Cathars living among the western residents in Constantinople: the whole tenor of his work makes this plain, particularly his references to the Orthodox churches and relics of the city and the cult of the icons. The tract was written at the request of unnamed noblemen in order to persuade the emperor to impose the death penalty on the Bogomils. Hugh's chief concern is therefore to supply his patrons with authorities which they can cite against Bogomil practices. The charges which he brings against the Bogomils are familiar ones, except that of their refusal to swear oaths. Hugh came from a society which was held together by ceremonies of oath-taking, and was very shocked by this: 'Without oaths the world could not and cannot be firmly based', he comments **[36]**.

His intervention had no effect. Manuel did not prosecute the Bogomils, nor did any of his successors in the troubled quarter of a century following his death in 1180, when the empire was beset by frequent palace revolutions, external attacks, and revolts in the Balkans which led to the creation of an independent kingdom in Serbia and a revival of the Bulgarian Empire.[145] The attack on Constantinople by the Fourth Crusade in 1203–4 caused further political fragmentation in the Byzantine lands. The Byzantine Emperor and the Orthodox Patriarch established their courts in exile at Nicaea, while other independent Byzantine states were set up in Trebizond and Epirus. The remaining imperial territory was divided between the Latin Emperor of Constantinople and the

---

143 Magdalino, *The empire of Manuel I Komnenos*, p. 393.
144 Dondaine, 'Hugues Éthérien et Léon Toscan'; Dondaine, 'Hughes Éthérien et le Concile de Constantinople'.
145 Brand, *Byzantium confronts the West*; Fine, *The late medieval Balkans*, pp. 1–59.

HISTORICAL INTRODUCTION

Venetians.[146] In the lands under western rule Orthodox bishops were replaced by Latins,[147] so that after 1204 there was no longer a unified secular or ecclesiastical authority in the Byzantine world to direct the fight against Bogomilism.

In the early thirteenth century the Papacy became involved in combating Bogomilism in Bosnia. Although the Slav rite was used there, Bosnia was part of Catholic Christendom, and its Bans, though in practice independent princes, were technically vassals of the Kings of Hungary.[148] Nicetas had listed a Church of Dalmatia among the Bogomil churches (it is called Sclavinia in the Italian sources) **[37(b)]**. From the *History of Split* written in *c.* 1260 by Archdeacon Thomas and from the correspondence of Pope Innocent III (1198–1216) it becomes clear that the Bogomils of Dalmatia were prosecuted for heresy by Archbishop Bernard of Split in the late twelfth century, and sought refuge in Bosnia. They were initially welcomed there by Ban Kulin, but under pressure from the King of Hungary the Ban agreed to a papal inquiry about their orthodoxy **[39(a–c)]**. This resulted in the Agreement of Bolino-Polje, made on 30 April 1203 between the legate, John of Casamaris, Ban Kulin, and the seven 'priors of those men who until now have alone had the right to be called Christians in the land of Bosnia' **[39(d)]**. The priors agreed to make their communities into orthodox, single-sex monastic groups within the Catholic Church.

J.V.A. Fine has questioned whether these men were Bogomils because there is no specific reference to their beliefs in the source.[149] We do not find his argument convincing. There would have been no point in requiring them to have chapels with altars, crosses and full texts of the Bible, and to celebrate Mass and recite the Divine Office unless they had previously failed to do so. But Bogomils rejected all those things, and lived in single-sex communities, as the followers of John Tzurillas had done in the early eleventh century **[19]**, and as western Cathars universally did at this time. Moreover, the seven priors were required solemnly to swear that 'henceforth we will not receive any known Manichaean or other heretic to live with us'. 'Manichaean' in the western Church at that time certainly meant Cathar, or in the case of Balkan heretics,

---

146 Nicol, 'The Fourth Crusade and the Greek and Latin empires'; Lock, *The Franks in the Aegean*, pp. 35–107.
147 Lock, *The Franks in the Aegean*, pp. 193–221; Fedalto, *La chiesa latina in Oriente*, pp. 219–487.
148 Fine, *The late medieval Balkans*, pp. 17–21.
149 Fine, *The Bosnian church*.

Bogomil **[39(d)]**. Moreover, the Agreement of Bolino Polje does not exist in a vacuum: the whole context of the correspondence leading up to it implies that these heretics were Bogomils.

In 1202 Kalojan, ruler of Bulgaria, wishing to secure independence from Byzantium, opened negotiations with the Pope which led to the union of the Bulgarian Church with Rome and the coronation of Kalojan by a papal legate in 1204.[150] In 1206 Innocent sent another legate to Bulgaria on an unknown mission,[151] and he may have persuaded the new Tsar, Boril, who came to power in 1207, to prosecute Bogomils. This is by no means certain, although the fact that Boril presided over a Synod at Trnovo in 1211 to legislate against Bogomilism at a time when the Albigensian Crusade was being fought in Languedoc seems too neat a match to be entirely fortuitous.

As Gouillard has pointed out, the legislation of this Synod consists of the anti-Bogomil pronouncements of the Patriarch Cosmas I arranged in a different order **[21]**, with two additional clauses, neither of which relates to Bogomilism **[41]**. The most valuable part of the Synodikon for the historian are the anathemas of Bogomil leaders which it gives, among whom is Peter of Cappadocia, *dedec*, or *dyed*, of Sredets (Sofia). Obolensky has argued that *dyed* must be understood to mean a Bogomil bishop.[152] This Peter was presumably the Bishop of the Bulgarian Bogomils in 1211.

The Agreement of Bolino-Polje did not mark the end of Bosnian Bogomilism. Honorius III (1216–27) tried to get King Andrew II of Hungary to take action against these heretics, but without success **[42]**, and was worried by the report of his legate in Languedoc, Conrad, Cardinal of Porto, that a heretical antipope had arisen 'in the regions of Bosnia, Croatia and Dalmatia, next to Hungary', who had appointed 'a certain Bartholomew of Carcassonne' as his vicar in southern France **[42]**. There was some truth in this rumour, because the Bogomil Bishop of Bosnia was trying to restore moderate dualism among the Cathars of Southern France at that time, but Cardinal Conrad supposed that this heretical *papa* was an antipope with jurisdiction over all the dualist churches.[153]

Pope Gregory IX (1227–41) deposed the Catholic Bishop of Bosnia for tolerating heresy and in 1234 licensed the Duke of Croatia to make war

150 Gill, *Byzantium and the Papacy*, pp. 21–2.
151 Alberic of Trois Fontaines, *Cronicon* (*MGH SS* xxiii, p. 886).
152 *The Bogomils*, pp. 240, 242–5.
153 Borst, *Die Katharer*, pp. 209–10.

on Bosnia with crusading privileges **[43(a)]**.[154] Gregory was also concerned about the presence of Bogomils in Bulgaria. Papal influence had ended there in *c.* 1232, when the Bulgarian Church returned to the communion of the Orthodox Patriarch living in exile at Nicaea.[155] In 1238 the Pope incited King Bela IV of Hungary to crusade against Tsar John Asen II because of his toleration of heresy, but nothing came of this because of the Mongol invasion of Hungary in 1241–42, which also brought to an end the prolonged crusade against Bosnia **[43(b)]**.[156]

No attempt was made to prosecute Bogomils in the Latin Empire of Constantinople. The emperors were too involved in defending themselves against the rulers of Nicaea, Epirus and Bulgaria to have time to deal with heresy; while the Latin bishops were separated by a language barrier from the mass of the population and would have found considerable difficulty in trying to seek out heretics, particularly because Bogomils often appeared indistinguishable from Orthodox monks.[157] It is known from the sermons of the Orthodox Patriarch Germanus II (1222–40) that there were Bogomils living in the Empire of Nicaea **[44]**,[158] but he was also concerned about the spread of heresy in the Latin Empire over which he claimed *de iure* spiritual authority, and he wrote an encyclical letter to the faithful of Constantinople on that subject. The Bogomils whom he describes are moderate dualists: 'they name the devil the Son of God and brother of Christ' **[44(d)]**. This, if true, would mean that the Bogomils of Constantinople had reverted to the moderate dualism which they had held in the time of the doctor Basil, and had renounced the absolute dualism of Dragovitia which *papa* Nicetas had introduced.

The papal Inquisition, created by Gregory IX in 1233 to deal with Cathars, was never established in Frankish Greece, but some of its officials were interested in what was happening there. Rainier Sacconi, a former Cathar minister who became Inquisitor for Lombardy, included a list of Bogomil churches in the *Summa*, or Treatise, about Catharism which he wrote in *c.* 1250: he names the Church of Sclavonia, the Church of the Latins of Constantinople, the Church of the Greeks in the same place, the Church of Philadelphia in Romania;

154 CICO III (iii), nos. 194, 197, 198, 207, pp. 268–9, 271–2, 283.
155 Gill, *Byzantium and the Papacy*. pp. 63–4.
156 CICO III (iii), nos. 229, 248, 248a, 248b, pp. 308–10, 325–8; Fine, *The Bosnian Church*. pp. 137–45.
157 Angold, 'Greeks and Latins after 1204: the perspective of exile'.
158 On the work of Germanus II, see Angold, *Church and society in Byzantium*, pp. 547–54.

and the Churches of Bulgaria and Druguuithia [*sic*] from which all the others trace their origin **[45]**.

There is a large measure of continuity between this list and that given by Nicetas eighty years earlier. The Churches of the Greeks in Constantinople, of Bulgaria, of Dragovitia (Druguuithia) and of Sclavonia are common to both.[159] Nicetas' Church of Melenguia is not listed by Sacconi. In the thirteenth century the Milingui were hemmed in by the Frankish princes of Achaea, with whom they were at war until 1248, so he may not have been able to find out anything about them;[160] alternatively the Bogomil Church there may have collapsed. Rainier lists two new Churches: Philadelphia in Romania, which almost certainly relates to the Bogomils in the Empire of Nicaea, against whom Germanus preached so vigorously;[161] and the Church of the Latins in Constantinople. The only information which we have about the origins of that Church suggests that it dates from the time of the First Crusade, and the hypothesis of such an early date for a Latin Cathar Church in the Byzantine capital might help to explain why Bogomil missions were able to work successfully in western Europe in the twelfth century without experiencing language problems.[162] Yet no such Church is mentioned either by *papa* Nicetas or by Hugh Eteriano, both of whom lived in the capital. A possible resolution of this problem might be that there were Latins as well as Greeks in the Bogomil community of Constantinople from the time of Alexius I, and that when the Bogomils adopted episcopacy in the twelfth century, there was initially one bishop in the city with authority over Greeks and Latins. It is known that Bishop Nicetas accepted the *ordo* of Dragovitia and its creed of absolute dualism, but that by the time of Germanus II the Greek Bogomils of Constantinople had reverted to the moderate dualist *ordo* of Bulgaria. It is arguable that when that first happened, some of the Latin Bogomils remained loyal to the *ordo* of Dragovitia and went into schism under their own bishop. This solution is entirely hypothetical.

Sacconi is the only authority to give any statistics of membership for the Bogomil Churches: 'The Church of the Latins in Constantinople has about fifty members. The Churches of Sclavonia and Philadelphia and of the Greeks [of Constantinople] and of Bulgaria and of Druguuithia

---

159 Italian writers always referred to the Church of Dalmatia as the Church of Sclavonia.
160 Lurier, tr. *Crusaders as conquerors*, pp. 126, 131, 160–1.
161 See map.
162 Hamilton, 'Wisdom from the East'.

have in total about 500 members' **[45]**. These figures presumably represent fully initiated members, whom the Cathars called the perfect, and the number of 'lay' adherents would have been far greater. Sacconi was trying, for propaganda purposes, to minimise the threat posed by organized dualism to orthodox Christianity in East and West. If one takes a multiplier of 100 to estimate the proportion of believers to perfect, this only produces a figure of 55,000 dualist adherents scattered throughout the Balkan lands and the Greek and Latin Empires of Constantinople, and it seems likely that the true figure was much higher.

No later western writer makes any reference to contemporary dualist movements in Bulgaria or the Byzantine lands, though the Papacy remained interested in Bosnia because it formed part of the western Church. Between 1247 and 1251 Innocent IV sought to establish stricter control over the Bosnian Church by making it subject to the primate of Hungary, but it seceded from papal obedience.[163] It is often assumed that Bogomilism became the established Church of Bosnia at that point, but J.V.A. Fine has questioned this. While not disputing that there were Bogomils in Bosnia, he argues that the established Church remained the Catholic Church, which went into schism from Rome for political reasons, because the Bosnians did not wish to be under Hungarian control.[164] The thirteenth-century evidence does not help to clarify this problem: the sources simply speak in general terms of the presence of heresy there and in the neighbouring regions.[165]

In 1325 Pope John XXII complained to Prince Stefan Kotromanič of Bosnia that 'a great crowd of heretics from many different regions has gathered together and migrated to Bosnia' **[47]**. This may have been true, because there are virtually no reports of any Cathar perfect in the West after that date.[166] A strategic withdrawal to Bosnia, where dualism had been tolerated since the late twelfth century, may have seemed the best solution to the Cathars of western Europe after ninety years of persecution, if, that is, they had retained enough organization to make concerted plans.

In this collection we have not attempted to deal with the subsequent history of Bosnian Bogomilism. Considerations of space have chiefly

163 Fine, *The Bosnian Church*, pp. 145–8.
164 *Ibid.*, pp. 148–57 (this is the thesis of the whole book). For a different view, see Sanjek, *Les Chrétiens bosniaques*.
165 E.g. CICO ser. III, V(I), no. 12, pp. 41–2; V (II), no. 49, pp. 92–5.
166 'The last [Cathar] bishop to be reported in Western Europe was captured in Tuscany in 1321; survivors continued for a time to find refuge, possibly in the Lombard countryside and the Alps' (Lambert, *Medieval heresy*, p. 144).

dictated this decision. There is a great deal of material about the Bosnian Church in the fourteenth and fifteenth centuries, and it would merit treatment in a separate monograph.[167]

The end of Bogomilism

In 1261 the Byzantine Emperor Michael VIII (1259–82) recovered Constantinople, and the Latin Empire came to an end. The restored Byzantine state was small and fragile, consisting of western Anatolia, Thrace, Macedonia, Thessaly and Epirus. Venetians held many of the Greek islands, while Frankish princes continued to rule much of central and southern Greece. In the reign of Andronicus II (1282–1328) almost all the Asian lands were lost to the Turks, and soon after his death the European lands of the empire were halved by the conquests of Stephen Dušan of Serbia (1331–55). Then in 1354 the Ottoman Turks seized Gallipoli and embarked on their conquest of the Balkans.[168] Evidence about the Bogomils during these troubled centuries is slight, but it shows that they continued to flourish, no doubt helped by the breakdown of centralized government.

In 1316 the parish priest of Bukovič, a village in southern Thrace, was accused of being a Bogomil, but although the case was dismissed by the Holy Synod in Constantinople, Bukovič remained a byword for Bogomilism, as is known from a secular lawsuit of 1330.[169] In the winter of 1316–17 the young St Gregory Palamas stayed in a monastery on Mount Papikion, 'on the borders of Thrace and Macedonia', where he disputed with some local heretics whom his biographer calls Messalians, but who were Bogomils, because they claimed that the Our Father was the only legitimate prayer and refused to venerate the Holy Cross, both distinctively Bogomil traits **[48(a)]**.[170]

Far more serious was the outbreak of Bogomilism in the early 1320s on Mount Athos, which was the monastic centre of the entire Orthodox world.[171] The authorities there reported to the Holy Synod of Constantinople that the heretics were Bogomils who rejected the cult of the icons, taught that baptism and the Eucharist had no value, and did not believe in the incarnation of Christ or the bodily resurrection of the

---

167 See Fine, *The Bosnian Church*; Sanjek, *Les Chrétiens bosniaques*.
168 Nicol, *The last centuries of Byzantium*, pp. 45–264.
169 The Italian term *paterene* is used to describe the heretics (*RP* V, no. 2071; Loos, *Dualist heresy in the Middle Ages*, p. 332).
170 Meyendorff, *A study of Gregory Palamas*, pp. 32–3.
171 For detailed studies of Athos, see Athos, *Le Millénaire du Mont Athos*; for a brief account, see Cavarnos, *The holy mountain*.

dead.[172] Nicephorus Gregoras gives an account of their trial and adds that some of them were given penances, but others were expelled from Athos, while some escaped during the trial and fled to Thessalonica, Berrhoea and Constantinople [48(b)]. The Patriarch Callistus I (d. 1363), in his *Life of St Theodosius of Trnovo*, reports that this heresy had entered Athos through the agency of an Orthodox nun in Thessalonica named Irene, who had a reputation for piety but was secretly a Bogomil, with whom brethren from Athos sometimes stayed when they went to that city on business [49]. No action seems to have been taken against the Bogomils who left Athos. Gregory Akindynus reports that in *c.* 1347 a group of Bogomils was still being led by George of Larissa (one of the leaders of the Athonite Bogomils), who preached openly and had the nun Porine among his disciples. She was that Irene whom Callistus claimed had first introduced Athonite monks to Bogomilism.[173]

The prevalence of Bogomilism in Macedonia and Thrace at this time is also attested in the law code issued by Stephen Dušan in 1349 (revised in 1353/4). Serbia had been remarkably free of Bogomilism, because its rulers had co-operated with the Orthodox Church in suppressing it when it first appeared there in the late twelfth century,[174] but as Dušan conquered Byzantine territory he found Bogomils among his subjects, and enacted: 'If any heretic be found to live among the Christians, let him be branded on the face and driven forth, and whoever shall harbour him, let him be branded. And whoso utters a heretical word, if he be noble, let him pay 100 perpers, and if he be a commoner, let him pay twelve perpers and be beaten with sticks.'[175]

Athos came under the protection of Stephen Dušan in 1345, and he accused the Greek *protos* Niphon, who was in charge of all the monasteries on the Holy Mountain, of being a Bogomil, but Niphon was successfully defended by St Gregory Palamas. This accusation seems to have been politically motivated, since the tsar almost certainly wanted to put a Serbian official in charge.[176]

This outbreak of Bogomilism on Athos coincided with the growth of Hesychasm there. This movement was rooted in the tradition of contemplative prayer taught by St Symeon the New Theologian (d. 1022)

172 Rigo, *Monaci esicasti e monaci bogomili*, p. 173.
173 Meyendorff, *A study of Gregory Palamas*, p. 36.
174 Obolensky, *The Bogomils*, Appendix IV (2), pp. 283–5.
175 Dushan, *Dushan's code*, Chapters 10, 83, pp. 41, 61. 'Perper' is the common Western form of *hyperperon*, the standard Byzantine gold coin, which by the mid-fourteenth century had become a money of account.
176 Meyendorff, *A study of Gregory Palamas*, pp. 91–2.

CHRISTIAN DUALIST HERESIES

and earlier by St Maximus the Confessor (d. 662). The Hesychasts claimed that it was possible to share in the experience of the apostles at the Transfiguration and see what they described as 'the uncreated Light of Mount Tabor' (Matt. 17.1–9). St Gregory Palamas became the leader of this movement, which met with great opposition from some circles in the Orthodox Church. Because the Hesychasts emphasized the importance of enlightenment through contemplation more than through the liturgy and the sacraments of the Church, they were sometimes accused of Messalianism, which had long been equated with Bogomilism (e.g. **[48(b)]**). Such accusations became untenable after a Church Council held in the Blachernae Palace at Constantinople in 1351 declared Hesychasm orthodox.[177]

In his *Life of Theodosius* the Patriarch Callistus relates that two of the Bogomils expelled from Athos in the 1320s, Lazarus and Cyril Bosota (the barefooted), fled to Trnovo in Bulgaria, where they preached and made converts. Lazarus is said to have been an Adamite and to have urged his followers to be castrated. He was later reconciled to the Orthodox Church, and in view of the eccentric character of his teachings, which were without parallel in Bogomil history, it is legitimate to question whether he was a Bogomil at all. He is not named in the Athonite anti-Bogomil tome, as Cyril is,[178] and it seems likely that Callistus made a mistaken inference about him **[49]**.

The Council of Trnovo in *c*. 1350 condemned the Bogomils for teaching cosmological dualism between the Good God of Heaven and the evil creator of this world. Obolensky finds this evidence of absolute dualism difficult to accept, because throughout its history the Bogomil Church of Bulgaria had been a bastion of moderate dualism.[179] But Cyril the barefooted may not have been a Bulgarian; he had come to Trnovo as a refugee from Mount Athos, and may therefore have been a member of the absolute dualist Church of Dragovitia. He and the priest Stephen, who refused to recant, were branded and exiled. St Theodore also accused the Bogomils of sexual excesses, but this was a standard part of the Orthodox repertoire of anti-dualist polemic, and no special significance need be attached to it **[49]**.

Bogomilism persisted in Bulgaria, for when from *c*. 1365–70 the province of Vidin was occupied by the Hungarians, who allowed Franciscan missionaries to work there, they claimed that they had found and

177 For a general study, see Meyendorff, *Byzantine Hesychasm*.
178 Italian translation by Rigo, *Monaci esicasti*, pp. 173–4.
179 *The Bogomils*, p. 262, n. 1.

converted innumerable Paterenes.[180] This is our last evidence about Bulgarian Bogomilism: by 1393 the country had been conquered by the Ottoman Turks.

That Bogomils survived in what remained of the Byzantine Empire right up to the eve of the Ottoman conquest is known from the Treatise against Heretics of Archbishop Symeon of Thessalonica (1416–29) **[50]**. He condemns a group called the *kudugeroi*, which Loos has suggested is a variant of the word *kalogeroi*, meaning 'good old men', a term used by the Byzantines to describe monks, but one which resembles the phrase 'bonshommes' used in thirteenth-century Languedoc to describe the Cathar perfect.[181] The *kudugeroi* were undoubtedly Bogomils. Symeon alleges that they believed in two principles, and if this is true, then they were members of the Dragovitian school rather than moderate dualists, and the last members of that group about whom anything is known.[182] Symeon gives little new information about the group except that 'at the end of life they lead many of the pious astray and sever them from Christ, for at the time of their end they summon them to denial'. This appears to refer to the initiation of the dying, a practice which was universal among the Cathars of the West, though not attested elsewhere in connection with the Bogomils. But if, as suggested above, the Cathars obtained their *Ritual* from the Bogomils, then it was from them also that they are likely to have derived this practice, for which the Cathar *Ritual* of Lyons contains a special form of service.[183]

In 1430 Thessalonica fell to the Ottomans, and during the next thirty years virtually all the surviving Byzantine lands passed under their rule. Nothing is known about the Bogomils under Ottoman rule, although it has sometimes been assumed that many of them were converted to Islam.[184] A more moderate and accurate conclusion is that of Yuri Stoyanov: 'Evidence for such a Bogomil influx into Islam is lacking, and the obscurity surrounding their disappearance seems to result from the insufficient knowledge of the early religious history of the Ottoman Empire, with its array of sectarian and syncretistic movements, still a controversial and largely unexplored field.'[185]

---

180 Loos, *Dualist heresy in the Middle Ages*, p. 334.
181 Duvernoy, *Le catharisme*, pp. 171–2.
182 Thessalonica is near Dragovitia; see map.
183 Clédat, *Le Nouveau Testament*, pp. xxii–xxvi; tr. Wakefield and Evans, in *Heresies of the High Middle Ages*, pp. 492–4.
184 E.g. Obolensky, *The Bogomils*, pp. 265–6.
185 *The hidden tradition in Europe*, p. 209.

1. PAULICIAN POPULATION TRANSFERS UNDER CONSTANTINE V (741–75)

Constantine V continued the campaigns of his father Leo against the Arabs. The transfers of populations recorded here followed the capture and destruction of Theodosiopolis and Melitene.[1] It is sometimes argued that the emperor's motive in moving Armenians and Paulicians to Thrace was an attempt to encourage Iconoclasm (which the emperor supported) in the areas near the capital, but the sources do not make this allegation. These chronicle accounts provide the earliest evidence in the Greek sources for the existence of Paulician communities in the upper Euphrates valley.[2] The authors write as if the Paulician heresy were familiar to their readers and needed no further explanation. For the Paulician community's own tradition of their origins see Peter of Sicily [7]. These traditions say nothing about this movement of population, presumably because Peter of Sicily's informants were only interested in the lives of those successive leaders of their community who had remained in Asia Minor. The Paulician account of the interrogation of their leader Gegnesius/Timothy by the patriarch who declared that his views were orthodox implies that the emperor Constantine had no reason to suspect the Paulicians and transferred them simply as an identifiable group (whose fighting skill he may have had reason to respect).[3] The passage of Theophanes shows that this reputation for orthodoxy did not last long.

(a) Theophanes (c. 760–817/18) wrote a chronicle of the years 284–803, continuing the work of George Syncellus (d. 810–11; his chronicle and ruler lists runs from the creation of Adam to 284). His history is heavily biased in favour of those rulers who were favourable to icons and to the monastic establishment. The translation has been made from the edition by de Boor (Leipzig, 1883), p. 429.

[AD 757] The emperor Constantine settled Syrians and Armenians whom he had brought from Theodosiopolis and Melitene in Thrace, and from them spread the heresy of the Paulicians. Similarly to the city whose inhabitants had been diminished by plague,[4] he brought settlers with their families from the islands and from Greece and the inhabited parts and made them settle the city and increase its population.

---

1 See map.
2 For the Armenian souces see Appendix 2.
3 For the later history of the Paulicians as a fighting force within the empire see below, [14], [17], [20].
4 For the plague of 748 see PS [7].

57

(b) Nicephorus the Patriarch (in office 806–15) wrote other historical works besides his best known work, the *Breviarium*, which covers the events of the years 602–769. The translation is made from the edition of de Boor (Leipzig, 1880), p. 66.

[AD 756/7] [Next] Constantine began to subdue the citadels of Thrace, in which he settled Syrians and Armenians, whom he made move from the city of Melitene and Theodosiopolis, giving them lavish gifts for their necessities.

2. THE EMPRESS IRENE (780–802) AND THE PAULICIANS

In the reign of the empress Irene, who was an enthusiastic iconodule, it appears that an attempt was made to convert Paulicians in the eastern provinces to orthodoxy – it is not clear to what extent the imperial authorities made a distinction between Paulicians and extreme iconoclasts. The empress summoned a general Council of the Church in 786 to reverse the policy of Iconoclasm, but elements in the army protested against this rejection of the policies of Constantine V with such violence that the council had to be postponed. When the council prepared to meet (as it did in September 787) units suspected of iconoclast sympathies were dismissed without pay. For a description of the historical works of Nicephorus the Patriarch see [1].

NICEPHOROS THE PATRIARCH (*PG* 100, col. 501b)

A few years earlier, when the pious empress was ruling the imperial power and displaying a worthy and godly zeal for our faith . . . by an inspired decree this city was well and truly rid of the evil and atheist throng which had filled it; they wandered like planets seeking a cult in which the icons and memorials of the incarnation of Christ should not be apparent. They found one, I mean the lack of faith and the atheism long embraced by Manichaeans, which matched their views and suited their opinions.

3. ALLEGED PAULICIANS IN CONSTANTINOPLE IN THE EARLY NINTH CENTURY

The chronicler Theophanes (c. 760–817/18) preserves a tradition hostile to the emperor Nicephorus (802–11) who imposed heavy taxes on church and monastic property in an attempt to pay for his army. The incidents described in the passages below are included as evidence that Paulicians were known as an identifiable group in the capital in the early ninth century.

(a) Despite the allegations made here, there is no evidence that the emperor Nicephorus was sympathetic to Paulicians or even to Iconoclasts, though the fact that his family originated in the eastern empire may have lent credibility to the charge. He was killed by the Bulgar Khan Krum on his return from an expedition to Bulgaria. The Bulgarians followed this success with the capture and destruction of Byzantine cities on the Black Sea coast, and (in 813) with the threat of an attack on Constantinople itself. Michael I, the successor of Nicephorus, was a pacific man.

The text has been taken from the edition of de Boor (Leipzig, 1883), I, p.488.

On the first of October, a Tuesday, someone unknown in monk's clothing seized a sword from one of the soldiers and rushed into the palace, seeking to kill Nicephorus. Two of the bystanders chased him and were seriously wounded. When he was caught and severely punished, he pretended to be mad and did not lay information against anyone. The emperor had him put in wooden fetters with those involved. From then on many thought that this was a sign of great evil for those in power and their subjects, as happened in the time of the impious Nestorius. He [Nicephorus] was a fervent friend of the Manichees who are now called Paulicians and of the Athingani who were his neighbours,[1] who live in Phrygia and Lycaonia, and took pleasure in their oracles and magic rites.

(b) This incident shows the survival of loyalty to the memory of the great general Constantine V and the assumption by monastic spokesmen such as Theophanes that such support identified those who showed it as iconoclasts and crypto-Paulicians. Text from de Boor, I, pp. 500–1.

About the beginning of June, Krum, the leader of the Bulgars, made an expedition with his troops since he had seen that the possessions of the Christians were very great. When he had marched to Bersinicia, at

---

1 An allusion to the eastern origin of the emperor's family; the Athingani were a dissident group who were alleged to practise astral magic and other non-Christian rituals; see Starr, 'An Eastern Christian sect'.

about mile-post thirty on the imperial road, Leo the patrician and *strategos* of the western forces and John Asplaces, patrician and *strategos* of Macedonia, were very anxious to attack them, but were prevented by the emperor, who was badly advised. While the city and the archbishop prayed in the church of the Holy Apostles some of the impious belonging to the foul heresy of Constantine[2] hated by God, who had levered up the door of the imperial tombs (while no one noticed them because of the people's distress) made it suddenly open with a crash, as if by some divine miracle. They rushed inside and fell on the tomb of that heretic, calling on him and not on God, saying, 'Rise up and help the city in its destruction.' They spread the rumour that he, who dwells with demons in hell, arose on horseback and went out to fight the Bulgars. The magistrate in charge of the city arrested them. At first they lied, claiming that the doors of the tomb had opened of their own accord through the power of God. But when they were brought before the magistrate and cowered in testimony, they admitted the act of leverage, when threatened with punishment. The majority of those who blasphemed in this way were Christians only in appearance. They were Paulicians in reality, who are not able to reveal their foul doctrines openly, but who corrupt the unlearned with this sort of trickery. They bless Constantine the Jewish-minded as a prophet and conqueror, and embrace his evil opinions in despite of the incarnation of Our Lord Jesus Christ.

4. THEODORE OF STUDIUM (d. 826) OPPOSES THE DEATH PENALTY FOR HERESY

After the first restoration of the icons, by the empress Irene (780–802), a debate developed about the appropriate punishment for heretics. Increased ecclesiastical pressure on Irene and on Michael I (811–13) meant that the civil authorities became more concerned to eliminate heresy, including that of groups such as Paulicians and Athingani, who had previously been left relatively undisturbed in the distant parts of Asia Minor where they lived. Ecclesiastical opinion agreed that heresy should be eliminated, but was divided on the question of whether heresy was in itself a capital offence, or whether heretics should be offered the opportunity of repentance and reconciliation.

2 Constantine V (741–75).

For Theophanes, the author of (a) see **[1]**. The text of Theophanes is taken from the edition by de Boor (Leipzig, 1883), vol. I, p. 494.

(a) The most pious emperor [Michael I, 811–13], inspired by great zeal for God, proclaimed capital punishment for Manichaeans, the present-day Paulicians, and the Athingani[1] who are in Phrygia and Lycaonia, at the urging of the most holy patriarch Nicephorus.

Theodore of Studium, the author of (b), was abbot of the monastery of Studios and a leading figure in the contemporary debate on the independence of church and state. The text has been translated from *PG* 99, col. 1481.

(b) LETTER TO THEOPHILUS OF EPHESUS

I have in my hands the letter which your sacred highness sent to our brother Athanasius, and, most worshipful of men, when I read it I was very grieved. Firstly because disputes and disagreements have arisen among those of us who uphold the word of truth against the heresy of the Iconomachi which now assails it, and secondly because I am obliged in all humility to adopt the opposing position. Your greatness will forgive me, for the argument is about truth, than which nothing is more important or more to be revered. What then is the content of the letter which disturbs me? It says, 'We have not decided whether to kill the Manichaeans or not to kill them. But if we were to allow it, we would make a very right decision.' What are you saying, most reverend? In the gospels the Lord forbade this, saying, 'No, lest when you collect the tares you root up the wheat with them. Let them both grow together till harvest.'

5. ST MACARIUS OF PELECETE CONVERTS A PAULICIAN IN PRISON

The subject of this life was abbot of the monastery of Pelecete, a house dedicated to Saint John the Theologian, situated on the coast of the Propontis, near Dascylium. The dates of his life have to be inferred; he was ordained priest by the patriarch Tarasius (780–806), was sent into exile as a supporter of the icons by the emperor Leo the Armenian (813–20), recalled from exile by the emperor Michael (820–29) and restored as abbot and finally sent once more into exile, this time to an island of the Propontis called Aphousia, during the reign of the

---

1 For this group see **[3]**, n. 1.

emperor Theophilus (829–42).[1] The life was apparently written by Macarius' successor as abbot. He refers to himself as an eyewitness to some of the events, notably the healing miracles, which he describes. This text is evidence for the systematic trial and condemnation of Paulicians; this should be seen in the context of the contemporary debate on the subject.[2]

The text is taken from pp. 158–60 of H. Delehaye, 'S. Macarii Monasterii Pelecetes Higoumeni'.

[Chapter 14] There were Paulicians, that is, Manichaeans, held in the prison under sentence of death, who begged the saint to pray for them at their death, but he said, 'There is no such fellowship as this between light and darkness. That is why you are receiving the fitting end of your impiety. Not merely are you undergoing punishment in this life, but you will receive unending correction hereafter.' So one of the condemned said that he would receive the pledge of salvation in place of food, and Macarius himself baptized him. So though all came to a fatal end, this man alone was saved and fulfilled the works of promise, laying aside the filth of heresy and putting on the shining doctrines of piety.

6. RENEWED PERSECUTION OF THE PAULICIANS IN ASIA MINOR AND THE MARTYRS OF AMORIUM

In 842 the empress Theodora, widow of Theophilus, became regent for the child emperor Michael III. In 843 she restored the icons and enforced the heresy laws against the Paulicians in the provinces, driving some of them to take refuge at Argaoun with the Emir of Melitene; see Introduction, pp. 21–2. In 844 the Paulicians of Colonea captured the imperial governor Callistus and handed him over to their fellow-believers at Argaoun. He was executed in 845, together with the Byzantine officers who had been captured at the fall of Amorium in 838.

Zonaras, the author of passages (a) and (c) below, wrote in the twelfth century. His own dates are uncertain; his history ends with the death of Alexius

---

1 There is a chronological problem here. The life is quite clear on the sequence of events, and therefore that Macarius lived into the reign of Theophilus, i.e. at least until 829. Among the letters attributed to Theodore the Studite, who died in 826, there is one (*PG*, col. 1457, letter cxlvi) offering condolences to the new abbot of Pelecete on the death of his saintly predecessor Macarius. The new abbot may be the author of the life; in the letter he is known as Sergius, while in the life he refers to himself as Sabas, but Greek monks customarily took religious names with the same initial as their secular ones.
2 See Introduction, pp. 19–22 for references, and [4] above.

Comnenus in 1118. He uses material contemporary with the events he describes, and is in general a reliable, though late, source.

(b) is a description of the death at Arab hands of forty-two members of the Byzantine army, high-ranking officers and their immediate followers. The majority of these had been taken prisoner at the capture of the great army base of Amorium[1] in 838; negotiations for their release had failed. The successful mission of Peter of Sicily some twenty years later should be set against this background. In addition to the captives from Amorium itself, there was a Byzantine commander, Callistus, on whose memory the greater part of the martyr story entitled *The Forty-two Martyrs of Amorion* is focused.

The text of Zonaras[2] is taken from the edition by M. Pinderi (Bonn, 1841–43). The *Martyrs of Amorion* is taken from the edition by V. Vasilevskii and P. Nikitin.

(a) [AD 843–44] In the East there was a large number of Manichaeans, who were called Paulicians in ignorance by the common people, who give them a name made up from Paul and John ... So then the empress[3] intended to convert them from heresy to orthodoxy, and sent some men from the nobility to achieve this. They handled their commission clumsily and to no avail, and not merely wasted their labour but drove the entire people (who number many thousands) to apostasize. Joining the Ishmaelites, they fought with them against the Romans and became the cause of many disasters for them.

(b) THE TESTIMONY OF THE FORTY-TWO MARTYRS OF AMORIUM: CALLISTUS THE *DOUX*, CONSTANTIUS THE PATRICIAN, THEODORE THE PROTOSPATHARIUS AND THEIR COMPANY

p. 23. Callistus, this noble soldier of Christ, had noble parents ... He became one of the picked troops of the emperor's army through the strength of his body, his good looks and the good name of his kinsmen. Later ... he held the rank of *comes* in the ranks of the Christ-loving *scholae* ...

p. 29. [at Colonea] he found ... some men of rank who suffered from the Manichaean heresy. At first he warned and exhorted and urged them to abandon the filth of this heresy ... When he saw that the wretches persisted in error and would not be converted, he made it plain that they were excommunicated from his sacred band. For this

---

1 See map.
2 For information on the date and reliability of Zonaras see **[14]** below.
3 Theodora (842–56), as regent for her son Michael III (842–67).

reason... they agreed to hand him over to their fellow Manichaeans who had abandoned the customs and lands of Christians because of their impiety, and had bound themselves by a treaty to the bloodstained race of the Agareni,[4] those who endure exile by the providence of God as befits their foul heresy. In accordance with God's decrees about him a plot was laid against Callistus, that man of peace and advocate of piety, as it was against his own master.[5] He was handed over to the apostates under the command of the thrice-wretched Carbeas. There at first he was condemned to close confinement and the penalty of irons on his feet, together with those of the servants who accompanied him, who were few in number.

When the Saracen chief learnt of this, he immediately sent him captive to Syria and ordered that he should be kept with the noble witnesses of Christ who were with the blessed Theodore and Constantine and Theophilus and Basoes. These holy men had spent six years in close confinement, in fetters and hungry and sleeping on the ground, after the capture of Amorium,[6] although they were men who had previously lived luxuriously and been soldiers on service with every comfort...

A few days after the arrival of the holy Callistus, the leading official made a statement to those in prison through the appropriate members of his command in these words: 'See, in addition to the time which has already elapsed, I am making you a present of five days. Reflect, then; you are noble and intelligent men, leaders in the Roman Empire. Don't throw yourselves away in death and lose the sweetness of this world. If you obey me, deny the Crucified one whom the Romans call Christ. You will have even greater honour than before and enjoy great wealth among us. If you do not listen to my advice, you will be executed by the sword....'.

[The offer was refused. After four days in which the martyrs prayed and fasted] On the fifth day, early in the morning, the Arab chief, that servant of Satan... gave orders that they should be brought from prison. The servants of the infidel seated the holy men on wretched animals, side-saddle, like women, as their legs were in fetters, and dragged them to be interrogated, mocking them as fools, and hitting them somewhat and uttering all kinds of insults, saying all the things which terrify and appal those who are condemned to death... [One of the group apostatised: 'they say that this man had earlier suffered from

---

4 Agareni; the children of Ishmael, the son of Hagar the slave-girl; see Gen. 18.21.
5 i.e. Christ.
6 The major military base of Amorium was captured by the Arabs in 838; for a similar use of captives see Peter of Sicily [7], chapters 4, 187.

heretical views concerning icons'. The others refused and were executed.]

After the forty-two martyrs of Christ had died in the confession of the faith on 6 March, their bodies were taken up and thrown into the river which flowed past. Guards were stationed on the banks for thirty miles to prevent any Christian taking anything belonging to them which the current might wash ashore. As the Tigris bore their holy bodies, as if by providential command, it made a deep inlet, and collecting them within it, united each head to its body, and so sent them out into the main stream . . . As it flowed on, it brought them all together to a place on the bank where there was a monastery of holy men [where they were given Christian burial]. From then onwards, those who approach them with faith receive in abundance all kinds of healing of disease to the glory of Christ, our true God.

(c) [c. AD 858] Then Michael led an expedition against the Agareni just as his beard was first starting to grow, and attempted to besiege Samosata (this is one of the cities on the Euphrates) . . . Then too the Manichaeans, fighting along with the Ishmaelites, took many of the noble officers captive and held them to ransom for large sums . . .

7. PETER OF SICILY'S *HISTORY OF THE PAULICIANS* (870)

Nothing is known of the author of this work or the circumstances in which it was written, beyond what he himself tells us, that he was sent to negotiate the release of some prisoners held by the Paulicians at the time when Paulician territorial power was at its height. These prisoners were held at Tefrice (see map), which was then the centre of the sect. For the historical circumstances, see our Introduction, pp. 21–2, for another set of prisoners captured (though not held) by Paulicians, and their less happy ending, see **[6]**.

There is a parallel account by the patriarch Photius, also edited in *T & M* 4 (1970), pp. 99–183. This was more popular, and exists in a dozen MSS, as well as the substantial quotations of it by Euthymius Zigabenus in the section of his *Dogmatic Panoply* against the Paulicians. This version appears to be almost entirely a rewriting of Peter of Sicily's account, and for that reason we have not included it. One point at which they differ is included in note 14, p. 72.

The text of Peter of Sicily is only known from one MS, Vat. gr. 511, ff. 80v–111v. This is an eleventh-century MS, damaged at both beginning and end. It contains:

1 The summary of Peter the Higoumenos (see **[8]** and notes).
2 The text of the present work, with an introductory title, 'By the same Peter, the Sicilian'.
3 Sermons, originally six in all, of which only two are completely preserved, together with part of the third; the remaining three are completely lost. The surviving texts can be found in *PG* 104, 1305–1350.

These contain Peter of Sicily's arguments against the Paulicians, based on biblical and patristic texts, but as they do not contribute anything about the beliefs and history of the group which is not to be found in the History or in the Summary of Peter the Higoumenos, they have not been translated here; for material which may be derived from the missing sermons see **[23]**. A modern edition of the work is contained in *T & M* 4 (1970), pp. 7–67, and the translation is based on this.

1. Even if it is appropriate that ignorance should not be displayed, yet we should not conceal in a lengthy silence what does not deserve silence. 'The Lord makes the blind wise' [Ps. 145/6.2] and accepts the stammerings of simple utterance which proceed from faith in preference to those of skilled speakers, who in their explanation make nets out of words like a labyrinth.

2. So then I too, although unskilled in speech, having invoked the Holy Trinity . . . and begging that you will support me with your prayers, O chief shepherd of the newly enrolled holy precious flocks of the Lord, together with all the holy shepherds who surround you, and with the whole company of the Church,[1] I determined to write to you a systematic account of the foul heresy of those who are called Paulicians, and describe from where and how and in what way this apostasy in its madness originated.

3. There are not two separate groups. The Paulicians are also Manichaeans,[2] who have added the foul heresy they discovered to the heresy of their predecessors, and have sunk in the same gulf of perdition. For even if, as the Paulicians themselves say, they do not share the licentiousness of the Manichaeans, they are careful guardians of their heresies.

---

1 The text of PS is addressed to the archbishop of Bulgaria, whose name is not given. The first Orthodox archbishop was appointed after the baptism of Khan Boris in 864 (Theoph. Cont. v.96, Bonn. p. 342). The first archbishop was in post by 870; see Lemerle, 'L'Histoire des Pauliciens d'Asie Mineure p. 21 for the dated epitaph of a member of his suite.
2 The use of the term 'Manichaean' to describe all Christian dissidents who held dualist views (and some, like Iconoclasts, who did not) is commonplace in Byzantine anti-heretical writing and central to the arguments of PS.

4. I have been obliged to do this, since I was among them on an imperial commission at the beginning of the reign of the autocrator Basil, our great emperor,[3] appointed by God ... who piously and reverently held the sceptre of the Romans ... and continued to hold it through many revolutions of years together with his holy sons, crowned by God, our emperors ... My task concerned an exchange of prisoners, which was successful in the time of, and by the favour of, their holy reign.

5. I spent some time on this same commission among the Paulicians in Tefrice,[4] and often conversed with them, and indeed I also made careful enquiries about them from the orthodox who lived there. Again, I had heard these blasphemers babbling that they intended to send some of their number to the country of Bulgaria to detach some from the orthodox faith and to bring them over to their own foul heresy. They were emboldened by the fact that the divine preaching had just begun, and thought that they would be able easily to sow their own tares in the pure and guileless wheat. These unholy people often do this, and eagerly accept many blows and dangers in order to share their personal plague with those they meet. So then I arrived at this solution.

6. Worthless, devoid of all virtue as I am, I entrust what I have diligently found out in the interests of the security of many to you, honoured fellow-bishops ...

PROLOGUE: PETER TO THE ARCHBISHOP OF BULGARIA

7. The presence of light scatters darkness, and the vigilance of shepherds chases off groups of bandits and wild beasts ...

10. The best plan for the simple is this, to avoid these corrupt people, and not be disgusted, nor try to answer their enquiries, but be silent when they make enquiry, and, if possible, run away from private audience with them, as if they were snakes. Such a person gains nothing from talking to them.

11. This is why they talk to ordinary people, to ... tear to pieces holy and divine doctrines, when there is no one who can oppose them sensibly ...

---

3 Basil I (867–86).
4 Otherwise known as Tibrice (see map). For the border wars of the period see **[6]** and our Introduction, pp. 19–22.

12. So it is best for an ordinary person to recognize them, but not to talk to them, in case the inexperienced should endanger themselves by conversing with them. It is difficult for the simple not to be swept away by them, as they quote all the sayings of the Gospel and the Apostle in conversation, and their craft is only recognized by those who are very familiar with holy scripture.

13. When they talk to anyone in authority, these foul people pretend to have an excellent character and deceitfully affirm and declare all the doctrines of orthodox Christians.

14. By an improper use of allegory, and in ignorance, they are able to say that they confess the Holy Trinity and to anathematize those who do not.

15. They say, although in an impious and ungodly manner, that our Lord and God became man in a virgin, and anathematize those who do not. And all the particulars of the incarnation of the Lord they admit, saying one thing with their mouth, another in their heart, and they anathematize enthusiastically Mani and all the foul heretics of his party,[5] and Paul of Samosata.[6]

16. They have other much worse teachers and leaders of their evil, as will soon be shown. In a word, like an octopus or a chameleon, they change both manner and appearance to suit the occasion, to catch some of the witless. When someone pays attention to their nonsense, then they show him a little of their mysteries . . .

18. The serpent, the father of evil . . . by his own counsel separated from God his precious creature man, and . . . enslaved man with his consent, and sold him to sin. God alone allowed this because of sin, and allowed the souls of men to be kept prisoner in Hades until the appearance in flesh of the son of God, our lord and God Jesus Christ, who is one of the Holy Trinity . . .[7]

---

5 See the abjuration formula below [11(c)], section 17.
6 Paul of Samosata (Bishop of Antioch *c.* 260–68) was accused of teaching a version of the Adoptionist heresy, that Jesus was born a man, but became the son of God by adoption at his baptism. Despite the similarity of name and their apparent connection with Samosata, Paulicians did not share this view; *contra,* see Garsoian, *The Paulician heresy.*
7 PS here sets out orthodox teaching, that the devil (identified with the serpent of Gen. 2.5) caused man to sin, and held the souls of the dead captive in Hell, until the righteous were released by Christ, who descended into Hell after the crucifixion (1 Pet. 3.19).

20. The only-begotten Son and Word of God ... in His ineffable love for men, determined to restore once again mankind whom He had formed from earth ... He humbled Himself with the Father's approval and the co-operation of the Holy Spirit, and took flesh from the Blessed Virgin, which was given a rational and spiritual soul and became man. He did not change what He is, for He is immutable, but took on what He was not, for He loves mankind. Passing through the Blessed Virgin, He left her once more intact, adorned with the light of her virginity and glorious within, as the prophet says [Ps. 45/44.14]. It is of her virgin seals that all the prophets long ago made paradoxical proclamations, and proclaimed her glory with foreseeing eye ...[8]

22. No one should think that the evidence which concerns Mary, ever-virgin, the mother of God, has just been introduced without good reason. For the enemies of truth teach that she gave birth to God in appearance and not in reality, and have the ridiculous idea that after the divine birth she had other sons from Joseph;[9] they do not accept the evidence of the prophets concerning her, as will be made clear in more detail later.

23. They claim that they follow the words of the holy Gospel and of the Apostle, but the fools craftily and untruthfully conceal the wolf under the sheepskin, although the pages of both the Gospel and the Apostle continually cite the evidence of the prophets, and reveal that they are trustworthy witnesses who revealed everything faithfully in advance, and bear witness to the truth. The prophets rouse their hearers to see clearly and think clearly, so that they may not miss the truth when it arrives, as if they were branded with the letters of their prophecy, and make their actions a base for contemplation ...[10]

25. From the time when our God and saviour Jesus Christ appeared on earth and lived among us men, all idolatry vanished, and true knowledge of God covered the earth like a flood ...

---

8 PS states the orthodox view that Jesus had a human body (which Paulicians denied), and was born of the Virgin Mary. He claims that the NT teaching about this is confirmed by OT prophecies, of which he cites four. Paulicians did not accept the OT.

9 The brothers of Jesus are mentioned in Matt.12. 40–42, Mark 3.31, Luke. 8.21; the sisters in Mark 6.3. Some early church writers believed that they were the children of Mary and Joseph, but this opinion came to be frowned on by orthodox opinion. See Graef, *Mary*, I, pp. 42, 70–71.

10 Paulicians rejected the OT, while accepting most of the NT as divinely inspired; yet NT writers cite OT prophets as evidence that the life of Jesus fulfils the law and the prophecies. PS is careful to identify this weakness in their position; see chapter 41.

26. Once the cross had been planted on earth and the bread of life for love of man came down from heaven together with the divinity – not that His body came down from heaven, He took that from earth with the same capacity for feeling as we have – and was raised upon the wood of the cross and watered the earth with the streams of His divine blood, He made it breathe out a sweet smell. Fertilized by the hallowing of His precious blood and water, it blossomed with different sorts of sweet-smelling spiritual flowers, as it still does.[11]

27. So the wood is venerated though which the gift of salvation came to mankind, and through which the enemy, the source of evil, was cast down to the ground and received a mortal blow. There is no other symbol of Christ's passion, through which so many miracles have happened, as through the venerable and life-giving cross of the Lord; the dead were raised even before the descent of our Lord and God to Hades. Then the curtain was torn and the earth quaked, the sun was darkened and then regained its light, revealing by the one the moonless darkness of the Jews, by the other foretelling the glory of the resurrection, and finally the deliverance of all the souls that were held in Hades (which took place when our Lord and God appeared to them) and the dissolution of Hades, so that it no longer holds the souls of those who fall asleep in the Lord.[12]

28. The unequalled power of the holy cross performed all these awe-inspiring wonders by the power of Him who was nailed to it, Christ our God. Let them be ashamed and turned backward and destroyed, those who do not admit its glory and do not venerate it with undoubting faith as the invincible trophy given by God.

29. The devil, that envious and evil hater of good, when once his head had been smitten and his heart pierced by the spear of the cross, could no longer carry out his abominable desires openly as he had before; but secretly he made the souls of some wretches frantic and deceived their minds 'through the pretensions of liars whose consciences are seared' [1 Tim. 4.2]; who deserve to be the fuel of the fire that is not quenched along with him.

---

11 In flowery language PS emphasizes the importance of the cross to orthodox Christians; the image is that of a tree bearing the fruits of the spirit.

12 It was believed that the empress Helena, wife of Constantine the Great, discovered the True Cross in Jerusalem before the emperor's death in 327; part of it was kept in Constantinople and greatly revered. For the miraculous powers attributed to it, see Drijvers, *Helena Augusta*, pp. 147–80; for the resurrection of the dead after the crucifixion see Matt. 27.52–3.

30. The Lord, who is ... superlatively good, did not abandon His accustomed benefits to His precious creation, man, but first 'appointed in the Church apostles' [1 Cor. 12.28] as eyewitnesses and ministers to announce clearly His descent in the flesh and His unlimited power, to give a true account of the evidences of His divinity, men who would not be ashamed of the bodily sufferings of Christ, nor claim that the miracles were a fraud, but would everywhere be concerned for the truth and declare the economy of the incarnation of the Word of God. 'Second, prophets' [1 Cor. 12.28], who would cut off at the root secret and unhallowed emotions by the sword of the Holy Spirit, and plant the healthy strong shoots of virtue. 'Third, teachers' [1 Cor. 12.28] to assist the others and give clearer explanations of what they said and did.

31. By their holy doctrines the whole Christian Church has been established of old, and is established still; destructive heresies, 'the gates of Hell', have never prevailed over it,[13] and do not now, as you well know, and as divine revelation promised. The waves of the verbosity of heretics always dissolve into froth. Whenever the various heresiarchs have taken on each of the champions of orthodoxy, the darkness of heresy has been defeated by the light of truth, and the Church of God has remained undisturbed ...

33. This filthy, darkened, divisive, foul and corrupting heresy of the Manichaeans is persecuted by all nations because it is poisonous and full of all kinds of filth, which they venerate and worship in the most profound silence. For this is what they are most concerned about, that their rites and heresies should not be shared with their nearest neighbours, far less with those who are strangers to them, but only with those few whom they perceive to be more perfect in impiety. A few years ago it gained force and was taught by the forces of rebellion, and confirmed under the errant guidance of Satan, the originator of evil; it conceived and gave birth to the apostasy which is his forerunner, revealing other incarnate demons together with their leader, the devil.

34. No one should doubt that they are demons: all those words and acts which demons do not dare to commit, they do and say against almighty God and all mankind, without shame or blushing. It is obvious that these corrupt hypocrites keep themselves from mixing with men because of their extremes of evil-doing, and live in lonely places as demons do, and utter strange and exotic blasphemies, claiming that they have based them on the words of the holy gospel and the Apostle.

13 Matt. 16.18.

35. Now as I begin my account, I shall explain what this heresy is, when and where it came from, making a list of numbered headings, briefly, so that it is easy to remember. Then later, after giving an account of them, I shall, with God's help, attack them in hand-to-hand combat, and will set out the scriptural proofs and evidence for every point, drawn up in parallel array.

36. The first mark of identification is that they confess two principles, an evil one and a good one; one who is the maker of this world and has power over it, the other has power over the world to come.[14]

37. It is often noticeable that when they are at leisure and one is talking politely to someone, they will say, regardless of the other person's rank, 'Tell me, what is it that divides us from the Romans?' (they call themselves Christians, and they call us who are truly named from Christ our true God, Romans).[15] They are trying to exchange for a tribal name the Lord in whom we, the real Christians, take more pride than in all the precious stones that there are in the whole world . . .

38. Paulicians say that this is what divides us, that they say that the maker of the cosmos is one god, and that another god, whom they call the heavenly father, has no power in this cosmos but does in the age to come, whereas we confess that there is one same God, creator of all, Lord of all, all-powerful. They say to us, 'You believe in the maker of the cosmos, we believe in him of whom the Lord speaks in the gospels (John 5.37), saying, "You have not heard his voice nor seen his face"'; they are talking empty nonsense, as will be shown later.

39. Second, the glorious ever-virgin mother of God is not even counted (in their hostility) among the bare number of good human beings. They say that the Lord was not born of her, but brought His body from heaven, and that after the birth of the Lord she had other children from Joseph.

40. Third, they refuse to accept the divine and awe-inspiring mystery of the body and blood of the Lord.[16] Not only that, but they think they can persuade others about this, saying that it was not bread and wine that

---

14 The parallel passage in the version of Photius, chapter 18 (*T & M* 4 (1970), p. 125, line 37) says: 'But some of them attribute to him lordship over heaven but not over what it surrounds.'
15 'Romans'; this term was used by the Byzantines to describe themselves as citizens of the empire, but the Paulicians used it as a religious description of those who held the faith of the Roman Empire rather than the true (Paulician) faith.
16 i.e. the Eucharist. The Orthodox Church believed in the real presence of Christ in the eucharistic elements.

the Lord gave to his disciples at the supper, but that symbolically he gave them his words as bread and wine.

41. Fourth, they do not accept the image, power and operation of the precious life-giving cross, but heap it with a thousand insults. Yet demons who see it merely drawn in the air flee trembling, with their leader the devil.

42. Fifth, they do not accept any book of the Old Testament, calling the prophets cheats and brigands, as will be shown at more length later, in its proper place. They accept only the four holy gospels and the fourteen epistles of St Paul, the catholic epistle of James, the three epistles of St John, that of St Jude and the Acts of the Apostles, using the same text as we do.[17]

43. They also have cursed epistles of their leader Sergius, full of impiety and arrogance.

44. They do not accept the two catholic epistles of the great and complete founder of the Church, the keybearer of the kingdom of heaven, Peter, the first of the apostles; they are hostile to him and heap him with a thousand insults and opprobrium, for some reason or other which I do not know. Perhaps, I suspect, and I have often said it to their face, because he prophesied what the future characteristics of their impious evil would be. The blessed apostle says in his second epistle [2 Peter 3.13–16]. 'And so, beloved, expecting all these things [obviously at the second coming of the Lord] be zealous to be found by him without spot or blemish and at peace. And count the forbearance of our Lord as salvation. So also our beloved brother Paul wrote to you according to the wisdom given him, speaking of this as he does in all his letters. There are some things in them hard to understand, which the ignorant and unstable twist to their own destruction.' This is the blame which is attached to the apostle, but it is in truth an encomium, because it is a prophecy which has been fulfilled without any rhetorical elaboration.[18]

17 In the margin there is a note in a late eleventh- or early twelfth-century script: 'I do not know if those then made use of the epistle of James and the Acts of the Apostles. Those of the present day only use the gospels, especially that of Luke, and the fourteen epistles of St Paul; in addition they have another epistle, that written to the Laodiceans.' The Epistle to the Laodiceans is mentioned in Timotheus of Constantinople, *De receptione haereticarum* (PG 86.21C). The version which survives bearing this title is known only in Latin and is a *cento* of passages from authentic Pauline epistles (*NTA* II, 128–32)

18 It appears that the Paulicians claimed that they rejected the epistles of St Peter because they criticized those of St Paul. PS argues that the real reason was that the epistles of Peter were a warning against misinterpretations of St Paul, such as those which he thought the Paulicians were guilty of.

45. Sixth, they turn away from the elders [*lit.* presbyters] of the Church. They say that the elders conspired against the Lord and so they ought not to name them, avoiding even the very name.[19] I will speak of this later more clearly in a detailed examination of each point . . .

46. Now it is time to make a beginning of historical notes. I shall begin by setting out what the blessed Cyril said in his catecheses and add the information I recently gathered, so that the enquiry may be more detailed . . .[20]

78. Socrates the Scholastic, who wrote a history of the Church, gives a brief account of what concerns Scythianus, Terebinthus, also known as Bouddas, and Manes, and agrees in every way with our great father Cyril.[21]

79. The successors who followed them, unable to withstand these refutations and also eager to disguise their evil, devised a wily plan; they rejected the impious Manichean books already mentioned[22] and taught the main theme to one another generation to generation, by tradition.

80. Moreover they held this as doctrine, that they may not read any other books at all except the Gospel and the holy book of the Apostle. Their reason for doing so is this, so that by the absence of Manichaean books and of the old books which are ours, by continual reading of the Gospel and the Apostolic book they might have a plausible pretext to attack the truth and deceive the unlearned and simple, saying that they had received their corrupt heresy from Christ and from the teaching of the preacher of the orthodox faith, the apostle Paul.

81. They try to hide the most central part of their error by the sweet-smelling and worshipful name of Christ, like a wolf in sheep's clothing. Recognizing these books alone, they can pervert the interpretation to their own intent, but not the other holy writings. So they reject the books of the Old Testament, as I said, because of the refutations which they

---

19 The Greek word *presbuteros* means both 'elder' and 'priest'. 'Elders' are frequently mentioned in the gospels as opponents of Jesus, e.g. Matt. 27.1.
20 The next thirty-two sections are a citation of the catechetical works of St Cyril of Jerusalem directed against Manichaeans. They have no relevance to the Paulicians.
21 Socrates (*c.* 380–439) was an ecclesiastical historian. The heretics named here are listed by Cyril as precursors of Mani. They are also to be found listed in an anathema formula (see **[10]**, section 11).
22 Also listed by Cyril. There were four fundamental Manichaean texts, the *Gospel* of Mani, the *Book of Mysteries*, the *Treasure of Life* and the *Kephalaia*.

contain, and those of our inspired fathers,[23] for fear that they may lead their kingdom of evil bound in triumph and everyone flee from them as from a fire. In our concern to triumph over this even more, I will set down evidence from another book to confirm even more the faith of those who come upon it.[24]

84. Some of the disciples of Mani came to Samosata in Armenia, and there sowed the tares of the evil one and deceived many of the Armenians there. After some years the root of the evil seed grew and shared its deadly fruit with many, reaching as far as Phanaroia.[25]

85. A woman from Samosata named Callinice had two sons, Paul and John. The viper mother reared these two snakes and taught them the corrupt heresy and sent them out of Samosata as preachers of error.

86. They reached the neighbourhood of Phanaroia and came to a village. Finding the inhabitants ignorant and unstable [2 Peter 3.11], they sowed the poison of evil and the malignant tares of the enemy. So to this day the village is called Episparis ['seed-bed'],[26] while the heresy took its name from its preachers. From that time instead of Manichaeans they were called Paulicians.

87. Our most orthodox and pious emperors, inspired with divine zeal that this plague might not spread further and infect many of us, have killed the Manichaeans they found in the Roman Empire, wherever and whenever they were found, in accordance with the Lord's saying in the Gospel, 'Those who did not want me to reign over them, bring them here and slay them before me' [Luke 19.27].[27]

88. So there have been many enemies of the Church of God at different times, and many sorts of victories have always been won by his grace. The devil, hater of God and 'inventor of evil' [Rom. 1.30], as is natural for one who is a fearsome and merciless enemy, having emptied his quiver in earlier heresies to no effect, shot his most lethal bolt at men in recent times, since he was permitted by the God of all things to perform

---

23 Orthodox Christians ascribed high authority to the writings of theologians such as St Basil, St Gregory and St John Chrysostom in their understanding of the Christian faith.
24 Chapter 82 is a citation from Epiphanius of Cyprus (c. 315–403) on the death of Mani.
25 Phanaroia (see Strabo 12.3.15, 30) is the fertile plain of the R. Iris. See map.
26 This village is not otherwise known. The name suggests wordplay on the image of the devil as the evil sower who plants weeds in the corn.
27 Legislation against Manichaeans was first enacted by the (pagan) emperor Diocletian in 297, and frequently confirmed thereafter.

all these wicked acts near the end of the ages, not in secret but openly, in accordance with the inspired and most holy sayings which say that antichrist, inspired by the devil, will perform signs 'so as to lead astray, if possible, even the elect' [Matt. 24.24].

90. The long-hidden lethal poisons of the corrupt Paulicians, which were unseen by almost all men, are now openly led in triumph by the sleepless prayers, the unwearied concern, the divinely given vigilance and skilful shepherding of our great, orthodox and peace-loving emperors . . .

93. How this foul heresy originated we have already explained in our detailed exposition, in which we spoke of Mani and the rest, of Paul of Samosata, the son of Callinice the Manichaean, and his brother John. Nevertheless, these of whom we gave a description, though they added some empty words to earlier heresies, as was shown in our account, were true disciples of the heresiarchs who had preceded them, as I showed in detail. Now something must be said about those who have recently appeared, on whom the Paulicians base themselves and whom they claim as their teachers.

94. In the days of the emperor Constantine, grandson[28] of Heraclius, there was born in the territory of Samosata in Armenia an Armenian named Constantine, in a village called Mananalis,[29] a village which even now rears Manichaeans.

95. This man entertained in his house for some time a certain deacon, a prisoner who was returning to his own country from Syria and came first to Mananalis. All this we found by careful enquiry. The prisoner was bringing back from Syria two books, one of the holy Gospel and the other of the Apostle, which he presented to Constantine in return for his hospitality.

96. When he had received the two books, that of the Gospel and of the Apostle, and realised that his heresy was unlawful and hateful and was hated and avoided by everyone because of the blasphemies and shameful acts it contained, he determined to give a new face to the evil. He determined, through the power of the devil, that no other book at all should be read than the Gospel and the Apostle, to conceal the harm

---

28 Since Constantine III, the son of Heraclius, only reigned for a few months in 641, this passage probably refers to Heraclius' grandson Constans II (641–68).
29 See map. There is confusion in the sources between Samosata in N. Syria and Arsamosata/Asmosata some 200 km. NE on the R. Murad. For the location of Mananalis see Bryer, 'Excursus on Mananalis'.

done by the evil, as those who give fatal poison to drink disguise it with honey.

97. He took the origin of every blasphemy from the Manichaean books already mentioned, and was able through the co-operation of the devil to twist the thoughts of the Gospel and the Apostle to his own opinion in his interpretation. He rejected the books of the Manichaeans . . . especially since he saw that many had died by the sword because of them.

98. For our most holy and orthodox and truly Christian emperors, in addition to all their most excellent decrees, have enacted that Manichaeans and Montanists[30] should be punished by the sword, and that their books, if found, should be burnt; and that if anyone should be found concealing them, he should be sentenced to death and his possessions be confiscated to the public treasury.[31]

99. To ensnare and totally destroy his disciples and make what he had to say more acceptable Constantine, the disciple of Mani, resolved to abandon the blasphemies of Valentinus[32] and his fabulous stories, the thirty aeons, I mean, and gods, and also the fabulous myth of Courbricus about rain. Courbricus said that rain originated from the sweat of a handsome young man who was chasing a girl.[33] Constantine rejected these and some other stories as being difficult to accept, not because he drew back from the height of evil, but to attract many to himself. He accepted the shamelessness and foulness and the evil-smelling mire of Basilides the mis-named[34] and of all the rest, and revealed himself as a new guide to the path of destruction.

100. For this reason the present-day disciples of Mani, knowing nothing of all this play-acting, willingly anathematize Scythianus, Bouddas and Mani, who were the chief guides of this evil.[35]

101. So then this Constantine, also known as Salo-anous,[36] left Mananalis and went to live in Cibossa, a *kastron* of Colonea,[37] saying that

30 See note 63 below.
31 *Ecloga* of Leo III (issued in 726, and so not in force in the Heraclian period), tit.xvii.5. For the implementation, see below chapter 114.
32 Valentinus of Alexandria (second century AD) was a celebrated Gnostic who originated one of the most elaborate Gnostic religious systems.
33 According to Cyril of Jerusalem (see note 20), Courbricus was the name originally given to Mani.
34 Basilides (also second century AD) was another Gnostic; the name means 'kingly', hence the wordplay in the text.
35 Despite what is said here, these names are included in anathema formulae, see **[10]**.
36 A derogatory parody of the name Silvanus.
37 See map for Colonea, the theme capital and ecclesiastical metropolis; Cibossa is not otherwise known.

he was the Silvanus mentioned in the letters of the apostle whom Paul sent as a faithful disciple to Macedonia.[38] He used to show his disciples the book of the apostle which he had got from the deacon, the prisoner already mentioned, saying, 'You are the Macedonians and I am Silvanus sent to you by Paul.' This he said 600 years after the martyrdom of St Paul, in the reign of Constantine, the grandson of Heraclius, as I said before.

102. He spent twenty-seven years there, and led many of the local inhabitants astray, and ended his life in a manner worthy of it.

103. For the emperor, having heard about him in some way or other, sent an imperial envoy called Symeon, with instructions to have the worker of evil stoned and his disciples handed over to the Church of God for conversion, on the grounds that they had been led astray through ignorance, and for correction if they still remained unconverted. All this took place.

104. Symeon arrived, took as his companion one of the local *archons*, named Typhon, and going to the place, gathered them all together and took them to the south of the *kastron* of Colonea. There he made the wretch stand with his disciples facing him, and ordered them to stone him. They picked up the stones, and dropping their hands as if to their girdles, they threw the stones behind them, so as not to hit their teacher, whom they believed had been sent to them by God. Now this Salo-anous had some time previously adopted a certain Justus and taught him the Manichaean heresy. He now received from him a fitting reward for his education and teaching. On orders from the imperial official, Justus picked up a stone, hit him like a second Goliath, and killed him ... Because of the stones thrown there, the place is called *Soros* ('Heap') to this day.

106. In accordance with the imperial order, Symeon handed over Constantine's disciples to the Church of God for conversion. But they remained unconverted, preferring to die in their own vice than by repentance to obtain forgiveness from God and eternal salvation. Symeon, who had conducted their trial, a man ignorant of divine learning and rather weak in intelligence, became a disciple of this fatal heresy.

107. He was recalled to the emperor and stayed for three years in Constantinople, living privately, and was completely taken over by the

---

38 In the RSV the names Silas and Silvanus are distinct. Acts 18.5 links Silas and Macedonia; for Silvanus see 2 Cor. 1.19, 1 Thess. 1.1.

devil. He abandoned everything and ran away secretly, and came to the aforesaid Cibossa. There he gathered together the disciples of Constantine and became his successor in the heresy. To give himself a better name he acted like his predecessors, calling himself Titus.

108. I will not call him Titus, for he was not the imitator of Titus whom Paul ordained as bishop in Crete,[39] but Ketos ('whale'). He was like the whale of the sea which lurks in the water. For of the sea-whale men say that it is called the shield-tortoise. In size it is like an island and has a deep voice. In ignorance sailors put down anchors upon it and driving in pegs, tie up their ships. When they light fires upon it, the beast feels the heat and immediately dives and plunges them all to the depths.[40]

109. So it was with this man. All those who knew nothing of the extent of his wickedness and who did not avoid, but rather obeyed his deep voice and placed in him the anchor of their hopes, all those did he whelm through fire to the depths of Hades . . .

110. He stayed there three years and deceived many. Later a dispute occurred, and there were many arguments between Justus . . . the one who killed Constantine by throwing a rock, and Symeon nicknamed the whale, about the saying of St Paul in the letter to the Colossians which goes: 'For in Him all things were created in heaven and on earth, visible and invisible, whether thrones or dominions or principalities or authorities. All things were created through Him and for Him; He is before everything and in Him all things hold together' [Col. 1.16–17]. Although Justus insisted, saying, 'Let us not deceive the people, and in ignorance destroy their souls, by teaching something other than the words of the apostle. We shall have to pay for their souls at the terrifying judgement,' Symeon did not agree; he persisted in twisting and perverting the sense of the words this way and that, as was his habit.

111. So there was a great quarrel between Justus and Symeon, and Justus went to the bishop of Colonea and, in his desire to understand the sense of the words of the apostle, told the bishop all about himself and the rest of those who accompanied him, and their teaching. Without delay the bishop informed the emperor Justinian (the one who succeeded Heraclius)[41] about this. When the emperor found out, he ordered

---

39 Titus 1.5.
40 The story of the whale becomes a commonplace in anti-heretical writings. For the original version of the story see *Physiologus*, no. 31, pp. 45–6.
41 Justinian II (685–93).

them all together to be brought to judgement, and that those who persisted in error should be burnt, as happened. A great pyre was constructed near Soros, and they were all burnt.

112. One of them, named Paul, an Armenian by race, had two sons, named Gegnesius and Theodorus. He ran away with them and came to Episparis, which I have already described in the detailed account, when I spoke of Paul and John, the sons of Callinice; the Paul from whom they were named Paulicians rather than Manichaeans.[42]

113. Paul then put forward his own son Gegnesius as teacher of atheism, and changed his name to Timotheus.[43] There was a rift between the two brothers, that is Gegnesius and Theodorus, one saying that he had received the divine grace of the spirit, the other making this claim for himself. So they quarrelled among themselves and hated each other completely, and so the leaders of this abomination remained to the end of their lives.

114. When the emperor heard all this (at the time it was Leo the Isaurian),[44] he sent for Gegnesius (who should be better called Thymotheus ['the anger of God']), and sent him to the patriarch of Constantinople.[45]

115. When the patriarch saw him, he said, 'Why do you deny the orthodox faith?' He replied, 'Anathema to him who denies the orthodox faith.' By orthodox faith he meant his own heresy.

116. Then the patriarch said again, 'Why do you not believe in and honour the precious cross?' He said, 'Anathema to him who does not worship and venerate the precious and life-giving cross.' By 'cross', he meant Christ making a cross by holding out his arms.

117. Again he asked him, 'Why do you not worship and venerate the holy mother of God?' He replied, 'Anathema to him who does not venerate the all-holy mother of God; into her entered Our Lord Jesus Christ, and she is the mother of us all.' He meant by this the Jerusalem

---

42 See chapter 86. It is not clear in the Greek which Paul is intended as the eponym of the Paulicians.
43 Timotheus/Timothy was a disciple of St Paul; see Acts 16.1.
44 Leo III (717–41).
45 There were two patriarchs in the reign of Leo III, Germanus I (715–30) and Anastasius (730–54). Germanus was forced to resign in 730 because he refused to accept the emperor's iconoclast policy. Anastasius was an iconoclast supporter, and perhaps the more likely candidate for the interview recorded here, as he would have been less inclined to press the interrogation.

which is above, which Christ entered as forerunner on our behalf [Heb. 6.20].[46]

118. Again the patriarch asked him, 'Why do you not partake of the stainless body and precious blood of Our Lord Jesus Christ, but dishonour it?' Thymotheus said, 'Anathema to him who does not partake of the body and blood of Our Lord Jesus Christ, or who dishonours it', but he meant his sayings.[47]

119. Again, being asked about the Holy Catholic and Apostolic Church, he answered in the same way, meaning by Catholic Church the assemblies of Manichaeans.

120. And about baptism similarly, he said that baptism was Our Lord Jesus Christ, and nothing else, because He said, 'I am the living water.'[48]

121. So Thymotheus twisted everything and anathematized it point by point, and so was considered guiltless of evil, and taking the emperor's *sigillion*[49] he went back to Episparis. There he gathered together all his disciples and fled with them, and came to the accursed town of Mananalis, from which had originated the Constantine I have already mentioned.

122. He stayed there for some time and then ... he was struck by plague[50] and ended his life, having been leader of the impiety for thirty years in all.

123. He had a son called Zacharias, and also a hired goatherd, whom he had found lying by the roadside in swaddling-bands because he was the result of an unchaste and befouled union. For this is how unchaste women cast their offspring by the roadside, for fear of the consequences.

124. When Gegnesius died, there was a schism among his disciples. Some followed Zacharias, and some Joseph the bastard, for that was his name. So there was great dissension between them, as in the earlier generation, and each of them was sure that he had received the grace of

---

46. The council of Ephesus (431) declared that Mary was the Mother of God. Since the Paulicians did not believe that Christ had become man, they did not reverence her, but apparently understood references to her in the NT as relating to the heavenly Jerusalem, described by St Paul as 'the mother of us all' (Gal. 5.26).
47 Paulicians understood Christ's words instituting the Eucharist in an allegorical sense; that He was giving his followers His words (as His body).
48 Paulicians rejected baptism with water because water was part of the material creation. They understood Christ's command to baptize as an allegorical reference to receiving Him spiritually.
49 An imperial safe-conduct.
50 Probably the great epidemic of 748.

the spirit, when they had rather received the power of the unclean spirit. Then Zacharias was angry because he might lose his paternal inheritance, and hitting Joseph the bastard senseless with a stone, he all but killed him.

125. After some time each of them resolved to take his own disciples and move away from the place in secret. They had gone a short distance from the villages when the Saracens, suspecting that they were going to Romania,[51] tracked them down. When Zacharias saw the attack of the Saracens he abandoned his disciples and ran away by himself. The Saracens caught up with his disciples and slaughtered them. So Zacharias was blamed by the others as being a 'hireling and not a shepherd' [John. 10.12].

126. Joseph the bastard, also called the senseless, having learnt this, turned his wagons towards Syria, and when the Saracens came up, he told them that he had come for pasture and cheese-making.[52] The Saracens were convinced by this excuse, and leaving them without further harassment, withdrew.

127. Joseph the senseless with all his followers took advantage of this opportunity, and escaped from that place. He came to Episparis, which has often been mentioned, and was warmly welcomed by the inhabitants. They all lit lamps and welcomed with great honour one worthy of all dishonour, as if he were a disciple of Christ.

128. A God-fearing man, one of the local *archons*, named Krikoraches, heard of this and surrounded the house where the disciple of Mani was with many soldiers, and arrested his disciples, but Joseph escaped and ran off as a fugitive towards Phrygia, and leaving there, he settled in Antioch in Pisidia.[53]

129. He too fought on behalf of evil for thirty years, and told his disciples he was Epaphroditus the disciple[54] of the apostle Paul, sent by him to them. I would more reasonably have called him Aphronetus. He was exceedingly lacking in education and judgement. Having made

---

51 At this time Mananalis was evidently on the Arab side of the shifting Arab/Byzantine frontier.
52 Compare the description of a Paulician unit in the capital as the '*tagma* of the herdsmen' (Nicephorus the Patriarch, quoted in Garsoian, 'Byzantine heresy', p. 98, n. 56).
53 This may be the incident described by Zonaras (*PG* 135,16B1–C3).
54 See Phil. 2.25. Aphronetus means 'senseless'.

many liable to eternal punishment by his vicious evil-doing he, too, ended his life there in a place called Khortokopeium.[55]

130. While he was still alive, a woman disciple of his in Armenia, having had an adulterous relationship with a disciple of his, had a son, as they say, 'of the Hebrews', Baanes the Foul, famous for vice.

131. This Baanes succeeded Aphronetus. He preserved the heresy safe which he had received from his predecessors, full of impurity, and led many of the insensate to complete destruction, becoming himself the instructor in evil.

132. Not much later another opponent of truth appeared in the neigbourhood of the city of Tavium. Near there there is a village named Annia, where lived a man named Druinus.[56] He had a son named Sergius, the champion of the devil, Sergius who made many of the sheep wolves, and through them scattered the flock of Christ, Sergius the terrible wolf in sheep's clothing who skilfully pretended to be virtuous and so deceived many, Sergius the enemy of the cross of Christ, the voice of impiety, the insulter of the mother of God and of all the saints, Sergius the arch-adversary of the apostles of Christ, who hated the prophets and turned his back on holy scripture, wandering away into lies and fairy-tales; Sergius the hater of Christ, the enemy of the Church, the one who trampled underfoot the son of God, who 'treated the blood of the covenant as common blood and outraged the spirit of grace' [Heb. 10.29].

134. Sergius who called himself the Paraclete and Tychicus,[57] and was adored by his own disciples as the holy spirit, Sergius the lover of darkness who called himself the star of daybreak . . .

135. So, then, this Sergius, while still a young man, had a relationship with a woman who was a Manichaean, and being led astray by her, became the forerunner of antichrist.

136. Some teachers of the most evil heresy were descended from Saracens, some from slaves, others were born from prostitution, and others took their error from women.

---

55 The literal meaning of the name is 'vegetable market'. The place is not otherwise known.
56 See map for Tavium. Annia is not otherwise known.
57 Mani also allegedly described himself as the Paraclete (Euodius, *De fide contra Manichaeos* (*PG* 42.1146), 24); for Tychicus see Eph. 6.21.

137. So that I may not seem to be accusing them for nothing, I will give a detailed account of him . . .

138. When he was a young man, it happened that he entered into a relationship with an immodest woman who belonged, it is said, to the Manichaean heresy. The devil's disciple, in her cunning and corruption, said to him. 'I hear of you, *kyr* Sergius, that you are practised in the knowledge of letters and education, and that in all ways you are a good man. Tell me then, why do you not read the holy gospels?' He was struck by her words, totally failing to recognize the hidden poison of evil in her, and said, 'It is not right for laymen like me to read them, but only for priests.'

139. She said to him, 'It is not as you suppose, "for God shows no partiality" [Rom. 2.11]. "The Lord desires all men to be saved and to come to the knowledge of the truth" [1 Tim. 2.4]. But since your priests are "peddlers of the word of God" [2 Cor. 2.17] and conceal the mysteries of the gospel, that is why they do not read to you all that is written in them for you to hear, but read some parts and not others, so that you may not arrive at knowledge of the truth.

140. For it is written that on that day some will say, "Lord, Lord, did we not cast out demons in your name and do many mighty works?" [Matt. 7.22]. And the king will answer, "Truly I say to you, I do not know you" [Matt. 25.12]. Search therefore and see, is this not how it is written? And there are some to whom the Lord will say, "I do not know you"' [Matt. 7.23]. Foolishly, in his ignorance Sergius was embarrassed and silent.

141. This is how the gospel saying should be interpreted: there are some even in our own day who live the life of Christ and seem to live piously, but who know how through incantation to put demons to flight frequently and to heal sickness and disease, just as long ago did the sons of Sceva or those who were called exorcists [Acts 19.13–14].

142. Even now there are people who act in this way and do not know that through incantation they are ruining their own salvation. They will cry out on that day, saying, 'Lord, Lord, did we not cast out demons in your name and do many mighty works?', and in reply the Lord will say to them, 'Truly I say to you, I never knew you.'

143. There are others who have undertaken a blameless and monastic life, but who have fallen into heresy from ignorance and lack of learning, and who for this reason will not attain the kingdom of heaven. So that on that day the just judge may owe them nothing, they receive in this life the gifts of healing, so that when they cry out, 'Lord, Lord, did we not do

many mighty works in your name?', they will hear, 'Friend, I am doing you no wrong, you received what was yours in this life, now take it and go' [Matt. 20.13].

144. Sergius, who did not know this or anything like it, searched in the gospels, and finding written the words which the wretched woman had quoted, said to her, 'Tell me, what did the Lord say these things about?' For a time she did not answer, but then she added, 'Who was the Lord speaking of when he said, "Many will come from East and West and sit at table with Abraham and Isaac and Jacob in the kingdom of heaven, while the sons of the kingdom will be thrown into the outer darkness?" [Matt. 8.11–12]. Who are the sons of the kingdom?'

145. He did not have the knowledge to say that they are the Israelites, 'to whom belong the adoption and the worship and the promises' [Rom. 9.4] . . . but they were cast out because they crucified Him.

146. So then the wretched Sergius, who did not know this, and thought that this Maenad was a guide to salvation, began to make careful enquiry of her about what she had already said. She [began] . . . to blaspheme against the saints in these words: 'These sons of the kingdom are your saints, who put demons to flight and heal men's diseases, whom you honour as if they were gods, abandoning the living and deathless Lord. They will hear on that day from the lips of the just judge: "I never knew you"' [Matt. 7.23].

147. So she went through what is written in the gospels, twisting the sense of every sentence, as she realised he was following, and little by little she made him a complete tool of the devil and herself sharpened a terrible weapon against humanity, such as none of his predecessors had ever been.

148. For some of those who appeared before him were exceptionally evil . . . nevertheless, they were obviously to be avoided by men and repulsive to all. For this reason few were led astray by them.

149. But this man cast off their defilements and their many acts of shamelessness, and embraced all their blasphemies as saving doctrines; he craftily laid claim to virtues and the appearance of piety, hiding the wolf under the sheep's skin. Although he rejected the reality of piety, he seemed to the ignorant to appear an excellent guide to salvation . . .

150. In this way until the present day these heretics deceive those who are not firmly based in the faith . . .

151. For until the heretics have led wretches to complete destruction, they do not reveal to them their great mystery, which is the denial of God.[58]

152. Sergius, the devil's champion, who had been taught her heresy by the destructive woman, came to think that all men who hold the pure and blameless faith of those who are truly Christian are liable to destruction. He was stirred by Satanic zeal, and became a new preacher of error. He called himself Tychicus, who is mentioned in the epistles of the apostle Paul,[59] and said to everyone that he was the apostle's disciple and sent by him to preach – not the word of God, but lethal error.

153. He went tirelessly round all the cities and districts in which 800 years earlier the apostle had preached the word of God, and detached many from the orthodox faith and brought them to the devil, as he himself claims in one of his epistles: 'From East to West, from North to South I have run, preaching Christ's gospel, weighed down to my knees.'

154. For all the thirty-four years that he was leader, from the reign of the Augusta Irene to that of the emperor Theophilus,[60] he established the apostasy which still survives, which the apostle Paul foretold to the Thessalonians [2 Thess. 2.3], through which he harmed a great part of the Church of Christ. Some he estranged from this temporal life by alienating them from their families and bringing them to death before their time, while those who followed him he deprived of eternal life by his abomination. He made many married couples divorce, and fouled their beds with his disciples; he tore many infants from their mothers' breast through his disciples, killed some and deprived others of parents; alienating them from the living God (who delivered them through His own blood), he sold them to the Saracens.[61]

155. He separated many good-looking young men and women, only children, from their parents, and sold them into slavery among the barbarians; he divided many brothers and sisters from their kinsfolk and those who were dear to them, and exiling them from their

---

58 The claim made here that Paulicians had an 'inner' teaching is not known from other sources, though it is frequently alleged against Bogomils and Cathars.
59 See note 57 above
60 Irene, 797–802; Theophilus, 829–42. The date of Sergius' death is given below, chapter 181, as 834/5.
61 Paulician communities profited from their position in the borderlands between the Byzantine Empire and the arab emirs. See **[6]** and Introduction.

own land, sent them into an alien country; their tears and laments reached the vault of heaven. Through his own disciples he destroyed many monks and nuns who had vowed their virginity to Christ, and alienating them from the monastic life, he made them strangers to God. He made many priests and Levites apostasize from the orthodox faith and transformed them from sheep into man-eating wild beasts. He caused many to die in bonds and in prison, and others who had been rich he made paupers.

156. So the one who is responsible for all these great evils should be worshipped as the Paraclete, should he? For his disciples pray in his name, saying, 'May the prayer of the holy spirit be merciful to us.'

157. He said, 'I am not responsible for these evils. I have often told them not to take Romans prisoner, but they did not obey me.' How can you claim to be guiltless? If they did not obey you, why did you agree with a disobedient people whom you are not strong enough to control? Why did you stay with them until death? If you were teaching them to walk in the way of Christ, why did you not teach them this too, as the Lord said, 'When they persecute you in one town, flee to the next'? [Matt. 10.23].

158. I will convict you from your own words. You wrote this to the people at Colonea: 'Having heard the reputation of your faith I remind you that, just as the churches which preceded you had shepherds and teachers (he means Constantine and the rest), so you have received a shining torch, a star of daybreak, a guide to salvation, as it is written: "If your eye is sound, your whole body will be full of light"' [Matt. 6.22]. Thrice-wretched, full of every sort of lawlessness! If, as you say, you are a disciple of Paul ... how can you untruthfully call yourself the star of daybreak, the shining torch, the guide to salvation (you, who destroyed so many souls), the eye of the body of the Church of Christ, madman and crazy as you are?

160. ... What sort of virtue of yours do they emulate, when you cry out, 'Be imitators of me, and hold fast the traditions which you received from me'? Look now, from your faith and teaching has grown the fruit of great impiety ...

161. A little later he says, 'Let no one deceive you in any way. You have these promises from God, be confident. I have written to you, having confidence in your hearts, that I am the door-keeper, the good shepherd, the guide of the body of Christ, the light of the house of God, and I am with you always to the close of the world [Matt. 28.20]. If I am absent

CHRISTIAN DUALIST HERESIES

in the body, still I am present in the spirit. For the rest, farewell, be strong, and the God of peace will be with you.'

162. Enemy of truth, son of the devil, worker of every kind of wickedness, how dare you say such things, 'making yourself equal to God'? [John 5.18].

163. Again he said, 'Again I say that Paul established the church in Corinth, Silvanus and Titus the church in Macedonia.' By Macedonia he means the assembly at Cibossa, and calls Constantine and Symeon Silvanus and Titus. 'Timotheus adorned the church of Achaea'. He says Achaea for Mananalis, and calls Gegnesius Timotheus, who was in reality Thymotheus. 'The church of the Philippians was served by Epaphroditus' – he means Joseph the goatherd, born out of wedlock, who was really Aphronetus, and his disciples he calls Philippians. 'The Church of the Laodiceans and the Ephesians together with that of the Colossians Tychicus taught.' By Colossians he means the Argaoutes, by Ephesians the people of Mopsuestia, Laodiceans the dogs who live in the country of the dog [*lit.* Cynochoritae]. He says of all these that the three are one, instructed by one man. Tychicus ...[62]

165. Tell me, you sycophant, attacker of truth, when Paul taught from Jerusalem to Illyricum and the areas round about, why did he establish only the Church of Corinth? If those whom you mention were Paul's disciples, how did he teach them and where were they, who were born eight hundred years later? ...

166. You ask to be accepted by all as an apostle of Christ, saying to Leo the Montanist,[63] 'As for you, give heed to yourself. Refrain from dividing the unwavering faith; what accusation do you bring against us? Have I claimed more than anyone or been haughty? You cannot say so; but if you do say so, your witness is not true. May I never hate you, but rather exhort you to accept shepherds and teachers just as you accept apostles

---

62 For the places mentioned here, see map. Cynochoritae literally translated means 'inhabitants of dog-country'. The use of the names of early Christian groups as titles for Paulician communities and those of the disciples of St Paul for their leaders is one of the strongest arguments for the view that they took their name from the apostle rather than from the various eponymous Pauls of the hostile orthodox tradition. See Introduction, pp. 7, 12.
63 It is uncertain whether 'Montanist' here is a description or a simple surname. If the former, Leo is the latest known member of a sect which originated in the second century, and placed great emphasis on the role of the Holy Spirit and of prophecy. Although condemned by the Orthodox Church, Montanist communities persisted in Asia Minor; systematic persecution which resulted in mass suicides is recorded in 721/2 in the reign of Leo III (Theophanes, ed. de Boor, I, p. 401).

and prophets, four in number,[64] so that you may not become the prey of wild beasts.'

167. Elsewhere you said, 'The first prostitution which we have inherited from Adam is a good work, but the second prostitution is more serious, about which it is said, "The immoral man sins against his own body"' [1 Cor. 6.18]. You go on to say, 'We are the body of Christ; if anyone separates himself from the traditions of the body of Christ, that is, our traditions, he sins, because he takes the part of those who teach otherwise, and does not believe sound doctrine.'

168. Say, you champion of iniquity . . . how dared you nullify through your incontinent hardness of heart the Lord's words, when he spoke about adultery even through a glance, in which he says, 'Everyone who looks at a woman lustfully has already committed adultery with her in his heart', but you would insist on your own views, for the sake of the worthless good opinion of men, and in order to attract to you people of slave mentality, who have no self-control, saying that there is no other fornication than flight from you? . . .

169. So having collected these few of his blasphemies to condemn him and his disciples, let us proceed to demonstrate the worthless treasury of his heart . . .

170. Let no one think that there are two different heresies, one taught by Sergius, the other by Mani; they are one and the same. When Sergius began to teach, since he wanted to attract many disciples and detach them from the Church of Christ, rather than have a few follow him, two and three times he stood face to face confronting Baanes, his corrupt fellow-disciple and fellow-initiate. Claiming piety, he began to attack him in the hearing of all, on the grounds not of belief, but the absurdity of his wicked acts.

171. Baanes said to him, 'You have appeared recently, you have never seen one of our teachers or stayed with him. I am a disciple of *kyr* Epaphroditus, and teach what he originally entrusted to me.'

172. Sergius had been disgusted by the evil-smelling filth which Baanes taught, and shaming him to his face, split the heresy in two; the ones who

---

64 Lemerle (*T & M* 5, p. 120), following Gouillard, thinks that a reference to Eph. 4.11 underlies this passage: 'And his gifts were that some should be apostles, some prophets, some evangelists, some pastors and teachers.' If we assume that the evangelists were originally included in Sergius' letter, the number 'four' here is more easily explained.

stayed with Baanes were called Baniots, while he called the disciples of Sergius Sergiots.

173. After the death of Sergius, his disciples were unable to bear the shame and reproach which they received from all sides, and began to kill the Baniots, to eliminate the shame of the Baniots from themselves.

174. Then one named Theodotus, a *synekdemos*[65] of Sergius, said: 'Let there be nothing between you and these men. We all had one faith until the revelation of our teacher.' So they ceased from slaughter.

175. The pious emperor Michael the abbot[66] and Leo, his successor,[67] seeing that this sort of heresy had defiled a large part of the Christians, sent out into all parts of the Roman Empire, ordering that those who were found involved in this foul heresy should be killed.

176. The order of the emperor came to Armenia, to Thomas, the bishop of Neocaesarea, and Paracondacus, who was the *exarch*.[68] So in obedience to the emperor's order, they killed those whom they found, on the grounds that they deserved death and were the guides to destruction.

177. Later some of Sergius' disciples, the ones called *Astatoi*,[69] by craft and treachery assassinated the *exarch*, while the Cynochoritae killed Thomas the metropolitan. So the *Astatoi* fled to Melitene.

178. The emir of the Saracens who were there was Monocherares. The *Astatoi* received Argaoun from him and settled there, and being gathered together in this way from all parts, they began to make raids on Romania.[70]

179. Sergius settled with his disciples in Argaoun for some time, but later by the judgement of God he was struck down with an axe, appro-

---

65 For this title among Paulicians, see below, chapter 183.
66 Michael 1 (811–13).
67 Leo V (813–20). For systematic persecution of Paulicians at this time, see Theophanes (de Boor, I, pp. 494–5): 'The most pious emperor [Michael], motivated by great zeal for God, proclaimed the death penalty against the Manichaeans – the present-day Paulicians – and the Athingani of Phrygia and Lycaonia. He was convinced by the arguments of the most holy patriarch Nicephorus and other pious men, despite other evil counsellors, who claimed their repentance, although it is impossible for those who are involved in heresy to repent.' For contemporary criticism of this policy, see Theodore the Studite, **[4]**.
68 For Neocaesarea see map. 'Exarch' in this context is the title of an official with oversight of monasteries (Photius, *Récit*, ed. Lemerle, *T & M* 4 (1970), 71, n. 58).
69 Literally, the wanderers. For Melitene, see map.
70 Monocherares is the Byzantine name of the emir known in Arab sources as Amr b. Abdullah al-aqta ('the one-armed'), who conducted several daring and destructive raids into Byzantine territory. He was killed in battle in 863. For Argaoun, see map.

priately for one who had cut the Church of God in half, and was thrown into eternal fire.

180. For Tzanion, who came from Castellon of Nicopolis,[71] found him in the mountains above Argaoun cutting planks, seized the axe from his hands, struck him and killed him.

181. So the last and worst of all wild beasts was snatched from this life below, in the year from the foundation of the world 6343 [= AD 834/5].

182. His most intimate disciples were Michael and Canacharis and John Aoratus, the three false priests,[72] and Theodotus already mentioned and Basileius and Zosimus and many others.

183. So then these disciples of his, who were called by them *synekdemoi*,[73] being false priests, infected the whole people that were gathered together in Argaoun after the death of their teacher Sergius with his teachings and those of his predecessors; they were always of equal rank, but no longer proclaimed one single teacher as their predecessors had done, but all were equal. They had subordinate false priests whom they called notaries.[74]

184. Now Carbeas appeared at this time and took his place at the head of this pernicious people; he increased their number so that there was no room for them in Argaoun, but they went and founded Tefrice[75] and lived there. So that at one and the same time he might escape the tyranny over them of the Agareni[76] of Melitene, and also, imitating the demons completely in the avoidance of mankind, might be near both Armenia and Romania.

185. So then he made those who obeyed him subject to treaty and had them as collaborators in the capture of prisoners, and those who did not obey him he sold to the Saracens. He pillaged the mountains of Romania towards Pontus.[77] At the same time he prepared the place as a convenient refuge for those who were being killed in Romania on account of this heresy. This was not all; he also summoned to himself to

---

71 *Castellon* usually means a fortified village, though here it seems to be used as a proper name. The place is not otherwise known.
72 The word used here is *miereus*, which appears to be a derogatory formation based on *me* ('not') and *hiereus* ('priest').
73 *synekdemoi* means 'companions in exile', 'companions on a journey'. Cf. 2 Cor. 8.19.
74 Cf. the anathema formula **[11(a)]**, section 15.
75 Or Tefrice, see note 4 and map.
76 Agareni means 'the children of Hagar' (Gen. 16.11), from whom, through her son Ishmael, the Arabs claimed descent.
77 For the Pontic Alps see map.

the same place the greediest and most licentious and foolish people from the frontier areas near Tefrice, by promising freedom for their most shameful feelings. So while he was still alive some of the false priests already mentioned ended their lives, but some were left.

186. When he too had left life, the leadership of the destructive people was taken in turn by Chrysocheir, who was his nephew and son-in-law.[78]

187. At that time I was in Tefrice, having been sent there in the imperial service to exchange some *archons* who were prisoners. This happened in the second year of Basil, Constantine and Leo, our great pious and just emperors.[79]

188. I spent a period of about nine months there, while Basileius and Zosimus, their polluted so-called *synekdemoi*, were still alive. I made careful and precise enquiry about the matters aforesaid, and I have endeavoured to make them clear to everyone, at the divine order of our great holy and orthodox emperors, like a slave obeying with great fear, though humble and unworthy.

189. Enough of all this; about some of their more complete heresies an account will be given to you in what follows, if God extends his hand to me, unworthy. To Him be the glory, to Father, Son and Holy Spirit, the one true God, creator, upholder and ruler of all the visible and invisible creation to all eternity. Amen.

8. PETER THE HIGOUMENOS: AN ABRIDGEMENT OF PETER OF SICILY

Unlike the description of Paulician beliefs and history attributed to Peter of Sicily (see **[7]** above) which survives in only one MS, this shorter version achieved a wide circulation. There are five MSS of the work as an independent treatise, and it also survives in the majority of the MSS of the chronicle of George Hamartolus (otherwise George the monk). One of the independent MSS, Parisinus gr. 852, attributes the work to 'Peter, monk and *higoumenos*'. For evidence that he and the author of the longer version **[7]**, known as Peter of Sicily, are identical, see the introduction to that version, pp. 65–6. The transla-

---

78 For the later battles between Chrysocheir and the Byzantine government see **[9]** below.
79 869/70. Basil became emperor in 867; his son Constantine became co-emperor between November 867 and February 868; he died in 879. Leo, the younger son, was associated in power in 870 and succeeded in 886.

tion has been made from the edition by Astruc, Conus-Wolska, Gouillard, Lemerle, Papachryssanthou and Paramelle in *T & M* 4 (1970), pp. 69–97.

1. The Paulicians (who are also Manichaeans) changed their name to Paulicians instead of Manichaeans from Paul of Samosata, the son of a woman called Callinice who had two sons, this Paul and John.[1]

2. She taught them the heresy and sent them from Samosata to the Armeniaci (*sic*) to spread their heresy. They came to a village of Phanaroia and there taught their heresy. From this the village changed its name to Episparis, and their disciples were called Paulicians.[2]

3. After some years of the teaching of this Paul (not Paul the great), the Paulicians had another teacher named Constantine, who changed his name to Silvanus. He it is whom they hold to be the chief of their teachers, and not Paul.[3]

4. He did not give them his heretical views in writing but unwritten, by oral tradition, while the Gospel and the Apostle were in writing. He handed them down unaltered in words and in writing as they are among us, but warped every chapter to his heresy, and made it a law for them that they should not read any other book of any kind than the Gospel and the Apostle.

5. After Constantine/Silvanus they had a second teacher called Symeon, who changed his name to Titus; the third was an Armenian by race called Gegnesius, who changed his name to Timothy; the fourth was Joseph who called himself Epaphroditus; after him Zacharias (but some of them reject him as a hireling and no true shepherd); the sixth was Baanes the Filthy, the seventh Sergius, who called himself Tychicus.

6. They willingly utter anathemas if anyone mentions to them Manes or Paul or John or anyone else. But Constantine, also called Silvanus, Symeon/Titus, Gegnesius/Timothy, Joseph/Epaphroditus, Baanes the Filthy and Sergius/Tychicus they will not anathematize, because they are their teachers and they regard them as apostles of Christ.

7. They say that there are six Churches in their confession; the Church of Macedonia, which is a *kastron* of Colonea; Cibossa, which was instructed by Constantine/Silvanus and Symeon/Titus; Achaea, which is a village of Samosata; Mananalis, which was instructed by Gegnesius/

---

1 See PS [7], c. 85.
2 For the place-names in this section see map.
3 For the Paulician leaders and the communities they founded, which are listed in sections 3–8, see PS [7], cc. 94–152 and notes there.

Timothy; the Church of the Philippians, by which they mean the disciples of Joseph/Epaphroditus and Zacharias whom they call the hireling shepherd; the Church of the Laodiceans, by which they mean the people of Argaoun, and that of the Colossians, meaning the Cynochorites. These three Churches were, they say, instructed by Sergius/Tychicus.

8. So these are the seven teachers and six Churches which they venerate and have in honour; all the others which one might mention to them they anathematize and reject.

9. Their first heresy is that of the Manichaeans, confessing two principles, as they do. They say, 'There is only one thing which separates us from the Romans, that we say that the heavenly father is one God who has no power in this world but has power in the world to come, and that there is another God who made the world and who has power over this present world. The Romans confess that the heavenly Father and the creator of all the world are one and the same God.' They call themselves Christians and us Romans.[4]

10. They say eagerly to those who do not know them, 'We believe in the Father and the Son and the Holy Spirit, the heavenly Father, and anathema to those who believe otherwise.' They conceal their wickedness with extreme care, for when they say 'the heavenly Father', they do not add 'the only true God, who made heaven and earth and all that is in them'. Anyone orthodox conducting the interview should ask the Manichaean to say the creed which goes 'I believe in one God the almighty Father, maker of heaven and earth, of all that is visible and invisible', and so on.[5]

11. Moreover, they blaspheme against the all-holy mother of God, without limit. If we force them to confess her, they speak allegorically, saying, 'I believe in the all-holy mother of God, into and out of whom the Lord went', but they mean the heavenly Jerusalem, into which the Lord entered 'as our forerunner', as the Apostle says,[6] and do not mean in truth 'Holy Mary, mother of God', nor 'from her the Lord took flesh'.

12. They also blaspheme the divine mysteries of the holy communion of the precious body and blood of our Lord Jesus Christ, saying, 'The Lord

---

4 See PS [7], c. 37.
5 i.e. the creed of the council of Nicaea (381), which had become the touchstone of orthodoxy. The words 'maker of heaven and earth and all that is in them' are not included in all the earlier creeds, though the ones which do not have them belong to the western credal tradition rather than to the eastern (Kelly, *Early Christian Creeds*, p. 62).
6 Heb. 6.20.

as he gave his words to the apostles said, "Take, eat and drink", but he did not say "bread and wine"', and they say that one ought not to make the offering of 'bread and wine'.[7]

13. They also blaspheme the holy cross, saying, 'Christ is the cross; it is not right to worship wood because it is a cursed tool.'[8]

14. They reject the prophets and the other saints; moreover, they insult and reject St Peter, the great chief of the apostles, most of all; they say that none of them are included in the number of the saved.[9]

15. In an allegory, when addressing us they refer to their own assemblies as the Catholic Church, but among themselves they refer to them as oratories [*proseuchai*].

16. They say that baptism is the words of the Gospel, as the Lord says, 'I am the living water.'

17. All this and more they say in an allegory when they are detected or surrounded. You must converse with them in all things sensibly and carefully. They have an untruth ready to hand, like their private rule, at all times, but especially when they are hard-pressed. They lie and say what they are told to or what is suggested, and in their own eyes they are innocent.

18. This is the tradition Manes gave them, saying, 'I am not heartless like Christ, who said, "Whoever denies me before men, I too will deny him" [Matt. 10.33]. I say, "If a man denies me before men and by the lie ensures his own safety, I accept with pleasure the statement and the lie as if he were not denying me, without holding him guilty".'

19. They reject our priests and other members of our hierarchy. They call their own priests *synekdemoi* and notaries; they are not distinguished from the others by dress or diet or the rest of their manner of life.

20. They turn all the words of the Gospel and the Apostle upside down; opposite to our views, but in agreement with their own, to fit in with their own heresy. As I have said, the text is exactly like ours in writing

---

7 For rejection of communion see PS [7], c. 40.
8 This is an abbreviated version of the doctrine attributed to Paulicians; that the cross which should be venerated is that made by Christ standing with arms outstretched, and that the cross used on Calvary was a gallows used for execution, and as such should not be honoured.
9 See PS [7], c. 44 for the Paulician view of St Peter, together with the community's explanation of it. For the rejection of apostles and prophets see PS c. 42; for a similar teaching among Bogomils see EZ [25], c. 11.

and in words, but they distort the sense, as I have explained more clearly in my detailed account.[10]

21. They honour our Gospel book when the occasion occurs – not the cross on it, but the book – saying, 'These are the words of Christ, and this is why we venerate them.'

22. Some of them, when they fall sick or are in pain, place the cross on themselves, and when they are healthy again, they break the cross and throw it into the fire to be burnt, or trample it under foot.

23. Some of them even have their children baptized by our priests if they are prisoners among them.[11] Others come secretly into our orthodox churches and receive the sacred mysteries to better deceive the simple.

24. They use these crafty ways and disguises, together with all sorts of licentiousness and corruption; they sleep with both sexes without distinction and without fear. They say that some of them abstain from their parents, and from them alone.[12]

9. THE DEATH OF THE PAULICIAN LEADER CHRYSOCHEIR (*c*. 878)

After the defeat of the Paulicians of Tefrice and the death of their leader Chrysocheir, as recorded in passage (a) below, it appears that their fighting men were included in the Byzantine army, though there was some pressure on their leaders to convert to Orthodox Christianity. The emperors obviously valued their fighting qualities, despite their heretical status. For later examples of Paulician fighting units, see **[14]**, **[17]**; for pressure to convert to Orthodoxy (perhaps seen as a way of ensuring political loyalty), see **[22]**.

(a) This passage is taken from the history of Genesius (p.124 in the edition edited by Lachmann, Bonn, 1834). He wrote a history of the period 813–86, at the request of the emperor Constantine VII. He probably wrote between 944–45; the imperial commission explains a bias in favour of the emperor's grandfather Basil I (867–86).

10 PS **[7]**.
11 See PS **[7]**; for Orthodox captives among the Paulicians, see **[6]**, **[7]**.
12 Cf. the anathema formulae **[11(b)]** and **(c)**. For similar charges of sexual licence made against Cathars, see Wakefield and Evans, *Heresies of the High Middle Ages*, pp. 102–4. Charges of sexual licence (with or without ritual cannibalism) are commonplace in the abuse aimed at minority groups.

THE DEATH OF CHRYSOCHEIR

[After the defeat of the main Paulician force] Chrysocheir took a few men with him and took to flight, pursued by a man whose name was well known, Pullades, waving a spear. He had been held captive in Tefrice, and had become familiar with Chrysocheir. So when he saw him, he recognized him and cried out loudly, 'Come here, soldiers, come here, domestic of the schools.' Chrysocheir escaped and shouted to Pullades, 'You wretch, Pullades, what wrong have I done you? Did I not do you many favours? Go away, do not get in my way.' Pullades replied, 'I know that you have done me many favours, Chrysocheir, and I trust in God my saviour that today I will return them.' As he rode, Chrysocheir found a ditch in front of him which his horse could not jump, but stumbled.[1] So Chrysocheir no longer had any thought of looking at Pullades, but instead looked straight in front of him to avoid falling into the ditch. Unseen by him, Pullades wounded him below the armpit with a spear. He was disturbed by the wound, and his horse shied and threw him. The most intimate of his grooms leapt down, a man named Diaconitzes, held his head and tended him, with his head on his knees. The noble emperor Leo converted this man to the better from the foul cult of the Paulianists [sic][2] and made him a *mensurator*, as the title goes in the Roman tongue. The officers found and seized him and, cutting off his head, sent it eagerly to the god-crowned emperor Basil as a trophy.

(b) This is taken from the work of the later chronicler Scylitzes, whose history covers the period 811–1057, and was probably written in the last quarter of the eleventh century. The later parts of his history are quoted at length in the works of Cedrenus, and have been translated from the edition of Cedrenus by I. Bekker (Bonn, 1839).

Stephen, surnamed Maxentius the Cappadocian, was sent to Lombardy[3] with a picked force of Thracians and Macedonians and Cappadocians. He accepted this, but having through cowardice and greed achieved nothing worth the name, he was relieved of his command, and in his place was sent Nicephorus Phocas, a man of good family, and energetic. He took with him an adequate force, including a unit [*tagma*] of Manichaeans, with Diaconitzes Chrysocheir as their commander.

---

1 *toutou dioklazen*; the translation is approximate.
2 For the use of this term rather than the more familiar 'Paulicians', see also **[10]**.
3 'Lombardy' in this context means the parts of Byzantine South Italy under Lombard control, to which an expeditionary force was sent under the command of Nicephorus Phocas the elder in 885.

10. THEOPHYLACT LECAPENUS (933–56) WRITES TO TSAR PETER OF BULGARIA ABOUT BOGOMILS

This letter provides the earliest evidence for the existence of Bogomilism in Bulgaria. In the reign of Tsar Peter (927–69), Orthodox Christianity was still a comparatively new faith there. The archbishop and the majority of the senior clergy were Greeks. The patriarch Theophylact was the son of the emperor Romanus Lecapenus (920–44); he had been appointed at the age of sixteen, and had the reputation of being more interested in the health of his race-horses than in theology. This letter, though sent out under his name to the Tsar, who was his nephew by marriage, was probably drafted by a professional who had access to the canon law collections of the Great Church (see also the letter of Theodore of Nicaea, [12]).

The text used is that printed by I. Dujčev, in his 'L'epistola sui Bogomili'.

TO PETER, KING OF BULGARIA, FROM THEOPHYLACT THE PATRIARCH, COMPOSED BY JOHN, *CHARTOPHYLAX*[1] OF THE GREAT CHURCH

A faithful and pious soul, my spiritual son, best of kinsmen and most illustrious, is a great matter, especially if it should happen to be royal and kingly as yours is, well-skilled to love and honour what is good and profitable ... Since I have already written to you about the heresy which has newly appeared in answer to your questions, now too I am writing more clearly and in greater detail, as you asked, now that I have learnt from you more of the abominable nature of the doctrine. I am writing in clear terms, setting out matters unadorned, in plain letters, as you asked.[2]

Let all those who are subject to your Christ-loving governance be divided into three groups, O lover of Christ. For it is neither just nor right that those who have erred through simplicity and ignorance should incur the same penalties as those who from evil and malice taught others and brought them to destruction. Let the first of these, those who have taught doctrines alien to those of the Church, if they repent and anathematize their own heresy, be rebaptized in accordance with Canon 19 of Nicaea, and let everything be done to them in accordance with the rule

---

1 The *chartophylax* was the archivist of St Sophia, and in this capacity had access to earlier documentation.
2 This presumes an earlier correspondence between Tsar and Patriarch, which has not survived.

of those who are being baptized. For this impiety is a mixture of Manichaeanism and Paulianism. So for this reason their priesthood is to be set aside. The others of them, those who have been led astray by the former and have been seduced, not by wickedness, but by their own simplicity and guilelessness, being unable to discriminate doctrines accurately – they have listened to and accepted the heresy while having baptism from the orthodox – let them not be rebaptized, but be sealed by being anointed with holy chrism, as is done to newly baptized children.[3] Similarly their priests, that is to say, when they have anathematized the heresy and given *libelloi* – a written denial of heresy and confession of the orthodox faith – let them be received. Those in the third rank, who neither taught nor learnt nor did nor had done to them anything in accordance with their foul customs, but in ignorance were united with them because they were ascetics and good and religious men, unsuspectingly, even if they spent some time with them to hear more completely about the heresy, if after hearing they recognized the foulness of the heresy and left and abandoned it, let all these be received after a separation of four months, so that their complete conversion may be certain. Let priests retain their priesthood without hindrance. As for a priest who has given information, let his suspension until now be sufficient punishment, and let him exercise his priesthood in the future without correction. Let your Christ-loving care make these provisions for those who are penitent; as for those who persist in vice and suffer from the disease of impenitence, the Church of God cuts them off totally like gangrenous and deadly limbs, handing them over to immediate punishment and anathema as well. The laws of the Christian state – since, O most prudent of men, you asked me to tell you about them – inflict death on them, judging the penalty a capital one,[4] especially when they see the evil creep and extend widely, harming many.

However, we do not want to hand them over in this way, nor is it right, and have revealed what is fitting for the Church's reputation and for ours, lest either all or some of them should never see the change of heart of repentance, and so that He should cure them Who alone is lover of men, who in His mercy desires not the death of a sinner, but rather that

---

3 In the Orthodox Church newly-baptized children are anointed with holy oil (chrismated). This corresponds to the rite of confirmation in the western Church, and is thought to confer the gift of the Holy Spirit on the child.
4 Death had been a penalty for heresy in the law code of Justinian, the basis of Byzantine law.

he should repent and live. Let the anathematization of all these together take this form. Let him be anathema from the holy and undivided and adorable Trinity, Father, Son and Holy Spirit, whoever does not think and believe as does the Holy Catholic Church of God in Rome and in Constantinople, in Alexandria, in Antioch and in the Holy City,[5] in sum the Church from one end of the world to the other, in accordance with the canons and rules and doctrines of the seven holy and ecumenical synods.[6]

1. Against him who says and believes that there are two principles, a good one and a bad, one the creator of light, the other of darkness, one of men, the other of the angels and other living bodies, anathema.

2. Against those who vainly say that the wicked devil is the maker and ruler of matter and of all this visible universe, and of our bodies, anathema.

3. Against those who abandon the law of Moses and say that the prophets do not come from the good, anathema.[7]

4. Against those who despise lawful marriage and say that the commandment to increase and preserve our race comes from the devil, anathema.

5. Against those who blasphemously say that the Son, who is one Person of the Holy Trinity, like in nature, the Word of God the Father, became man without sin in appearance and seeming, but not in reality, anathema.

6. Against those who vainly imagine that the cross and the death of Christ and the resurrection are only appearances, anathema.

7. Against those who do not believe in what is really the body and blood of Christ, which He gave to His apostles, saying, 'Take, eat', and entrusted to them, but fantastically assert that it is the gospel and the epistles of the apostle,[8] anathema.

8. Against those who nonsensically say that the all-holy Mother of God is not the virgin Mary, the daughter of Anna and Joachim,[9] but Jerusalem which is above, which they say Christ entered and left, anathema.

---

5 These five patriarchates, in the view of the Orthodox, made up the universal Church.
6 The councils of Nicaea I (325), Constantinople I (381), Ephesus (431), Chalcedon (451), Constantinople II (553), Constantinople III (680–01) and Nicaea II (787), which for the Orthodox had defined Christian doctrine.
7 For similar Paulician views, see PS [7], c. 42.
8 Cf. PS [7], c. 40.
9 These names are given to the parents of the Virgin in the apocryphal infancy gospel known as the *Protoevangelium*.

9. Against those who malignly invent the story that after the ineffable birth of the Son and Word of God the ever-virgin mother of God had other children from contact with a man,[10] anathema.

10. Let the leaders and teachers of this ancient heresy which has newly reappeared be anathema.

11. Let Scythianus the Egyptian, the originator of these blasphemies, who in his audacity did not hesitate to call himself God the Father, and his disciple Terebinthius, also named Boudes, the son of perdition, who did not shrink from calling himself the son of God, and Courbicus, also called Manes, who in his sinful madness gave himself the title of the Paraclete and Holy Spirit, let all these three enemies and opponents of the Trinity, who lay claim to the glory of God, together with the twelve disciples of Manes and their doctrines, be anathema.[11]

12. Let Paul and John, the infamous children of Callinice the infamous, from whom the group of apostates takes its name, and Constantine the Armenian of Mananalis, also called pseudo-Silvanus, and Simeon, also called Titus, be anathema.

13. Let Paul, the other Armenian, and Theodore and Genesius, his abominable sons, Joseph, also called Epaphroditus, Zacharias and Baanes the foul be anathema.

14. Let Sergius, also known as the son of Druinus, or as Tychicus, the accursed, who again under the inspiration of the evil one boasted that he was himself a second Paraclete and Holy Spirit, may he and his writings and all the members of his group be consigned to eternal anathema, together with all those who have anything in common with them or knowingly harbour them, whether in their own house or outside, just as they have tried to expel our God, and have expelled Him as far as they could from His own creation and kingdom, and have handed it over to their fellow-apostate, the devil.

O wisest and best of men, let those who anathematize all these persons, together with their doctrines and writings in church, according to the form laid down, be deemed to have deserved appropriate restoration. Let those who do not believe in accordance with the understanding of your piety be subjected either to the ecclesiastical proclamation of anathema – for the apostle says, 'After one or two admonitions,

---

10 Cf. PS [7], c. 39.
11 For the names of the heretics in this section and in those which follow, and the connection with Paulicians, see *ibid.*, cc. 94–172.

denounce a heretic in the knowledge that such a man is perverse and sinful; he is self-condemned' – or to the legal punishment of the state. Nevertheless, over and over again, care must be taken in every way, either with threats and clear proofs, or with constant teaching and encouragement, and their salvation must never be despaired of.

11. ABJURATION FORMULAE (TENTH CENTURY) FOR PAULICIAN CONVERTS TO ORTHODOXY

These formulae represent the summaries of their heretical views to which ex-heretics who desired to be reconciled with the Orthodox Church were required to give formal assent. The Bogomil formula **[26]** survives in a liturgically complete version which may be useful as a guide for how the Paulician formulae were used. Several collections of such formulae are known; the most complete is Vindob. gr. 306. An account of the contents of this and similar collections may be found in Eleuteri and Rigo, *Eretici, dissidenti, musulmani ed ebrei a Bisanzio*. Individual formulae have been dated on internal evidence, especially where there appear to be verbal echoes of other anti-heretical material. In all cases it should be remembered that the formulae do not necessarily express the beliefs of the new converts from heresy, but rather what the churchmen who conducted the service of reconciliation thought were their beliefs. The Bogomil formula suggests that it was read out section by section while the ex-heretics repeated 'anathema' at the end of each section in the presence of witnesses. Peter of Sicily's claim that Paulicians were willing to anathematize Mani and his disciples, but not the community leaders they revered, is most easily explained if we assume a cleric taking his candidates through a pre-written text. In the form in which they have survived, the formulae, especially (b) and (c), appear to be composite documents, representing both a summary of the heterodox views being abjured by the candidates and a theological explanation of the origin of such views. This latter may represent nothing more than a guess, more or less prejudiced, on the part of the orthodox, and should be accepted with a degree of caution.

Formula (a) is to be found in MS Sinaitus graecus 383, fos 148v–9r. This is a tenth-century MS, in which the abjuration formula follows the text of Peter the Higoumenos **[8]**, with which it has verbal links. The reference in the last clause to 'the Great Church' suggests that this may represent a patriarchal collection like that of MS Coislianus 213. Formula (b) is that described by Garsoian in *The Paulician heresy*, p. 26, n. 2 and thereafter as 'the Manichaean formula.' Sections 12–16 are also to be found in MS Coislianus 213, a *euchologion* (or collection of prayers for particular occasions), whose colophon says that it was completed in August 1027 for 'Strategius, priest of the Great Church and of the patriarchal oratories'. These anathemas are also included in the *Synodikon of orthodoxy* **[16]**. Formula (c) is contained in MS Scorialensis R.1.15, a twelfth-century MS.

All three formulae have been translated from the edition in *T M* 4 (1970), pp. 190–208 by Astruc, Conus-Wolska, Gouillard, Lemerle, Papachryssanthou and Paramelle.

(a) HOW REPENTANT MANICHAEANS OUGHT TO ANATHEMATIZE THEIR HERESY

1. Anathema to him who believes or thinks or says that there are two opposed Gods, a good one and a bad one, that there is one God the Father and Son and Holy Spirit, God of the world to come, and another who is the maker and creator of this age or world.[1]

2. Anathema to him who does not confess and believe with heart and mouth that there is one God and not another different one; that there exists the Father, Son and Holy Spirit, our only true God, that He is the maker and preserver of all that is, seen and unseen, that is, of the heavens we see above us and the air we breathe and the fire we see and the earth we tread and the sea and everything that is in them, man and beasts, reptiles and birds and all other living things.[2]

3. Anathema to him who does not believe with heart and mouth that the Son of God, one of the Holy Trinity, was born in the flesh of holy Mary without change or confusion, that is, that He was incarnate of her substance.[3]

4. Anathema to him who thinks or believes or says that the Lord brought His body from above and made use of the womb of the mother of God like a bag.[4]

5. Anathema to him who says that after the Lord's birth the holy mother of God had other sons or daughters from Joseph.[5]

6. Anathema to him who does not agree with heart and mind that it is the sinless body and precious blood of our Lord and God, not a type or antitype, which we receive in church, and which is offered in sacrifice by

---

1 Cf. PH, c. 9.
2 Cf. PH, c. 10.
3 Cf. PS, c. 20.
4 Cf. PS, c. 39. The image more commonly alleged against unorthodox theories of the Incarnation is that Christ passed through the body of the Blessed Virgin Mary 'as through a pipe'.
5 Cf. PS, c. 22.

orthodox bishops and priests 'for the forgiveness of sins', as the Lord said.[6]

7. Anathema to him who does not accept with heart and mind the law of Moses, as being given by the one true God, together with the holy prophets, apostles, martyrs, and all the saints as the Holy Catholic and Apostolic Church teaches.[7]

8. Anathema to him who does not worship with a true heart and mouth the venerable wood of the precious and life-giving cross, on which was nailed our Lord and God, and all the figures of it which are made of any material, for the salvation of our souls and bodies.[8]

9. Anathema to Constantine the Paulician who called himself Silvanus, who left the village of Mananalis near Samosata and taught the Manichaean heresy at Cibossa, a *kastron* of Colonea, and was there stoned by Symeon because of his evil deeds and blasphemy.[9]

10. Anathema to Symeon who called himself Titus, who, after he had stoned Constantine on the emperor's orders, became the second teacher at Cibossa, was denounced by Joseph his disciple to the bishop of Colonea, and was by the emperor's orders burnt near the heap of stones where Constantine had been stoned.

11. Anathema to Genesius who called himself Timothy and was summoned to Constantinople by the emperor Leo the Isaurian.[10] By allegorizing the heresy he deceived those who were holding him and went from Constantinople to Episparis, a village near Phanaroia where he had lived before, and from there went to Mananalis and there ended his life.[11]

12. Anathema to Joseph who called himself Epaphroditus, who taught at Mananalis and went to Episparis in Armenia and from there to Phrygia to the village of Annia, and died there.[12]

13. Anathema to Zacharias, son of Genesius, who taught with Joseph.

14. Anathema to Baanes the Filthy, their fellow-initiate.

6 Cf. PS, c. 40.
7 Cf. PS, cc. 23–9.
8 But *contra* PH, c. 22, which alleges that Paulicians made some use of images of the cross as healing charms.
9 For these place-names see map and PS, c. 94, with note there.
10 In 717–41. Genesius' death from plague probably occurred in the epidemic of 747/8.
11 Episparis is otherwise unknown. The name means 'seed-bed' and may be an abusive allusion to the parable of the devil sowing weeds in the corn (Matt. 13.24–30, 36–42).
12 Cf. PS, cc. 128, 132.

ABJURATION FORMULAE (TENTH CENTURY)

15. Anathema to Sergius who called himself Tychicus, the son of one called Druinus, who was taught the Manichaean heresy by a woman and preached the error for thirty-four years from the time of the empress Irene to the emperor Theophilus, as he wrote himself in his letter.[13] He had as more intimate disciples and *synekdemoi* Michael and Canacharis and John Aoratus, Theodotus and Zosimus and Basil. Anathema to them. This Sergius lived in Argaoun with his disciples, and was hacked to pieces on the mountain by Tzanion the Castelliote in the year of the world's foundation 6343.[14]

16. Anathema to those who say that there are six Paulician Churches, Macedon, which is a *kastron* of Colonea called Cibossa, which Constantine/Silvanus taught, and Symeon/Titus; Achaea, which is Mananalis, a village of Samosata, which Genesius/Timothy taught; the church of the Philippians, taught by Joseph/Epaphroditus; the Church of the Laodiceans, that is the people of Argaoun; the Church of the Ephesians, who are the people of Mopsuestia; the Church of the Colossians, who are the Cynochoritae; these three Churches were, they say, seduced by Sergius/Tychicus.

17. Anathema to all Paulicians, wherever they may be, those who persist in this filthy heresy and remain there and do not walk in the orthodox faith of the Great Church of Constantinople.

(b) HOW THOSE WHO APPROACH THE HOLY CATHOLIC AND APOSTOLIC CHURCH OF GOD FROM THE MANICHEES SHOULD GIVE A WRITTEN ANATHEMA OF THEIR HERESY

1. Moreover, I anathematize those who later in these latter days have been leaders of the heresy, Paul and John, the children of Callinice, Constantine, also known as Silvanus, Symeon/Titus, Genesius/Timothy, Zacharias the hireling, Joseph/Epaphroditus, Baanes the Filthy, Sergius/Tychicus and his disciples and *synekdemoi* Michael, Canacarius, John, Theodotus, Basil and Zosimus, of whom the more senior are called notaries.[15]

---

13 Cf. PS, c. 132. The place Annia (see PS, c. 12 above) is given there as his birthplace. The empress Irene reigned from 797 to 802; the emperor Theophilus from 829 to 842.
14 Cf. PS, cc. 181–4. Sergius was killed in 834/5.
15 For these two ranks of Paulicians and a different account of their relative seniority see PS, c. 183.

2. In addition I anathematize the accursed Carbeas and his nephew and son-in-law Chrysocheir.

3. Anathema to what are called the Churches of the Manichaeans which are these: Macedonia, which is Cibossa in Colonea, Achaea, which is Mananalis in Samosata, Laodicea, which is Argais in Lycia, the Church of Colossi or Cynochoritae, the Church of Ephesus, Mopsuestia and the Church of the Philippians.

4. Anathema to those who say that the Father is not the all-powerful maker of heaven and earth and of all that is seen and unseen, but is simply the heavenly Father with authority only over the world to come, because the present age and all the cosmos were not created by Him, but by his enemy the evil cosmocrator.

5. Anathema to those who insult Mary the holy mother of God, although they claim to honour her, and think instead of her of the heavenly Jerusalem into and out of which (they say) the Lord came, and to those who despise the holy cross, although they pretend to honour it, and think instead of Christ, who (they say) extended his arms and so made the sign of the cross; and to those who turn away from the communion of the precious body and blood of Christ, although they pretend to receive it, and think instead of the sayings of the teachings of Christ which (they say) he said while giving it to the apostles, 'Take, eat and drink'; and to those who belittle baptism, but pretend to regard it highly, and think in its place of Christ, who said, 'I am the living water'; and to those who reject the Catholic Church by saying that they honour it and thinking in its place of their own assemblies and meeting-places; and to John, the brother of Paul and originator of their heresy.[16]

6. Anathema to all those aforesaid and to those who reject the Church of Christians whom they call Romans, and who insult Mary, the holy mother of God, and the precious cross and the holy icons and saving baptism, and who reject the communion of the holy mysteries, but use the burnt umbilical cords of children for the purification (but rather the pollution) of their souls, and with them defile their food.

7. Anathema to those who pollute themselves by eating the flesh of dead animals, and to those who reject all Christian fasts, and at the season of what they think is Lent enjoy cheese and milk.

8. Anathema to those who deny or bastardize the four gospels of Christ and the letters of St Paul the apostle, and who, instead of God, the

16 John, although mentioned in the narrative accounts, is only given a position of importance in the sect here.

creator of everything, worship him who is called 'the Lord of this world', and in place of the apostle Paul, honour Paul, the son of Callinice, and receive his four disciples as a type of the four evangelists, and give the other three the name of the Trinity.

9. Anathema to those who are polluted with their sister or mother-in-law or sister-in-law, and those who gather to celebrate a feast on the first of January, and after the evening drinking-session put out the lights and have an orgy, sparing no one on the grounds of age or sex or relationship.

10. Anathema to those who do not tell the truth on oath, but always tell a convenient lie and commit perjury, following the teaching of the thrice-cursed Manes, who said, 'I am not harsh like Christ, and I will not deny anyone who has denied me before men. Anyone who lies for his own safety and who denies his own faith through fear I will receive with joy.'

11. If I do not think and say these things with all my heart, I so-and so, but have made the foregoing anathemas hypocritically, may I be anathema katathema in this world and in the world to come, and may my soul be condemned and destroyed and consigned to hell for ever.

12. If anyone does not confess that the Holy and undivided Trinity is of one nature, but confesses some imported angel, named Amen, as the Son, and some further different and lesser nature for the Spirit (who is equal in power to the Father and the Son),[17] may he be anathema.

13. If anyone does not confess that God is the creator of heaven and earth and of all that has been made and the maker of Adam and inventor of Eve, but says that the adversary is Lord and maker of all and moulder of the nature of man, let him be anathema.

14. If anyone does not confess that the Son of God, the Word, was begotten of Him without alteration before the ages, and in the last times was incarnate of the unsullied Mary, mother of God, through His great pity, and for our salvation became man and took on all that was ours except for sin, and if he does not share the immortal and life-giving mysteries with fear, as being the Lord's flesh and His blood poured out for the life of the world, but as simple bread and ordinary wine, let him be anathema.

---

17 In this section there appear to be echoes of much earlier controversies over the nature of the Trinity, for which see Hanson, *The search for the Christian doctrine of God*, pp. 100–9.

15. If anyone does not revere the cross of our Lord and God and Saviour Jesus Christ, not as an instrument of tyranny, but as the salvation and glory of all the world, which has finally brought to nothing the plans and weapons of the enemy and destroyed them, and has redeemed the creation from idols and brought victory to the cosmos, let him be anathema.

16. If anyone does not honour the august and holy icon of our Lord and God and Saviour Jesus Christ as an effigy of the word of God incarnate on our behalf, and does not consider that he sees Him in the the likeness of the icon, and His immaculate mother and all the saints, but calls icons idols, let him be anathema.

17. Anathema to Paul of Samosata and Luke and Blasius and Barnabas and Antonius and Ronidace and Anthes and Nicolaus and Leo and Peter and all the other thrice accursed teachers of this new heresy, forerunners of antichrist and creatures of Satan, anathema to them.

(c) CONCERNING HOW A CONVERT FROM THE PAULICIANS OUGHT TO ANATHEMATIZE THE PAULICIAN HERESY

1. Anathema to those who call our eternal God Satan.

2. Anathema to those who confess that our Lord Jesus Christ suffered, but teach that He was not born in reality from the holy and ever-virgin and wholly pure mother of God, but was born only in appearance.

3. Anathema to those who do not confess and adore the holy and immaculate mother of God.

4. Anathema to those who insult the holy mother of God, Mary, and the precious cross and the holy icons of all the saints and the august and holy icon of our Lord Jesus Christ and of his holy mother, the mother of God, and of the angels who have the form of God and baptism which brings salvation.

5. Anathema to those who avoid all Christian fasts, but who at the time which they think is Lent enjoy meat, cheese and milk.

6. Anathema to those who deny or corrupt the four gospels of Christ and the letters of St Paul, and in the place of God, the creator of the universe, worship him whom they call the ruler of this world, and instead of the holy apostle Paul, honour Paul, the son of Callinice, and accept his four disciples as types of the four evangelists, and give the other three disciples the name of the Trinity.

ABJURATION FORMULAE (TENTH CENTURY)

7. Anathema to those who practise consanguinity and defile themselves with their sister and mother-in-law and sister-in-law, and to those who on the first of January assemble, as they say for a feast, but who after an evening's drinking extinguish the lights and engage in a sexual orgy with no respect for sex or age or relationship.

8. Anathema to those who call our God, the creator of the universe, Satan, and teach that the body was made by Satan, and say blasphemously that man received his soul from him, inserted into the body through the nostrils, and tell the absurd story that he receives it back again.[18]

9. Anathema to those who do not accept the twelve disciples and apostles of Christ and their teaching, but receive and honour six who have corrupted the evangelic tradition and the entire Gospel and falsely interpreted it, whose names are these: Paul, Silvanus, Timothy, Epaphroditus and Tychicus.

10. Anathema to those who accept the teaching of these men and the book which is written in opposition to the Gospel and is called Power [*Dynamis*], and honour it.[19]

11. Anathema to those who confess our eternal God is seated above the heavens, but blasphemously claim that His Son and co-ruler, our Lord Jesus Christ, is borne on a cloud below the heavens and teach those who think as they do.[20]

12. Anathema to Paul of Samosata, and his teaching, and to those who share his views and all his writings, and those who accept them and honour them, and are trained in and preserve their traditions.

13. Anathema to those who do not think as the Holy Catholic Apostolic Church thinks.

14. Anathema to those who do not revere and honour and accept and welcome the holy teachings of the apostles and their traditions, and the canons and traditions of the holy and inspired fathers, but revere their own assemblies and teach their own doctrines.

---

18 Cf. the Bogomil legends of the creation of Adam recorded in EP **[19]** and EZ **[25]**, c. 7.
19 A Gnostic work with this name is known, but this is the only mention of it in connection with Paulicians or Bogomils. The reference here may reflect the use by the orthodox compiler of earlier anti-heretical material.
20 Cf. PS **[7]**, c. 36 and note 14.

CHRISTIAN DUALIST HERESIES

15. Anathema to those who do not honour and accept the seven ecumenical councils[21] which met to safeguard the august doctrines, and who do not agree to love and preserve the doctrines they defined.

16. Anathema to those who do not also revere and love the other local regulations which have been established at different times and places by the holy and saintly fathers.

17. Anathema to all the Paulician heresy and all its heresiarchs, and all who follow them.

18. On all Paulicians, anathema.

19. On those who do not accept holy and saving baptism and value it as the purification of mind and body and the passport to the kingdom of heaven, anathema.

So I oppose all the sect of the Paulicians and all their doctrines and customs, and 'I believe in one God almighty, maker of heaven and earth', and the rest of the holy creed.[22]

12. THEODORE, METROPOLITAN OF NICAEA (956–), WRITES ABOUT PAULICIANS IN EUCHAITA

Two generations after the Paulician military threat, led by Carbeas and his nephew and successor Chrysocheir, had been defeated by the emperor Basil I in 878, Paulicians were still present in sufficient numbers in northern Asia Minor to make the question of how they should be reconciled with the Orthodox Church a pressing one. This letter, which reveals the problem, can only be approximately dated. Its author Theodore was ordained priest by St Peter, bishop of Argos (who died *c.* 925), and became metropolitan of Nicaea after 956. Some of his letters in the collection appear to date from the period before he was promoted to this position, when he was *chartophylax*.[1] The use of archaic parallels in the explanation of the canon law position in this letter may support a dating to the period when he was *chartophylax* and would have had ready access to reference collections, but this cannot be given too much weight. The metropolitan Philotheus of Euchaita, to whom the letter is addressed, was appointed at some time after 945. Euchaita (see map) was a prosperous town in the

21 For the names and dates of these councils see **[10]**, note 6.
22 The final reference is to the liturgical recitation of the creed by those about to be received; see also PH **[8]**, c. 10.

1 An official of the Great Church of St Sophia, who was responsible for keeping all ecclesiastical records.

Armeniakon theme.[2] A century later the fair held there in honour of the patron saint, St Theodore, was famous.

The letter is printed in *Epistoliers byzantines du Xe siècle*, ed. J. Darrouzès, pp. 274–5.

TO PHILOTHEUS, METROPOLITAN OF EUCHAITA

I should have shared your pain and your distress if I had known anything of them, but since you yourself admit that you did the same for me (since I had not told you anything of what had befallen me), we should return thanks to God, who does not allow us to be tried beyond our strength, with mutual exchange as far as we can.

Since a host of heretics have approached you on your arrival and, as if abominating the foul and alien doctrine of their teachers, begs to be united with the fair body of the Church, to be numbered among us and to learn the truth, and since you need to gain more information from us about them (though you are far from ignorant), and about how they should be received when they approach, we will refresh your memory from the holy and divine canons themselves.

Dionysius the Elder[3] and the synod assembled with him determined that all who had not submitted to the one baptism of the universal Church should be rebaptized, because they utterly refused to accept the baptism of heretics. The holy fathers who succeeded him, in the interests of economy,[4] made a distinction between different heresies and their degree of connection with the whole body of the Church.[5] So it was determined that Arians and followers of Macedonius and Sabbatians and Novatians (that is, the Enlightened who call themselves Pure),

---

2 For the buildings and status of Euchaita in the middle Byzantine period, see Crow, 'Alexios I and Kastamon', pp. 26–33 and the bibliography there.
3 Dionysius the Great, bishop of Alexandria (d. AD 264), who devised rules for the readmission of various classes of heretics and schismatics.
4 This untranslatable word does not imply financial planning, but flexibility.
5 Most of the heresies listed here were historical phenomena at the time that the letter was written. Arians and Macedonians were the followers of Arius (250–326) and Macedonius (d. 362), who disagreed with the orthodox on the divine nature of Christ. Novatians were the followers of Novatius (martyred 257/8). He refused to compromise over the readmission of those Christians who had compromised themselves with paganism to avoid persecution. The Sabbatians formed a later internal schism within the Novatians, over the calculation of the date of Easter. The Tesserakaidekatai were another group with a different way of reckoning the date of Easter. Some of them were reconciled with the orthodox by the patriarch Photius (858–67; 877–86). The Apollinarians were followers of Apollinarius (d. 390), who taught that the human nature of Christ was unlike our own.

Aristeri and Tessarakaidekatai (that is, Tetradites) and Apollinarians should give *libelli* and anathematize every sort of heresy which has opinions other than those of the universal Church, and particularly that to which they had belonged. Then that they should learn the creeds of the Church and be anointed in all their senses with holy chrism, and so be received and share the holy mysteries with us. This, according to the great Basil, for the sake of the economy of the majority. But he enjoined that Eunomians,[6] who baptize with a single immersion, or Montanists, also called Phrygians, Sabellians, who teach the identity of the Father and the Son, and those Paulianists of whom you speak at most length, and all other heresies, should be treated as if they were pagans. They should be catechized and spend time in listening to the Holy Scriptures, and then be baptized or rebaptized. Since the heresy of the Jacobites[7] seems less serious than other heresies, we do not anoint those who were converted from them with chrism, nor indeed rebaptize them, but when they have given *libelli* and anathematized all heresy, especially their own, we receive them, and include them in the number and ranks of the orthodox.

Most holy of men, in obedience to these precedents which serve economy and command severity, refuse to accept local customs[8] on the grounds that they are unreasonable, and endeavour to take measures to reject and decline those customs which are in opposition to the divine commands. May you be a light and a way to those under your charge, enlightening them and guiding them, so that with them you may attain eternal life, and say confidently to God, 'Lord, here am I, and the children you gave me', and may He favour you in body and spirit all your life, on our behalf.

---

6 The Eunomians were followers of Eunomius, an extreme Arian. The Montanists were followers of Montanus, who believed in the outpouring of the Holy Spirit, and rejected other Christians who did not share his charismatic views. The Sabellians were followers of Sabellius (date uncertain, probably early third century), whose Trinitarian doctrine was suspect. Paulianists: there appears to be confusion here between the followers of Paul of Samosata and the later Paulicians. See PS [7], c. 85 and PH [8], c. 1.

7 The Jacobites were the followers of Jacob Baradaeus. They rejected the doctrine of the Person of Christ defined at Chaldedon (451).

8 Nothing is known of these local customs.

13. ST PAUL OF LATRUS (d. 955/6) CONVERTS PAULICIANS NEAR MILETUS

St Paul of Latrus who died in 955/6, lived for the greater part of his religious life as an ascetic at various sites on the slopes of Mt Latrus[1] in Caria, near the city of Miletus. Later he founded a monastery there,[2] and still later crossed to the island of Samos nearby, to avoid the crowds of disciples who had followed him. The life is evidence of the presence of dualist heretics on the coast in the early tenth century, but the use of the archaic term 'Manichaean' to describe them leaves it uncertain whether they were Paulicians (for whose dispersal at this time see the Introduction) or early Bogomils, who are first recorded in Asia Minor with certainty in a document written in *c*. 1045 (Euthymius of the Periblepton, [19]), which gives an account of an earlier trial. The life of St Paul records (c. 27) that the saint received letters from Tsar Peter of Bulgaria, but makes no allusion to the problems the Tsar was having with dualist heretics in his kingdom, for which see [10] above.

The translation has been made from the text edited by I. Sirmondi, with revision and introduction by H. Delehaye, *Analecta Bollandiana*, 11 (1892), 136–82; this passage is on p. 156.

Chapter 41 Indeed the saint greatly despised, or rather hated, fame among men. That is why he did not seek, but rather avoided, the palaces of princes and rulers and preferred the humble, especially those who love God. Nevertheless, there were many ways in which he did not fall short of the zeal of the saints, but outdid Phineas and came in no way short of Elias. An indication of this was his zeal against the Manichaeans. He arranged the removal to a great distance of those who were most notable and prepared to do harm, I mean those of the territories of Kibyrrhaeotis and Miletus, using letters to the emperor which, indeed, were sweet to his throat and better than honey to his mouth.

---

1 See map.
2 The foundation date is uncertain, but the monastery received offerings from Romanus Lecapenus in 924; see the text of the chrysobull recording the gift in *PG* 113, col. 1065.

14. JOHN I TZIMISCES (969-76) SETTLES PAULICIANS AT PHILIPPOPOLIS

The emperor John I Tzimisces came to the throne by organizing the murder of his predecessor Nicephorus Phocas while both were on campaign in northern Syria. At the same time the northern frontier of the empire was under threat from a Russian invasion of Bulgaria. The transfer of Paulicians recorded in the chronicles (the second of its kind; for the first, see [1]) served two purposes; the new emperor was enabled to ingratiate himself with the ecclesiastical authorities who were most likely to have accurate information about his implication in the assassination, and at the same time to use the Paulicians' well-known abilities as a fighting force to reinforce the northern defences. The settlement at Philippopolis had a long life: see [20], [22] and [40] for information about their later history and chequered relations with the central government.

The text has been translated from the chronicles of Zonaras, who wrote a history ending in 1118 with the death of Alexius Comnenus, and whose own death occurred probably about 1149. His history is based on earlier sources, some now lost, but is in general reliable. The edition used is Zonaras, *Epitome historiarum*, ed. Dindorf (bk. 17.1, pp. 92.26–93.4).

When [John Tzimisces] had been proclaimed in this way, since Antioch the Great was without an archbishop, he approached a certain monk Theodore, who had prophesied to him that he would be emperor, and that he should not be hasty nor snatch at it, but wait to be offered it by God. When he received the archbishopric, he made a request to John to remove the Manichaeans from the East to the West, as they were destroying many with their foul heresy. The emperor fulfilled this request, transferring the race of the Manichaeans to Philippopolis.[1]

15. THE DISCOURSE OF THE PRIEST COSMAS AGAINST BOGOMILS (AFTER 972)

The discourse of the priest Cosmas has been conventionally dated to the late tenth century, after the death of Tsar Peter (927–69), who is referred to as a 'good Christian' – a normal Slav formula for the dead – but to whose canonization in 972 no allusion is made. On this dating Cosmas gives the Bulgarian account of those heretics whose views are condemned in the letter of the patriarch Theophylact [10]. He is writing half a century before the account of Bogomil beliefs given by Euthymius of the Periblepton [19] and a century before the Greek letter of the patriarch Cosmas, on which the Bulgarian *Synodikon* of Tsar Boril was based [21]. Some Bulgarian scholars have argued

1 See map.

THE DISCOURSE OF COSMAS AGAINST BOGOMILS

against this dating; their views are conveniently summarized in Dando's article, 'Peut-on avancer de 240 ans la date de compostion du traité de Cosmas le prêtre contre les Bogomiles?' For arguments for accepting the conventional dating, see our Introduction, p. 27.

This translation is based on the French translation of Puech and Vaillant (Paris, 1945), but it has been amended by Yuri Stoyanov, who has collated it with the new critical edition of the Old Slavonic text of O. Bégunov, which is based on many additional manuscripts and on citations in later works, and therefore contains a large number of variants. No modern translation exists of this new edition of the text.

1. All the commandments of Our Lord Jesus Christ are wonderful, dear to those who read them, since they were spoken for our salvation. Even if we are far from his commands, like a loving father He bears with our wickedness; He does not will the loss of any, but desires to bring us all back to Himself and to save us: He admonishes and teaches us, some by the holy Gospels, others by inspired teachers, so that we may not fall into the pit of heresy . . .

Our enemy the devil knows this, and he has never ceased to lead mankind astray; beginning with Adam, the first man, until today, he has not ceased to try to entice all men from the faith, so that a large number of men might be with him in torment; his deceptions have led some to worship idols, others to kill their brothers, yet others to commit fornication and other sins. But since he saw that all these sins cannot be compared with heresy, he entered first Arius,[1] who set himself to blaspheme the son of God, claiming that he is not equal to God, but is like an angel, subordinate to God, forgetting the word of Christ, 'I and the Father are one' [John 10.30]; he also entered Sabellius, who undertook to unite the divine persons into one, saying that what suffered in body on the cross was at the same time Christ and the divinity of the Holy Trinity; while Macedonius used to blaspheme the Holy Spirit, claiming that he is inferior to the Father and the Son, not equal in divinity. Their teachings were anathematized by the holy fathers at the council of Nicaea: they rooted them out of Christianity like the tares out of the field, with the help of God and of the emperor Constantine. Later there were various heresies in various places, not about the Holy Trinity but about divine creation; some devised one error and some another, but the teachings of the holy apostles and the fathers banished them from everywhere.

---

1 The list of earlier heretics resembles those found in other anti-heretical texts.

CHRISTIAN DUALIST HERESIES

This, then, is what happened in the land of Bulgaria. In the reign of the good Christian Tsar Peter[2] there was a priest called Bogomil, 'worthy of God's compassion',[3] but in reality Bogunemil, 'unworthy of God's compassion', who started for the first time to preach heresy in the country of Bulgaria. Later we shall expose his errors . . .

Indeed externally the heretics appear sheep: they are gentle and humble and quiet. They seem pale from their hypocritical fasts, they do not utter vain words, they do not laugh out loud, they do not show curiosity, they take care not to be noticeable and to do everything externally so that they may not be told apart from orthodox Christians. Inside they are ravening wolves, as the Lord said [Matt. 7.15]. People who see this great humility of theirs, who think that they are good Christians[4] and able to direct them to salvation, approach them and take their advice about their souls' salvation; while they, like a wolf about to snatch away a lamb, at first pretend to sigh, and answer humbly. They pass themselves off as knowing in advance what happens in heaven,[5] and when they see anyone simple and ignorant, there they sow the tares of their doctrines and blaspheme the traditional teaching of the Holy Church, as I will show in what follows.

As for you, faithful army of Christ, let none of you be their friend; you would be enemies of Christ. Apply yourselves to reading holy scripture, so that you may not go to endless torment . . .

To return to our subject. Scripture says, 'As Jesus sat on the Mount of Olives, the disciples came to him, saying "Tell us, when will this be, and what will be the sign of your coming and of the close of the age?" The Lord answered them, "Take heed, for many will come in my name, saying, 'I am the Christ' and they will lead many astray." But, he added, 'You be on your guard so that no one leads you astray" [Matt. 24.3–5]. "You will recognize them by their fruits; a good tree cannot produce bad fruit, nor a bad tree good fruit. Men do not gather grapes from thorns, nor harvest figs from thistles"' [Matt. 7.16, 18]. All the same, you ought to recognize these men from their fruits, that is their hypocrisy, their pride, their blasphemies: and when you have recognized them, avoid them, lest you share their condemnation. If a man who allies himself to the enemies of an earthly king does not even deserve to live, but is put

---

2 927–69. The phrase 'good Christian' is normally used of the dead.
3 This name is probably the Bulgarian translation of the Greek name Theophilus.
4 Cf. the description of Cathars as 'good Christians'.
5 An alternative reading gives: 'as if they were in heaven'.

to death along with them, how much more those who are the enemies of the heavenly king; they will perish in the everlasting fire, as it is said, 'Every tree that does not bear good fruit is cut down and cast into the fire' [Matt. 3.10]. What do the heretics say? 'We pray to God more than you do, we keep vigils[6] and prayers, we do not live in laziness as you do.' Alas, words like those of the proud Pharisee who boasted of himself, saying, 'I am not like other men, extortioners, criminals, adulterers' [Luke 18.11]. We shall answer them, 'What are you boasting of, you arrogant heretics? By this reckoning the devil does not sleep either, he does not taste food . . .'. 'But', they say to us, 'we call on God in our prayers.' We shall answer them, 'Do you hear demons calling out to the Lord, "What have you to do with us, Son of God? Have you come here to torment us before the time?"' [Matt. 8.29]. As for us, let us leave them to go their own way to perdition; you can correct an animal more quickly than a heretic. The pig turns from the pearl to gather excrement; similarly heretics stuff themselves with their filth and distance themselves from divine teaching. Just as when you shoot arrows at marble, you do not pierce it, but the arrow, glancing off, is likely to hit someone behind you, similarly when you try to instruct a heretic, you should not consider merely that you will not succeed in instructing him, but that you might even corrupt someone whose spirit is weak.

What shall we compare them to, what shall we liken them to? They are worse than deaf blind idols, for idols are made of wood and stone, and of their nature neither hear nor see, whereas heretics have human thoughts; they have voluntarily made themselves stone so that they may not recognize the teaching of truth. Shall I compare them to demons? They are worse than the demons themselves, for the demons are afraid of the cross of Christ, while the heretics chop up crosses and make tools of them.[7] The demons are afraid of the image of the Lord painted on a wooden panel, but the heretics do not venerate icons, but call them idols.[8] The demons are afraid of the relics[9] of God's just; they dare not approach the reliquaries where lies the priceless treasure given to Christians to save them from every danger; while heretics deride them and laugh at us when they see us prostrating ourselves in front of them and asking for their help, forgetting that the Lord said, 'He who believes in me will do the works that I do, and greater works than these will He do'

---

6 For the nightly prayers of Bogomils see EZ **[25]**, c. 19.
7 Similar allegations of hostility to the cross are made against Paulicians in PS **[7]**, c. 27, and Bogomils in EZ **[25]**, c. 14.
8 Cf. EZ **[25]**, c. 11.
9 For hostility to relics and the cult of the saints see EZ **[25]**, c. 12.

[John 14.21]. At the same time as they refuse to give glory to the saints, they insult the miracles of God, such as are done by the relics of the saints through the power of the Holy Spirit, and say, 'The miracles did not take place according to the will of God, but it was the devil who did them to trick mankind'; they utter still more nonsense on this subject, wagging their heads like the Jews when they crucified Christ.

O patient God, how long will you watch the human race provoking your wrath to this degree? Yes, indeed, they are worse and more hateful than demons, for what demon ever made himself the adversary of the divine, or dared to blaspheme God's creation as the heretics do? Indeed, what do they claim? That it was not God who made heaven and earth or all the visible universe.[10] And because they are truly blind and deaf they do not understand the words of John the Theologian: 'In the beginning was the Word, and the Word was with God, and the Word was God; all things were made through Him, and without Him was not anything made, that was made . . .' [John 1.1–3]. In many places the holy prophets, the apostles and other just men proclaim that God is the creator of everything visible and invisible. Why speak of the just? Ask anyone you like, a barbarian, someone ignorant, ask the devil himself who is the creator of everything visible and invisible, and they will answer you, 'Why, my friend, are you so crassly ignorant? What can exist or be without the order of God?' Heretics, who showed you that God is not the author of this created world? Woe to your unbelief, for you are piling fire on your own heads.

As for the Lord's cross, here are the blasphemies they produce: 'How can we adore it? It was on it that the Jews crucified the son of God, and the cross is even more the enemy of God.' So they teach their followers to detest rather than to adore it, saying thus: 'If anyone killed the king's son with a cross of wood, would the wood be dear to the king? The same is true of the cross for God.' O the devil's hatred of mankind! To what chasm of perdition has he not led them! Just as formerly the Jews read the prophecies but did not realize that they were teaching about the Lord's passion, and it was those who read the prophecies daily and every sabbath who became the murderers of Christ, thinking that they could put the Immortal One to death, so the heretics who read the words of the Lord and the apostles constantly do not understand what is said to them. Blessed Paul was right to give them the description 'those who are lost', saying, 'the word of the cross is folly to those who are lost, but for

---

10 For Bogomil views on creation see EP **[19]** and EZ **[25]**, c. 7.

us who are saved it is the power of God' [1 Cor. 1.18] ... I could cite from other books proof that our Lord's cross is holy, but the heretics would not believe them ...

Indeed, what Christian has not been enlightened by the Lord's cross? Who has not rejoiced to see crosses set up in high places, where once men sacrificed to demons, immolating their sons and daughters? Who has not saved himself from evil when confronted by any sort of trial, by making the sign of the cross on his face or his heart? The Saviour spoke of his cross to the apostles before his crucifixion, saying, 'As Moses lifted up the serpent in the wilderness, so must the Son of man be lifted up, so that whoever believes in Him may not perish, but have eternal life' [John 3.13–14]. Truly, my brothers, those who look lovingly on the Lord's cross will not perish. As we gaze on the cross with the eyes of the flesh, but with the eyes of the spirit contemplate Him who is crucified there, we glorify Him and say, 'Glory to you, Christ our God, who graciously willed to bring death by your cross to him who long ago brought death to our ancestor Adam in Paradise, and who have given us your cross for victory in our fight with the devil.' We hope in this way to shut the mouth of the heretics God hates, who utter untruths against God, and to gain everlasting life. As for me, I will not cease denouncing godless heretics to 'build up' the Church of God, that is the Christian faith, which they try to overturn.

Indeed, what do they say about holy communion?[11] 'Communion was not instituted by a divine command; the Eucharist is not really, as you claim, the body of Christ, but a simple food like all others. For it is not Christ who instituted the Mass, and that is why we do not honour holy communion.' Their blindness! Their hardness of heart! Tell me, godless heretic, what was the Lord talking about when He gave bread to the apostles and said, 'Take, eat, this is my body which is broken for you for the remission of sins'? And again, when He held the cup in His most pure hands and gave it to His disciples, saying, 'Drink of it, all of you; for this is my blood of the covenant, which is poured out for many' [Matt. 26.26–8]. What was Paul talking about in his epistle to the Corinthians? [1 Cor. 11.2–9].

There it is, heretics, clearly proved – I have not spoken of myself, but in the words of holy scripture and the apostle – that the holy Eucharist is not ordinary food, as you think, but really the most pure body of Our

---

11 For rejection of the Eucharist by Paulicians see PS **[7]**, c. 40; by Bogomils see EP **[19]**, EZ **[25]**, c. 17.

Lord Jesus Christ. Indeed, just as earlier when He created the world he said, 'Let there be light', and there was light; 'Let there be heaven', and there was heaven; 'Let there be earth and all it bears' [Gen. 1.3, 8, 11], and in an instant all came into existence as Holy Scripture says, so now by His power the Holy Spirit transforms this bread into the Lord's body, this cup into His blood, just as the holy men who were the true witnesses of the mysteries of God have told us in scripture . . .

Tell us, who have shown you that these words do not apply to this consecrated bread and cup, as you heretics claim in your madness? In your deceits you tell that they refer to the four Gospels and the Acts of the Apostles, not to holy communion; by 'body', you understand the four gospels and by 'blood', the Acts of the Apostles.[12] As for us, let us ask them the question, 'Tell us, you who are blind, if you have common sense; when the Lord gave this bread and cup to his disciples and said, "This is my body, this is my blood", when He gave them this commandment, was He still on earth or had He ascended to heaven?' Even if they are blind, they have tongues to answer with, and they cannot say that the Lord had ascended to heaven when He said these words; it was during the night when He gave Himself up that He made all these arrangements; He sanctified them and entrusted them to the apostles, and in obedience to them the apostles transmitted them to us: we believe that it is the real body and blood of the Lord, not an image.

After the Lord ascended to heaven, the holy apostles wrote the four Gospels so that true believers might remember and be saved, as they told us. Matthew wrote eight years,[13] Mark ten years, Luke fifteen years and John thirty-two years after the Ascension. The Acts of the Apostles were written many years later; Luke the evangelist, who knew what Paul had said and done, wrote it down and transmitted it to the churches; to this day the holy churches are happy to read them out loud, to do as the Lord said: 'No one, after lighting a lamp, puts it under a bed, but puts it on a stand, so that those who enter may see the light' [Luke 8.16]. So how can you, heretics, say that the words of Christ do not apply to holy communion, but to the four gospels?' . . .

Again, why do you blaspheme against the holy rules transmitted to us by the holy apostles and by the fathers inspired by God (I mean the office and other prayers used by good Christians). How can you say, 'It is not

---

12 This allegorical interpretation of the words instituting the Eucharist resembles that given by Paulicians; see PS **[7]**, c. 40.
13 These traditional dates for the composition of the gospels are found in many medieval MSS; see von Soden, *Die Schriften des neuen Testaments* I, pp. 297–9, 323–7.

the apostles who bequeathed the liturgy to us, or the communion, but John Chrysostom?' From the incarnation of Christ to John Chrysostom more than three hundred years elapsed; did the churches of God remain bereft of liturgy and communion for all those years? Did the apostle Peter not compose the office which the Romans still follow? And James, the Lord's brother, the first bishop, established by the Lord himself, did he not compose an office at Jerusalem which is still sung to this day, as we have been told, at the Lord's tomb?[14] Later Basil the Great in Cappadocia gave us a liturgy, following the instructions which he had received from God, and regulated the communion, dividing it into three parts, as the Holy Spirit had bidden him. So how can you say that communion and the religious office are not part of divine tradition?

You insult priests and the whole religious hierarchy by treating priests who are true believers as blind Pharisees, yapping at them like dogs following a mounted man; the eyes of your spirit are blind; when you read the epistles of the blessed Paul, you are incapable of realizing who has established priests, bishops and the rest of the clerical orders over all the world, but, as Paul says, 'Seeking to establish their own, they did not submit to God's righteousness' [Rom. 10.3].

Even if priests whose faith is sound lead idle lives, as you say when you condemn them, still they do not blaspheme the divinity as you do. All the same, they will have gained some hidden merit,[15] and 'who are you to pass judgement on the servant of another?' as the apostle says? [Rom. 14.1]. 'In a great house there are not only vessels of gold and silver, but also of wood and earthenware, and some for noble use, others for ignoble. If anyone purifies himself from what is ignoble, he will be a vessel for noble use' [2 Tim. 2.20–21]. So if they were good for nothing, they would not be hallowed ... The heretics who hear these words answer us, 'If you are sanctified, as you claim, why do you not live as you are bidden to? As Paul says in his epistle to Timothy, "Now a bishop must be above reproach, the husband of one wife, temperate, sober, dignified, hospitable, an apt teacher, no drunkard, not violent but gentle, not quarrelsome, and no lover of money. He must manage his own household well ... Deacons likewise must be chaste, not double-tongued, not addicted to much wine, of good reputation. Let them be tested first; then if they prove themselves blameless, let them serve" [1 Tim. 5.2–4, 8–10]. Now we see that you are not like this; priests act quite

---

14 For pilgrimages to Jerusalem at this period see EP **[19]**.
15 An alternative text reads: 'even if they have committed secret sins'.

otherwise. They get drunk, they commit robbery and have other hidden vices, and nobody forbids them to do these evil deeds, despite the words of Paul, "As for those who persist in sin, rebuke them in the presence of all so that the rest may stand in fear" [1 Tim. 5.20]. Bishops instead of preaching self-denial as we do, deny us their prayers, but do not forbid their priests to sin.'

Let us answer them with this: 'Heretics, do you not understand what Paul said on this subject in his letter to Timothy? "Never admit any charge against a presbyter except on the evidence of two or three witnesses" [1 Tim. 5.19]. The lewd and arrogant heretics have no shame, but continue, 'Even if their sin is in secret, yet still they live openly according to the flesh and not according to the spirit, as we do; for the works of the flesh, says Paul, are "fornication, impurity, licentiousness, idolatry, sorcery, enmity, strife, jealousy, anger, selfishness, dissension, party spirit, envy, drunkenness, carousing and the like" [Gal. 5.19–21].' Let us answer them, 'Why do you raise yourselves so high above us, heretics? Do you not hear what the Lord said to you: "everyone who exalts himself will be humbled, but he who humbles himself will be exalted?" [Luke 18.14] . . .

Priests are honoured by God; listen, heretics, to what the Lord says about them to the apostles: 'The priests sit on Moses' seat, so practise and observe whatever they tell you, but not what they do, for they preach but do not practise' [Matt. 23.2–3]. Do you see, heretics, that you are commanded to hold priests in honour, even if they are wicked? If the Lord orders the apostles who are so great and so holy to obey those who sit on the seat of Moses, how much rather ought you and everyone to honour those who are seated on the seat of Christ? Just as Christ is far more venerable than Moses, so those who sit on His throne are far more venerable than those who sit on the seat of Moses . . .

For all sin is less serious than heresy. Even Jews did not spit on anything but the Lord's flesh, while heretics spit on His divinity, but this rebounds on their own face. So heretics are greater sinners than the very Jews who crucified Christ; they insulted His body, while the others insulted His divinity. In fact, the devil, who could not oppose divine holiness on his own, took them as his assistants, as once he did Judas at the Lord's crucifixion. He incites them to blaspheme all the traditions of the Holy Church, in his desire to destroy the rites of prayer which the holy apostles and fathers have handed down to us. This can never be, as the Lord said: 'It is on this rock I will build my Church, and the gates of Hell (that is to say, the teaching of heretics) shall not prevail against it' [Matt. 16.18].

Indeed, which apostle or holy man taught you, you heretics, to spurn the law God gave to Moses? What falsehood have you found in the prophets to insult them and reject the books they wrote? How can you claim to love Christ, when you reject what the holy prophets prophesied about Him? The prophets said nothing of themselves; they gave us their predictions, as the Holy Spirit ordered them to. If you do not believe the words which God spoke once through the mouths of the prophets, listen to what the holy apostles say about the prophets; if you do not believe the apostles either, you are still more unbelieving than the heathen themselves, more malevolent than the demons. Peter, the great leader of the apostles, cried, 'What God foretold by the mouth of all the prophets from of old' [Acts 3.18, 21]. Listen also to blessed Paul proclaim the same: 'And his gifts were that some should be apostles, some prophets, some evangelists, some pastors and teachers, for the perfecting of the saints' [Eph. 4.11–12].

Do you see, heretics, that the prophets are holy, and that the Holy Spirit has proclaimed everything to us through their lips? . . . What does Scripture say about David, from whose race Christ became man? 'I have found in David, the son of Jesse, a man after my heart, who will do all my will' [Acts 13.22]. Of the same David, Matthew writes at the beginning of his gospel: 'The book of the genealogy of Jesus Christ, the son of David, the son of Abraham' [Matt. 1.1]. The heretics make nothing of this David who is so great and holy, and reject the words that the Holy Spirit uttered through his mouth. They do not accept Abraham, 'the friend of God' [James 2.23] or Daniel, Azarias and his companions, or the other prophets whom even wild beasts feared, before whom fire shrank back. As for John the Forerunner, the dawn of the great Sun, they insult him and call him the precursor of antichrist, the man whom the Lord Himself called greater than all the saints: 'Truly I say to you, among those born of women there has risen no one greater than John the Baptist' [Matt. 11.11]; the Lord Himself bowed His head before him to receive baptism at his hand. In truth they are themselves the antichrists, according to the words of the evangelist John the Theologian, 'Children, it is the last hour; and as you have heard that antichrist is coming, so now many antichrists have come' [1 John 2.18].

Surpassing all their evil, see this that the wretches commit; they do not honour the most glorious and pure mother of Our Lord and God Jesus Christ,[16] and utter madness against her. It is impossible to record in this

---

16 For Paulician and Bogomil rejection of the cult of the Blessed Virgin Mary see PS **[7]**, cc. 22, 39; EP **[19]**; EZ **[25]**, cc. 8, 22.

book their words and their insults with regard to her whom the prophets foretold...

If the Lord is with her, as He always is, always without end, what do you heretics count on, when you neglect such a path to salvation? We put our trust in you, blessed mother of God; be merciful to us now and on the dreadful day of judgement. It is you who appear most holy in all the world, visible and invisible. Truly blessed is the house of David in which you were reared: 'God is in the midst of you; you shall not be overturned, for the Most High has hallowed you his tabernacle.' You are the support of Christians, the protectress of sinners, the boast of those who live the life of virginity, the bulwark of our faith. Now then, blessed mother of God, gain from your Son by your prayers that we may be saved from all evil; it is through you that we have known the Son of God, and that we have been found worthy to be partakers of His holy body and blood. When we see His image in an icon, carried in your arms, we sinners rejoice and we bow low before it, and kiss it with fervour, in the hope that through your prayers we may attain the life of heaven.

'Cult paid to an image passes over to its original', as great Basil[17] said. The heretics have heard the apostle Paul speaking about idols: 'we ought not to think that the deity is like gold or silver made by the art of men' [Acts 17.29], and because these wretches think that this applies to icons, they have made these words a pretext for not reverencing the icons when they are on their own. They visit churches and kiss the cross and the icons for fear of men, as some of them who have been converted to our true faith have told us, 'We do all this for man's sake, not from our heart; we keep our faith in secret.' As for us, the people of true believers, when we see the Lord's image painted on an icon, we lift our hands towards it, we sigh deeply, and turning the eyes of our spirit to heaven, to the Lord Himself, who is there with the Father and the Holy Spirit, we cry out: 'Lord Jesus Christ, who revealed yourself on earth for our salvation, who were willing of your own free will that your hands should be nailed to the cross, who gave us your cross to put all our enemies to flight, have mercy on us, who put our trust in you.' Then when we see the icon of Mary, the holy mother of God, again, from the depths of our heart, we cry out to her, 'Most holy mother of God, do not forget us, us who are your people, for it is in you that we have our protection and sinners their support; thanks to you we hope to obtain the remission of our sins, etc.' When we see the image of some saint, we say the same:

17 St Basil the Great (330–79).

'Saint of God' – here we name him – 'you who suffered for the Lord, you have influence with your master, pray for me, that I may be saved by your prayers.'

Do you see, heretics, how false your words are, and full of deceit, when you say, 'Those who venerate icons are like the pagan Greeks'? As we venerate an icon, we do not prostrate ourselves in front of its paint or its wooden panel, but in front of him whose image is reproduced, him whose portrait is painted with the appearance he ought to have, whether young or old. Just as a woman with a good heart, who loves her husband, if she sees in the house a tunic or a belt of his, when he is away from her on a long journey, takes it in her hands, kisses it, holds it to her eyes; it is not the bright colours of the garment that she loves, but she does it because it carries the name of the one she loves. So we too, we Christians, who love Christ, if we find some piece of clothing in which one of God's pious servants has been martyred, or a bone of his body or powder from his tomb, we think of them as most holy, we lay hold of it with awe and kiss it with love; it is not the dust or the bright-coloured cloth which we are venerating, but the saint himself, or rather Christ, whom he has served well, as the prophet David said: 'I have held your friends in honour, my God.'

But, they say, we do not listen to David or the prophets, but only to the gospel, and we do not live in accordance with the law of Moses, but that of the apostles. Come then, listen, you heretics, if you have ears, while I prove to you that those who do not obey the Law and the prophets deny Christ himself. For what does the Lord say?: 'Think not that I have come to destroy the Law and the prophets. I have come not to abolish them, but to fulfil them' [Matt 5.17] . . . Indeed, what is so wrong and reprehensible that the heretics have seen in the Law and the prophets, that they insult and reject them, and claim that they cannot save us? . . .

They insult every law which is part of the tradition of God's Holy Church, and honour their own teachings, muttering goodness knows what fables that they learn from their father, the devil. It is unwise even to denounce their absurd ideas in front of you – their words, as I have already said, defile everything under the heavens. All the same, I will tell you something, passing over the rest in silence: 'for it is a shame even to speak of the things they do in secret' [Eph. 5.12].

Many people do not understand what this heresy represents; they think that these people are suffering in the interests of justice, and that they will receive some reward from God for the prisons and fetters they have suffered. Let them listen to what Paul says here, too: 'an athlete is not crowned unless he compete according to the rules' [2 Tim. 2.5]. How could they deserve any compassion, even if a host of them suffer, when they claim the devil as creator of mankind and all the divine creation? And because of their great ignorance, some call him a fallen angel, others call him the 'steward of iniquity'.[18] These terms they use make men of good sense laugh, as their arguments are not consistent, and fall to pieces like a scrap of rotten cloth; in their desire to surpass one another in ingenuity, each of them invents his own imagined name for his own father and teacher. They have conceived such veneration for him that they call him the creator of God's works, and think that the glory of God is the glory of the devil, in spite of God's words through the prophet, 'I will not give my glory to another' [Isa. 42.3].

The heretics have heard the lying devil say to Jesus: 'All these I will give you, if you will fall down and worship me' [Matt. 4.9.]; they put their faith in this, and think that he is the master of God's creation. Again, they hear the Lord say, 'the ruler of this world is judged' [John 16.11], and then, 'Now the ruler of the world is coming, and has no power over me' [John 14.30], and, hearing these words, call the devil master and prince of God's creatures. But they should learn why he was called 'prince'. Before the Lord's crucifixion, when idols were multiplied all over the earth, and impure sacrifices were being offered everywhere, the devil exalted himself, and sin and death reigned with him; after the only Son of God did us the favour of destroying his power by His cross he was no longer called 'prince' or 'master', but enemy and adversary; we see him trodden underfoot daily, not just by men, but also by women, the feebler sex, as those will know, who have read the life of the holy virgin Justina, of bishop Cyprian[19] and those of the other saints of God. The devil is still called prince and father and master of those who do his will, brigands and the debauched, heretics and all those who obey him, not because God has given him power but because they have run to him of their own free will. In every heart he sows evil thoughts, but he does not reap a harvest everywhere. If he does not have power over pigs, how much more does he not have power over men made by God's hand?

We hear many of our people ask – why does God let the devil attack

18 Compare EZ **[25]**, c. 6.
19 The existence of the popular edifying legend of the conversion and martyrdom of the sorcerer Cyprian of Antioch and the beautiful young Christian Justina is recorded by the year 379, when Gregory of Nazianzen included allusions to it in his sermon in praise of the (historical) Cyprian of Carthage. See Delehaye, 'Cyprian d'Antioche et Cyprian de Carthage'.

men? These infantile remarks do not come from a healthy mind; it is for the sake of his brave men that God has allowed the devil to sow evil thoughts in the minds of men, so that those who do God's will may be recognized, and those who do the will of the devil . . . As, my brothers, when a thought which inclines us to any sin assaults the heart of any one of us, let us take hold of the rod and staff of the Lord, I mean the cross of Christ, as we make it on our face and on our hearts, and instantly that cowardly and shameless dog [the devil] will turn away from us; if he repeatedly tries to attack us, let us chase him off with the same sign of the cross.

As for the heretics, since they have made themselves aliens to the cross of Christ, and have driven him far off from themselves, they allow themselves to be wholly led by the devil, as he wants. Just as those who fish with a hook cannot catch fish unless they put a worm on the hook, so heretics cloak their poison under hypocritical humility and fasts, and again they take the Gospel in their hands, and, giving it an impious interpretation, they try to catch men this way and lead them to perdition; they think they can destroy all charity, all the Christian faith . . . burning it up by their prayers, vainly and senselessly. For it is said: 'If I give away all I have, and if I deliver my body to be burned, but have not love, I have nothing' [1 Cor. 13.3].

If this is said of man, how much more is it not true of the Church of God, which they teach men not to love. And through their ruin the holy Gospel suffers in their hands like 'a gold ring in a swine's snout' [Prov. 11.22]; so sweet a food becomes deadly, through the poison they introduce into the soul of those who listen to their falsehoods. Just as a cup of honey becomes bitter if you add to it a single drop of vinegar, so their deadly poison acts in the same way on those who listen to it, even if they think they are doing no evil. Such is the habit of the devil; he blinds the eyes and shrinks sin, so that those who do evil think they are doing nothing wrong.

If a bird is trapped by a single claw, it is bound to die; how much more ought heretics to die, who are trapped by so many different fingers! What words of scripture have they not twisted, what part of the divine ordering of the world have they not blasphemed? They have not just blasphemed the earth, but have hurled their blasphemies at the heights, saying that it is by the devil's will that all exists; the sky, the sun, the stars, the air, mankind, the churches, the cross; all that belongs to God they ascribe to the devil; in short, everything that moves on the earth, whether it has a soul or not; they ascribe it to the devil.

When they hear the Lord in the gospel tell the parable of the two sons [Luke. 15], they make Christ the elder son and the younger son, who has deceived his father, the devil. They themselves have given him the name Mammon;[20] they call him the creator and architect of things terrestrial. They say that it was he who bade men take wives and eat meat and drink wine; in short, they insult all we have, and pass themselves off as inhabitants of heaven, while they term servants of Mammon men who marry and live in the world; they refuse all these things with repugnance, not for the sake of abstinence, as we do, because we do not think that they are impure. The Holy Spirit has prophesied about this, too, by the mouth of Paul, who says in his letter to Timothy: 'Now the spirit expressly says that in later times some will depart from the faith by giving heed to deceitful spirits and doctrines of demons, through the pretensions of liars whose consciences are seared, who forbid marriage and enjoin abstinence from foods which God created to be received with thanksgiving: for then it is consecrated by the word of God and by prayer' [1 Tim. 4.1–5].

Heretics, did you see these words of the Holy Spirit, declaring that legitimate marriage is pure, instituted by God, and that food and drink taken in moderation cannot condemn a man? . . .

What we have written here is not to desire or permit anyone to get drunk or to eat to excess, but to shut the mouths of the odious heretics who totally forbid us to touch meat or wine, which they treat as impure. We are well aware that a drunkard is a being hateful to God and man; holy scripture is full of attacks on those who drink to excess; a drunkard makes fools laugh and wise men weep, for he loses the intelligence and reason which are God's gifts to him, and of his own free will turns himself into a brute beast instead of a man. Next day his head and his stomach hurt, his muscles shake, so that from it comes two sorts of harmful consequences, sins of the soul and illnesses of the body. So wine taken in moderation, as the body needs it, is a good thing, but taken in excess it whelms a man in great evils.

I hear one of these heretics saying, 'Who has made you teacher among us?' Let them remember scripture: 'Every good endowment and every perfect gift is from above' [James 1.17]. What I am saying is not to boast or set myself up, God forbid – I know that pride could even cast the angels out of heaven – but to refute these heretics . . .

---

20 In the account of ps.-Psellus [34] the devil is the elder and Christ the younger son. See also EZ [25], c. 6.

THE DISCOURSE OF COSMAS AGAINST BOGOMILS

That is why, faithful people of Christ, we priests, who are your unworthy teachers, beg you in the words of the apostle, 'Beloved, do not believe every spirit, but test the spirits to see whether they are of God, for many false prophets have gone out into the world' [1 John 4.1].

If you trust in these men or welcome them with love in your houses, or do something for them that gives joy, look, I have warned you in advance; you are condemning yourself with them to eternal torment. So, faithful people of Christ, even if you see a heretic drive away demons, give sight to the blind, raise the dead, do not have faith in him. The Lord says, 'They will do prodigies and miracles, so as to deceive even the elect, if it is possible.' If it is your father or mother or brother or son who falls into these errors, and after a first and second remonstrance he does not listen to you, separate yourself from him, and have him in aversion, for it is said: 'As for a man who is factious, after admonishing him once or twice, have nothing more to do with him, knowing that such a person is perverted and sinful; he is self-condemned' [Titus 3.10–11].

Do you see, my brethren, the deadly blows of the devil? – they also reject holy baptism and loathe little children who are baptized. If it happens that they see a young child, they shrink from it, as if from some evil smell; they spit and cover their faces, when they themselves are filth to men and to angels. Even if they want, lyingly, to maintain that they are Christians, as is their habit, do not believe them; they are liars, like their father, the devil. Now how can they claim to call themselves Christians, when they have no priests to baptize, when they do not make the sign of the cross, they do not write down the priests' prayers and do not honour priests? If it ever happens that a priest joins their belief, it is because he has turned his back on all our faith; if he keeps it, it is for fear of the earthly masters, but his heart and mind are wandering far away from the law the Lord gave to the holy churches.

Little children are pure, without sin; let us listen again to what the Lord said of them, addressing the apostles: 'Let the children come to me, and do not hinder them; for to such belong the kingdom of heaven' [Matt. 19.14]. And again: 'Unless you turn and become like children, you will never enter the kingdom of heaven' [Matt. 18.3]. The heretics are so inflated with pride, even higher than the famous Pharisees, that they go so far as to claim that the little children whom the Lord declared are pure are not worthy to be brought to them, but turn away from them in horror, inventing new names without cease, in their great ignorance. They call them children of Mammon, intending to say, children of the devil . . .

As for holy baptism, I am not constrained to speak to you of it in this writing; everyone knows, even if he has a mind deranged, that it is God who instituted baptism and transmitted it to us. He said, 'Go, therefore, and make disciples of all nations, baptizing them in the name of the Father and of the Son and of the Holy Spirit, teaching them to observe all that I have commanded you' [Matt. 28 19–20]. What the holy apostles have set up and what they have taught with great effort, this it is that the heretics have set themselves to destroy . . .

How, indeed, are they not the enemies of God and man, they who do not believe in the Lord's miracles? Because they call the devil the creator, they do not admit that Christ performed any miracles. Although they hear the evangelists proclaim out loud the Lord's miracles, they 'twist them to their own destruction' [2 Peter 2.16], saying: 'Christ did not restore any blind person's sight, he cured no cripple, he did not raise the dead; these are only parables. The evangelists present sins which were cured as if they were diseases.' Nor do they believe in the crowds in the desert fed on five loaves; they say, 'What was there was not bread, but the gospels of the four evangelists, and the fifth was the Acts of the Apostles.' In short, they have 'twisted the sense of everything to their own destruction'.

Their prayers swarm with thousands of errors. They pray, shutting themselves in their houses four times a day and four times a night,[21] and they open the five doors[22] which should be kept closed. As they pray, they say, 'Our Father, who art in heaven', but even this condemns them, because in their words they call the creator of heaven and earth Father, when they make his creation the creation of the devil. As they pray, they do not make the sign of the cross on their face.

We ask them this question. If, as your madness claims, the devil created this visible world, why do you eat bread and drink water, since all this is the devil's work? Why do you wear our clothes? You condemn us at the same time as the one who made them, but without your volition, it is God to whom you referred; God is the creator of us and of all things visible and invisible. Your thoughts and words are sown by the devil; when he could find no place for himself under heaven, he made his nest in your hearts and there, like a bird, hatched out your thoughts and your doctrines. Indeed, who taught you to fast, to make prostrations, to give yourselves to manual work on the day of the Lord's resurrection [Sun-

---

21 EZ [25], c. 19: 'seven times a day and five times a night'.
22 Of the senses.

day]? You say that it is men who have instituted these rules; it is not written in the gospels. You do not observe any of the feasts of the Lord or any commemoration of the holy martyrs or holy fathers.

See all the tangles of their delusion, the signs of perdition. I omit the other abominations they teach, which are a web of various errors; the sort you might expect from them, as they are not in their right mind. If they had their reason, they would not claim that the most holy mother of God sinned; if they had their reason, they would not call the devil the creator of heaven and earth; if they had their reason, they would not call the holy cross the enemy of God; if they had any sense, they would not blaspheme against the holy institutions of the Church, which have been handed down to them; if they had any sense, they would not label as deceits the miracles which take place over the holy relics, but would listen to the Lord, saying, 'He who believes in me will also do the works that I do, and greater works than these' [John 14.12]. When the heretics refuse to give glory to any saint, they are also decrying the miracles of God.

Let a man ask them, 'Is this what you do and say?' – then they deny it and swear on oath, 'We are not such as you believe.' They deny their practices and prayers so forcefully that you would think there was no harm in them: 'Everyone who does evil hates light and does not come to the light, lest his deeds should be exposed' [John 3.20]. This is a trick they teach their followers, to whom they explain, 'If our prayers and our works came to be known among men, then all our labour would have been wasted.' They try to conceal themselves behind the words of scripture, which the Lord uses: 'When you pray, you must not be like the hypocrites, for they disfigure their faces so that their fasting may be known among men. But when you pray, go into your room and shut the door, and pray to your Father in secret. And in praying, do not heap up empty words, but Our Father who art in heaven.' For, he says, the hypocrites 'love to stand and pray at street-corners' [Matt. 6.5,16.6–7.9]. The heretics twist all this that they read; they claim that the 'street-corners' are the churches; 'excess of words' means the offices and the other prayers which take place in churches. Woe to them, in the Lord's words in which it is written: 'Woe to the world for temptations to sin! For it is necessary that temptations come, but woe to the man by whom the temptation comes!' . . .

I would like to report to you some other opinions they hold, which they make use of to entrap ignorant souls: 'You ought not to weary yourself with earthly labours: since the Lord said: "Do not be anxious about what you shall eat, or what you shall drink, or what you shall put on; for the pagans seek all these things" [Matt. 6.25, 31–2]. That is why some of them go about in idleness and are unwilling to employ their hands with any task; they go from house to house and eat the goods of others, those of the men they have deceived. As the Lord says, they shall be the more condemned. Let us listen to the apostle Paul: . . . 'If anyone will not work, let him not eat' [2 Thess. 3.10]. The heretics, then, incur a double condemnation, both for spreading an alternative doctrine and for being the new apostles and precursors of antichrist, preparing for people to welcome the son of perdition.

They teach their followers not to obey their masters; they scorn the rich, they hate the Tsars, they ridicule their superiors, they reproach the boyars, they believe that God looks in horror on those who labour for the Tsar, and advise every serf not to work for his master. On this point we shall recall to the Christ-loving faithful the words and teaching of the apostles and prophets to confound the shamelessness of the heretics. It is the wisdom of God which says that 'emperors and lords have been instituted by God' [Prov. 8.15–18]. Listen to it: 'It is by me that kings reign and rulers decree what is just; by me princes rule and nobles govern the earth. I love those that love me and those who seek me diligently find me. Riches and honour are with me . . .'.

Much has been written on the same subject in the other sacred writers, but there is nothing there to support the heretics, with their contradictory absurdities. As for the words: 'Do not be anxious about what you shall eat or what you shall drink' [Matt. 6.25], the Lord did not say this to forbid manual labour, but because he does not want us to waste care on terrestrial goods, rather than to concern ourselves with our soul. 'The soul', he says, 'is worth more than food, and the body more than clothing.' We are not forbidden to betake ourselves to manual labour, but as we work with our hands, we should occupy our souls with considering divine matters. If God had ordered men not to work, plants would grow grain and woods grapes; as things are, when God bids men work and share with the needy the product of their toils let the lazy and those who blaspheme shut their mouth . . .

I would like to tell you another opinion of the heretics which the devil, the enemy of men, uses to catch them in a trap. They hear it said by James, the Lord's brother: 'Therefore confess your sins to one another, and pray for one another, that you may be healed' [James 5.16], but do not realize that these words are said to priests. James says, 'Is any among you sick? Let him call for the elders of the Church, and let them pray over him, anointing him with oil in the name of the Lord, and the prayer of faith will save the sick man, and the Lord will raise him up, and if he has committed sins, he will be forgiven' [James 5.14–15]. The heretics practise confession to one another and loose sins when they are themselves caught in the toils of the devils. It is not just the men who do this, but the women as well, which is worthy of condemnation. For the apostle says, 'I permit no woman to teach or have authority over men; she is to keep silent' [1 Tim. 2.12].

But heretics blaspheme everything they do not know, as the blessed apostle Jude said: 'But these men revile whatever they do not understand, and by those things they know by instinct, as irrational animals do, they are destroyed. Woe to them! For they walk in the way of Cain, and abandon themselves for the sake of gain to Balaam's error, and perish in Korah's rebellion. These are blemishes on your love-feast, as they boldly carouse together, looking after themselves; waterless clouds, wandering stars, for whom the nether gloom of darkness has been reserved for ever' [Jude 10–13].

For mankind's sake, the holy apostles have written this about heretics even more: 'You are a chosen race, a royal priesthood, a holy nation, the people of the renewal' [1 Peter 2.9], as the chief of the apostles says. You should all honour priests and approach those who are good and learned, 'for there are some who long ago were designed for this condemnation, ungodly persons who pervert the grace of our God into licentiousness' [Jude 4]. John says, 'If anyone comes to you and does not bring this doctrine, do not receive him into the house or give him any greeting, for he who greets him shares his wicked work' [2 John 10–11]. 'For', he says, 'many deceivers have gone out into the world; look to yourselves, that you may not lose what you have worked for' [2 John 7–8].

If you recognize anyone who shares the heretical faith, and if anyone among you is competent to instruct him, teach him and set him back on the right path: 'Whoever knows what is right to do and fails to do it, for him it is sin' [James 4.17]. If they do not listen to you and do not accept this saving teaching, shake the very dust off your feet and say, 'Your blood be upon your own heads.' When you have marked the heretic in this way, separate yourself from him, soul and body. 'Let him be to you as a pagan and a Gentile', as the Lord said [Matt. 18.17]. And know this, that at the day of judgement it shall be better for Sodom and Gomorrah than for this man. So do not give this teaching to dogs who refuse to obey, and do not scatter your pearls before swine. But if they listen to these holy words and repent and turn away from the deceptions of the heretics, welcome them with enthusiasm, taking care to be certain that their repentance is real and not pretended, for they are very cunning, and hide their thoughts in the depths of their heart. If, as I say, their conversion is real, and they truly confess with tears their deceiving delusions, lead them affectionately in the right path, in the knowledge that in the next world we shall receive a great reward . . .

Listen to the words of John the evangelist [actually James 5.19–20]: 'My brethren, if any one among you wanders from the truth and someone brings him back, let him know that whoever brings back a sinner from the error of his ways will save a soul from death and cover a multitude of sins.'

16. THE *SYNODIKON OF ORTHODOXY*: CLAUSES ABOUT BOGOMILS

The *Synodikon of Orthodoxy* originated as part of the feast decreed to preserve the memory of the celebrations which took place at the restoration of the icons in 843. The feast took place and the *Synodikon* was read annually on the first Sunday of Lent.

The original text of the *Synodikon* summarized orthodox teaching, condemned the doctrines of the Iconoclasts and their named supporters, and commended their (sometimes martyred) opponents. In later recensions additions were made to the text which summarized developments in doctrine as it emerged from the theological controversies of the eleventh and twelfth centuries; for these see Gouillard, 'Le Synodikon d'orthodoxie', pp. 186–226. These additions are found in all the MS traditions of the text. Besides these generally accepted additions there were others which are only found in some MS families. The anti-Bogomil material belongs in this category. (a) and (b) below are found only in one MS, Vindob. hist. gr. 73. This is a thirteenth century document, Cc in Gouillard's stemma. (c) consists of five anathemas which appear to have existed independently of the synodikon tradition. They are also found in MS Coislianus 213, a *euchologion* (or collection of prayers for special occasions) made in August 1027 for 'Strategius, priest of the Great Church[1] and of the patriarchal oratories'. (d) consists of thirteen further anathemas, which are to be found in five MSS of the *Synodikon*, all of which come from one group associated with the province of Athens. For a detailed discussion of the problems raised by this section, see Gouillard, 'Le Synodikon d'orthodoxie', pp. 232–3. None of the anti-Bogomil material is found in the Constantinopolitan text of the *Synodikon*.

1 St Sophia.

THE SYNODIKON OF ORTHODOXY

The translation has been made from the text edited by Gouillard, 'Le Synodikon de l'orthodoxie', *T & M* 2 (1967), pp. 1–313.

(a) p. 59. To *papa* Bogomil who, in the reign of Peter of Bulgaria, stirred up this Manichaean heresy and spread it through every town and countryside.[2]

(b) p. 61 [and additional reading in variants to line 243]

To the Bogomils who have been discovered at Panormus and the catepanate, anathema.[3]

(c) pp. 61–3. To those who do not confess that the unity of the Holy Trinity, indivisible, equally honoured, sharing one throne and co-eternal, is of one nature, Father, Son and Holy Spirit, but say that some angel they have introduced called 'Amen' is the Son and say that the Holy Spirit, equal in power to the Father and to the Son, is of some other still lower nature, anathema.

To those who do not confess that God is the creator of heaven and earth and the whole creation, the shaper of Adam and the maker of Eve, but say that the Adversary is the ruler and creator of all, the shaper of human nature, to such, anathema. To those who do not confess that the Son of God, the Word, begotten by Him before all the ages and at the end of time incarnate from the immaculate mother of God, Mary, through his great compassion, for our salvation became man and took on all that is ours except sin, to those who do not share His holy and immortal mysteries with fear, as being the very flesh of the Lord and His holy and precious blood shed for the life of the world, but as mere bread and ordinary drink, to such, anathema.

To those who do not revere the cross of our Lord and God and Saviour Jesus Christ as being the salvation of the whole world and its glory, which brings to nothing and destroys the devices and weapons of the enemy, which frees the creation from idols and displays victory to the universe, but regard it as an instrument of tyranny, to such, anathema.

---

2 This is the first Greek source which mentions Bogomil by name. The place where it is inserted in the text (immediately following the details of the condemnation of John Italus (1076, 1082) may suggest a connection with the trial and condemnation of Basil; see **[24]**, **[25]**.

3 The identification of Panormus ('harbour' in Greek) is uncertain. The well-known Panormus, modern Palermo, in Sicily, had been under Arab and later Norman control from 831. There was a Panormus on Cephallonia on the Dalmatian coast, one near Cyzicus in the Straits, and one on one of the islands in the Bosphorus now known as the Princes' Islands. See EP **[19]** for the association of the main naval base on the Bosphorus, Hieron, with heretical activity. A *catepan* was a high-ranking naval officer; see Arhweiler, *Byzance et la mer*, p. 57 for one associated with Hieron; *ibid.*, pp. 124–5 for those associated with the Panormus in Sicily.

To those who do not venerate the holy and august image of our Lord and God and Saviour Jesus Christ as a representation of the Lord and God incarnate for us, and do not glorify Him as represented in His image, nor that of His holy and immaculate mother, or of all the saints, but call them idols, to such, anathema.

(d) pp. 63–9. Our Lord and God and Saviour Jesus Christ, through his holy disciples and apostles, handed down to us the pure mystery of the faith, and said that in the last days there would come many false apostles and false prophets, and warned us to keep away from such people. Likewise Paul, the herald of God, when writing to Timothy warned that 'in the last days some will abandon the faith and follow a spirit of error and the doctrines of demons who give false teaching, in pretence, whose conscience is branded; they will forbid marriage and enjoin abstention from foods which God created for the faithful and those who have knowledge of God to partake of with thanksgiving; since everything God has created is good when taken with thanksgiving. It is hallowed through the word of God and prayer'.[4] And again, 'there will be some of these who sneak into houses and take captive women who have sinned, ensnared with various desires, who are quite incapable of learning and coming to the knowledge of the truth of God'.[5]

Since our God and Saviour gave us forewarning and in the apostle preached this, let us be on our guard, beloved, in accordance with these prophecies, now that we have come to the last days. The heresy of the Messalians or Bogomils, confused and many-named,[6] is now prevalent in every city and countryside and province, and those who introduce it do not cease to destroy the simpler folk. These enemies of Christ call themselves Christians, and by the good sound of the name are confused with the orthodox; without being recognized as hiding the wolf under the sheep's clothing, they make the beginning of their empty preaching, starting from the scriptures which we venerate; and when they have been accepted in this mask and the listeners begin to attend to them, they spew forth their poison. Now that they have become familiar, they vomit forth the foul teachings of Satan, which together with them we subject to anathema as being foul and spurious and alien to the Catholic Church.

To Peter, the leader of the heresy of the Messalians or Lycopetrians,

4 1 Tim. 4. 1–5.
5 1 Tim. 3.6.
6 The confusion between Manichaeans, Messalians and Bogomils is widespread in the sources. It may reflect the use of archaic descriptions of heretics, but sometimes there is also confusion in the doctrines attributed to more recent heresy. See [23] below.

Phoundatai or Bogomils, who called himself Christ and promised that he would rise again from the dead, and for this reason was called Lycopetrus [wolf–Peter], because when he was justly buried under stones through his infinite sorceries and foul deeds, he promised his wretched followers that he would rise again after three days: as they surrounded his abominable remains, after three days he appeared there like a wolf emerging from the heap of stones, anathema.[7]

To Tychicus his fellow-initiate and disciple,[8] who destroyed and misinterpreted other holy scriptures, especially the whole of the gospel of St Matthew, misinterpreting all the sayings which concern God the Father as well as those about the Holy Spirit, applying them to his spiritual father, and so perverted the glory of God to the leaders of his abominable sect, anathema.[9]

To Dadoes, Sabas, Adelphius, Hermas, Simeon and the rest who vomited forth the poison of such heresy and led astray the more rustic people, both men and women, and plunged them into the pit of destruction, anathema.[10]

To those who say of the holy and life-giving Trinity – that is God the Father and the incarnate Word, the son of God, our Lord Jesus Christ, and the most Holy Spirit – that there is some other trinity, or again a superior power seated on the uppermost of the seven heavens, in accordance with their abominable apocryphal 'Vision of Isaiah', anathema.[11]

To those who introduce other scriptures besides those uttered by the Holy Spirit and handed down to us by the holy fathers, anathema.

To those who say that marriage in the Lord and eating meat as God allows are abominable to God and therefore forbid them both, anathema.

To those who reject the prayers and hymns which have been handed down to us, first by the holy apostles and then in succession by the holy

---

7 For Peter Lycopetrus and the various legends associated with him see EP **[19]** and note 49. The charge that heretical leaders had falsely promised their own resurrection is found made against Simon Magus in Hippolytus, *Refutatio*, VI.20.2–3.

8 Presumably Sergius/Tychicus, for whom see Peter of Sicily **[7]**, cc. 132–73 and note there.

9 The heretical commentary on the gospel of St Matthew cited in EZ **[25]**, cc. 28–52 does not fit this description.

10 These five names are cited from earlier anti-Messalian material; see St John of Damascus, *De haeresibus* (*PG* 94, col. 735 B8).

11 The 'Vision of Isaiah' is available in translation in Wakefield and Evans, *Heresies of the High Middle Ages*, no.56 (pp. 447–64).

and blessed fathers and teachers of the Church, to those who reject and attack all these as vain repetitions, and in the beginning of their separation from God, teach men only to use the Our Father with prostration to the ground, without the sign of the Lord's cross on the face, on the pretext that this prayer was transmitted by our Lord Christ, but in reality to invoke their abominable father Satan (for it is for this reason that they reject the sign of the cross as well, and cannot bear to hear the ancient final sentence[12] transmitted by the inspired luminaries and teachers of the Church, to the glory of the holy and consubstantial Trinity, 'for Thine is the kingdom, the power and the glory, Father, Son and Holy Spirit'); to those who think and teach thus and persist to the end in their perverse position, anathema.

To those who detest gatherings in church and take their seats in private places and there teach, on the excuse of quiet, but in reality so that their abominable errors may remain unrecognized and unrefuted, so that in this way they might pour out in a corner all the poison of their heresy to those they have led into error, to all who persist in such error to the end, anathema.

To those who attack the tradition of building churches to the glory of God, which has been handed down to us by the apostles, as works of men's hands, and similarly reject the venerable setting-up of the sacred and holy icons and their honour and veneration, to those wholly corrupt and gangrenous ones, anathema.

To those who strive to reverse the teaching of our Lord and God and Saviour Jesus Christ, which he enjoined on his holy apostles, that they should baptize those who believe in Him in the name of the Father and of the Son and of the Holy Spirit – to those who are blind to all this, and under the influence of the power of Satan at work in them dare to say absurdly of holy baptism that it is just water, since they are outside our faith and the Church and are, once for all, strangers to God, anathema.

To those who consistently with such nonsense and absurdities call the holy and life-giving cross a gallows, holy baptism mere water which does not give forgiveness of sins or come from the Spirit, but claim that they give the baptism of the Spirit, when they dress their abominable initiates in the mock monastic habit and at the same time perform over them such an invocation which is rather a ruin of their souls and bodies, anathema.

12 The Orthodox Church regularly uses the doxology to the Lord's prayer. In the West, where it was not regularly used, Cathars said it and were again criticized for so doing; see Appendix 1.

To those who say that the communion of the precious body and blood of our Lord and God and Saviour Jesus Christ is a communion of mere bread and wine, so that they tell those of the laity who make their communion to come forward after food and make their communion as a pretence to escape notice, and command those priests who have been converted to have a meal and then celebrate the divine and awful mysteries, to these, as being manifestly antichrists, even though they call themselves 'Christopolites', anathema.

To those who, in order to overturn all faith in God, perform other evil rites for those they blasphemously initiate; instead of the holy and divine inspiration which we receive from our master Christ by the mystic inbreathing of the Holy Spirit, they spit on those they initiate (as they deserve), and so do the same to those they are initiating as we do to demons, and moreover wipe them from head to heel with a sponge of dirty water, to wipe off holy baptism and the light-giving presence of the Holy Spirit, anathema.

These are the seeds of perverse blasphemy, the growing shoots of the ungodliness of Satan, the evil one. But may we, the chosen people of Christ, hold fast with all our hearts to the divine and apostolic doctrines and the traditions of the fathers, fleeing with all our soul from the foul teaching of blasphemy, keeping our distance from their pernicious cult, and rather serve God in purity, He who is honoured and worshipped in the Trinity of persons, to whom be glory and power to endless ages, Amen.

17. PAULICIANS IN ELEVENTH-CENTURY SOUTHERN ITALY

In the eleventh century the Byzantine provinces of Italy were ruled by a catepan stationed at Bari.[1] In 1041 the catepan was Michael Douceianus, who was attacked by the South Italian Normans; he called for support in the Byzantine regiments stationed in Sicily, but suffered two defeats, first in March, when the Normans occupied Melfi, then again in May. He was then relieved of his command, but his successor Boiannes fared no better, for although supported by fresh troops from Sicily he was defeated and captured by the Normans near Montepeloso on 3 September 1041.

The texts used are (a) *Annales Barenses* (*MGH SS* 9, p. 248); the *Annals of Bari* are a near contemporary western source and report the presence of a Paulician

[1] See map.

regiment among the Sicilian reinforcements; and (b) the *Gesta Roberti Guiscardi*, which William of Apulia began writing at the request of Urban II (1088–99) and completed before 1111. While remembering that Paulicians had taken part in this important battle half a century earlier, his informants had clearly confused them with some other Eastern-rite Christian contingent. This translation is made from *La Geste de Robert Guiscard par Guillaume de Pouille*, ed. M. Mathias (the text is also printed in *MGH SS* 9, p. 239).

(a) [Entry for the year 1041]

Here came from Sicily into Lombardy[2] Michael the *protospatharios* and *catepan* ... then in the month of May, having collected all the Greeks together in one place at Mons Maior, near the river Aufidius, battle was joined as the fourth day began, where perished many Nalulichi[3] and Obsequiani,[4] Russi,[5] Trachici,[6] Calabrians and Lombards, and people from the catepanate.

Retreating from there in confusion with a few men, the rest only half-alive, for fear of the savage Normans, Michael wrote to Sicily and there came the wretched Macedonians themselves and the Paulicians and Calabrians.

(b) [In September 1041] Together with the Greeks there were some whom evil error had made senseless, and from this they took their name.[7] These people used to say that the Father suffered together with Christ, and made the sign of the cross on their forehead with one finger.[8]

---

2 i.e. the area of southern Italy under Lombard rule, not the modern Lombardy.
3 Anatolians.
4 Opsikiani? (for the Opsikion theme, see EP **[19]**).
5 Varangians, recruited from the cities of Russia.
6 Thracians.
7 [Cum Graecis aderant quidam quos pessimus error / Fecerant *amentes* et ab ipso nomen habebant.] This is a reference to Manichaeans, i.e. Paulicians: the usual pun Mani/maniac underlies it.
8 Making the sign of the cross with one finger is allegedly a Jacobite (or Armenian) error.

18. ST LAZARUS THE WONDER-WORKER CONVERTS PAULICIANS NEAR EPHESUS (BEFORE 1054)

This extract from the life of St Lazarus of the monastery on Mt Galesius, on the western coast of Asia Minor between Smyrna and Ephesus, provides evidence of the survival of Paulician communities in that area after the fall of Tefrice and the collapse of the independent Paulician state.

The text is printed in *Acta Sanctorum; Nov. iii; Vita S. Lazari auctore Gregorio Monacho* vol. 3, pp. 508–88 (1910).

p. 512. When he learnt from the brethren who had been there before him that in the mountain opposite the monastery there is a cave convenient for those who desire quiet, he asked leave of the superior and going away, made his dwelling in it. There he displayed many remarkable acts of asceticism. These the enemy of mankind could not endure, but undermined him another way; the evil one incited heretics[1] of the village near the mountain – for there were many in it – intending to use them to drive him from the mountain. They came up and hurled mockery and insults at him, indeed, they attempted to strike him unless he rapidly withdrew from the mountain, but he bore it all meekly and gently, for he knew well who it was who had incited them to this. So he did not cease to exhort and admonish them with gentle words until he made them not merely cease their hostility to himself, but deny their inherited heresy, and approach the Orthodox Church. As he saw them yielding to his arguments, he wrote to the bishop of Philetus[2] and received them into fellowship when they had first anathematized their heresy in church. Some of them, after they had made their denial, approached him and begged him to tonsure them and to make their dwelling with him. He was not persuaded to do this, but they continued to beg him more earnestly. When he had been unable to convince them, after much discussion he wrote to the superior and on his instructions received them.

[p. 543] Another, a Paulician, came to the father and the moment he saw him had no need for further arguments to receive the true word of piety in his soul, but immediately abjured the heresy of which he had

---

1 That this heresy was Paulicianism is inferred from the second passage translated; there is no evidence in this text.
2 Philetus was a suffragan see of Myra. Throughout this life there is emphasis on the care taken by St Lazarus to observe ecclesiastical discipline. For the forms used for the reception of heretics see **[10]**, **[11]**.

been fond. When he had anathematized it at the bidding of the holy father he was deemed worthy of holy baptism in the monastery. Indeed later, against all expectation, through the good pleasure of God he became a monk. After he had spent some time in the monastery, being scandalized for some reason, or rather swept off his feet through lightness of mind, since he was still a layman,[3] he left the monastery and went away to his own country. But God, that lover of men, through the prayers of our holy father provided that he should go to Jerusalem and receive the tonsure in the monastery of St Sabas.[4]

19. EUTHYMIUS OF THE PERIBLEPTON CONDEMNS BOGOMILS (*c.* 1045)

This is the earliest account in Greek of the activities and beliefs of Bogomils. Nothing is known of the author except what he himself tells us, that he originated from (or at least had family connections with) the diocese of Acmonia,[1] and was of age to accompany his mother to a lawsuit 'in the reigns of the emperors Basil and Constantine' (976–1025). The case was to be judged by 'the late Romanus, who subsequently became emperor' – so we must assume that Euthymius was born at least twenty years before the accession of Romanus III (1028), and that the text was written after Romanus' death in 1034. There are verbal similarities between his condemnation of Bogomils and an abjuration formula **[11]**, which is found in a *euchologion* dated August 1027.[2] Euthymius speaks as though he were in a position of authority in his monastery, which was founded by the emperor Romanus in 1030.[3] His text is evidence that Bogomils were active in the capital and in a monastery with imperial patronage.

The text of Euthymius survives in five MSS, of which three are only fragmentary. One of these fragments is printed in *PG* 131; the others are printed in Ficker, *Die Phundagiagiten*. These are cited as C.

Two MSS, Vindob. 307 (= Ficker A) and Vindob. 193 (= Ficker B) contain the whole text. The relation between these is complex. A is the longer, but B is not a shortened version, since at many points it is fuller than A, while A itself has been substantially interpolated. Internal evidence suggests that Euthymius him-

---

3 That is, he had not yet taken monastic vows.
4 For the monastery of St Sabas at Jerusalem see Hirschfeld, *The Judean desert monasteries*, pp. 24–6; for the relationship of St Lazarus and the monastery of St Sabas see Morris, *Monks and laymen*, pp. 34, 197.

1 See map.
2 For the details of this MS see **[16]**.
3 See note 5 below.

self wrote more than one anti-Bogomil document, and that these were later reworked by other authors.

We have printed the translation of a composite text, based on B. Variations in A are recorded in the footnotes; important variations from C (which is incomplete) are included in the main text, but are underlined for ease of identification.

A LETTER FROM EUTHYMIUS, MONK OF THE MONASTERY[4] OF THE PERIBLEPTON,[5] SENT FROM CONSTANTINOPLE, FROM THE MONASTERY AFORESAID, TO HIS NATIVE LAND,[6] IDENTIFYING THE HERESIES OF THE MOST GODLESS AND PROFANE HERETICS, THE PHUNDAGIAGITAE,[7] OR, AS THEY ARE ALSO CALLED, BOGOMILS[8]

All my Christian brothers, let us urge one another because we have come to the end of the ages and we have reached in these days all that our Lord and God Jesus Christ has revealed to us in his gospel. For He speaks of the last great error: 'Watch lest you go astray; false Christs and false prophets shall arise and lead many astray, if possible even the elect; these are they who wear sheep's clothing, but inwardly they are ravening wolves' [Matt. 7.15], and so on. The apostles of antichrist[9] go round everywhere and lead and have led many astray, not just laity, but priests and monks as well ... The blasphemers of whom I have already written do not honour or confess God as the maker of heaven and earth, or the mother of God or the holy cross or the holy sacrifice or holy baptism or

---

4 C adds 'imperial'.
5 The monastery of the Mother of God Seen by all (The Periblepton) was built by Romanus III after his unsuccessful expedition to Syria in 1030; he was buried there on Good Friday, 12 April 1034. The expensive style of the church attracted contemporary criticism; the only surviving description of it confirms that it was luxuriously adorned. See Janin, *La Géographie ecclésiastique*, 1ᵉ partie, III, p. 218.
6 The diocese of Acmonia, north-west of Smyrna; see p. 160 below and map.
7 This name for the heretics otherwise called Bogomils has not been satisfactorily explained.
8 A adds: 'and Massalians, together with the heresy of the Armenians and the remaining ... heresies'. C has two variants: the *PG* text reads: 'the atheist Phundagiagitae, who call themselves Christopolitai, but in the west are called Bogomils'; the fragment printed by Ficker reads: 'These are the so-called Bogomils, those who are called Massalians in the Syrian language, which in Greek means Euchites. Anathema katathema on them.' For the use of Messalian/Massalian as a description of heretical groups who almost certainly have no structural continuity with the Syrian group from whom they are named, see Rigo, 'Messalianismo = Bogomilismo', pp. 53–82.
9 See our Introduction, p. 29.

sacred churches; they do not confess them, but insult and dishonour them all.[10] They believe in and worship the ruler of this world, who is Satan (Satanael).[11] Craftily the crafty play-act Christianity, the appearance of monks and the priesthood.

My brethren and dear kinsfolk, as I have already told you in my worthless letters of the ... error ... of the Phundagiagitae, I would like to remind you again ... to be on your guard against them ... By their interpretation of the holy scriptures they deceive the ignorant and those of little faith ... They are difficult to identify, and so some people cannot recognize them ...

I happened to share my way with one of these people unknowingly; later, when I asked him who he was and where he was going, I learnt his details and what his opinions were ... He was a false priest, as he told me and [from] the country of Gozas.[12] He said to me, 'There is no resurrection of the dead', advancing scriptural evidence from the epistles of St Paul ... .[13] Altogether if I had not known how to answer him back ... but had accepted his blasphemous opinion, how many other things would his filthy mouth not have uttered, and into what spiritual harm might I not have fallen? He seemed to say what was sensible, to a rustic, advancing ... evidence from the apostle ...

[Here a long passage has been omitted, in which Euthymius expounds the orthodox faith in the resurrection as found in the creeds, citing various miracles which had occurred to corroborate the decisions of the General Councils of the Church which had issued these creeds.]

[I said to him] ... 'All the saints, the ecumenical lights and teachers, have confirmed and ratified by faith the holy creed in which it is written, 'I look for the resurrection of the dead and the life of the world to come.' Do you think they were all holy and wise, yes or no?' ... The devil's

---

10 All these points are considered at more length later in the text, except the reference to the mother of God. In the Orthodox Church the Blessed Virgin Mary is revered as the *Theotokos* (God-Bearer). Since Bogomils did not believe that Christ had become a human being, they did not give her this title.
11 'Satanael' only in the *PG* text. For a similar oscillation between forms see EZ **[25]** and note 3 there.
12 Gozas/Gozen is not otherwise known, unless it is to be identified with the place to which the Israelites were deported in 2 Kings 17.6. This may be Gaulanitis (Ptolemy 5.18.4) in the north Syrian plain near Nisibis.
13 The Orthodox Church affirms the bodily resurrection of the dead. Bogomils did not accept this, apparently basing their views on 1 Cor. 15.50 'Flesh and blood cannot inherit the kingdom of God'.

labourer, the forerunner of antichrist, answered in turn, 'The saying of the apostle is more powerful, and how, my friend, do you understand it?' I said, 'Were all these holy men unaware of the saying of the apostle? . . . "that flesh and blood cannot inherit the kingdom of God"' [1 Cor. 15.50], and so on. As I said, 'Either you have chanced among heretics, or perhaps you are one of them, since you do not have an argument to add as a support for this blasphemous saying.' Immediately he began to curse and swear: 'I am not what you say.' These habitual liars and cheats are in the habit of answering Christians like this, in their anxiety to conceal the snake which lurks in their hearts. 'But', he said, 'for profit's sake I will make enquiry' . . .

[Some 2,000 words on the scriptural basis of the doctrine of the resurrection have been omitted.]

As I explained the subject like this . . . the man who had been and still was in error agreed to believe; but in his opinion the faithless one remained faithless . . .

While I was absent in Jerusalem,[14] those who shared the aforesaid blasphemy found my disciple and persuaded him, who had no skill in letters and was unlearned, to adhere to their opinions, to believe, not in God, who is in heaven, but in the Lord of this world, who is the devil [John 12.31] So when I had separated from this evil fellow-traveller and returned, as I say, from my journey to Jerusalem, I found my unhappy disciple in the monastery of the Periblepton, led astray. Blasphemers of this kind were all around, teaching everywhere within the city and outside it . . . My pupil, who was affectionately disposed towards me, told me the blasphemous sayings of the atheists, as if for my profit. When I heard this and understood what had happened and showed him a smiling face, I asked to see the teachers who had told him things of this sort, saying to him in pretended ignorance, 'I want to profit from them, because I can't believe you, who are my pupil.' He did so with great pleasure, and brought them to me, men who were at that time in that very monastery. I did not drop the pretence to them, but called them fathers, saviours of our souls, teachers, rather than blasphemers, who had led men astray. I had no other way to discover the secrets of their

---

14 Presumably on pilgrimage. The Church of the Holy Sepulchre had been destroyed on the orders of the Caliph Hakim in 1009; rebuilding at the expense of the Byzantine government was begun by Romanus III Argyrus under the terms of a peace treaty with Syria made in 1030 and completed by Constantine Monomachus in 1048. See Coüasnon, *The church of the Holy Sepulchre in Jerusalem*, p. 20.

impiety. I kept them in my cell for some days and talked to them. It was a sight to see, brethren, their impious leader. Not merely did the heretic have the sayings of the gospel and the epistles of the holy apostle Paul on his lips, but works of theology of St John Chrysostom, sayings from the Psalter, of the holy old men from the Sayings of the Fathers,[15] [saying] that later on he taught men to err, bidding them not to believe or heed as holy writings what he himself had previously advanced as instruction. No wonder, for it was not he who toiled and learnt the scriptures, as we were informed by the heretic himself later, but it was the devil who said these things through him ... Do not disbelieve this, for we too have found in scripture that it is so. It is written in the Sayings of the Fathers that demons often answered a monk, though they were spirits, and entered the monks' cells and prayed and sang psalms with them, singing verse and verse about in psalm 119 ... and the other psalms ...

There were four atheists. Having overpowered them, we determined to separate them from one another and to shut them in solitary confinement, in fetters, and to threaten them with death unless they gave a clear and complete account of their error and heresy. This we did. Being interrogated one at a time, I think that they left out nothing of their error which was not identified. The first villain among them we asked whence came their knowledge of Scripture: 'How do you have it on your lips if you do not believe it?' [He replied]: 'I cannot deceive a Christian otherwise than by pretending to be a monk; we call ourselves Christians and appear in every way to act as Christians do, and put forward the holy scriptures as our teaching. He who sends us out to this preaching enables us to have holy scriptures on our lips.' The blasphemers call the lord of this world (who is Satan) Christ, and the power of the holy gospels and the epistles they ascribe to him, as they themselves confess, and as my deluded disciple told me. They call themselves true Christians.

The accursed ones made confession, saying: 'From a certain heretic Peter, a miserable clothes-carder nicknamed Lycopetrus,[16] we have a

15 C adds: 'The polluted ones insult St John Chrysostom [golden-mouth] as foul-mouth.' This charge is repeated by EZ **[19]**, c. 21, note 64. 'Sayings of the Fathers' is a general description of the collection of the sayings of early monks, of which the most accessible is that printed in *PG* 65, 74–439.
16 Lycopetrus means Wolf–Peter. There is confusion here between Peter the Fuller, the Monophysite Patriarch of Antioch, who died in 488, Peter Lycopetrus and Peter of Cappadocia. The last two may be alternative names for the same person; see Gouillard, 'Le Synodikon de l'orthodoxie', *T & M* 2 (1967), p. 65 and commentary.

satanic spell, which we call the Revelation of St Peter.[17] When by a variety of teaching we have persuaded someone to distance himself from God and induce him to our will, or rather to the will of the devil himself, and we know that the grace of the Holy Spirit which he received in baptism has left him, then', he said, 'we have a custom of reading this same satanic spell above his head as a seal.[18] The moment it has been read, the grace of the Holy Spirit leaves him, which he has received from holy baptism, and a satanic energy comes upon the one who has been led astray, and from then on if he wants anything, he speaks.' When he was asked to say whether the person who is led astray knew that the spell was being read over him, he said that he did not know: 'We trick him, saying, 'We intend to read the four gospels over you.' We put the book above his head and begin with well-known words from the holy gospel, so that he is not aware. So secretly, together with the words of the gospel, we recite the spell as well over his head.[19] When this has happened, and the grace of the Holy Spirit has left him, he receives the seal of the devil, and an evil spirit enters and lurks in his heart. In future no one can take such a one out of the devil's hands; I don't know whether God himself could.'

This he admitted he had himself gone through, giving a detailed narrative, and cursing his teacher. Then in turn we said to the atheist, 'Since, as you admit, you are in heresy and your teaching is heresy, and anything like this is worse than all other evils, why are you zealous to deceive others as well?' The accursed one answered: 'Those who have the knowledge of evil and who have been ordained as apostles and teachers by the devil have no life with the foul demons, unless they do this with great zeal.' Then we asked him again to say, 'Does the one who has been led astray know later about the imposition of the spell?' He said, 'No, he does not know. Only the teachers of evil know this.' Then again we said to him, 'Since, as you admit, everything you do and play-act comes from the devil, why do you play-act everything that belongs to Christians?' The wretch answered thus: 'The apostle says: "Whatever

17 Three apocryphal works with this title are known. The most complete is printed in translation in *NTA* 2, pp. 663–83. This is an early apocryphal work, known to and considered non-genuine by Eusebius (*HE* 3. 3.25). It gives a vivid description of the rewards and punishments of the afterlife. Another work with the same title (which has not survived) is attributed to Peter the Iberian, a Monophysite who died in 491, and may be intended here; see Gouillard, 'L'Hérésie dans l'empire byzantin', *T & M* 1 (1965), pp. 299–324.
18 The term 'seal' was used in the early Church to describe baptism.
19 EZ [25], c. 16 says that the Gospel of St John was used in Bogomil initiation. EP appears (wilfully?) to misunderstand the rite.

does not proceed from faith is sin" [Rom. 14.2–3]. If we do everything, yet we do not do it with faith, either baptism, or priesthood, or monastic vows, or anything else that is Christian.[20] We do everything for show, or rather in mockery, in the interests of concealment. Our ruler [*archon*] has told us to act like this, saying, 'No one will be in danger for my sake.[21] Pretend in all things. I am not hard-hearted like Christ, to say to my disciples, as he does: "Whoever denies me in the sight of men, I will deny" [Matt. 10.33], but in case of need deny me, and curse me. Do and say everything against me, pretend to all the activities of Christians, then turn back to me and I will receive you again with joy.'

'I will tell you another point', said the heretic to us: 'If the orthodox priest makes a small slip in his liturgy, he has involved himself in a serious fault. In our cult, if he starts on his liturgy and makes a mockery of the entire liturgy and defiles all those orthodox who share in the liturgy or in prayer, how much the greater is his praise . . .'.[22] <u>I do not dare, my brethren, to set down in writing all the blasphemies of these impious men, which they utter against the precious life-giving cross, the saints, the holy icons, against Christ himself and God . . . Yet these crafty folk walk round among us, and by their hypocritical behaviour appear to share our views.</u> The impious, atheists and heretics, found churches, not from faith, but to insult them[23] and regard them as ordinary buildings . . . A reliable man swore an oath to me that he had seen with his own eyes that within the district called the Narrows, near Hieron,[24] there was an apparent monk and priest of this most evil cult . . . This man founded a church, adorned and beautified it with paintings inside and out[25] in variety and beauty. Now it happened that

20 A similar doctrine can be found in the works of Constantine Chrysomallus, condemned by the patriarchal synod in 1140 for unorthodox teaching; see **[28]** and Gouillard, 'Constantin Chrysomalle sous la masque de Syméon'.
21 This remark is elsewhere attributed to Mani.
22 This passage makes clear the anxiety felt by Euthymius about nominally orthodox priests who held Bogomil views, and how this might affect their performance of their religious functions.
23 C adds: 'not scrupling to perform . . . foul matings on the very altar'.
24 Probably the naval base and customs post which derived its name from the earlier temple of Zeus Ourios by Ophrou Limen, the entrance to the Black Sea. There was a monastery (of *kyr* Nicholas) there, in which the monks condemned as followers of Constantine Chrysomallus were ordered to be detained; for the monastery see Janin, *Les Églises et les monastères des grands centres byzantins*, p. 101.
25 Despite their rejection of the material world, not all dualists rejected representational art; cf. the Manichaean miniatures from Turfan, (Klimkeit, *Manichaean art and calligraphy*) and for Cathar illuminated bibles, the testimony of Pierre de Luzenac to the Inquisition of Carcassonne in 1308, cited in Guiraud, *Histoire de l'Inquisition au Moyen Âge*, I, p. xi.

this evil sinner was revealed. It was discovered in the church that he had built behind the altar ... because he had made a great pit and had put above the pit a bench, leaving a little hole in it; in that hole behind the table of the altar, the accursed man performed his bodily functions. Such is the faith which the polluted people have in the churches which they founded. So they benefit from them ... They design icons, not in faith but in fun, and to insult them they make them as a show and deception, so that when they want and if they like, they may approach them secretly and trample them secretly. They do not baptize in faith, but make game of holy baptism ... saying to their disciples that it is water and oil,[26] and neither helps nor harms ... <u>They baptize their godless infants openly in church, and then returning home, they sponge them immediately with water that has been befouled, and with urine, reciting a satanic spell to them. This filthy water they pour away in a foul and shameful place, rejecting what partakes of the grace of holy baptism.</u>[27] In short ... the crafty people imitate all Christian activities craftily, not just to avoid detection, but to insult what is holy ... The ... Phundagiagitae go round with the sayings of the saints on their lips, through the power of Satan, not to teach and save the unwise, but to ensnare them through familiar words and to catch them in the snare of their father, the devil, and destroy them. For men looking at them, at their monastic appearance and name and Christian behaviour, and their false and humble manner and the holy and familiar scriptures which they have on their lips, do not recognize the evil and blasphemy which lurks within them, but fall readily into the devil's snare, and come to eternal destruction. Nor can those who are instructed by the atheists clearly perceive this ... impiety, hearing said to them the name of the Father and of the Son and of the Holy Spirit, of Peter and Paul, the great preachers and apostles, the sayings of the Lord and of the apostles as instruction ... When they know that the Holy Spirit has left them, that they are alienated from holy baptism, and that an unclean spirit has taken up its dwelling in them through a foul spell, then they begin to

26 In the Orthodox Church candidates for baptism are also anointed with the oil of catechumens and the oil of chrism.
27 A adds: 'In the same way they say concerning the holy, spotless and life-giving body and blood of Christ, our true God, that it is ordinary bread and wine. Such a person tries in every way in front of ordinary Christians to partake in pretence, and if he is not seen, he spits out the elements on to the ground and tramples on them, and if he does this he claims it as something to boast about. But if someone like this is seen and recognized, he eats and drinks them, but not as though they are holy, but as if they are common; at a time when he is not fasting, but stuffed with food. They say of these too, that they neither help nor harm.'

encourage in them the [initiation- (supplied from A)] rites of the devil... They do not entrust everything all together, only one thing. When they see the poor wretch firmly established in that one first evil, then they tell him another. So little by little over a year, they slowly reveal all their madness and heresy to him.[28] In the future they gain him; he worships the devil knowingly, and so as they work on the person they have led astray, he himself becomes a demon, one of their teachers for the future, rather than a disciple.

<u>Those who have been instructed by the atheists are not able to join this foul impiety at once. At first they enjoin on their disciples a severe fast, prayers seven times a day and seven times a night,[29] the possession of only one tunic and to have no contact of any kind with their wife (in which the impious overturn the law of God).[30] When they see that they have observed this rule for some time, then they promise them baptism, the sponging-off and removal of holy baptism, and the recital of a satanic hymn which the blasphemers call baptism. Not even thus are the blasphemers bold to give them the mysteries of impiety, but demand securely sworn oaths not to reveal to the majority what they have learnt from them. When they see that they accept this gladly, they tell them the rest, and so, little by little, over time and with difficulty, they reveal the blasphemy to their disciples. In the end they have taken it all in and knowingly worship the devil, the lord of darkness, and then the wretches become teachers, no longer disciples. Those who worship him see nightmare visions, as if they were asleep, and they also demand a signed undertaking that they will never return to the faith of Christians.</u>[31]

Do not be astonished, my brothers, at the impious diabolists, when you hear them say that they believe in Father, Son and Holy Spirit,[32] that they keep the apostles and saints in memory, and call themselves Christians. On such things the wretches have reference to their father, the devil. I shall explain to you how, as I heard from the blasphemers myself and found it written when I read about heresy... They call themselves

28 For allegations of progressive initiation see also EZ [25], c. 16.
29 EZ [25], c. 19 says five times a night; Cosmas [15] four times a day and four times a night.
30 See also EZ [25], c. 39 for Bogomil opposition to sexual relations of any kind.
31 This appears to claim that Bogomils demanded a *libellum*, a signed undertaking of faith, of their converts, as the Orthodox did of those heretics who were received back into the Church. See Theophylact [10] and the Abjuration formula [26].
32 A adds: 'all heresies say this, the Paulicians and the rest'.

Christians, not from Christ, our true God, but from their father, antichrist, the devil.[33] When they speak of Father, Son and Holy Spirit, they do not mean the holy, life-giving and undivided Trinity which we orthodox worship and adore. When they say 'Father', they mean the devil, as is written in the holy gospels, 'You are of your father, the devil' [John 8.14]. By 'Son', they mean 'the son of perdition' [2 Thess. 2.3], and 'spirit', the 'spirit of wickedness' [perhaps Eph. 6.12]. This is the atheists' opinion and their trinity. On this subject, listen to what the apostle said: writing to the Thessalonians: 'For the mystery of lawlessness is already at work; whom the Lord will slay with the breath of His mouth and destroy him by His appearing and His coming [2 Thess. 2.3–4].[34] So do not be surprised if when they pray, they say the Our Father which art in heaven. They have not learnt how to chant or pray the Thrice Holy, or the Glory be to the Father and to the Son, or Lord have mercy, or anything else besides the Our Father alone.[35] The corrupt advance as justification indeed quoting from the gospel that Christ commanded the use of no psalm or prayer except the Our Father . . . The atheists refer their prayer to the devil in two ways. They say the Our Father which art *in* heaven, as though they were summoning him *from* heaven; in one way, then, as it is written in Job about him, 'Now there was a day when the sons of God came to present themselves before the Lord, and the devil also came among them. The Lord said to the devil, "Whence have you come?" The devil answered the Lord, "from going up and down what is under heaven, and from walking up and down upon the earth"' [Job 1.6, 7].

Elsewhere those who are stuffed full of every sort of blasphemy dare to call all God's creation, heaven and earth and all that they contain, the devil's, and say that the devil is the creator of all this, not God. Indeed, they say that he made Paradise as well, and modelled man. They say that there are only two things in the visible universe which belong to

33 C adds: 'Concerning the son of destruction, whom the godless atheists honour instead of the Son of God, and call Christ, the apostle . . . says (2 Thess. 2.3–4).'
34 St Paul taught that the forces of antichrist had been secretly at work from the beginning of the Christian dispensation, but that finally antichrist would be openly manifested and would rule on earth as the prelude to the second coming of Christ.
35 The exclusive use in ritual of the Our Father is also alleged against Cathars. Of the other prayers in this sentence the Thrice Holy (Holy, holy, holy . . .) is first recorded in use at the Council of Chalcedon (451), and forms part of the eucharistic liturgy of the Orthodox Church. 'Glory be to the Father . . .' is said at the end of each psalm in the divine office. 'Lord have mercy' is a common response made by the people to the litanies which form an important part of Orthodox worship.

CHRISTIAN DUALIST HERESIES

God's creation, the sun and the human soul.[36] Why these ? They say that once upon a time God became angry with the *archon* and expelled him, so that he should no longer be before his face.[37] When he was expelled from the face of God, he stole these two things from God, the sun and the human soul. There are eight heavens; seven which God made, and He has taken His seat above them. The eighth, they say, is the lowest of all, the one we see, and the ruler of this world, the devil, made it, and takes his ease above it.[38] He is the object of the atheists' prayer, Their (not Our) Father, as they invoke the devil from heaven ... The crafty atheists say as well that the ruler [*archon*], when he was chased out by God, departed from heaven and made this visible heaven, and fixed the stars and the sun (which he had stolen from God), and the moon. When he had made the earth and the sea and all that is in them, he planted paradise as well. When all this had happened, he formed Adam, and came to inserting into Adam (when he had formed him) the soul which he had stolen from God. He inserted it starting from the mouth, and it went out through the anus. Again he inserted it, starting from the anus, and it went out through the mouth. Although he did this many times, the soul went out, refusing to accept habitation in what he had formed, and went out now by the mouth, now by the anus. Since he could not force it into the body so that Adam might have life, he abandoned it, and it lay lifeless for 300 years.

After this the *archon* made a plan. He ate all sorts of unclean animals, like snakes and scorpions and dogs and cats and frogs and weasels,[39] and everything similar. When the god of the Phundagiagitae, that is, the foul demon, had eaten of all the foul and unclean beasts as they strengthened and taught him, then he came to the form of Adam which he had shaped and cast the soul into by way of the mouth, and put his hand under the anus and prevented it doing what it used to do, and coming out. Having done this and shut in what he had made, he expelled into Adam those things which he, the foul one, had eaten, on top of the soul, and the soul was contaminated and remained in the body, and Adam came to

36 For the devil as the creator of the visible universe see PH **[8]** and EZ **[25]**, c. 7. The exception for the human soul is implicit in the Bogomil creation account as given by EZ, but there is no mention there of the sun.
37 Cf. Luke 10.8; 'I saw Satan like lightning fall from heaven.'
38 For a detailed account of the fall of Satan as part of Bogomil cosmology see EZ **[25]**, c. 7. The heavenly Father created the spheres of the seven planets and is seated in the Empyrean – the fiery sphere which surrounds them. The creator of the world rules the sublunary sphere of change and decay. For another version of the legend of the creation of Adam, see EZ **[25]**, c. 7.
39 A adds: 'and foxes and wolves and jackals'.

life.[40] That is why, when a man is angry, he rages like a snake or a dog;[41] they say that because of this contamination the soul has something in common with all kinds of beast. I forgot to ask them, my brethren, whether a man is angered like a weasel or a frog. Do you ask them who know that; I mean the Batani,[42] Zurillas, Racheas[43] and the earlier leaders of the sect and those who surround them. For, as you well know, there are not a few of them there . . .

Those who taught us . . . this impiety were close kinsmen and fellow initiates of the Batani, Zurillas, and Racheas, and, as they themselves said, they wanted to winter near them.[44] As I said, they knew these mysteries clearly. So . . . [they] say to their disciples, 'It has been given to us to know the mysteries of God as they are written in the gospel, and not to others, except in parables.'[45] They name the holy gospels and the epistles of St Paul to those who are not yet completely their followers, and cite their sayings to them. After they have completely led them astray and read over them the demoniac spell,[46] then they teach them to despise and think false what they previously held out to them, that is, all holy scripture, old and new, the holy gospel itself and whatever else any prophet or apostle or teacher revealed . . .[47] As we have said, the corrupt teach also that we should not await the resurrection of the dead or the second coming or the judgement of God, but that all power over what is on earth, either punishment or paradise, is in the power of the *archon* of this world, that is the devil; that he sends his friends to paradise and his enemies to punishment, and that he has nothing in common with God, that God rules all that is above the heavens and the devil rules what is on earth . . . I know, you enemies of God, the devil's picked troops, that you do not read the Old Testament. You pretend to breathe

---

40 Since Bogomils rejected the account of the creation of Adam in Genesis, they produced this version to explain why man, though part of the material creation, had spiritual capacity.
41 A adds: 'or a cat'.
42 Perhaps related to the Arab word 'Batini', used of Ismaili Shi'ites who accepted an esoteric interpretation of the Koran (*taiwal-Batin*; Lewis, *The Assassins*, p. 28).
43 For Tzurillas see below, pp. 159–60; the name appears Slav. For Slavs in Asia Minor see Charanis, 'The Slavic elements in Byzantine Asia Minor' and Lemerle, 'Invasions et migrations dans les Balkans, pp. 306–7. Racheas is not otherwise known.
44 This suggests that these Bogomils, like some Paulicians (PS c. 125) were transhumant herdsmen, but see Angold, *Church and society in Byzantium*, p. 476 for a different translation and interpretation.
45 This claim to possess the true apostolic teaching is based on Mark 4.11.
46 A adds: 'they rub them down with befouled water'.
47 For other evidence about the Bogomil canon of scripture see EZ [25], c. 1; for the Paulician canon see PS [7], c. 42.

CHRISTIAN DUALIST HERESIES

out the epistles of St Paul and the sayings of the holy gospel; these not in faith, but only in appearance.... In the beginning they do not reveal the nonsensical and blasphemous sayings of their doctrine, but pretend to piety and upright teaching. If they realize that there is someone with knowledge, they argue with him dogmatically, since they have dogma in their mouths, and in accordance with what they think is the knowledge of each, they come down to their level...[48]

Let me speak to you also about their foul apostles, whom these godless people honour, especially Peter and Paul, whose names they always craftily bring forward, because they are trying to conceal them craftily through their having the same names as the chief of the apostles. Let us speak of... those who are the apostles of the foul devil, whom the godless Phundagiagitae honour and venerate... They accept as [their] first and great apostle Simon Magus – I know that you all know the life of the Magus from the works of Clement[49] – and next to him Montanus[50] and Peter, whose namesake is Peter the Worthless whom we have mentioned before and will speak of again, revealing his tricky life, Paul of Samosata, the teacher of the Paulicians from whom the Paulicians take their name, as if from Paul himself, Tychicus and Scythianus, and Terebinthus, also known as Boundas, and Courbicus, also known as Manes, the teacher of the Manichees, Phoundas, Hermas, the disciples of Manes and all the other heresiarchs, like Arius and Sabellius,[51] these the godless Phundagiagitae[52] honour and call apostles and saints. All those who are truly saints, the apostles and teachers and holy men and martyrs, whom we Christians venerate and honour, they loathe and

48 A adds: 'and from there unveil their argument by degrees'.
49 Simon Magus was first found in Acts 8.9–24. Many legends were later associated with him, the earliest in the works of Hippolytus (*Refutatio omnium haeresium* 6.20.2, 3). The story of his fatal flight is in Cyril of Jerusalem's *Catechesis* 6.15, and in the pseudo-Clementine 'Apostolic Constitutions'. Many other legends about him are collected in the pseudo-Clementine Homilies and Recognitions ('Clement' here), which survive in a Latin translation of the early fifth century (available in translation in *The Ante-Nicene Christian Library*, vol. 17, ed. A. Roberts and J. Donaldson).
50 A heretic of the second century who held apocalyptic views, emphasizing the continuing work of the Holy Spirit, inspiring prophecy in both sexes.
51 A adds: 'Boundas... Dascoes and Sabbas, Hermas and Simeon... Macedonius, Apollinaris, Origen, Nestorius, Eutyches, Dioscorus, Severus, Jacobus, Theodosius, Zeno, Cyrus, Maearius, Sergius, Novatus, the other Sergius, the disciple of Peter the worthless, Nicolaus, from whom come foul heresies; to wit the Courcoudigetae, Montanists, Artotyritae, Quattuordecimans, Orthopeucatae, the Cateuchiatae, the Cathari, who are Anthegani, the Aeti, the Montanists, the Messalians, the Hellenes, the Copritae; the second Nicolaus, and all who are like them'.
52 A adds: 'That is, the Bogomils'.

dishonour. The atheists call all the saints false apostles and false prophets, especially the great lights and teachers of the orthodox ...[53]

[The story of Peter and the wolf][54]

I shall reveal in part the conduct ... of Peter the worthless ... this worthless man, although he was a heretic, was not identified by the orthodox through his feigned humility and falsity, and also because his madness and heresy was concealed. So in ignorance they elected him archbishop and unworthily he who was wolf, rather than shepherd, ascended the apostolic throne. At the end the impious one did not escape, but his madness was recognized in synod. When the emperor[55] heard of his impiety, he was very angry with him, and sent messengers to arrest him. The worthless wretch, hearing of the emperor's anger and that he was on the razor's edge, fled at speed to a wizard, the devil's craftsman, his dear kinsman and relative, and told him of the emperor's anger against him and the danger that hung over him, and asked for the assistance that he could give. Then the wizard, hearing this, said to the worthless wretch, 'Do not be downcast, master, since you have me as a friend. Only tell me where you want to escape to, and I will swiftly convey you there.' The wretch answered, 'In the Roman Empire there is no place for me; I would like to go to Great Armenia since I have a good knowledge of the Armenian language ...'.

[The wizard] filled a dish with water and performed over it his magic and diabolic spells and workings, and then he summoned [Peter] the worthless, and gave him a glass bottle full of satanic perfume ... and also a spell, a satanic one written on paper, and said to him, 'Take all these things I give you, for they are essential. Early tomorrow you will find yourself in Great Armenia. When day comes, bid the men who are your servants go forth and proclaim to all the inhabitants of great Armenia as follows: "A great apostle and teacher has come to live in your country. All of you come to see him and venerate him." When the people come to venerate you, anoint the palm of your right hand with

---

53 A adds: 'St Basil the Great, Gregory the Theologian, St John Chrysostom'.
54 The legend of Peter Lycopetrus (Wolf–Peter) is alluded to elsewhere (see [16]). This is the most complete version. Its purpose is perhaps to make a link between Paulicians and Bogomils. Sergius/Tychicus is one of the sequence of Paulician leaders, but PS ([7], c. 138–44) gives an alternative account of his initiation into Paulicianism. The legend of a heretic's false claim to resurrection is told of Simon Magus in Hippolytus, *Refutatio omnium haeresium* 6.20.2–3; see also note 49 above.
55 A adds: 'Marcian and the Empress Pulcheria'. The emperor Marcian was remembered as a pillar of orthodoxy, perhaps because the council of Chalcedon (451) was held in his reign.

the perfume which I put into the bottle I give you, on both sides. Make those who intend to come to venerate you first kiss the back of your hand, on which the perfume has been smeared, and after they have kissed it, put your anointed hand above their heads, and recite over each of them this spell of yours, which I wrote for you and gave you, as if you were praying for them and blessing them. After this has been done, the devil will make his home in them, because the Holy Spirit will loathe the pollution and will withdraw from them the effective grace of baptism; in future you will have them all following your doctrine straightaway, and your will.'

The wizard . . . bade him and the servants go immediately to the jar which had been bewitched. Acting on this, the worthless wretch was snatched by the demons, together with his servants, and was found at first light transported to Great Armenia. When these things had happened and he had done as the wizard instructed, the wretch wandered preaching through all the land of Armenia, and preached as we described earlier. Many were gathered to him. He led astray and destroyed all the Armenians, not just the laymen, but even their king himself. [The king of the Armenians] wrote to the king of the Iberians[56] in these words: 'I want you to know, my lord and dear brother, that a great leader and apostle has come to live this day in my land. His arrival has greatly enlightened and aided me; if your majesty gives the order, I will send you this man, and you will be greatly benefited by him . . .'.

The Iberian king received him, and summoned the most knowledgeable of his bishops. When they had examined all that concerned him closely and carefully, they did not find him a light and a holy man, as the king of Armenia had revealed, but a devil, a heretic led astray, and a deceiver. Immediately afterwards the heretic was stoned by order of the king of the Iberians, to such an extent that there was a large heap over him of the stones that had been thrown.

When he learnt of this the king of the Armenians . . . wanted to take vengeance for his teacher's blood, and marched against the king of the Iberians, to make war on him. When he heard of this, the king of the Iberians sent to him, saying, 'My brother, you are angry with me for nothing, because he was a wretched and heretical man, and a deceiver. We Christians believe . . . that he who dies for the true orthodox faith is

---

56 Unlike the Armenians, who did not recognize the council of Chalcedon, and were therefore considered Monophysite by the Byzantine Church, the kingdom of Iberia (modern Georgia) remained strictly Orthodox. 'Great Armenia' was historically centred on Theodosiopolis (see map).

a saint, and that his remains work miracles and have a sweet smell. Come in peace, so that we may excavate and discover the remains of this man. If we find that they are as has been said, we will honour them in unison, and we shall believe that his doctrine is true, and we shall punish the bishops who attacked him as slanderers; but if the opposite is discovered, why are you angry with us for nothing?'

So the plan of the Iberian king pleased the [king of] Armenia. [Both] set out and dug up the heap of stones which was lying on top of the heretic ... They found his foul body unexpectedly transformed into the shape of a wolf. Finally, when the stones were taken off him, the wretch leaped up like a wolf, as they all watched, and ran off as a fugitive into the mountains. When the Armenians saw this, they returned with great shame, repenting of their errors. Notwithstanding, the disciple of the wicked wretch, Sergius[57] [the heretic, did not let them][58] repent completely. [For the future] this heretic was not called [Peter] the worthless, but Lycopetrus. This is the Peter, the apostle of the Phundagiagitae, and the satanic spell which the wizard gave to Lycopetrus is the one which they claim contains the revelation of St Peter the apostle.[59] If the heretics get in first, reading this to a man, the devil makes his house in him, and brings him to complete destruction. From then onwards, no arguments about knowledge of God enter his soul ...

They have Paul of Samosata, of whom we have spoken earlier, and Thomas, the disciple of Mani ...[60]

Reflecting on these things ... I found a book which the blessed St John of Damascus had carefully written, identifying all the heresies, so that men should not go astray in ignorance.[61] I went through the whole of the aforesaid book to try to discover what sort of evil heresy and blasphemy this was, and what it was called, since the people of the Opsikion [theme][62] call those who are members of this most evil blasphemy Phundagiagitae, but towards the Kibbyrrhaiot [theme][63] and towards the west and in other places they call them Bogomils ... For this reason

57 Sergius/Tychicus: see above, pp. 19–21.
58 These words are supplied from A for the sake of clarity.
59 See above, note 17.
60 See Cyril of Jerusalem, *Catechesis* 6.31.
61 St John of Damascus (*c.* 675–*c.* 749) was a theologian whose *On the Christian faith* provided a summary of Christian heresies which became the standard textbook on the subject.
62 See map.
63 See map.

I read all the names of heresies till I could discover what sort of evil heresy this is, and what it is called. I could not find out.

All the heresies have heresiarchs; one has Peter the worthless, who is also called Lycopetrus, another has Paul of Samosata, another Montanus, another Manes . . . But this evil, which surpasses all in blasphemy and lack of faith in God, was not found to have its origin in a man, but, as I believe, in the devil himself, the prompter of all heresy.[64] . . . [The Paulicians] say that they have St Paul as their teacher, as these people do, and have the gospels on their lips, and the epistles of St Paul, as they do. Their teaching is very like that of these blasphemers, but their heresy is obvious and cannot harm anyone except those who hold it as inherited tradition; no one is grieved or upset on their account.[65]

But as for these secret wolves, [they] play-act the monastic and priestly way of life; they travel round all the Roman Empire, and wherever the sun sees Christians, they lead souls astray and deceive them, to snatch them from the hands of God and give them into the hands of their father, the devil. Attend, my brothers, to what I want to tell you. These incarnate demons, these rational wolves, show such zeal for the devil's work that they share out all the regions of Romania[66] and cast lots over them as did the holy apostles of Christ our God,[67] and these heretics call themselves apostles, not of Christ, our God, but of antichrist, their father, the devil. They withstand blows and fear and oppression and imprisonment and often dangers, too; they despise even death to accomplish the devil's work, to damage the flock of Christ and to destroy their souls . . . About them the apostle Paul wrote in his first epistle to Timothy [1 Tim. 4.1–5][68]

My brethren, do you not recognize that these words apply to the blasphemers we have here? Are they not those who forbid marriage? Are

---

64 Euthymius evidently knew nothing of the account of Bogomilism written some eighty years earlier by Cosmas, presumably because this was written in Old Slavonic.
65 If true, this would mean that by the time of writing (mid-eleventh century) Paulicians were a recognized sect who did not attempt to proselytize.
66 'Romania' refers to the Byzantine Empire.
67 An apocryphal tradition recorded that the Apostles fulfilled Christ's command to preach the word to all the world literally, by dividing the world among them by throwing lots.
68 Euthymius was living at the end of the first Christian millennium. There was some expectation that this represented the sixth age of the world, which would end in the final Sabbath and the second coming of Christ. The Pauline texts appeared to link heretics who had similar views to those of the Bogomils to the last days before the second coming.

they not those who teach abstention from worldly foods? Are not they those who in pretence falsely quote holy scripture? Are not they those who apostatize from the faith and go to error and the teaching of demons? If you want to learn precisely that they are liars and that they quote holy scriptures in pretence, listen closely. They teach that whoever does not put away his wife will not be saved, as you yourselves know well that they teach and practise this . . . I will give you an account of what I saw with my own eyes. I know that most of you are well aware of it. You know well John Tzurillas; I cannot call him Papa, as you are in the habit of doing,[69] or abbot, for he is not one, but an initiate and apostle of the devil. You all know that he left his wife, making her a mock abbess when he himself became a mock abbot.[70] . . . not only he, but many of his disciples acted in this way. Now hear something else about him, which I know you are well aware of. In the reign of Basil and Constantine Porphyrogenitus[71] there was a *krites* in the theme near[72] us, the Opsikion, the late Romanus Argyropolus, who became emperor.[73] I remember that he came to my diocese, Acmonia, and I came too, with my mother who had a lawsuit against someone else. The officials had provided a temporary building near the *archistrategos*, whose name was Strouthopolites. The lawcourt was there. They brought this blasphemer Tzurillas, whom you recognize because he is the leader of their newly assembled cult of blasphemy, and [said] that he had spent three whole years on the preaching of the devil and had persuaded entire towns in the parts of the Thracians and in the district [*topothesia*] of Smyrna[74] and in many other places, to deny Christ and worship the devil. That famous countryside in which he had his dwelling, which is populous and well-inhabited and large, where in my memory all who lived were orthodox Christians, people whom you saw recently, he had made in a short time agree to worship and adore the devil and deny the orthodox Christian faith. As I think, there are a thousand hearths in the place, and as I carefully found out from you, no more than ten Christians are left. They

---

69 The Bulgarian founder of the sect was called *pop* Bogomil, according to Cosmas (p. 116), and in the twelfth century a Bogomil *papa* named Nicetas from Constantinople visited western Europe; see **[37]**.
70 In the Orthodox Church a marriage might be ended if both parties took monastic vows. Since Bogomils rejected marriage, married converts might be true to their new faith without appearing to be heretics if both took monastic vows.
71 Basil II emperor 976–1025; Constantine VIII, his brother, co-emperor 976–1025, sole emperor 1025–28.
72 *hypo*; the literal meaning is 'under'.
73 Romanus III Argyrus, 1028–34. There is no other evidence that he was governor of the Opsikion theme.
74 See map.

have been distressed and upset by the insults and mockery of the blasphemers, so that they themselves have almost been persuaded to destruction. You all saw this blasphemer, who caused all this upset and is still active,[75] you observe and know well that this is true, and that this is what he teaches, that whoever does not put away his wife is not saved. He did so, and so did many others. Listen carefully, that you may realize that they do not teach this from purity and chastity, but to overturn the law of God. They brought the blasphemer in chains before the judge. What was the charge? That he had raped a girl in an uninhabited mill which was at a distance from the place. The young girl brought the charge, she who had been ruined by the blasphemer, weeping bitterly. Not only the girl, but her father, weeping bitterly, accused him. There was present Obarnakoumenon,[76] a noble eunuch, who grasped the blasphemer's *pallium* with his hand and said mockingly, 'It's a seemly thing, holy father, that we put on these holy things to make a show and parade of them before such a crowd of lay people.' The lord Constantine, the archdeacon and *oikonomos* of the diocese of Acmonia, whose surname was Galenus, answered,[77] 'It is not as you suppose, my lord; he did not put on these dark representations, the black *pallium* and the wide *apostolokis*[78] for the sake of Christ, but for that of antichrist, because he is the chief of the heretics.' When the bishop heard this from the archdeacon he was astonished, for he did not know the blasphemer; leaving him, he stood at a distance from him, and heaped many curses and reproaches on him, and so did many others who were there to witness that these charges were true and not false. This assures you that it is not from chastity that they teach men to leave their own wives and wives to leave their husbands. You should learn that the blasphemers have the words of the gospels and of the epistles of St Paul on their lips, but where does the gospel or the apostle say, 'Whoever does not divorce his wife is not saved'? ...[79]

The blasphemers teach about holy baptism, saying this: there is no holiness or grace in it. It is simply water and oil, and it is a good thing

75 Evidently no charge of heresy was brought against John Tzurillas, who appears still to be active at the time when Euthymius is writing.
76 Or 'the bishop of the Barnakoumenoi' (no bishop of this name is known).
77 An *oikonomos* was the financial officer of a bishop. The family of Galenus continued to have local importance; see Ahrweiler, 'L'Histoire et la géographie de la région de Smyrne', *T & M 1* (1965), p. 130; John Galenus, the *katepan* of Smyrna, is the addressee of a letter from John Tzetzes.
78 A *pallium* is the distinctive neckscarf worn by a bishop; *apostolokis* is the general term used to describe a bishop's complete robes.
79 The very long defence of marriage, based on scriptural quotations, has been omitted.

that those whom we teach should not be baptized at all; but if someone is baptized through fear of men, he will be neither harmed nor helped by it.[80] ... The blasphemers teach people not to accept that the venerable and life-giving cross should be revered, for it is not holy.[81] ... The atheists also blaspheme about the holy communion, saying that it is common bread and wine.[82] ... The blasphemers say no one is or should be called holy; only God is holy ...[83]. The atheists also reject the priesthood, saying, 'What is a priest [*lit.* "an elder"]'? ... All this the blasphemers do not dare to say or to teach openly to everybody, but reply ... that they believe all that we do, but in their own darkness the sons of darkness teach their own disciples not to believe the passages of holy scripture which have been mentioned earlie ...[84]

I tracked them down at such length so that I might understand their craft and madness, as from the freedom of speech they enjoyed with me they might make their foul prayer in my presence. Hear how their prayer is conducted. The leader of the blasphemers takes his stand and begins by saying, 'Let us adore the Father and Son and Holy Spirit.' Those who pray with him answer, 'It is right and fitting.' He begins the Our Father in the way we have already described, making a genuflection thus; they bob their heads up and down like those who are possessed. They do not pray facing east, but wherever they happen to be standing.[85] ...

I will tell you another crafty trick of the blasphemers; they are in the habit of joining in pretence in religious assemblies with the orthodox, to avoid detection. As they read the holy scriptures, whenever the scripture speaks against sinners or blasphemers, they say secretly to their own disciples, 'This is about them', that is the orthodox; but wherever it speaks of the just and holy they say 'This is ... about us.' ...

Earlier I promised to tell you about the prayer Our Father; listen. The blasphemers add to their own teaching the claim that Christ said: 'But when you pray, go into your room and shut the door, and pray to your Father, who is in secret, and your Father, who is in secret, will reward you openly' [Matt. 6.6]. He did not say, 'Into the church', but 'Into your

80 For the Paulician attitude to baptism see PH **[8]**, c. 16; for Bogomils see EZ **[25]**, c. 16.
81 For the Paulician view see PH **[8]**, c. 13.
82 See also EZ **[25]**, c. 17; for similar charges against Paulicians see PH **[8]**, c. 12.
83 The word 'holy' here is also translated 'saint'; for the selective rejection of saints by Bogomils see EZ **[25]** c. 11–12.
84 A selection of proof-texts justifying the orthodox position is omitted here.
85 See Appendix 1 for the text of the Radoslav ritual.

room', that is, your guest-room [*hospitis*]. In this the blasphemers attack the services of the Holy Church and say that the psalms are vain repetition, and that we ought to chant nothing else than the Our Father.[86] Why then do you continue, you blasphemers, teaching the gospel hypocritically, when you have elected the devil as *archon* and lord of all that is visible? Does not authority over the heavens and what is on earth belong to Christ our Lord, as is written in the holy gospels? [Matt. 28.18] ... Did not the Lord with his own hands impress his undefiled likeness on a pure cloth and send this to Abgar, the holy likeness which he also impressed on the holy tile?[87] Did not Luke the holy apostle and evangelist of Christ our God with his own hands draw the most holy mother of God, holding the child Christ, our true God, in her arms?[88] Are not these same holy icons, together with the holy letter that was sent to Abgar, preserved among us to this day in the God-guarded palace? We Christians all gaze on them and adore them with longing and deep faith, and kiss them ...

I exhort you to persuade the laity most continuously, especially those who have kinship and friendship with the blasphemers, and those orthodox who have blasphemers as neighbours. Let each of you exhort the other to what is good, so that you may not go astray. Those who have gone astray have fallen once, an extraordinary fall, and for them there is no rising again ... Even if one of them were to be willing to repent, he would be quite unable to, being held fast bound by the devil ...

During my absence the corrupt heretics who led my pupil astray would not have succeeded in doing all their habitual evil actions against him, they would not have recited the spell over him or bowed down to the devil visibly as they do, if their father had not been persuaded to help them in their teaching.[89] The mysteries which we have already described

---

86 See Matt. 6.7–9.
87 The Mandylion of Edessa – a piece of cloth on which a portrait of Christ had been miraculously impressed) was brought to Constantinople by John Courcouas in 944. Its cult was associated with that of the Keramidion – the tile to which the portrait had also miraculously been transferred. This was brought to Constantinople from Edessa or Hierapolis in the later tenth century. Some accounts attribute the transfer to Nicephorus Phocas in 966, some to John Tzimisces in 974. Both Mandylion and Keramidion were a focus for the devotion of icon-supporters and the object of popular cult. See Cameron, 'The history of the image of Edessa' and Runciman, 'Some remarks on the image of Edessa'; see also Hugh Eteriano **[36]**.
88 For the belief that St Luke had painted a portrait of the Blessed Virgin Many and that one such portrait had been given by the empress Eudocia to the empress Pulcheria, see the account of Theodore Lector (*Ecc. Hist.*) in *PG* 86.1, 165a 9–12. Later several such portraits were believed to exist.
89 'Their father' here means the devil.

gave him encouragement, and an unclean spirit took up its dwelling in his heart. For four whole years he repented and wept and beat himself, and made petition of God night and day without ceasing and I prayed with him and beat myself with him. I could find no alleviation of the evil demon which was assaulting him, until wearily he came to the life-giving tomb of Christ, our God. There, like Peter, he wept bitterly, not once, but many times, and was able to get relief from the evil demon. This did not just happen to my pupil; the devil struggled hard with me as I slept. The evil one showed me an open book and angrily ordered me to read it, and as I read, I found the passage of the gospel which says: 'Whoever denies me before men, I also will deny before my Father, who is in heaven' [Matt. 10.33]. Again he said harshly to me, 'Did not God say this?' When I agreed that this was so, he said again: 'Why do you dare to reconcile to God one who has openly denied him?' With this the accursed one left, not merely angry, but wanting vengeance. But we have God to help us, and we will not be afraid of the threats of the evil one.

All this I have explained to reveal to you the impiety of the atheist Phundagiagiatae, so that you might know in what the error consists. Loathe and avoid them ... I tell you, as I have been informed by the blasphemer we arrested under interrogation, that where there is one of them, all the rest of the household share his opinions. Pretending to fast and be pious and pray, whether man or woman, he is a true initiate of the devil, a guide and teacher of the rest and all those who share the same household as he does think as he does in it ... When you have heard all this about the blasphemers, realize the magnitude of their error and impiety and destruction; hate and reject them totally, so that to our God may be glory for ever and ever. Amen.

APPENDIX

The heretic Sergius and his dog

[This story is found only in the A text.]

Let us say a little of the many things which concern Sergius the disciple of Lycopetrus the worthless.[1] This Sergius was taken instead of the worthless Peter in Armenia ...

---

1 Although this story is only found in the A text, the figure of Lycopetrus occurs elsewhere, see **[16]** and note 7. There does not seem to be any connection with Bogomils, although the figure of Lycopetrus is linked to that of Sergius/Tychicus. The whole episode may be intended to link two separate heretical movements; hence its inclusion.

But concerning the fast of Arzeberius which the Armenians keep, [Sergius] gave them this tradition.[2] This Sergius... being taken in Great Armenia as a teacher had a little dog, and called it Arzeberius. When he was going to some town or village, he practised his magic art and skill, and sent this same dog ahead of him. When it came to a town or village to which it had been sent, it entered the place and going to every door in that place, it barked, as if to announce the presence of their teacher Sergius. The deluded wretches took this as the usual sign, and assembled to greet him and honour him and welcome and make requests of him... and he taught them. One day it happened that the little dog was coming to a village to which Sergius had sent it in accordance with his habit, and it encountered a hare on the way and began to chase it. While the dog was chasing the hare, they met a wolf, which seized the little dog and devoured it. A farmer who was ploughing saw this. When Sergius came to the village and no one came to meet him from the people of that village, to which he had sent the dog, as was his habit, which they knew, he began to reproach them and blame them. But they answered, 'No one told us you were coming.' Sergius said, 'Where is Arzebourtzius [*sic*]?' They replied that he had not come there, and none of them had seen him. Hearing this, Sergius was greatly upset. A search was made for the little dog, and great commotion; as they made a great search and did not find him, disquiet and fear and grief overcame them all, until there arrived the aforementioned farmer who had been ploughing on the previous day, and he told them everything, and how Artzebourtzius had been eaten by the wolf.

20. THE PAULICIANS OF PHILIPPOPOLIS ALLY WITH THE PATZINAKS (*c.* 1050)

Some of the Paulicians survived the destruction of their citadel at Tefrice; for their later employment in the Byzantine army in S. Italy see **[17]**. Some remained in the group's original heartland in eastern Asia Minor and were moved to Philippopolis by the emperor John Tzimisces (for the circumstances see **[14]** and Introduction, p. 23). The emperor's intention had been that they should help to defend the northern frontier from attacks from beyond the Danube, but they proved unreliable, as this passage shows. Their value as fighting men and their continued unreliability can be seen in **[22]**.

2 The story of Sergius and the dog is an attempt to provide an insulting explanation of the Armenian fast of Arzeberius (also called the fast of Nineveh), kept for three days in the week preceding Lent.

John Scylitzes, the author of this account, wrote in the second half of the eleventh century a *Synopsis historiarum* covering the period 811–1057, aiming to continue the work of Theophanes (for whom see the introduction to **[1(a)]**). The text used for the translation is John Scylitzes, *Synopsis historiarum*, ed. Thurn, 1973, p. 741.

A certain Lacas, one of the Paulicians of Philippopolis,[1] set out from Epigambria and deserted to the Patzinaks,[2] and plotting with them, seriously threatened the Roman state. Moreover, a certain Dobromir made trouble in Mesembria.[3] These men intended to rebel against the emperor, but being fearful and having learnt prudence by the misfortunes of others, before the attempt they bowed their necks to the servile yoke and approached him as suppliants of their own volition.

21. A LETTER OF THE PATRIARCH COSMAS (1075–81) AGAINST THE BOGOMILS

This letter was written by a Patriarch named Cosmas, who was almost certainly Cosmas of Jerusalem (1075–81). Cosmas II Atticus (1146–7) spent most of his brief reign defending himself against almost certainly false charges of complacency towards Bogomils (see **[32]**). It was written to the metropolitan of Larissa in Thessaly, but this may be a surviving copy of a more widely distributed encyclical. As Gouillard has shown, it forms the basis for the *Synodikon* of Tsar Boril of 1211, and the twelve anathemas from this letter have been printed there **[41]**.

The translation has been made from the edition of Gouillard, 'Une Source grecque du synodik de Boril', *T & M* 4 (1970), pp. 361–74.

LETTER OF COSMAS, OUR MOST HOLY LORD AND ECUMENICAL PATRIARCH, TO THE METROPOLITAN OF LARISSA, MOST BELOVED OF GOD, CONCERNING THE ATHEIST HERETICS

... The darkness of Manichaeanism, which long ago was deservedly destroyed and brought to nothing by the holy fathers, but now, as our

---

1 See map.
2 Otherwise spelt Petchenegs, they were a nomadic Turkic tribe, based to the north of the Danube, who from the mid-eleventh century made raids on Byzantine territory.
3 A Byzantine town on the Black Sea coast; see map.

Mediocrity has learnt, has secretly entered almost all the country of the Bulgars, indeed, the greater part of what is called the western area,[1] has become widespread, and has brought it to the pit of perdition. Our Mediocrity has taken thought about this, together with the holy and divine synod, and has devised and found no other cure for evil of this kind than this; that on every Sunday and feast day all the holy Catholic churches in your jurisdiction should proclaim an anathema of the corrupt doctrines and actions of the heresy aforesaid, so that the unlearned people, knowing that their false doctors are rejected by the Orthodox Church, may reject those who led them astray, may recognize what is true and upright, and may take refuge in the Orthodox community.

Those who are about to be subject to anathema are these, and they should be anathematized in the following way: [here follow twelve anathemas reproduced in the *Synodikon* of Tsar Boril, see **[41]** below].

Let all who are like this be anathemetized in this way. Do not yourselves be slack in your treatment of this matter, and do not let your subordinates, the priests and bishops of your jurisdiction, take it lightly. Know that whoever is careless concerning such most salutary correction of the brethren, or has regard to appearance, or allows himself to be corrupted by bribes, incurs God's curse and ours. Farewell.

22. ALEXIUS COMNENUS (1081–1118) AND THE PAULICIANS

Anna Comnena, the eldest child of Alexius Comnenus, who lived from 1083–*c.* 1153, wrote a history of the life and times of her father in laudatory terms. Her propaganda purpose sometimes distorts the chronology of her account; for the best known example of this see the introduction to **[24]**, below, but in these passages the problem does not arise.

Although their religious views were heterodox, Paulicians were employed as mercenaries in the Byzantine army at all periods.[1] Similar use was made of the Patzinaks (who were pagan). These three passages supply evidence that they were not always reliable allies, and that the emperor tried to make them adhere to the Byzantine value system by forced conversion, in an attempt to make them

---

1 For Bogomilism in 'western' areas, cf. EP **[19]**.
1 See **[17]**; Zonaras (Bk.18.23, p. 242) gives an alternative version: 'He dismissed the Manichaean unit from the army, which until then had been serving illegally. Ancient law totally forbids Manichaeans to serve in the army.'

ALEXIUS COMNENUS AND THE PAULICIANS

throw in their lot with the empire. That this attempt might backfire can be seen from the second passage.

The text has been translated from the Budé text, edited by B. Leib.

(a) 5.3.2. [The Paulicians of Philippolis were summoned to join the Byzantine army in its campaign against the invading Norman army under Robert Guiscard, in 1081/2. After the initial defeat of the Byzantine army, the Paulicians went home.]

The Manichaeans Xantas and Couleon, with the 2,000 men under them, returned home without being ordered to. Although the emperor summoned them frequently, and they promised to come, they put off their arrival. He insisted, and in his letters promised them gifts and honours, but still they did not come.

(b) 6.2.1–3. [In 1083, having defeated the Normans, Alexius determined to punish them. The interest of the passage lies chiefly in the evidence it gives that leading Paulicians might be employed in the capital in senior positions, despite their religious views.]

Until then [the Paulicians] had been peaceful, living in their own country, and had not yet turned to any acts of brigandage or raids. So on his way back to Byzantium he summoned them by letter with many promises. As they had heard of his victories over the Celts[2] ... however reluctantly, they set out to join him. When he reached Mosynopolis,[3] he stayed in the neighbourhood ... awaiting their arrival. As they arrived, he pretended that he intended to review them and to write down the names of each. Then, stern of face, he took his seat and ordered the leaders of the Manichaeans to march past in an orderly fashion, ten at a time, promising that there would be a general review on the following day, and that then, when their names had been written down, they might go through the gates. Men were stationed with the duty of seizing their horses and arms, putting them into fetters and shutting them in the prisons which had been assigned.

They advanced in order, in total ignorance of what was happening, and so entered without suspecting what was going to happen to each of them. So then he had control of them. He confiscated their property and distributed it among his noble soldiers who had fought with him in the battles and dangers they had endured. The person in charge of this task chased their wives from their houses and held them under guard in the

---
2 i.e. the Normans. The use of the archaic term, like that of Byzantium for Constantinople in the previous line, is a feature of Anna's consciously archaizing style.
3 See map.

citadel. Shortly afterwards the emperor took pity on the Manichaean prisoners. All those who chose to avail themselves of holy baptism were not refused. He investigated them thoroughly, and when he had discovered those who were responsible for folly of this kind, he banished them to imprisonment on islands. The others he dismissed, giving them safe conduct to go wherever they pleased. They immediately returned to their native country, preferring it to all others, to arrange their affairs as best they might.

Passages (c) and (d) describe a later attempt by Alexius to convert the Paulican leaders during his northern campaigns of 1114. These were directed against the Cumans, another nomadic people who threatened the northern frontiers of the empire. The emperor appears to have believed that conversion to Orthodoxy would make the Paulicians more committed to the Byzantine cause.

(c) 6.4.2. [The punishment of the Paulician leaders did not have the desired effect.]

At the time when the autocrator was elevated by Nicephorus Botanaiates to the rank of Domestic,[4] he took a certain Traulus, a Manichaean, and included him among his familiar servants. Having obtained for him holy baptism, he arranged that he should marry one of the waiting-maids of the Basilissa. Now this man had four sisters. One day he saw them being led off to prison like the others, stripped of all their possessions. He was moved to anger and could not bear it, but looked around to see how he might be freed from the autocrator's power . . . All those who were his kinsmen joined him and betook themselves to Belyatovo.[5] This is a small fortress situated on a ridge which dominates the valley below it. Finding it uninhabited, they considered it their personal property and made their dwelling there. Then they made daily sorties from there, and getting as far as the city of Philippopolis, they returned with much booty.

Not content with this, Traulus made a treaty with the Scythians who live in the Paristrion,[6] winning over by intrigue the chieftains round Glabinitza and Dristra[7] and the adjacent areas, and betrothing himself to the daughter of one of the Scythian nobles. He tried with all his might to harm the autocrator by means of a Scythian attack. When the em-

---

4 c. 1079.
5 Exact position unknown, but somewhere in the valley of the Marica (for which see map).
6 The Scythians here are probably the Patzinaks.
7 The Paristrion is the district immediately south of the Danube. See map.

peror got news of this every day and realized what might happen . . . he composed a chrysobull of immunity and total liberty, and sent this to him. A crab never learns to walk straight. Traulus was the same as yesterday and the day before; he continued making overtures to the Scythians and sending for many more from his own country and raiding all the area round about.

(d) 14.8.3. [Philippopolis] consists of three hills, each surrounded by a strong and lofty wall. As the wall descends towards level ground, there is a moat which runs near the Eurus. . . . There were several ways in which [the city] was unfortunate, but especially in the presence there of many impious people. For the Armenians had taken possession of this city, together with those called Bogomils, about whom and about their heresy I shall speak when it is appropriate,[8] as well as the most impious Paulicians.

[. . .]

5. John Tzimisces, that admirable emperor,[9] defeated [them] and took them as slaves from Asia. From there he transferred them from the lands of the Chalybi and the Armeniakon to Thrace. He obliged them to live in the area round Philippopolis. Thus at one and the same time he withdrew them from the strongly fortified cities and forts which they had held like tyrants, while establishing them as a secure garrison against Scythian incursions, which the areas round Thrace had frequently suffered.

[. . .]

7. So John Tzimisces made his Manichaean opponents our allies, and established them as a force under arms capable of fighting these Scythian nomads. Then the cities drew breath, relieved from the frequent attacks. But the Manichaeans, who are independent by nature and unwilling to accept orders, acted in character and reverted to their nature. The whole population of Philippopolis with very few exceptions were Manichaeans, who tyrannized over the Christians there and pillaged what they had, taking little or no notice of the envoys sent by the emperors. They increased, and all in the area round Philippopolis were heretics. Into this flowed another foul stream, that of the Armenians, and another from the stinking spring of the Jacobites.[10]

8 See [24].
9 For John Tzimisces and the transfer of Paulicians see [14].
10 For the spread of the Armenians westwards in the tenth century, see Dédéyan, 'L'Immigration arménienne'. The Jacobites were the followers of Jacob Baradaeus (500–78), the Monophysite patriarch of Antioch. For confusion between them and Paulicians see [17].

[...]

9. When Alexius came to Philippopolis . . . because the Cumans had not arrived he embarked on a greater task . . . that of converting the Manichaeans . . . From dawn to afternoon or even evening, sometimes till the second or third watch of the night, he sent for them and taught them the orthodox faith, disproving the errors of their heresy. There was with him Eustathius of Nicaea,[11] a man learned in religious and secular knowledge . . . and also the bishop who occupied the see of Philippopolis. In addition to all these, and superior to them all, the emperor made use of my Caesar, Nicephorus,[12] whom he had trained in the study of the sacred books. So, then, many of the Manichaeans approached the priests immediately, confessed their sins and received holy baptism. But it was possible to see many . . . men who cited examples and evidence from holy scripture, thinking that in this way they would confirm their detestable doctrine. Still by continuous contact with the emperor and his constant exhortations the majority of them were convinced and shared holy baptism. [Alexius then marched against the Cumans, who withdrew without fighting, and he returned to Philippopolis.]

[...]

14.9.3. He sent for Couleon[13] and Cousinus and in addition to them, Pholus, leaders of the Manichaean heresy, who for the most part shared the views of the other Manichaeans, but were especially obstinate in their heretical opinions and adamant in their resistance to argument, extremely ingenious in tearing the word of God to shreds and frivolously pushing it to extremes. Every day he engaged in a war of argument with them . . . [But] as he had totally failed to convince them, at last he flagged in the face of their folly. He sent them on to the imperial city and assigned them as lodging the porticoes which surround the Great Palace. His hunt was not entirely fruitless, for every day there were added to God here a hundred, there more than a hundred, so that the total of those that were now and had previously been persuaded by his tongue was a huge one, thousands or tens of thousands.

4. . . . In different ways he converted to our orthodox faith entire cities

11 Eustathius was himself condemned in 1117 for holding heretical views on the relationship between the divine and human natures of Christ, though he was later reinstated.
12 Nicephorus Bryennius (1062–1136), the husband of Anna Comnena.
13 See (a) for this man's earlier history.

and districts which had been contaminated by heresy of every kind. He gave great gifts to those of the first rank among them and enrolled them in the elite of his army; he assembled the common people and those of them who were peasants, who laboured with ploughs and oxen, together with their wives and children. He built a city for them near Philippopolis on the other bank of the river Eurus, and settled them there. This city was named Alexiopolis (or Neocastron, which became the dominant name). He distributed fields and vineyards among them, as well as houses and immovable goods. He did not leave these donations without confirmation . . . but ratified the gifts he had made with chrysobulls. He enacted that these gifts were not limited to the recipients only, but might be inherited by their children and grandchildren; if any one of them were to disappear, his wife should have a share of the property given . . .

5. . . . When the emperor had completed all that was necessary . . . he returned to the imperial city. Again the same arguments and discussions between the followers of Cousinus and Couleon and the emperor took place constantly. He won over Couleon, who was I think the more intelligent . . . and made him into the meekest sheep of our fold. As for Cousinus and Pholus, they continued to rage . . . For this reason he threw them into the prison known as Elephantine, because they were the most blasphemous of the Manichaeans, and drove men to obvious insanity. While making generous provision for all their necessities, he abandoned them to die in their evil ways.

23. EXTRACTS FROM EUTHYMIUS ZIGABENUS' *DOGMATIC PANOPLY* AGAINST THE PAULICIANS AND THE MESSALIANS

The circumstances in which Euthymius Zigabenus was commissioned to write his *Dogmatic Panoply* are described by Anna Comnena in her account of the trial of Basil the Bogomil, **[24]** below. He was concerned to collect materials which gave an account of earlier heresies from authoritative accounts, and is careful to give his references. The greater part of his description of the beliefs and history of the Paulicians is derived from the account of Photius, itself a rewriting of the account of Peter of Sicily, for which see the introduction to **[7]**. There is a relatively small amount of information which is not accounted for in this way, some of which appears to be based on a Paulician explanation of biblical texts. It is possible that this may be derived from the lost three sermons of Peter of Sicily (for which also see the introduction to **[7]**), but this is speculative. Extracts from his account of the Messalians are also included because the name was frequently applied in the eleventh and twelfth century material to Bogomils, to give some idea of how the term Messalian was understood at the time.

AGAINST THE PAULICIANS

(a) *PG* 130, 1200A1–14. [The Paulicians] say that the evil one has been begotten from fire and darkness; so we should ask them, 'Why was darkness not adequate for his creation, or fire? Who united these two elements for the origin of the creation of the evil power?'... If fire is perceptible, whose product is it? If it comes from the evil one, how can they say that he proceeds from fire and darkness? If from the good, how can they say that the Good made nothing perceptible? They could not say that what produces the evil one is intelligible, because they ascribe all intelligible things to the Good.

(b) 1200 B2–8. Some of them say that the Good God is the creator only of the heaven, and introduce some other maker of the earth and what lies between. Some of them (for the error takes many forms) have the audacity to say that the very heavens and all that lies between them and the earth are the creation of the evil one.

(c) 1207 B2–D8. 'He came to his own', it says, 'and his own did not accept him' [John 1.11] If the apostates say that by 'his own' are meant 'the words of the prophets', and that Christ came to them and they did not accept him – see their overweening folly and shamelessness. Firstly, how do they say that the words of prophecy are Christ's own, while saying that the prophets themselves are creations of the evil one, in so far as it is from him that they take their inspiration? Then, how did Christ come 'to the words of the prophets'? Firstly, by their own account, he came to strangers, and the words of the prophets are strangers because they are inspired by a stranger[1] and not by the Good God. Then, to whom did Christ give power to become the sons of God? To the words of the prophet? Surely this is long-winded nonsense. If the words come from God, it is from there that they have the power to become the property of God; if they come from the evil one, how could they become sons of God? Then, what sort of prophetic word has its origin 'from blood and the will of man' and 'from the will of the flesh'? For the passage continues: 'Those who were born not from blood, nor from the

---

1 The use of the term 'stranger' to describe the God of the Old Testament is commonly alleged in the patristic sources to be part of the belief system of the second-century heretic Marcion.

will of the flesh, but of God' [John 1.13]. What words are those which were 'born of blood' and what are those that are not? So, then, he calls 'his own' the world, as in another place he says to the disciples, 'Lo, the hour is coming, and indeed it has now come, when you will be scattered, every man to his own' [John 16.32]. What sort of 'own' does he mean here? Is he talking about the words of the prophets, or each disciple's own dwelling and property? So, then, here too, 'own' does not mean 'prophetic words', as the nonsense mentioned claims, but each man's house and property. So when you read, 'he came to his own, and his own did not receive him', 'own' means 'the perceptible world' – this is his property and creation.

(d) 1209 D1–11. As confirmation of their blasphemy that the evil one rules everything on earth, the heretics quote this. They are led astray by the fact that when he showed Christ all the kingdoms of the world, he said, 'I will give you all these, if you fall at my feet and worship me' [Matt 4.9]. In fact this argues against them, because the evil one rules none of them. He is a liar, the chief of lies, who never stands by the truth as our Lord taught, and so he proved that he was not the master of things of earth.

(e) 1215 D1–3; 1217 B6–11, B15–C11;1220 B10–C1. Why do you call Jerusalem 'which is above' the mother of God?[2] What holy scripture, or which of the saints taught you this folly? ... There are many other pieces of evidence that the most holy virgin Mary gave birth according to the flesh to Our Lord Jesus Christ, who is both God and Man, both in the gospels and in the writing of the apostle, the only books you accept, since you despise all others ... If they are driven into a corner by such texts and make up the absurd story that Christ brought His body down with Him from heaven, let us answer them like this: 'If Christ's body were heavenly, it would not be subject to human experiences – those that are innocent, I mean, like hunger and thirst and sleep and fatigue and grief and tears, and things like that. If he were a heavenly man to whom the Word was united in person, it would not have been mortal and corruptible like terrestrial bodies'. ... But they say, 'In the Gospels the Lord said: "No one has ascended into heaven but He who descended from heaven, the Son of man, who is in heaven" [John 3.13], and again the apostle says, "The first man was from the earth, a man of dust; the second man is from heaven" [1 Cor. 15.47]. See, both passages call him a heavenly man.'

2 See PH [8], c. 11.

(f) 1225 C5–12. If the evil one is the lawgiver of the old dispensation, how is it that the Source of truth says: 'Search the scriptures, because it is in them that you will find eternal life'? [John 5.30]. By scriptures, he means the books of Moses and the prophets, for the books of the New Testament did not then exist.

AGAINST THE MESSALIANS

(g)1273 B2–C3, D9–12; 1276 A5–8, B6–7, C13; 1277A 12–B11; 1288 C5–10; 1289 C1–5. The Messalian heresy originated in the time of Valens and Valentinian. The name, if translated into Greek, means 'those who pray'. They make much talk of prayer ... by this they mean either supplication, such as the Our Father, which the Lord gave to his apostles, or some other prayer which is known only to those more initiated into their impiety, but which is unknown to all the others who could not endure it because of its absurd language and satanic spell [*epode*][3] ... They say that the three persons of Father, Son and Holy Spirit will be dissolved into one person. They have stolen this idea from the Sabellians ... They say that the divine nature can easily change and convert itself into what it likes, and so be admixed into souls that are worthy of it ... They say that the seed and Word of God fell into the womb of the Mother of God ... They claim that holy baptism cannot eradicate the roots of sin ... They say that every child which is born inherits from our forefather Adam both his nature and his enslavement to the devils, and has combined with that nature a demon that dwells in it and inspires it, and that neither holy baptism nor any other holy practice is able to expel it; it only leaves as a result of being coughed up and spat out by the person praying ... After the expulsion of the inborn demon, the person is the indwelling of the Holy Spirit and perceives the Holy Trinity and has no need of any sort of devotional practice ... They pretend to elect clergy, ascending the grades of deacon and priest, so that they may claim some power and authority. Indeed, they also put on the monastic habit, intending in this way to escape notice and deceive the majority ...

They swear and forswear fearlessly ... especially if charged with Messalianism ...

---

3 Cf. the use of the same word in EP **[19]**.

24. ANNA COMNENA'S ACCOUNT OF THE TRIAL OF THE BOGOMIL BASIL (*c.* 1098)

Anna Comnena (1083–*c.* 1153) wrote the biography of her father Alexius in her later life, when after her failed attempt to depose her brother John in favour of her husband, she was confined to a convent, where she could be the patron of scholars, away from the political arena. The biography lays particular stress on Alexius' role as the scourge of heresy; Anna records her father's prosecution of John Nilus and of the Paulicians of Philippopolis (see [22]) and gives this detailed and graphic account of the trial and execution of the Bogomil leader in Constantinople. In her narrative the trial appears late in the reign; this must be misleading. The determining dates are those of the death of the Patriarch Nicholas Grammaticus (1084–1111) and of the *sebastocrator* Isaac (*c.* 1103), for which see Papachryssanthou, 'La Date de la mort du *sébastocrator* Isaac Comnène'.

The text used is that of the Budé edition, edited by B. Leib (3 vols, Paris 1937–45).

8.1. After this, in the ••[1] year of the reign a vast cloud of heretics arose; a new form of heresy never previously known to the Church. Two most evil and worthless doctrines combined, which had been known in earlier times, the impiety . . . of the Manichaeans, which we call the heresy of the Paulicians,[2] and the loathsomeness of the Massalians.[3] That is what the Bogomils' doctrine is like, a combination of the Manichaeans and the Massalians. It appears that it existed even before my father's time, but unrecognized; the sect of the Bogomils is very skilful at counterfeiting virtue. You would never see a lay hair-style on a Bogomil; the evil is hidden under a cloak or a cowl. A Bogomil has a grave expression; he is muffled to the nose, walks bent forward and speaks softly, but inwardly he is an untamed wolf.

3. The fame of the Bogomils had already spread everywhere. A certain monk, Basil, was very clever at spreading the heresy of the Bogomils; he had twelve disciples, whom he called apostles,[4] and took along with him, as well some female disciples, women of depraved and evil character, and spread the evil everywhere. The evil had attacked many souls, like a fire. The emperor's soul could not endure this; he made enquiry into the heresy. Some of the Bogomils were brought to the palace. They all

---

1 The date is left blank in the MS.
2 See [7], [8].
3 See EZ [25], note 4.
4 The same allegation that he had twelve 'apostles' was made against Mani. There must be some doubt whether this charge against Basil is historically true. See the description of Basil's followers in EZ [25], c. 22.

said that a certain Basil was their teacher, and the outstanding leader of the Bogomil heresy. One of them, Diblatius, was captured, and when unwilling to give answers to his interrogation, he was subjected to torture. He denounced the aforesaid Basil and the apostles whom he had chosen. So the emperor embarked on a search for this man. At length Satanael's[5] commander-in-chief Basil appeared, a monk from his habit, with an austere face, a scraggy beard, and tall.

4. Immediately the emperor . . . summoned the man with a pious excuse. He rose from his chair for him, shared a seat and his own table . . . he pretended that he wanted to become his disciple, and not he himself alone, but also his brother Isaac the *sebastocrator*,[6] and that he took everything Basil said as divinely inspired, saying that he would obey him in everything if only Basil would procure his soul's salvation 'Most venerable father,' said he, 'I admire you for your virtue. I beg you to teach me some of the doctrine of your reverence, because our doctrines are all useless, and do not lead to virtue at all.' . . . The brother of the emperor, the *sebastocrator*, appeared at the same time, and played his part in everything.

5. Basil spewed out the doctrines of the heresy. How? A curtain was stretched between the women's quarters and those of the emperor. While this wretch was vomiting forth everything and explaining it all clearly, a clerk inside the hanging was writing down all that was said . . . That accursed man . . . called the churches, alas – our holy churches – the temples of demons; the Body and Blood of the great high priest and sacrifice consecrated by us he set at naught, and made nothing of it.

6. What happened next? The emperor tore off the mask, he drew back the curtain. All the senate was assembled, the general staff were gathered, and the ecclesiastical synod was there.[7] At that time the throne of the imperial city was occupied by that most blessed of patriarchs, the Lord Nicholas the Grammarian.[8] He read out the abominable doctrines; the truth could not be gainsaid. Immediately, with bared head, Basil went on the offensive and promised to stand firm against fire and whips and a thousand deaths. These deluded Bogomils are convinced

---

5 For the use of this name for the devil among Byzantine Bogomils and the alternative version, Samael, see note 3 to EZ **[25]**.
6 For the date of the death of the *sebastocrator* Isaac, see Papachryssanthou, 'La Date de la mort du *sébastocrator* Isaac Comnène'.
7 For a similar assembly of the governing class of the empire to condemn heresy, see the preamble to the condemnation of the patriarch Cosmas below **[32]**.
8 Patriarch 1084–1111.

THE TRIAL OF THE BOGOMIL BASIL

that they will bear any punishment without pain, because angels will snatch them from the very pyre . . . Although the pyre and other tortures threatened, [Basil] was tightly held by the demon, and held his Satanael tightly. He was put in prison. The emperor sent for him repeatedly, and repeatedly exhorted him to forswear his impiety, but he remained the same, in the face of the emperor's exhortations.

7. I must include the marvel which took place concerning him. Before the emperor began to regard him more harshly (after his confession of impiety), in the mean time he went to a small building situated quite near the emperor's apartments, which had been recently built for him as its first occupant. It was evening, and the stars above shone in the clear air, and the moon gave its light for the evening after their synod. As the monk entered his cell about midnight, stones fell, like hail on the cell, of their own volition. No hand threw the stones, and no human being cast stones at that diabolic abbot. It seems likely that it was an expression of anger on the part of the enraged demons of Satanael, who were furious that he had made revelations to the emperor and incurred an obvious persecution of this error . . . Immediately after the rain of stones there was an earthquake; the ground shook, and all the roof timbers creaked.[9]

[. . .]

9. I intended to give an account of the entire heresy of the Bogomils, but shame prevented me, as Sappho the fair said (because I am a historian and a woman, the most honourable and eldest of the children of Alexius), from saying what deserves to be left in silence . . . There was a monk named Zigabenus, who was known to the princess,[10] my grandmother on my mother's side, and to all the clergy. He had reached the peak of literary skill, and while not ignorant of rhetoric, was better informed on doctrine than anyone else. The emperor sent for him and commissioned him to set out all the heresies, each individually, and to write out the holy fathers' refutations of each, and to include that of the Bogomils, as the blasphemous Basil had explained it. The emperor named this book 'The Dogmatic Panoply'; and it is still known by this title.

Now let us return to the execution of Basil. The emperor had summoned the disciples and fellow-initiates of Basil from all the land, especially those who were called his twelve disciples, and made trial of their views. They were truly disciples of Basil. The evil had weighed heavily even on

---

9 See section 5 of the anathema formula in **[41]**.
10 Mary of Bulgaria.

the greatest houses, and the plague had infected a great number. Once for all, then, he condemned these heterodox [lit., 'aliens'] to the pyre, leader and chorus alike. When the Bogomils who had been detected were arrested, some of them laid claim to their heresy, while others vehemently denied it ... The emperor was not ready to believe them ... he devised a new method by which those who were really Christians might be recognized. So the next day he took his seat on the imperial throne. Many members of the senate were present, and of the holy synod and those leaders of the Nazarites[11] who were knowledgeable. All those who were accused of the Bogomil heresy were assembled in the middle together, and the emperor ordered each of them to be interrogated again individually. Some of them confessed that they were Bogomils ... others absolutely denied it, and called themselves Christians ... The emperor looked fiercely upon them, and said, 'Today two pyres shall be built, and by one a cross will be fixed in the ground. Then you are given a choice. All those who want to die today in the Christian faith should separate themselves from the others and approach the pyre with the cross, while those who adhere to the Bogomil heresy shall be thrown on the other. It is better for those who are Christians to die than to live and be persecuted as if they were Bogomils, and outrage the consciences of many. Go then, and let each of you approach which pyre he chooses.'

[...]

The prisoners were taken away at once, and a large crowd assembled. Immediately the pyres were constructed ... in the so-called Tzykanisterion.[12] The fire went up into the sky. The cross stood by one pyre. The choice was given to the condemned to go to whichever they chose, because they were all going to be burned. Seeing that their fate was unavoidable, those who were orthodox approached the pyre with the cross ... while the atheists ... approached the other.

At the moment when they were all about to be thrown on to the pyres together ... an imperial order was received, which forbade the executioners to carry out their task. In this way the emperor obtained firm knowledge of who were really Bogomils, and set free the Christians who had been denounced ... He had the others returned to prison, the apostles of the impious Basil separated from the rest. Then he sent for them individually and gave them much instruction, encouraging them

---

11 A deliberately archaic description of monks, based on the Old Testament term for those under ascetic vows.
12 The polo-ground.

to abandon their foul cult. As for the others, he ordered some senior members of the Holy Church to approach them individually and teach them the orthodox faith . . . Some of them converted and were released from prison, while some died in their heresy while still in prison, although they were kept amply supplied with food and clothing.

10. As for Basil, who was in reality a heresiarch and completely unrepentant, all the members of the holy synod and the Nazarites and the very patriarch Nicholas himself judged that he deserved the pyre. The emperor shared their opinion . . . So he had a very large pyre built in the Hippodrome. A great pit had been dug, and the quantity of wood, all lofty trees piled together, made the entire mass seem like a mountain. When the pyre was lit, a large crowd slowly gathered on the flat ground and on the steps of the Hippodrome, all anxious to see what would happen. On the other side a cross had been set up, and the blasphemer was given the choice . . . to change his mind and approach the cross. In this way he would immediately be set free from the pyre.

The crowd of heretics were also present to see their leader Basil. He showed himself contemptuous of all threats and all punishment, and while still some distance from the pyre he mocked it . . . saying that angels would snatch him out of the midst of the fire. He recited that psalm of David, 'It will not come near you; you will only see it with your eyes' [Ps. 90.7–8]. When the crowd parted and gave him the opportunity for a leisurely sight of the terrifying spectacle of the pyre (for even from a distance he felt the fire and saw the flames rising and, as it were, thundering and sending sparks as high as the top of the stone obelisk which stands in the middle of the Hippodrome), then that rash man seemed to be afraid of the fire and to be troubled. He kept turning his eyes, and struck his hands and beat his thigh, as though he were completely at a loss . . .

Since there were many stories and tales about him circulating on everyone's lips, the executioners were afraid that the demons who surrounded Basil might perform some wonder, with the permission of God, and the villain might be snatched from the centre of the pyre, big as it was, and appear in some crowded place, and so the last error should be worse than the first. So they decided to try an experiment . . . They took his cloak and said, 'Let us see if the fire will touch his clothes'. Immediately they threw it into the middle of the flames. Basil was so far beguiled by the demon who deceived him that he said, 'Look, my cloak is flying into the air.' They recognized the weaving from the selvage; they seized him and threw him, clothes and shoes and all, into the middle of the furnace.

The fire, as if furious with him, devoured the blasphemer so completely that there was no smell of burning flesh nor any alteration in the flame, but simply a thin line of smoke appeared in the middle of the flames ...

As for the remaining number of the destructive sect of Basil, the excited people tried to have them thrown on to the fire by force, but the emperor would not allow it. He ordered that they should be imprisoned in the porches and galleries of the Great Palace ... They were transferred there, and having spent some time there, died in their impiety.

25. EXTRACTS FROM EUTHYMIUS ZIGABENUS *DOGMATIC PANOPLY* AGAINST THE BOGOMILS

Euthymius was given the task of interrogating the Bogomil leader Basil, whose trial is recorded by Anna Comnena[1]. As she reports, he was commissioned to write up an account of the sect in his encyclopaedia of heresies, the *Dogmatic Panoply*. The most accessible version of that text is that of Migne (*PG* 130.1289d–1331d). Another account by Euthymius of his interrogation of the Bogomil leader exists in a twelfth-century MS at Utrecht, published by Ficker (*Die Phundagiagiten*, Leipzig, 1908), who called it the *Narratio*. This would appear from internal evidence to have been written earlier than the *Dogmatic Panoply*. In the *Narratio* Euthymius is concerned to give factual information about the heresy, interspersed only occasionally with comments which make his disapproval clear. In the anti-Bogomil chapter of the *Panoply* he has rearranged the material in a more logical order, and has taken pains to refute the heresies and to state the orthodox position. He also cross-references the reader to other chapters in his work where he has refuted the arguments of earlier heretics holding similar views. Almost all the information about Bogomilism contained in the *Narratio* is incorporated in the *Panoply*, though it is arranged in a different order. Both texts end with a long section containing citations from a Bogomil commentary on St Matthew's gospel. This is the only Christian dualist commentary which has so far come to light,[2] and is, therefore, of unusual interest.

The translation is based on the text of the *Dogmatic Panoply*; significant variants in the *Narratio* text are given in footnotes.[3] Euthymius' refutations have been

1 [24]above.
2 There is an allusion to another commentary on the gospel of St Matthew in [16, d], but the description of its contents does not match the text given here.
3 The commonest of these is the use in the Ficker text of Samael (rather than Satanael) as a name for the evil spirit. The section describing how Satanael, after his fall from heaven, became known as Satan (p. 187) makes it clear that the Bogomils of Constantinople used the form Satanael. Both versions of the name are otherwise familiar.

omitted in most cases, except where they help to elucidate his comments about Bogomilism, or in a few cases (identified in the footnotes) where they show that he and his opponents shared a common thought-world. The section from the *Narratio* in which Euthymius describes what he terms the 'archaeology' of heresy, that is, the instruction given to new converts, has been printed as an appendix. Although this does not contain any significant information which is not found in the *Panoply*, it is the only coherent account which we have of Bogomil catechetics.

PREFACE

The heresy of the Bogomils arose not long before our own generation. It is a part of the Messalian heresy, and for the most part shares their doctrines,[4] but with some additional points which increase the pollution.[5]

It was identified in the time of the emperor Alexius,[6] who skilfully and altogether admirably tracked down its leader. He was Basil, a doctor, or rather, a destroyer, a plague, one full of destruction and a tool of every sort of evil. The emperor summoned him, received him with respect, honoured him with a seat by his own, talked to him pleasantly with kindly and agreeable conversation and, cleverly pretending discipleship, easily deceived the one who had deceived many to their destruction. With acuteness of mind and dexterity of spirit, he tracked down all the malignancy which lurked within the body of this corrupt and abominable old man. So like all kinds of wild beast from their lair, he dragged out the defilement from the darkness of his heart, the multiform poisonous teachings, by the ingenuity of his enquiry. So he outwitted the foolish old man, that ancient ill, and ordered me to write this down and triumph over the ridiculous secrets of the aforesaid heresy.

Samael is the angel of death in Jewish tradition; the earliest record of the name is found in the Ethiopic *Book of Enoch*, c. 6, and the legend that Samael was present in the garden of Eden and there took the form of a snake is in the *Apocalypse of Baruch*, 4.9. He also occurs in the *Ascension of Isaiah* (*NTA* II, p. 645). That he was the father of Cain is recorded in the Targum on Genesis 3.6 (*Sources chrétiennes 245; Targum du Pentateuque*, I, 91 R. le Déaut and J. Robert). Satanael is first recorded in the *Gospel of Bartholomew* (*NTA* 1, 497) – a work dating perhaps from the fifth century. The existing text appears to support the Bogomil view that Christ and Satan were brothers. See also Dando, 'Satanael'.

4 The Messalian/Massalian heresy originated in Syria in the fourth century. EZ's account of it in *PG* 130.1273 **[23 (g)]** shows that he believed that its main characteristics were the teaching of a technique of ecstatic prayer as the only way to expel the evil demon who indwelt every human being.
5 Here the Ficker text adds: 'Until recently it was concealed by the appearance of piety, and for this reason was difficult to detect, not only by those whose sight is simple, but by the keen-sighted, who see more clearly than many.'
6 Alexius Comnenus (1081–1118).

1. They reject all the books of Moses[7] and the God who is described in them, together with the just men who are well pleasing to Him; indeed, all the books which follow, as being written in accordance with the plan of Satan. God be merciful to us who record their views! They accept and honour only seven, and highly respect them; that is, the Psalter, the sixteen Prophets, the Gospel according to Matthew, Mark, Luke and John, and as the seventh book, the Acts of the Apostles together with the Epistles and the Apocalypse of John the Divine. For, they say, 'wisdom hath builded her house, and she hath hewn out her seven pillars' [Prov. 9.1]. They interpret this as meaning by 'house', their corrupt assembly, and by 'pillars', the books which equal them in number. They have learnt to reject the books of Moses and what follows them from the Paulician heresy... You must realize that in despising the books of Moses they often cunningly select sayings from them to support their positions. And even if one of them is driven into a tight corner by some saying from these seven books I have revealed, and is forced towards the truth, straightaway in their anxiety to escape they turn to allegory.[8]

2. They put forward, as a way of deceiving the simple, that they believe in the Father, the Son and the Holy Spirit, but they refer these three appellations to the Father, and suppose that He has a human face, sending forth a ray from each temple, one of the Son, one of the Spirit. So their faith is perverted to some sort of monstrous physically formed God, who could not exist in any way. They have taken from the Sabellian heresy this laying hold of the Father under three appellations.[9]...

3. They say that the Son and the Holy Spirit dissolve back into the Father, from whence they came, and that He who has three faces will, when 5,000 and 33 years have elapsed, become single-formed again, but bodiless, though in human shape. Alas for that vast lack of sense, the extent of the matter for laughter.[10]

7 Both Paulicians and Bogomils refused to admit the Pentateuch as canonical; see Peter of Sicily [7].
8 See Glossary, p. 298.
9 Sabellius (early third century) is commonly cited by Byzantine authors as the originator of an erroneous view of the Trinity. He emphasized the singleness of the Divine Nature, and so had problems with the incarnation. The teaching here attributed to him is that described in the fourth-century debates on the relationship of Christ to God the Father.
10 The Byzantine era for the age of the world supplies the start date here; Bogomils evidently thought that the resurrection of Christ (at the end of his thirty-three years of earthly life) marked the end of time and the beginning of the new creation. F. Loofs ('Das Nicänum' *Festgabe K. Muller*, pp. 68–82) believes that the idea that the Trinity was in some sense limited to a period from the beginning of creation to the end of time was a widely-held early Trinitarian doctrine. None of the authors he cites mentions a

4. They say that there was neither Son nor Spirit until the year 5000,[11] and that they then took their origin and name, despite the evangelist John's voice of thunder, which says: 'In the beginning was the Word, and the Word was with God, and the Word was God' [John 1.1]...

5. They say that the Father begat the Holy Spirit[12] and that He, in a spiritual way, begat the traitor Judas and the eleven apostles. They quote the gospel, saying, 'Abraham begat Isaac, Isaac begat Jacob, Jacob begat Judas and his brethren,' [Matt. 1.2], and claim that this is written about the Holy Trinity.[13]...

6. They say that the demon whom the saviour called Satan himself is also a son of God the Father, called Satanael;[14] he came before the Son, the Word, and is stronger, as befits the first-born; that they are brothers one of the other. Satan[15] is the steward, second to the Father, having the same form and dress as He does, and he sits at His right hand on a throne, and deserves honour next after His. He was intoxicated by this, and being carried away by loss of sense, he plotted a rebellion, and having done so, he seized the opportunity to test some of the ministering powers. He said that if they wanted to lessen the load of their service, they should follow him and join him in breaking away from the Father. As confirmation of this nonsense, they quote the parable in St Luke's gospel of the unjust steward who reduced the liability of the debtors [Luke 16.1–13]. They say that he is Satanael, and that this parable is written about him. Then to the aforesaid angels who were enticed by the lightening of their burdensome services and other excessive demands, he said: 'I will place my throne upon the clouds, and I will be like unto the Most High' [Isa. 14.14]; they were attracted by this, and joined the plot. When God perceived this, He threw them all down headlong together...

---

date for the extension or retraction of the divine power, or the human shape of the Trinity. 'Human shape' here is either an instance of unsophisticated Bogomil thinking or a tendentious presentation of their views. Ficker adds: 'They say that the Son is the Word of the Father, and the Holy Spirit is the Word of the Son.'

11 Ficker has 5500.
12 Ficker has 'They say that the heavenly father begat the Son and the Son begat the Holy Spirit.'
13 The allegation that to say the Holy Spirit is begotten means that he is the younger brother of Christ is made against the followers of Macedonius of Constantinople (Hanson, *The search for the Christian doctrine of God*, p. 754). Bogomils, who did not accept the Old Testament as canonical, had to make sense of the genealogies of Christ in the gospels.
14 Ficker has: 'they say that Samael [*sic*] son of the Father, preceded the Son and Word'.
15 Ficker has 'Samael'.

7. They say that Satanael[16] was cast down from above, and was unable to sit upon the waters; 'For the earth', they say, 'was invisible and unprepared'. But since he had the form and dress of God and possessed the power of the Demiurge[17] to summon the powers which had fallen along with him and to embolden them, he said, 'Since God made the heaven and the earth' (for he said, "in the beginning God made the heaven and the earth"), I too will make a second heaven, being the second God,[18] and the rest in order.' He said, 'Let the firmament be created', and it was created; 'Let such and such be created', and they all were created. He adorned the second heaven, and withdrew the water from the face of the earth, and arranged it in places as seemed good to him, as the book of Genesis describes. He adorned it and beautified and created all that grows from the earth and animals and anything else, and allotted this as a home for himself and for the powers which had rebelled. Then he moulded the body of Adam from earth mixed with water, and made him stand up, and some moisture ran down to his right foot, and leaking out through his big toe, ran twisting on to the ground and made the shape of a snake. Satanael[19] gathered together the breath that was in him and breathed life into the body which he had moulded, and his breath, running down through the emptiness, ran down to the right foot in the same way, and, leaking through the big toe, ran out into the twisted drop. This instantly became alive, and separating from the toe, crawled away. That is why it is clever and intelligent,[20] because of the breath of Satanael[21] which came into it.[22]

When he, the new creator, saw this, and realized that he had laboured in vain, he sent an embassy to the Good Father, and asked Him to send His breath, saying that the man would be shared if he were to be endowed with life, and that the places in heaven of the angels who had been thrown out should be filled by the man's descendants. Because God is good, He agreed, and breathed into what Satanael[23] had

---

16 Ficker has 'Samael'.
17 The Demiurge; the Creator.
18 For Satan as the elder son of God see Ps.-Psellus **[34]**.
19 Ficker has 'Samael'.
20 Ficker has: 'they say that the serpent alone among irrational beasts has mind and reason, even if not perfect, and that he is called cunning in the scriptures (Gen. 3.1), because the soul breathed in by Samael trickled through Adam and ran into him, and stayed there.'
21 Ficker has 'Samael'.
22 For a similar but not identical Bogomil creation myth see EP **[19]**.
23 Ficker has 'Samael'.

moulded the breath of life; immediately man became a living soul, splendid in his body and bright with many graces.[24]

Eve was made similarly then, and shone forth with the same splendour. Satanael[25] became envious and repented, and was moved to plot against what he himself had made. He slipped into the inward parts of the serpent, deceived Eve, slept with her and made her pregnant, so that his seed might get a start on and master the seed of Adam, and as far as possible destroy it and not allow it to increase and grow. Soon she fell into labour and brought forth Cain from her coition with Satanael,[26] and his sister like him, named Calomena.[27] Adam became jealous. and also slept with Eve, and begot Abel, whom Cain immediately killed, and so brought murder into life. That is why the apostle John says that 'Cain was of the evil one' [1 John 3.12]. As Satanael[28] coupled shamelessly with Eve through the medium of the serpent, immediately there were taken from him his divine appearance and dress and, as they say, his creative power and the appellation of God. Until now he had been called God. When he had been stripped of all these he became dark and ugly. Until this point the good Father had stayed His anger and pardoned this lord and cosmocrator, himself a creator, who had fallen from above. These are their myths.

But how was he unable to sit upon the water, or rather, since sitting is a property of a body, how could he and the powers that fell with him not make their dwelling in the waters? For even now they inhabit waters, springs and rivers, marshes and lakes, and stay underground like immaterial spirits, even less material than the spirits of the winds[29] ... The doctrine that Satanael created the firmament, that he gathered together the waters into the channel prepared for them, that he adorned the firmament and the earth and all that follows, as far as the breathing of spirit into the first created, they have stolen from the Mosaic account of Creation; but the Bogomils, following the Paulicians, ascribe all this creative work to Satanael. The Paulicians assign the making of this and

---

24 Ficker has: 'they say that man is shared between God and the devil; the body was moulded by the devil, but the soul was breathed in by God. That is why some men are friendly with God, and others with the devil.'
25 Ficker has 'Samael'.
26 Ficker has 'Samael'.
27 This name for the sister of Cain is otherwise found in a late Jewish source, *The Chronicles of Jerahmeel*.
28 Ficker has 'Samael'.
29 For the belief that demons are associated with damp places, particularly subterranean ones, see Pseudo-Psellus [34].

of the first heaven, the earth, indeed, to sum it up, everything in the world, to the evil one...

8. They say that while men endured harsh rule and were cruelly destroyed, a few of the Father's party came into being with difficulty, and crossed over to the ranks of angels. These are they who are recorded in the genealogies of the Gospels of Matthew and Luke.[30] At length the Father realized that He had been outwitted and knew that He had been wronged, because although He had provided the most important part of man and supplied what was most essential for his completion, He could lay claim only to an infinitely small part of the human race. At the same time He felt pity for the soul which He had himself breathed in, which was suffering so piteously and was oppressed; He determined to defend it, and in the year 5000 he sent forth from his heart the Word, that is the Son, who is God. For it is written, 'My heart has uttered a good word' [Ps. 44.2].[31]

They claim that this word and son is the archangel Michael, 'For his name shall be the angel of good counsel' [Isa. 9.6]. They believe that he is called archangel because he is more divine than all the angels, Jesus because he cures all weakness, and Christ because he is anointed with flesh;[32] that he descended from above and crept through the right ear[33] of the Virgin, and put on a body which seems physical, like a human body, but in reality is immaterial and divine, that he went out again as he had entered, while the Virgin perceived neither entrance nor exit, but simply found him lying swaddled in the cave. He accomplished the incarnate plan and did and taught what is set out in the Gospels, except that he only appeared to undergo human sufferings.[34] When he had

30 Ficker, chap. 20: 'they say that all men from Adam to Christ have died, some through their own sin, some because they pleased the God who is described in the books of Moses, for he is Samael. Only those listed in the genealogies in the Gospels of Matthew and Luke achieved salvation. So they are recorded as just by the evangelists.'
31 A literal translation of the LXX Greek has been used to make the wordplay clear. Ficker (introduction, p. 5) says: 'He taught him his own words, "I will address my verses to the King." That is why in the gospels he says, "If I am not doing the works of my Father, then do not believe me"' [John 10.37].
32 Jesus means 'deliverer' in Hebrew; Christ means 'anointed' in Greek. For the association of the figures of Christ and the archangel Michael in early Christological thinking see *Shepherd of Hermas, Sim.* 8.1.
33 The idea that the Virgin Mary conceived through the ear (by responding to the message of the angel) is found in the poetry of St Ephraim Syrus (Graef, *Mary*, I, p. 59). Bogomils, who were concerned to deny that Christ took human flesh, appear to have welcomed this image and interpreted it in a literal sense.
34 Ficker, chap. 10: 'They say that the Son was incarnate but in immaterial flesh, godlike, needing no food. "For my food", he said, "is to do the will of my Father."'

appeared to be crucified and to have died and to rise again, he rang down the curtain, made the play apparent, took off the mask and imprisoned the rebel. He bound him with a thick and heavy chain and shut him in Tartarus, taking from his name the syllable 'el', which is angelic. He allowed him who had been called Satanael to be called Satan,[35] and then, having fulfilled the service he had undertaken, he returned to the Father and sat at his right hand on the throne of Satan,[36] who had been cast down.[37] Then he returned whence he came and was dissolved back into the Father, in whose womb he had been enclosed in the beginning ... The taking of immaterial flesh and all the heretical ideas about appearance which follow and the true birth from the Virgin has come to them from the madness of the Manichaeans and similar heresies which preceded them ...

9. They say that the angels which fell, having heard that Satanael[38] had promised the Father to fill up their places in heaven from the race of men, looked shamelessly on the daughters of men and took them to wife, so that their descendants might ascend to heaven to take the place of their fathers. For they say, 'the sons of God saw the daughters of men, that they were fair, and they took them as wives for themselves' [Gen. 6.2].[39] From their union came the giants who resisted Satanael[40] and triumphed over his overthrow on men's behalf. He was enraged and brought down on them the flood, and destroyed along with them all human flesh. Only Noah, who had no daughter, knew nothing of the rebellion of Satan,[41] and continued to worship him. Satanael,[42] pleased with his devotion, suggested all that concerned the Ark [Gen. 6.5–9.18], and he alone was saved with those who were in it ...

10. They say that Moses was led astray by Satanael,[43] and returned to Egypt, that he deceived the people of the Jews and led them out, having

Holding this doctrine, they say that the whole plan of the incarnation of the Saviour took place only in appearance.'

35 Ficker (introduction, p. 6): 'But having been called not only Samael but Satanael, he became Satan.'
36 Ficker has 'Satanael'.
37 Ficker, chap. 5: 'They say that the Son and Word took over the first rank which was Samael's and took his position as first born and this throne.' In Bogomil doctrine the effect of the life (and apparent death) of Christ was to strip Satan of his divinity.
38 Ficker has 'Samael'.
39 Ficker, chap. 19: 'They call them the sons of God, begotten from him.'
40 Ficker has 'Samael'.
41 Ficker has 'Samael'.
42 Ficker has 'Samael'.
43 Ficker has 'Satanael'.

done some signs and wonders through the power of Satanael.[44] They came to Mount Sinai and received the Law, led by Satanael.[45] Countless thousands of them were destroyed, and the Apostle bears witness to this, when he says, 'I had not known sins but by the Law' [Rom. 7.7, 9, 12] and again, 'When the commandment came, sin revived.' O learned in evil, why do you dishonestly leave out the next phrase? It is written immediately: 'The law is holy, the commandment holy and just and good...' [Rom. 7.12].

11. They say that the only saints are those in the genealogies of Matthew and Luke, as is said above, and the sixteen prophets and the apostles and martyrs, all those who were executed for refusing to bend the knee to idols. They reject all the bishops and the Fathers altogether, on the grounds that they are idol-worshippers, because they bow the knee to icons. And they banish all the pious emperors from the fold of Christians, and they say that only the Iconoclasts are orthodox and faithful, especially Copronymus.[46] They do not honour the venerable icons, saying, 'The idols of the heathen are silver and gold, the works of men's hands' [Ps. 115.4], in their ignorance that an idol is one thing and an icon another. The prototypes of idols are insubstantial and false, for they call gods those who are not gods, but demons, falsely claiming divinity. The prototypes of our icons really are in truth what they are called. Those are the idols of criminals, these the icons of saints...'[47]

12. When I asked the leader of this heresy of theirs, 'Why do you reject the bishops among the saints and the blessed Fathers whose relics we venerate?', opening his polluted lips and vomiting forth an evil word, he said, 'Because the demons are among their number, who taught them while they were still alive, who remain near their tombs[48] and do wonders to deceive the foolish and persuade them to honour the impure as saints. The demons can do all they want, taking power from above, as far as the boundary of the seven aeons.'[49]

---

44 Ficker 'Satanael'. For Bogomils all the stories about the Exodus from Egypt; Moses and the Burning Bush, and the giving of the ten commandments, are told of Satanael, not God the Father.
45 Ficker 'Satanael'.
46 Constantine V (741–75).
47 For the theory of the relationship between image and prototype see the proceedings of the Second Council of Nicaea (AD 787), Mansi XIII, 204–364. For the theology of icons see Germanus **[44]** and Introduction.
48 Ficker, chap. 29 adds: 'being in possession of their souls'.
49 'Aeon' (originally a period of time), later also a sphere of influence. Here it is used of the seven planetary gods who control both the days of the week and the concentric planetary heavens which surround the earth, all of which are part of Satanael's

13. They say that it is by them, that is, the Bogomils, alone that the demons are always put to flight like arrows from the bow. Every other man has a resident demon, who teaches him evil and leads him to evil actions, and when he is dead, it inhabits his remains[50] and stays in his tomb, and awaits the resurrection, to be punished along with him, and is not separated from him, even in punishment. They have this view that each man has his own indwelling demon from the Messalian heresy.[51] That demons do not flee from Bogomils alone, but rather stay with them, and are at their ease with them, is clear from the rest of their error, and because they appear to them in different shapes, as you will find later.

14. They do not honour the holy cross,[52] because it is the murderer of the Saviour, when they should rather honour it, because it destroys the devil. Until that time it was an instrument which brought death, but from then on it became a weapon which brought life, most royal and terrible to its enemies, inasmuch as it was sprinkled with the Lord's blood and water.

15. Again when I asked the man who had been revealed as leader of the heresy, 'Why do those who are possessed by demons run to the cross and howl?', he replied, 'The demons who live in them love the cross especially because it is their own work. For they prepared it for the murder of the Saviour. Sometimes they pretend to insult it, play-acting, and often run away from it of their own free will, so that men may look at it and revere it more as a persecutor of demons.' But the truth, as we see it, is not like this. They are dragged unwillingly by the power of the cross to be tested. For the howling and contortions of body of those possessed by demons, and their writhings, are witness to the torment of the demons. They insult it because it is hostile, and flee from it because it puts them to flight.

16. They say that ours is the baptism of John, being accomplished in water, but theirs is the baptism of Christ, achieved, as they think, through the Spirit [John 3.5–6]. So they rebaptize anyone who converts to them, first fixing for him a time for confession, purification and earnest prayer. Then they place the gospel of John[53] on the candidate's

> creation, and thus subject to demons. Above the spheres of the planets is the eighth sphere (otherwise known as the Ogdoad), that of the fixed stars, which is not subject to change or decay.
> 50 Ficker has 'soul'.
> 51 See note 4 above,
> 52 An attitude they shared with Paulicians; see above, PH **[8]**, c. 13.
> 53 Ficker, chap. 28 adds: 'and read: "In the beginning was the Word."'

head, and invoke what they call the Holy Spirit, and chant the Our Father.[54] After a baptism like this, they again fix a time for a more searching training, a more continent way of life and purer prayer. Then they look for evidence to see if he has observed all this, if he is judged to be enthusiastic. If men and women give such evidence they bring him to a public initiation. They place the wretch facing East,[55] and again put the Gospel on his impious head, and those men and women who happen to be present put their unhallowed hands on him and chant their unholy rite. This is a hymn of thanksgiving because he has kept the impiety that was entrusted to him. So they complete, or rather totally finish off and overwhelm one, who deserves the abyss of destruction.[56] If our baptism were accomplished with water alone, then ours would be the baptism of John. But it is not accomplished with water only, but with the Holy Spirit as well, as the Lord taught, when he said, 'Except a man be born of water and of the spirit, he cannot enter into the kingdom of God' [John 3.5]. So they howl in vain.

17. They do not honour the mystic and awful sacrifice and the holy communion of the Lord's body and blood, saying that it is a sacrifice of the demons who inhabit temples. O impious lips and still more impious tongues. They adduce as witness the prophet Isaiah [Isa. 65.11], who says, 'Those who prepare a table for Fortune and fill a cup for the demons.'[57] In their stupidity, the fools do not realize that he is speaking of idol-worshippers. The bread of fellowship they say is the prayer Our Father, for they say 'our daily bread' [Matt. 6.9–14]. Similarly they say that the cup of fellowship is the covenant quoted in the Gospel; 'this cup is the new testament [covenant]'. So the mystic banquet is the sharing of both these. If any ask, 'How can the Our Father, being the Lord's body, be broken and divided? or how can the phrase "the Son of Man has been glorified" and what follows be taken as said of the blood of the Lord spilt for us?', they admit that they do not know.[58]

18. They say that demons live in all the holy temples, dividing up each

---

54 For the use of the Our Father in Cathar worship, see Wakefield and Evans, *Heresies of the High Middle Ages*, pp. 469–72. EP claims that what the Bogomils used in initiation rituals was a 'satanic spell' (*satanike epode*), a phrase used by EZ in his description of Messalians (*PG* 130, 1273).
55 Compare EZ in *PG* 130, 1181; 'at baptism we turn West to renounce Satan and then East to glorify God'.
56 See EP **[19]**.
57 Following the LXX text; the RSV differs here.
58 Since Bogomils rejected material sacraments as being part of the evil creation, but had to explain the words of Christ instituting the Eucharist, they did so allegorically. For similar behaviour by the Paulicians, see PS **[7]**, c. 40.

his own order and power proportionately.[59] Satan has of old allotted to himself the very popular temple in Jerusalem; after it was overthrown he laid claim to the superlative and renowned temple of the Holy Wisdom[60] in the queen of cities. For, they say, the all-highest does not dwell in temples made with hands [Acts 7.48], since He has the heavens as His dwelling. Yet 'My house', says the Lord, 'shall be called the house of prayer' [Matt. 21.13]. And again Christ said, 'Make not my Father's house a house of merchandise' [John 2.16], and said this about the temple of Jerusalem made with hands. If the temple in Jerusalem was the house of God, how much rather the one in this queen of cities? To put it briefly, all those temples in any places which are hallowed for God, the mother of God, and all the saints, are holy, and are sanctuaries and places which banish demons. For wherever divine grace lives, there the evil spirit is chased away, together with all the powers of the demons.

19. They say that the only prayer is the one the Lord handed down in the Gospels, that is, the Our Father. This alone they pray, seven times a day and five times a night. Wherever those stand to pray, they say this prayer, some ten times over with genuflections, some fifteen, some more or less. All other prayers they despise, calling them idle repetitions, appropriate to the gentiles; they refer what is called idle repetition in the Gospels to this ...[61]

20. The leader of the heresy said that in the[62] Gospels was written a saying of the Lord's which says: 'Honour the demons, not to gain their help, but so that they may do you no harm.' And interpreting the saying, he added that they ought to honour the demons who inhabit the temples made with hands, worshipping them[63] so that they might not be angered and destroy those who did not do so, as they have great and irresistible power to harm. Neither Christ nor the Holy Spirit with Him can stand against this, since the Father still spares them and does not take away their strength, but allows them the government of the whole cosmos until the consummation. When the Son was sent down into the world at the beginning, He asked for their complete destruction, but did not gain

---

59 The idea that demons inhabited particular churches and divided up their spheres of influence must reflect popular devotion to the saints commemorated in individual churches.
60 St Sophia, the cathedral of Constantinople.
61 For similar use of repetitions of the Lord's prayer in the Cathar ritual see Appendix 1.
62 Ficker has 'their'.
63 Ficker adds (chap. 14): 'and through the sharing of the sacrifice offered to them and worship of their physical icons which are put up to their honour pay them cult'.

his request through the goodness of the Father . . . they have learnt this nonsense from the heresy of the Messalians . . .

21. He said that this saying of the Lord was written too, 'Be saved by craft'; that is, 'with craft and guile imitate the faith of those who put pressure on you, so that you will be saved from danger and death which comes from them'. To this this passage [Matt. 23.5] refers: 'all therefore, whatsoever they bid you observe, that observe, and do' (that is, in pretence), 'but do not do after their works'. For indeed, the Lord himself spoke to the disciples straightforwardly, but to the unbelievers in parables [Matt. 13.3], so that the unbelievers might see the surface of the pretence, but might not see what is hidden in our hearts, and might hear, but not hear; for deception and deceit they call a parable. I took the Gospel book of the man who taught this in my hands and searched carefully, but failed to find either the passage which preceded this or the one which followed. The four evangelists were just like our genuine ones. I asked him about this. He looked sullen and upset, as one who has been caught out, and agreed that he had never himself been able to find the two sayings, although he had often read the Gospel. 'When I bought the present book of the Gospels', he said, 'I met an old man in a deserted place. He called me by my name, and said to me, "I will give you a great treasure. This is the only book which escaped the hands of John the Swollen-throated – this is what those of unclean lips call Chrysostom[64] – it has written in it the two sayings I mentioned, which have been expunged from the other Gospels." I believed his words and I preach them as being in my book of the Gospels.' Such was his explanation, and I immediately realized that it was Satan who had played the part of the false old man.

22. They say that those of their faith, in whom dwells what they think of as the Holy Spirit, are all, and are called Mother of God.[65] They bear the word of God and give birth to It by teaching. The first God-bearer had nothing more than they . . . They say that people of this sort do not die, but are changed, as if in sleep. They take off this covering of clay and flesh without pain, and put on the incorruptible divine robe of Christ. Becoming like Him in form and body, they come with an escort of angels and apostles to the kingdom of the Father, and their abandoned body dissolves into dust and ash, and will never rise again. But that they do not

---

64 Phrysostomos ('Swollen-throated'). John Chrysostom ('Golden-throat' c. 347–407) was Patriarch of Constantinople and, especially through his commentary on the Gospels, a central figure in the teaching tradition of orthodox Byzantine theology.

65 Orthodox Christians reserve this title for the Virgin Mary. For the use of a similar expression by Paulicians, see PS [7], c. 117.

have a painless death, like sleep or the taking-off of a covering, was revealed by the leader of the heresy himself, who was struck with many pains after the sentence of burning was proclaimed against him.[66] He was devoured with fear, received deep blows to the heart, and when the play was over and he realized that he had been tricked, that the mysteries of his faith had been made public and written down to be mocked, that his disciples (especially his kinsfolk and relations by marriage) were in prison in chains, that all help was lost, and his hopes vanished – when he saw his disciples and kinsfolk in such a pitiable condition, as I have said before, against all his expectation (for until the last day he had thought that they were all in a good state, as the emperor had promised), he claimed that they had betrayed him, and wept floods of bitter tears, and uttered deep sighs which revealed the fire that burnt in his heart. As if felled by the hurricane of his misfortune, he fainted, revived, fell again; unable to stand until propped up by those who had been ordered to bring him, he was lifted up and carried to the pyre. His voice failed and his breath came in gasps; he was thrown into the fire and became a holocaust to the demon he worshipped. So he went to the place of darkness and other evils prepared for him. The body of this wretched old man will rise completely on the day of universal resurrection, as the Saviour promised, when he said that those who did evil will go to eternal punishment [Matt. 25.46], even though he taught that there was no resurrection of the dead . . .

23. They say that they see the Father, not just in dreams but even waking, like a long-bearded old man, the Son like a man just getting a beard, and the Holy Spirit like a beardless youth.[67] The demons easily take on these shapes and deceive them, and teach them that the holy Trinity is not equal, but differs according to the difference of these shapes and the Arian division of the single nature divided among them.[68]

24. They dress as monks and put on their appearance as a bait,[69] they hide the wolf under the fleece, so that they may be welcomed for their appearance and find a place to meet people. There, unsuspected, they drop poison into the ears of their audience through pleasant conversation.

25. They command that one should fast every week on Monday,

---

66 For a detailed account of the trial and execution of Basil see **[24]**.
67 Ficker has 'eunuch'.
68 See Hanson (note 13 above) *passim*, for the Trinitarian controversies of the fourth century.
69 Anna Comnena also describes the Bogomils of Constantinople as dressed like monks.

Wednesday and Friday, until the ninth hour.[70] But if anyone invites them to a meal immediately, forgetful of this commandment, they eat and drink like elephants. From this it is obvious that they behave licentiously, even though they attack fornication and other impurity in word as if they were fleshless and bodiless.

26. In the beginning they teach the newly converted simply, exhorting them to believe in the Father and the Son and the Holy Spirit, to know that Christ was incarnate and gave the sacred gospel to the apostles. They order them to keep the precepts of the gospel and to pray and to fast and keep pure from all uncleanness and live in purity[71] and be long-suffering and repent and tell the truth and love one another. In brief, they teach everything worthy, beguiling them with excellent teaching, hunting them little by little, and unseen bringing them to destruction. As time goes by, they sow tares in the wheat. When they have made the poor wretches tame and obedient and got them within their nets, then, indeed, they give them the deadly potion, blaspheming openly and initiating them into the teaching of the devil.[72]

27. They interpret all of the seven books previously listed[73] by twisting their words and distorting them from the correct sense and perverting them to their own opinions. All that is said in them about sinners and the impious and idol-worshippers they apply to those who believe as we do. All that is said of those who are pleasing to God they apply to themselves, and with full assurance say that they are the elect, just and chosen of God. It would be a long task, taking much time, and clearly a waste of labour, to consider their explanation, or rather distortion, of each book, the change of what is fitting and a toil leading to nothing valuable. Those who have read so far and have been immediately worn down by the absurdities of their blasphemy will be like seasick people who are full of dizziness and vertigo, and will, I know, vomit up the information about this and spew it out and will turn away, saying that we are unseasonable. So that we should not appear to shape an apologia and try to run away from the labour of this, I will expound a few of their crazy sayings[74] on St Matthew's gospel. I will show the jar from a taste, the

---

70 Orthodox tradition enjoined a fast on Wednesday and Friday.
71 Ficker has 'poverty'.
72 Ficker (chap. 36) adds a point not found in the *Panoply*: 'They say that in their dreams when asleep demons make sexual advances in bodily form to their human bodies, taking either the active or passive role'.
73 In c. 1.
74 A detailed comparison of this commentary with those of EZ himself and of Theophylact of Ochrida shows many similarities of exegetical technique.

spring from a stream, the garment from a selvage; I will not bring arguments to counter their interpretations.

THE BOGOMIL COMMENTARY[75]

28.

[Now when Jesus was born in Bethlehem of Judea in the days of Herod the king, behold, wise men from the East came to Jerusalem, saying, 'Where is he who has been born king of the Jews? For we have seen his star in the East, and have come to worship him.' (Matt. 2.1–2)]

They call their assembly Bethlehem. They say Christ is born there, that is, the Word of God preaching the truth of the faith. They think that Herod is our Church, which tries to murder the Word of truth born among them. Again they say that they themselves are the Magi,[76] and in this they tell the truth. Truly they are wizards, corrupt and destructive. Again they call our Church Jerusalem, and the star the law of Moses. For they say that by it they are led as far as our faith, and then learn from its high priests and scribes and teachers that Christ has been born in what has been revealed as Bethlehem. Their first teachers came from us.

29.

[Then Herod, when he saw that he had been tricked by the wise men, was in a furious rage, and he sent and killed all the male children who were in Bethlehem . . . 'A voice was heard in Ramah, wailing and loud lamentation, Rachel weeping for her children; she refused to be consoled, because they were no more.' (Matt. 2.16, 18)]

They tell the story that Rachel was a widow woman who had two young daughters. When Herod gathered together the male children, she altered them to look like boys, thinking that they would deserve honour and favour from him, and brought them forward as sons. When the same thing happened to them as to the other boys, the other mothers simply wept, but Rachel was inconsolable, because in her attempt to outwit Herod she had herself been outwitted and had destroyed her daughters for nothing.[77]

Allegorising the story, they say that Rachel is the heavenly Father and

---

75 The text being commented on is printed here in brackets for ease of reference. These texts are not present in the original.
76 'Magi' or wise men; the word used in the gospel is used to describe a class of professional astrologers, often with negative associations.
77 This account of the passage, with its apparent allegorization of a folktale explanation, has no parallel in the orthodox commentators.

that her children are the soul of Adam and the soul of Christ[78] which were murdered by Herod, that is, the cosmocrator; the Father weeps inconsolably for their loss.

30.

[Now John wore a garment of camel's hair and a leather girdle around his waist; and his food was locusts and wild honey. (Matt. 3.4)]

They say that John had a garment of camel's hair and a leather belt about his loins. His food was locusts and wild honey. This is the Gospel account. Let us see what the mad and crack-brained and half-wits say about this. The camel-hairs are, they say, the commandments of the Mosaic law. This is impure like the camel [Lev. 11.4], and allows those subject to it to eat flesh and marry and swear oaths and offer sacrifice and kill and many other similar actions. They say that the leather belt is the holy Gospel, which is written on sheep-skin. The locusts [*akrides*] are the precepts of the Mosaic law which cannot judge [*krinousas*] what is right, nor distinguish what is better. Wild honey is the holy Gospel, which seems honey to those who receive it: 'How sweet', they say, 'are your words to my mouth' [Ps. 119.30], but it is bitter to those who do not accept it, because of the sharpness of the saying, 'Strait is the gate and narrow is the path' [Matt. 7.14]. They say that the Forerunner is in the middle between the Old Law and the New, and has a share in both the earlier and the later.

31.

[But when He saw many of the Pharisees and Sadducees coming for baptism, He said to them, 'You brood of vipers! Who warned you to flee from the wrath to come?' [Matt. 3.7]

Those who believe as we do are the Pharisees and Sadducees who come to the baptism of John. How shameless! They insult us and call us a generation of vipers, that is, the children of the serpent who slept with Eve, as was explained earlier. They exhort us not to be upset that we have truly been given this name by John the Baptist.

32.

['He who is coming after me is mightier than I, whose sandals I am not worthy to carry ... His winnowing fan is in His hand and He will clear His threshing floor and gather His wheat into the granary, but the chaff He will burn with unquenchable fire.' (Matt. 3.11–12)]

78 For Christ as the second Adam see Romans 5.14, 1 Corinthians 15.45.

They say that Christ's sandals [*hypodemata*] are the marks [*hypodeigmata*] of the signs which He revealed to the disciples and the crowds, which the Baptist could not endure, because he could in no way reveal such things. They think that the winnowing-fan [*ptuon*] of Christ is the word of the Spirit, which was breathed out [*apoptusthenta*] through his mouth, and the threshing-floor [*halos*] is Christians, because there are different groups [*allous kai allous*], some orthodox, others heterodox. The wheat is their faith, which is clean and nourishing; the chaff ours, as being useless and fit only for the fire. What pious soul could endure such blasphemies? My soul swells at this nonsense and my senses quiver, as the prophet says [Jer. 4.19]. I wish to cut short the argument and to go no further, nor give to light and memory what rather deserves darkness and oblivion. But we must go on and endure for a while the wordiness of their endless nonsensical and disgusting talk.

33.

[Again the devil took him to a very high mountain and showed him all the kingdoms of the world and the glory of them; and he said to him, 'All of these I will give you if you will fall down and worship me.' (Matt. 4.8–9)]

They say that the high mountain is the second heaven, and that Christ was taken up there by the devil and saw all the kingdoms of the cosmos. They say that the devil would not have gone up to it if he had not recognized it was his own making. And he would not have said he would hand over all the kingdoms if sovereignty over them had not belonged to him because they originated from him.[79]

34.

[And leaving Nazareth he went and dwelt in Capernaum, by the sea. (Matt. 4.12)]

And Jesus, leaving Nazareth, went and dwelt in Capernaum. They say that we are Nazareth but they are Capernaum. They say that Christ has left our assembly and now lives with them.

35.

[Blessed are the poor in spirit, for theirs is the kingdom of heaven; blessed are those who mourn, for they shall be comforted; blessed are the meek, for they shall inherit the earth; blessed are those who hunger and thirst after righteousness, for they shall be satisfied; blessed are the merciful, for they shall obtain

---

79 Ficker, chap. 46 adds: 'as was revealed in the *archaeologia* of these sorcerers, which has been already set out'. The 'second heaven' is the heaven created by Satan, from which the earth (at the centre of the universe) could be fully surveyed; cf. c. 7 above.

mercy; blessed are the pure in heart, for they shall see God; blessed are the peacemakers, for they shall be called the children of God; blessed are those who are persecuted for righteousness' sake, for theirs is the kingdom of heaven. (Matt. 5.3–10)]

They claim that Christ said all the Beatitudes about those of their faith, the Bogomils, for they are like this, poor in spirit and mourners, and hunger and thirst for righteousness, and so on. They are called the salt of the earth and the light of the cosmos and all the other things which Christ said of the apostles.

36.

[For truly I say to you, till heaven and earth pass away, not an iota, not a dot, will pass from the law till all is accomplished. (Matt. 5.18)]

No iota or dot shall pass away from the Law until all things are accomplished. They say that the *iota* is the ten commandments of the Law and the *keraia* [the dot] the same,[80] for if one straightens up a *keraia* which is lying horizontally, it becomes an *iota*. So they interpret it that the ten commandments of the law will not pass away, but remain kept by the Jews until heaven and earth pass away. 'For', they say, 'I did not come to undo the law of Moses but to fulfil' heaven which had been emptied of its angelic inhabitants and to fill up again the ranks of the fallen angels.

37.

['For I tell you, unless your righteousness exceeds that of the scribes and Pharisees, you will never enter the kingdom of heaven.' (Matt. 5.20)]

'Unless your righteousness exceeds that of the scribes and Pharisees,' they say, 'you will not enter the kingdom of Heaven.' They call us the scribes, because we are trained with a scholarly education and take pride in it. They say that their righteousness exceeds ours because they teach what is truer and share a lifestyle which is more austere and pure, abstaining from meat and cheese and marriage and everything like that.[81]

38.

[But I say to you, 'Love your enemies.' (Matt. 5.44)]

80 The Greek letter *iota* was also used as the numeral 10; it is a short vertical stroke. The *keraia* is a short horizontal stroke used to distinguish between two otherwise identical Hebrew letters.
81 Abstention from meat, cheese and eggs was the fasting diet for periods such as Lent in Orthodox monasteries. Cathars ate fish (in the belief that fish did not reproduce sexually); there is no reference to this in the Bogomil material.

'Be kindly to your enemy.' They say that the devil is the enemy of man, and by a crazy interpretation, that we ought to be kindly to him and pay court to him with genuflection, as we showed earlier, so that he should not trip up and overthrow those who do not believe and hand them over to the judge, that is, God, to endure the sentence of condemnation on the day of judgement.

39.

['But I say to you, that everyone who divorces his wife except on the ground of fornication makes her an adulteress.' (Matt. 5.32)]

Since 'Anyone who divorces his wife except on the charge of fornication' and the rest of this saying contradicts their teaching about not marrying a woman, they say that all this is secret, inexplicable and only known to those who have put off the flesh. They strongly affirm the doctrine of celibacy and adduce the word of the Lord, 'In the resurrection they neither marry nor are married' [Matt. 22.30], thinking in their stupidity that 'resurrection' means repentance and the life of the gospel.

40.

[Do not swear at all . . . by Jerusalem, for it is the city of the great king, (Matt. 5.34, 36)]

'Do not swear by Jerusalem, because it is the city of the great king.' Now they say that the great king is the devil, because he is cosmocrator. Lord be merciful to us as we explain their blasphemies!

41.

[You have heard that it was said, 'An eye for an eye, and a tooth for a tooth.' (Matt. 5.38)]

'You have heard it said that an eye should be taken for an eye, and a tooth for a tooth.' They say that the eyes are the two laws, that of Moses and that of the Gospel.[82] Christ came to give a law instead of a law, the gospel law for the law of Moses, a way for a way, the narrow for the broad. How broad is the stupidity of the ignorant!

42.

['When you pray, go into your room and shut the door.' (Matt. 6.6)]

'When you pray, go into your room.' They say that the room is the mind, and starting from this point, that none of them should pray in

---

82 Ficker adds: 'the teeth (*odontes*) are the two ways (*hodoi*), the broad and the narrow'.

assemblies,[83] although they have clearly heard the prophet David ordering us to pray in the assemblies [Ps. 22.22].

43.

['Look at the birds of the air; they neither sow nor reap. [Matt. 6.26] ... Consider the lilies of the field, how they grow; they neither toil nor spin; yet I tell you, even Solomon in all his glory was not arrayed like one of these.' (Matt. 6.28–9)]

'Look at the birds of the air, that they do not sow nor reap.' They think that the birds of the air are the monks who live on columns[84] and who lead a life without labour and are nourished for nothing by the heavenly Father. They call themselves the lilies of the field because they are white in purity of heart and fiery in virtues. Solomon could not compare with any of these, as the covering of his soul was stained.

44.

['Do not give dogs what is holy, and do not throw your pearls before swine.' (Matt. 7.6)]

'Do not give what is holy to dogs, nor throw your pearls in front of swine' [Matt. 7.6]. What is holy is their simpler faith; the pearls are the more secret and more valuable doctrines of their error. By dogs and swine – what overweening arrogance – are meant the pious among us, as being idolaters. I shudder even to mention the remainder of their unspeakable opinions. They add that they receive one who converts to them as a dog or a pig. First they mortify him with prayer and fasting, and then baptize him, as we have shown before. Then to one who distinguishes himself more by small steps and additions, little by little they entrust what is holy and the pearls.

45.

['Beware of false prophets who come to you in sheep's clothing, but inwardly are ravening wolves.' (Matt. 7.15)]

'Beware of false prophets.' They say that false prophets – how absurd – means Basil, who was great in teaching, and Gregory the star of theology, and John the Golden-tongued, because they taught the received

83 In the Greek the word for 'assembly' and for 'church' are the same.
84 'Stylites' – ascetic monks who spent their lives on pillars – had existed in some numbers in the fourth and fifth centuries. It is not certain that there were any contemporary with Euthymius, but they were commonly represented on icons and in illuminated manuscripts, so the image would have been familiar.

doctrine.[85] I leave out the other absurdities of the sect, which they utter against these saints more than the rest, and which deserve thunder and a chasm and punishment of every sort.

46.

[On that day many will say to me, 'Lord, Lord, did we not prophesy in Your name and cast out demons in Your name? . . . And then I will declare unto them, 'I never knew you, depart from me, you workers of iniquity.' (Matt. 7.22–3)]

'Many will say on that day, "Lord, did we not prophesy in Your name, and in Your name cast out demons?" Then I will say to them, "I never knew you, depart from me, ye workers of iniquity" [Matt. 7.22–23]. When they interpret these words of the Gospel, they say that these are those whom we consider holy bishops and godly fathers, all who were esteemed for their prophetic grace, and who cast out demons and did many other wonderful works. All these wonders were done by their indwelling demons to impress the unlearned. And yet demon does not cast out demon [Mark 3.23], as Christ himself said, who is the truth. Rabid dog, the poison of asps is on your lips.

47.

['Every one, then, who hears these words of mine and does them, will be like a wise man who built his house on the rock; and the rain fell and the floods came and the winds blew and beat upon that house, but it did not fall, because it had been founded on the rock. And everyone who hears these words of mine and does not do them, will be like a foolish man who built his house upon the sand, and the rains fell, and the floods came, and the winds blew, and beat against that house, and it fell; and great was the fall of it.'. (Matt. 7.24–7)]

They say that the prudent man is they themselves, who built his house on the rock of the Our Father. The foolish man they say is us, who have built our house on the sand of other prayers which, though they are many, are foolish and weak – so these foolish folk think.

48.

[And a scribe came up and said to him, 'Teacher, I will follow you wherever you go.' Jesus said to him, 'Foxes have holes, and the birds of the air have nests, but the Son of man has nowhere to lay his head'. (Matt. 8.19–20)]

---

85 Basil (*c.* 330–79), Gregory (either of Nazianzus, 329–89, or of Nyssa, *c.* 330–*c.* 395) and John Chrysostom (*c.* 347–407) are leading figures in the theology of the Greek Church.

'And coming forward, a scribe said to him, "Master, I will follow you wherever you go." Jesus said to him, "Foxes have dens, and the birds of the air have nests, but the Son of man does not have anywhere to lay his head."' They say that by 'scribe' is meant anyone who is learned, and they advise one another not to accept anyone educated among their pupils, in imitation, as they say, of Christ, who did not accept the scribe. They say that 'foxes' means those ascetics who live confined in narrow cells, like dens. The 'birds of the air' are stylites, as I said before, with whom Christ totally refuses to dwell, as not being worthy of His company. The throat of these destroyers is an open tomb which gives off a bad smell and pours forth destructive poison through its impious mouth.

49.

[And when he came to the other side . . . two demoniacs met him, coming out of the tombs . . . The demons . . . came out and went into the swine, and, behold, the whole herd rushed down the steep bank into the sea and perished in the waters. (Matt. 8.28, 32)]

They say that the two men affected by demons who came out of the tombs are the order of monks and the order of clerics. They always live in sanctuaries made with hands, and these are tombs enriched with the bones of the dead. This is what these accursed call the relics of the saints. These two orders are supremely feared by the Bogomils, so that none of them is strong enough to go down that road. The 'herd of pigs' is the common herd of unlearned swinish men whom they approach and teach and throw headlong and overwhelm in the sea of sin.

50.

[Neither is new wine put into old wineskins; if it is, the skins burst and the wine is spilled . . . but new wine is put into fresh wineskins . . . (Matt. 9.17)]

The 'new wine' they say is their teaching, but the old wineskins are those who do not accept it. The 'new skins' are those who accept it and keep it inside them.

51.

[A woman who had suffered from a haemorrhage for twelve years came up from behind him . . . (Matt. 9.20)]

The woman who suffered from a haemorrhage for twelve years is the Church in Jerusalem, which haemorrhaged with the blood spilt in sacrifices by the twelve tribes of Israel. This haemorrhage Christ made cease, and soon afterwards he destroyed Jerusalem. How could the twelve tribes mean twelve years? For a year is a movement and interval of time, but a tribe is a class of men. What a difference there is between man and time!

52. Listen to the most ridiculous interpretation, and from that you will learn the stupidity of those who tell such fairy-tales, like drunken old women. For instance, 'Jesus rebuked them [*enebrimesato*]' [Matt. 9.30] they interpret as 'Jesus gave them a word to eat [*enebromatisen*]'. Here I seem myself to be ridiculous when I answer their absurdity.

That is why I have run through many things and have noted the headings summarily. Anyone who encounters it should recognize from these few notes the rest of what comes, as they say, from the same workshop. We have uncovered a vast sea of impiety which needs many days to cross it; we are still a little way from land. I realize that you are seasick; I too suffered in the same way before you. It seems to me better to let down the sail of my argument and, turning the prow, to put into the harbour of silence. All the more, since that evil and babbling tongue is silent, those polluted lips are closed which uttered all that unhallowed nonsense. The mouth of those who spoke evil is stopped. Our most wise and magnanimous emperor summoned him, revealed the defence of his writings and, testing it, found it rang hollow, like copper alloy. Although he announced a change of heart, immediately, like a dog, he returned to his vomit.

The emperor considered the matter, took as his council all those in office, both the civil and ecclesiastical, and judged that he should undergo the sentence of burning, because he had sent many to the burning fires of Gehenna. Now he has been burnt and departed, and taken his blasphemy as a shroud. Is there anyone knowing how to equal a lament with its cause who would weep adequately for him, who studied erroneous doctrine for fifteen years, taught it for more than forty[86] and dragged thousands of disciples to the pit of destruction, and who in the end did not join them easily? He was struck out of both lives and gained fire in this one and in that, and passed from the extinguishable to that which cannot be quenched. We ought to take heart for the future, The dragon's head is off.[87] Some of its limbs and parts have already received what is most appropriate, some are about to, some are being individually denounced. We are nourished by the hope that not even the tail will escape the careful concern of the emperor, who is God's fellow-worker,

---

86 Ficker has 'fifty-two'.
87 The imagery here is taken from Revelation 12.3, where the enemies of the Church are symbolized by a great red dragon.

and his zealous search, which with great care strains to catch them all within his net and reveal the field of piety, clean of tares.

The 'origin myth' of Bogomilism: the instruction given to new converts according to the *Narratio* of Euthymius Zigabenus

So that my argument may proceed in order, an explanation is necessary of what precedes, which the heretics call their origin myth and theology, but we call foolishness and the study of atheism. This they entrust to those whose feathers are beginning to sprout, to nurture them after their original instruction, preserving the fouler doctrines for later, and entrusting them to the more initiated in impiety as mysteries. Since many of these are strange, erroneous and contradict one another, they must be put down to the stupidity of the heresiarchs, who so openly contradict and are conquered by their own arrows, as the proverb goes; in this way evil fights both good and itself, and is pierced by its own weapons.

They tell the story that the good God and Father, when He had created thousands upon thousands and ten thousands upon ten thousands of angels, had Samael as second to himself, his steward, who had the same dress and shape as He, who sat at His right hand and received honour next after Him. He was intoxicated by this and fell into madness; he plotted rebellion, and then, having done so, he took the opportunity to test all the powers that served, asking them if they wanted to lighten the burden of their service and follow him in rebelling against the Father. As evidence for this nonsense, they cite the parable in the gospel of Luke of the steward of unrighteousness who reduced the sums owed by the debtors. They say that he is Samael, and that this parable is written about him. The aforesaid angels were enticed by the lightening of their toilsome service and the other burdensome commands, for he said, 'I will place my throne above the clouds and will be like the most high' [Isa. 14.14]. They joined him in rebellion and shared his plot. God perceived this, and threw them all down headlong together.

Then Samael was at a loss and was unable to sit upon the waters, for, they say, 'the earth was invisible and unprepared' [Gen. 1.2]. But since he still had the appearance and dress of God and possessed the divine grace of creation, he called the powers together and encouraged them in these words: 'God created heaven and earth. I will create a second heaven, as I am the second God, and the rest in order.' He said, 'Let the firmament be created', and it was created; 'Let such and such be created', and they were all created. Having adorned the second heaven, he drew back the water from the face of the earth and arranged it in the places which seemed fit to him, as the book of Genesis tells. Having beautified it and established it, he assigned it to himself and the rebellious powers to live in. Then he moulded the body of Adam from earth mixed with water, and made him stand upright. A little moisture ran down from him into Adam's right foot, and, running through the big toe, it ran out on to the ground, twisting, and made the shape of a snake. Samael gathered together the breath that was in him and breathed life into the body which he had moulded, but the breath ran down through the empty space to the right foot in the same way, and, trickling through the big toe, it ran out into the twisted drop. All at once it came to life, separated from the two, became a snake and crawled away. For this reason it became intelligent and knowledgeable, because Samael's inspiration had come into its soul. When this new creator saw this and realized that his labour was in vain, he sent an embassy to the good Father and asked Him to send breath, saying in the message that if man came to life, he would be common to them both, and that from his race the places in heaven of the outcast angels might be filled. Because God is good, He breathed out and instilled the breath of life into what Samael had made. Immediately man became a living soul, glorious in body and adorned with many graces. Next in order, Eve was made similarly, and gleamed with the same brightness. Samael was envious and repented, and turned to plot against what he had moulded. He slid into the insides of the snake, deceived Eve, slept with her and made her pregnant, so that his seed might get a start and overcome the seed of Adam, and as far as possible might destroy it and not allow it to increase or grow. Soon she was taken with labour pains, and gave birth to Cain from her union with Samael, together with his twin sister who was like him, named Calamena.[88] Adam was jealous, and himself slept with Eve and begot Abel. Immediately Cain destroyed him, and brought murder to life. That is why the apostle John says, 'Cain is of the evil one' [1 John 3.12]. When Samael slipped shamelessly into Eve through the intermediary of the serpent, at once he lost his divine shape and dress and, as they say, his gift of creation and the name of God. Until then he too had been called God. He was stripped of all these, and became dark and unpleasant to look at. Until then the good Father had held back His anger and given free rein to this cosmocrator and lord of what he possessed, as he fell from above.

So he had possession of these things and was lord of all. Then since men were under bitter tyranny and were being cruelly destroyed, a few of the

---

88 See note 27 above.

Father's party came into being with difficulty, and rose to the rank of the angels. Then at length the Father realized that He had been tricked, recognized that He was wronged, because although He had provided the most essential part of man and supplied what was most essential for his completion, He was deprived of the greater part of the race. At the same time he took pity on the soul, His own creation, which was suffering so grievously and unable to rise to safety, so in the year 5500 He poured forth from His heart a Word, that is His Son, God. 'My heart', they say, 'has uttered a good word' [Ps. 45.2]. He taught him his own words, 'I will address my words to the king.' That is why in the gospels He says, 'If I am not doing the works of my Father, then do not believe me' [John 10.37]. They affirm that this Word and Son is the archangel Michael, and 'His name' they say 'is the angel of good counsel' [Isa. 9.6]. He is called archangel because he is more divine than all the angels, Jesus because he heals all disease and weakness, Christ as anointed with flesh. He descended from above and slipped in through the right ear of the Virgin, and took on flesh which in appearance was physical and like a human body, but in reality was immaterial and godlike; he went out again as he had come in, and the Virgin knew nothing of his entrance or exit, but simply found him lying swaddled in the cave. He accomplished the plan of the Incarnation and did and taught what is set out in the Gospels. He was crucified and died, and, appearing to rise again, he rolled back the curtain, revealed the play, laid by the mask and imprisoned the rebel. He bound him with a thick and heavy chain and shut him in Tartarus, having taken the 'el' from his name, as being angelic. For having been called not only Samael but Satanael, he became Satan. Then, when he had fulfilled the duty laid upon him, he returned to the Father and sat at his right hand on the throne of Satanael, who had been cast down. Then he returned whence he came, and was dissolved back into the Father, in whose womb he had been enclosed in the beginning. When he taught his disciples in the world, he gave them the Holy Spirit, that is, the apostolic teaching. Now the Father is presented as something with three faces, a monstrous being; the middle one is of human shape, from which man was created, 'according to His image and likeness' [Gen. 1.26]. From each of the Father's temples shines forth a ray, that of the Son to the right and the Spirit to the left. So finally the Father becomes three-faced; before he had only one face. Satanael, as has been shown above, used to have the same shape as he. That is why, when he moulded man, he said, 'Let us make man in our image and likeness'; clearly the image of himself and of the Father.

Such is the teaching of the old relic of evil days [Sus. 52], their great teacher and the producer of apostles among them, truly a creature of the evil one, the chosen instrument of the devil [Acts 9.15], the treasure-store of Satan, the tool of all impiety. He called it a summary of their profane heresy ...

26. ABJURATION FORMULA AND FORM OF RECEPTION INTO THE CHURCH FOR BOGOMIL CONVERTS

The anathema formula (a), with its attached draft *libellum* or formula for written abjuration (b) and the discharge certificate (c) can only be dated by MS evidence. (a) and (b) are both contained in an eleventh-century MS, Vindob. th. gr.306, which is a collection of anti-heretical material. The most recent study of this collection, by Eleuteri and Rigo (*Eretici, dissidenti, musulmani ed ebrei a Bisanzio*), suggests that it was made *c.* 1150–60, though some elements in it are earlier. The anathema formula (a) shares most of its condemnatory clauses with the *Synodikon of Orthodoxy* [16]. This part of the *Synodikon* was probably added after all the Comnenian heresy trials, and certainly after the trial of the Bogomil Basil, *c.* 1098 (for which see [24]). The certificate (c) is included here because of its similarity of content. The only MS from which it is known is from the thirteenth century, dated on the evidence of notarial formulae to 1258/9. It appears to be the only surviving example of the formula used for the reconciliation of Bogomils, especially the lay members of the group, though the existence of something similar can be inferred from other material.

(a) was originally published by von Thalloczy, 'Bruchstücken aus der Geschichte der nordwestlichen Balkanlander, V', and it was re-edited and reprinted in Ficker, *Die Phundagiagiten*, p. 172. A more recent edition is to be found in Eleuteri and Rigo, pp. 136–55, together with the texts of (b) and (c).

(a) CONCERNING THE BLASPHEMOUS MANY-FORMED HERESY OF THE ATHEIST MESSALIANS WHO ARE ALSO KNOWN AS PHUNDAITES[1] AND BOGOMILS AND EUCHITES AND ENTHUSIASTS AND ENCRATITES AND MARCIONISTS

Those of the foul heresy of the Bogomils who approach the most holy great Church of God, those who derive from the Manichaeans and are worse than they, should be received like this.

1 *sic*; for the same spelling see [46].

One who has already associated and mingled with them, has shared their table and accepted the heresy, but has not received the *epode*[2] or approached the *cosmocrator* or worshipped him in their demonic nocturnal initiatory rites in their customary places, nor abjured Christ, should be received and be instructed, after he has been shriven and prayed for forty days on end. After this period he should prepare himself, and take his stance in front of the holy font with his head uncovered, and anathematize the *kephalaia*[3] of the Bogomils. Next he should set this out in writing in a *libellum*, and so say the propitiatory prayers and the one written against those who have apostasized. Then immediately he is worthy of the pure and life-giving mysteries and Christ, while they impose on him that he should be instructed by some spiritual monk.

If anyone has spent some time in this sort of heresy, has received the *epode* and worshipped the evil one, as he should not, whether he approaches the holy Church of God of his own accord or because he has been detected, he is to be accepted and instructed, and needs the anathemas and the *libellum*, but he is not wholly worthy of the anointing of holy chrism or of the holy mysteries. When he has completed twice forty days in church, let him be entrusted to some well-known monastery. The abbot should command him[4] to remain within the monastery all his life and not permit him to leave it; all the more experienced monks should observe his way of life and make sure that he does not entice any of the monks into his heresy; anyone who has experienced this is hard to cure or to change. He ought to be isolated within the monastery, to eat dry food and to bend the knee as the pastor may determine, and observe his penance, and this must continue for the whole of his life, even if he appears to approach the holy icons with fervour of soul, as is the way of Enthusiasts and Euchites. If he is near to death, then he shall be deemed worthy of the holy sacrifice, so that he may not be without the good viaticum. If he persists in his heresy and is recognized as being of this opinion, he shall not share the divine mysteries even on his death-bed. If, when he has spent three years in the monastery, as has been enacted, it is then clearly seen and witnessed that he has been converted to the Lord

---

2 For the 'reception of the *epode*' as the initiation ritual among Bogomils see EP **[19]**.
3 Mani was the author of a work with this title; perhaps the use of the term here is designed to suggest a link? No other source makes a specific reference to a Bogomil teaching work with this title. Alternatively some general meaning such as 'teachings' may be meant.
4 Reading *paranggelon*, with Eleuteri and Rigo.

in sincerity and simplicity, he shall be deemed worthy of holy chrism and the sacraments.

The anathematization takes this form. After the candidate's head has been anointed by the priest in front of the holy font, he says three times, 'I, so-and-so, who have approached the holy great Church of God today from the blasphemous and manifold heresy of the atheist Messalians, that is the Bogomils, not from any force or necessity, nor in craft or hypocrisy, but with my whole soul and a sincere and pure heart, for the love of Christ and with faith in Him make this present written *libellum* as a guarantee to you, catechists, so-and-so and so-and-so, and through you to our most holy lord, the ecumenical patriarch, the divine and holy canons and the pious laws, as shall be made clear. So then, having anathematized these views with my own lips in the presence of the great Church, see, I also subject to anathema through this present written *libellum* of mine all those who are involved in the satanic heresy of the Messalians or Enthusiasts and Epeuchites and those who share their views, saying as follows:

1. To Peter, the leader of the heresy of the Messalians or Lycopetrians and Phoundaiates and Pogomils [*sic*], who called himself Christ . . . [*The text continues as in the parallel anathemas in the Synodikon of Orthodoxy* **[16]**. After these anathemas there is a concluding paragraph.]

(**b**) So then, having insulted and anathematized all the heresy of the Manichaeans in the presence of the Church of God, and having forsworn it in writing, I confirm and with this *libellum* declare that if from this time forward I should ever be found at any time or season in the company of any of the Bogomils, whether it be monk or nun or layperson of any kind, mixing with them or eating or drinking with them, or appearing to pray with them or secretly defiling the holy churches of God or the holy icons within them,[5] or am accused of any other Bogomil misdeed and am convicted, may I not merely be deprived of all ecclesiastical aid, but may I be transferred to civil justice and be liable to every penalty without remission, and be condemned for my entire life to be sent into perpetual exile.[6]

(**c**) So-and-so together with his wife[7] so-and-so are alleged to have been

---

5 See EP **[19]** for charges that Bogomils defiled churches and icons deliberately.
6 See Balsamon **[29]** for an alternative version of the penalties for heresy which might be imposed by the civil authorities and **[4]** for the controversy this had given rise to earlier.
7 Since Bogomil leaders did not marry, these must be lay members of the sect.

contaminated by evil neighbours and to have been infected with the wicked heresy, the cult hateful to God and men, of the Bogomils. Since they were infected through ignorance and eagerly await the second coming of Our Lord and Saviour Jesus Christ, who will punish for ever with the fire He has prepared all those collaborators who have abandoned Christ our Lord and God and Saviour and have adhered to the crooked and rebellious devil, they have come with all their hearts, with contrite spirit and appearance and glance, with humble choice, to the most worthy *kathegoumenos*[8] and spiritual father so-and-so, and have made a sincere confession, in case they have in any way gone astray (as is human) and have been infected by their evil neighbours and their enchantments,[9] and have accepted from him the canonical penalty. Then they have approached the Holy Church and, having admitted such appalling behaviour and anathematized the heresies and teachings of the Bogomils in the presence of me, unworthy, I have instructed them and catechized them and taught them and done everything that the canons and the Church enjoin to them. I have brought them into the Holy Church of God and numbered them among the pious flock of Christ our God, the chief shepherd. In addition I have issued to him [*sic*] the present written evidence of pardon as a guarantee in the month and indiction so-and-so.

27. A SERMON AGAINST THE BOGOMILS FOR THE SUNDAY OF ALL SAINTS (*c.* 1107)

The printed text of this homily follows the MS, which attributes it anachronistically to the patriarch John Xiphilinus (1064–75), but the contents make it clear that the sermon was preached after the trial and execution of the Bogomil Basil in *c.* 1098 (see **[24]**, **[25]**). Its phraseology has some echoes of Euthymius Zigabenus and also of the Bogomil section of the *Synodikon of Orthodoxy* (**[16]**, section d). In the MS title it is dated to the second Sunday after Pentecost – the feast of All Saints in the Orthodox Church – but the order of the collection and thus the dating of individual sermons to particular Sundays may not have authority.[1]

The text is that published in *PG* 120, 1289–92, from a Venetian MS of twenty-five sermons attributed to John Xiphilinus.

8 The superior of a monastery.
9 See note 2 above.
1 See Gouillard, 'Le Synodikon d'orthodoxie', pp. 232–3.

ON THE SUNDAY OF ALL SAINTS

On the gospel of Matthew, chapter 10

I think it is a good time to speak briefly to you about the foul heresy of the Messalians,[2] since we celebrate their overthrow and condemnation today. Our most pious and Christian emperor[3] disproved and condemned what had been for the most part hidden and had been unnoticed by the simple; then sentenced their leader, their instructor in wickedness, to the fire of justice and ordered their evil teaching to be anathematized by the Church. Know then that there are people like this, who go round dressed as monks[4] and appear like bait, hiding the wolf under the sheep-skin, foul wretches that they are. That is why the simple accept them as pious; they mix the poison of evil into fair words and stir a deadly drug into their honeyed syrup. At first they teach that they believe simply in Father, Son and Holy Spirit; that they acknowledge the incarnation of Christ, and claim to obey the commandments of the Gospel; they teach people to pray and to fast and to keep themselves pure from all pollution. As time goes on, they sow tares in the wheat; when they have made the wretches tame and have caught their prey within the net, then they pour out the poison and blaspheme openly, revealing the doctrines and dogmas of the devil. What these are and how many they are, this is not the time to tell, for they are a mixture of all the worst heresies. This at least you ought to know. At the outset their teaching is such as we said earlier, but it is only in name that it agrees with us; in reality it is entirely different. Since they are darkness like their father, they pretend to be light; when they teach that they honour the Father and the Son and the Holy Spirit with their lips, they extol a different Trinity from the holy and life-giving one that we venerate.[5] They blasphemously imagine some power seated on high in their mythical highest of the seven heavens[6] and say that this power of theirs has a human shape.[7] They are keen to lay claim to virginity, in opposition to us. For we embrace it, thinking it more valuable and lofty than marriage,

---

2 For the historical Messalians and the use of this term by later heresiologists to describe the Bogomils see EZ **[25]**, and note 4 there.
3 Alexius I Comnenus (1081–1118).
4 For claims that the Bogomils of Constantinople dressed as monks see EZ **[25]**, c. 24 and Anna Comnena **[24]**, c. 1.
5 i.e. the Bogomils honoured God the Father, Satan, his elder son and Christ, his younger son. See EZ **[25]**, c. 6 and note there.
6 See EP **[19]** and note 38.
7 This seems to be an allusion to the language used (according to EZ **[25]**, c. 3, note 10) by the Bogomils of Constantinople to describe their Trinitarian doctrine.

and established for those who have received training,[8] but they do so from their hatred of marriage, which the Lord blessed, saying, 'Marriage is honourable, and so is an unstained bed.' They teach continence, but not as a way of quieting passions, but in distaste for food, as having been made by the evil one. They pretend to love retirement and claim to settle in lonely places[9] because they are avoiding the churches and want to remain undetected...

28. THE POSTHUMOUS TRIAL OF CONSTANTINE CHRYSOMALLUS FOR HERESY (1140)

This is the official record of a trial held in the church of St Alexius in Constantinople in May 1140 at a synod presided over by the patriarch Leo II Stypes. The bishops present examined the writings of Constantine Chrysomallus, a layman who had recently died in the monastery of St Nicholas at Hieron,[1] which had circulated among monks and influential laymen. The synod found evidence of Messalianism and Bogomilism in these works, and ordered them to be burnt. Modern scholars incline to view Chrysomallus' teaching (as reported by the synod) as an attempt to cultivate the spirituality of personal illumination advocated by St Symeon the New Theologian.[2]

The text is translated from that published by Gouillard, 'Quatre procès de mystiques à Byzance'.

Month of May, third indiction, under the presidency of our most holy lord and ecumenical patriarch *kyr* Leo, in the right hand catechumenate of St Alexios; joined with him in session the most holy bishops of Ancyra, Cyzicus, Amasea, Melitene, Laodicea, Crete, Antioch in Pisidia, Trajanopolis, Philippi, Amastris and Mesembria, and in the presence of the patriarchal officials... [A paragraph follows which stresses the need for theologians to be trained experts.]

So then, taking cognizance of the fact that many have taken upon themselves of their own initiative to teach others, and in our concern for the salvation of the majority (especially simple folk, who are not compe-

---

8 i.e. in the religious life.
9 i.e. to behave in the same way as orthodox hermits did.
1 Hieron in this context may be the naval base on the Bosphoros mentioned in the writings of EP **[19]**. For monasteries there, see Janin *Les Églises el monastères des grands centres byzantines*, p. 10.
2 See our Introduction, p. 40.

tent to discern the difference between nourishing plants and those which are poisonous), we have learnt from some monks who were fulfilling their vocation in the monastery called Of *kyr* Nicholas at Hieron that they had found some writings of the late Constantine Chrysomallus. When they came upon these, they were not a little scandalized, because they contain much that was strange and bizarre, as they said. These writings had already been widely distributed, because people thought they were very profitable and very appropriate as providing a rule of life for many. As we took this very seriously, we took possession of the books which had come into the hands of those who had obtained copies of them, and learnt by enquiry that there was one in the hands of a certain Peter, monk and abbot of the monastery of St Athenagoras, another in those of the *proedros* George Pamphilus, and a third in the possession of the monks aforesaid, who had brought the matter to our attention. They said that they had got theirs from Euthymius, a monk of the monastery of Gerocomeion. When we compared all three together, we found that the contents were the same in all, as if derived from the same original, but that the copy belonging to Peter was fuller than the other two. In these two the material was divided into 150 chapters . . .

He says that any Christian who has been baptized (because in accordance with prevailing practice this happens in infancy and, as he puts it, 'without catechism') is not truly a Christian, even though he may be so called, and even if he has practised some of the virtues, he has done so like a pagan; that he ought not to read the words of the teaching of the gospel, but first be rebaptised, initiated and converted, that is to say, removed from the power of Satan.

He also says that all those called Christians who have not received their regeneration from holy baptism, even if they attain the rank of bishop and have all holy scripture on the tip of their tongue and give instruction in their conceit at the knowledge which puffs them up, it profits them nothing unless they have been catechized and receive regeneration and the formation of the disposition of their souls through the mediation and laying-on of hands of the expert stewards of this great mystery, who are skilled in holy knowledge . . .

Surely such opinions are clearly the characteristics of the heresies aforesaid. That he demands from the baptized a spiritual perception, or an intellectual perception, or merely a perception (as he says elsewhere) and illumination and revelation and comprehension of the Spirit, and says that otherwise their baptism is useless, even if they devote themselves to all kinds of good actions – this is completely part of the heresy of the

Enthusiasts,[3] who imagine that they receive divine revelations by the deceit of demons.

That even after holy baptism those who have been baptized, inasmuch as they have been reborn without catechism (as they say) – that is, all of us Christians, including teachers, priests and even bishops – need to be catechized again from the beginning, initiated and regenerated by means of an initiation he introduced, the imposition of hands by the skilful stewards of some mystic grace. Such men he says must be sought out with all care, since it is rare to find those who alone are able to renew those who approach them and make them sharers in the grace of God – this belongs to the Bogomils who introduce a second holy baptism of their own which brings perfection and provides the Holy Spirit.

That a Christian has two souls, or is no Christian, as they say, is explicitly taught as doctrine by the foul heresy of the Messalians or Bogomils.[4] . . .

So then . . . we determined that the books themselves should be burnt forthwith; we have subjected to anathema all those who share these views . . . We threatened Pamphilus with the penalties laid down if in future he were to have or to share these views. As for the monk Peter – thinking that it was not appropriate for him to have charge of others in the future, both because of the injury done to the conscience of many through him and because it might give rise to dispute or suspicion, and also because he was inadequate for this position, for how can a man be judged capable of guiding and instructing others, who was so completely ignorant as he claims to have been, and so unable to detect impiety that was evident to everyone else? – we determined that he should be sent to another monastery to be placed under another master and director, as he grovelled at the feet of our Mediocrity, and that of all the assembly of bishops.

---

3 Another name for Messalians?
4 This is a Messalian doctrine, there is no other evidence that Bogomils shared it.

29. THE PATRIARCH MICHAEL II (1143–46) ORDERS THE BURNING OF BOGOMILS

The author of this extract, Theodore Balsamon, who lived from c. 1130–40 until some time after 1195, was a canon lawyer. His commentary on the *Nomocanon*, the collection of Byzantine canon law, was probably started in the 1170s and includes references to material now lost. There is no other reference to the burning of Bogomils in the reign of Manuel I.

The translation has been made from the version of the text in *PG* 104, col. 1111.

Commentary on *Nomocanon IX*. 25. Do not be surprised that the synod of Constantinople in the time of the most holy patriarch *kyr* Michael Oxites[1] enacted and enjoined that Bogomils should be burnt. For it is probable that the law was not then enforced, and especially because the Bogomils, unrepentantly adhering to their personal heresy, seized on burning as a form of martyrdom. I know that no canon has ever enjoined punishment, and ecclesiastical law has not known corporal penalties, but rather the civil law has. I am still surprised that the synod enjoined a punishment of this kind, for we have been told to cut heretics off from the body of Christ, but we have not learnt to punish them, but rather to hand them over to the civil power if they are unrepentant, and that sentence against them be given by the magistrates.

30. TWO CAPPADOCIAN BISHOPS ARE CONDEMNED FOR BOGOMILISM (1143)

The trial of these two men was one of the first ecclesiastical acts in the reign of the emperor Manuel (1143–80), who was careful to appoint two members of his own family to the synod which condemned them, a fact which underlines its perceived importance. The charges brought against them do not substantiate the allegation that they were Bogomils. The cities to which they had been appointed as bishops were deep in Asia Minor, in areas under Turkish control and suffering from a lack of clerical manpower, which was the cause of the irregularity of their consecration. Both men had to improvise solutions to the problems of ecclesiastical discipline created in a frontier area, and neither appears to have had the personal qualities necessary to bring pressure on local Christians without local public opinion to back them up. For reasons which the synod proceedings do not make clear, they fell foul of the new metropolitan. The charge of Bogomilism is evidence of the fear that this heresy created; little in their teaching as recorded in the synod proceedings confirms the charge.

1 For heresy trials during this patriarchate see [30], [31] below.

The text translated has been taken from the version published by Gouillard in 'Quatre procès de mystiques à Byzance.'

Semeioma of the deposition of the pseudo-bishops of the province of Tyana, those of Sasima and Balbissa, on the grounds of uncanonical ordination. They were afterwards convicted of Bogomilism. On the 20 August, the sixth day of the week, the sixth indiction[1] under the presidency of our most holy lord and ecumenical Patriarch *kyr* Michael[2] in Thomaitis; associated with his Holiness in session the most holy bishops of Ephesus, Heraclea, Ancyra, Nicomedia, Nicaea, Gangra, Antioch in Pisidia, Hierapolis, Mesembria and in the presence of the patriarchal officials.

We were joined today as a result of the imperial rescript issued at the request of Basil, the most holy metropolitan of Tyana, by the *pansebastos sebastos* and Great Drungarius,[3] the most blessed archbishop of Bulgaria[4] and the most illustrious *protoasecretis*,[5] who had been commanded to join our Humility and our divine synod in judgement on those charges of the Bogomil heresy which had been brought by the aforesaid most holy metropolitan of Tyana, in his capacity as metropolitan of the district and not as an accuser, against two so-called bishops, that they taught and thought erroneously and had spread such a foul cult to many Cappadocians to their destruction . . .

[The report of the proceedings of the first session of the synod has been omitted. In it it was established that Leontius and Clement had only been consecrated as bishops by the then metropolitan, not by the three bishops demanded by canon law, and that their consecration was therefore invalid.]

Semeioma of the judgement passed on the monks Clement of Sasima and Leontius of Balbissa (previously stripped of the rank of bishop on the grounds of uncanonical ordination) on the charge brought by the most holy metropolitan of Tyana, *kyr* Basil, that they belonged to the most foul heresy of the Bogomils.

1 October, sixth day of the week, seventh indiction, under the presidency of our most holy lord and ecumenical Patriarch Michael, in

1 1143.
2 Michael II Curcuas (1143–46).
3 Constantine Comnenus, son of Isaac, the brother of Alexius I.
4 Adrian (John in religion) Comnenus, son of Isaac, brother of Alexius I.
5 For this man and his position see **[31]**, note 3.

Thomaitis . . . [The list of members of the synod follows, containing the same senior members of the imperial family, officials and bishops. The metropolitan of Tyana, Basil, was represented by a clerk named Leo.]

The *kanonikos*[6] of Tyana submitted a deposition which . . . most clearly demonstrated that anyone who acted thus was not motivated by orthodox piety, but truly suffered from the Bogomil disease. The deposition had been put together . . . by clerics and officials and people who simply lived in the metropolis of Tyana, and gave evidence of activities of this kind on the part of the accused:

that they taught that men should abstain from cohabitation with their lawfully married wives, from meat and fish and wine, for three years. After this every kind of enjoyment of this sort is permissible.

again, [they also taught] that no layman can be saved, even if he practises every virtue, unless he becomes a monk.

that those who have just been married should be barred from all intercourse with one another till some days have passed.

[they were also charged] that they give the tonsure to men without the knowledge of their wives, and let wives take the veil without the permission of their husbands.

that they had left some Christians who had died unburied and without funeral rites, and had not admitted them to penitence even in their lifetime.

that they disinterred the remains of Christians (buried both inside and outside churches), saying that those who had died were sinners and that demons inhabit the bodies of the dead.[7]

that they would not allow veneration to be paid to the cross unless it bore the inscription 'Jesus Christ the Son of God'.

that they rebaptized the children of Christians, claiming that those who baptized them were sinners.[8]

that they had ordained women as deaconesses and given them permission to make the customary prayers in church, to read the holy gospel and to join in the liturgy with Clement.[9]

---

6 The canon law official of the diocese.
7 For a similar belief allegedly held by Bogomils see EZ [25], c. 13.
8 For the orthodox position on the problems raised by the administration of the sacraments by clergy whose own morality was suspect, see Hugh Eteriano [36].
9 One of the functions of the deacon in the liturgy of the Orthodox Church is to lead the litanies to which the congregation respond, as well as reading the gospel.

that they destroyed holy icons.

that as concerns the holy cross of the Great Commander [of the heavenly host], they claimed that the many miracles which it performs result from diabolic activity.[10]

that they anathematized the God in whom bishop Acacius[11] believes, a man acknowledged by those from whom the deposition originated as an orthodox Christian.

in addition, that they had handed over Christian women into pagan hands on the pretext of adultery . . .

Leontius admitted that he had rebaptized, but only because the original baptism had been performed by a priest who had been deposed on manifest charges, and after the latter's deposition. He was asked to establish how the baptism was debatable. Since he could not do this – the explanation was lengthy – what had taken place was adduced as evidence of the heretical views of Leontius, on the grounds that he had the audacity to rebaptize in accordance with the foul cult of the Bogomils,[12] and that the case presented by Leontius, that the priest who had performed the first baptism had been deposed, was totally inadequate to justify the proceeding.

In addition Leontius admitted that he had left some corpses unburied and without funeral rites, and said that he had done so because the dead had been sinners in their lifetime and had not obeyed him when he counselled them to amendment.

He also admitted that he had handed over a Christian woman to the Emir's representative in the *kastron*, saying that she had had the audacity to commit adultery with her husband's brother, and that he had been unable to think of any other way of bringing the evil to an end.

He also admitted that he had burned down a divine temple, for this reason. He had often told a man who stored hay in the church to stop doing so, but found that he paid no attention. For this reason he had set light to the hay that had been stored there even after he forbade it, and the result of the fire was that the church had burnt down, contrary to his

10 The Great Commander of the heavenly host is St Michael. This wonder-working cross is not otherwise known; perhaps it should be linked with the great pilgrim church of St Michael at Chonae, some sixty miles from the dioceses of the accused.
11 Gouillard, 'Quatre procès de mystiques à Byzance', p. 42 suggests that Acacius was an earlier incumbent of the see, of impeccably orthodox opinions. Otherwise this reference is unexplained.
12 Other sources suggest Bogomil opposition to orthodox baptism, but not re-baptism by Bogomils. See EZ [25], c. 16.

intention... The monk Clement admitted the ordination of deaconesses.

As they remained obdurate in the face of the other charges and were not willing to admit them [further witnesses were called]. These made many other accusations beside the ones contained in the deposition which they did not accept, much more serious than those recorded, which clearly showed that they did not have orthodox and pious views.

Since we had formed a firm conviction from what they had admitted and thought that it was unnecessary to submit to oaths men who were more than ready to take them from their zeal for piety, we were satisfied with their own admissions. Judging that the rejection of sinners and refusal of forgiveness to them even after death was a product and teaching of the cult of the Bogomils, to omit the other important points, we agreed to determine that they thought and taught as Bogomils do. So therefore it is our care to safeguard them for the future, keeping them solitary, so that they may not share their corruption with others either in conversations or in any other way, and simultaneously to keep a watch on them to see if they veer towards amendment, and root out the heretical doctrines which they have sown.[13]

[In the original a third document follows, recording the fact that the accused had anathematized their errors and sending a signed copy of the entire proceedings to the province where the case had originated.]

31. THE MONK NIPHON IS CONDEMNED FOR BOGOMILISM (1144)

The condemnation of the monk Niphon on charges of heresy is connected with both [30] and [32]. He was initially condemned at the same sitting of the patriarchal synod as Leontius and Clement (for whom see [30]). His own views are not reported in sufficient detail to explain his condemnation, apart from the allegation that he supported Leontius and Clement with intemperate enthusiasm. Even the reported exclamation 'Anathema to the God of the Hebrews', which might suggest Bogomil-related hostility to the Old Testament, is scarcely enough. The emperor John II (1118–43) had respected him; perhaps in the new reign the attack had a political dimension. It was claimed that his friend, the later Patriarch Cosmas Atticus (for whose trial and deposition see [32]) had

---

[13] For a parallel programme of observation and solitude see the anathema instructions [26].

CHRISTIAN DUALIST HERESIES

been a supporter of the new emperor Manuel's brother Isaac; for a more detailed account of this see below, pp. 222, 224–5.

The text has been translated from that published in Mansi 21, col. 597.

Decree passed for the banishment to the monastery of the Periblepton[1] of Niphon the entirely foul Bogomil, on Friday 1 October, seventh indiction. Under the presidency of our most holy lord and ecumenical Patriarch *kyr* Michael in Thomaitis, joined in synod by his great holiness the *pansebastos sebastos* and great drungarios, the most blessed *sebastos* the archbishop of Bulgaria[2] and the most noble *protoasecretis* Icanatus,[3] with the most reverend archbishops of Ankara, Cyzicus, Nicomedia, Nicaea, Tyana, Antioch in Pisidia, Dyrrachium, Alania, Maduti, Mesembria, Cyzica, Garei and Gothia, and in the presence of noble lords.

Our Mediocrity has received many evil tidings sent by numerous persons concerning the monk Niphon, which contain much that is to his disadvantage. Now we have seen his writings which he sent to many in Cappadocia, addressed by name, which he has admitted are his, and that he insults the entire Church, calling them all heretics, as the blameless Domestic of the Secrets, Basil Cyminianus, and George, Secreticus of the second entry, and John, Secreticus of the Wine Service, whom we sent to him reported to me. So indeed did also some monks from the monastery in Cotya, and many other distinguished people . . .

It was greatly feared that if he were at large and went freely wherever he wished, mixing without hindrance with whomever he wanted, he would be responsible for spiritual harm to many, since, as far as we had heard, he did not appear to have orthodox opinions. For this reason, until we had gained more accurate information, clearly and exactly, we ordered that he should be sent to the venerable monastery of the Periblepton, and that an order should be given to the most pious abbot, to the *oeconomus* and to the other monks, that he should live quietly in one of the cells of the monastery with no visitors from outside, be served by only one servant, and speak freely to no one, either lay or ecclesiastic, not even to the monks in the monastery; that he should neither write nor teach nor send messages to anyone, either directly or through intermediaries, but should live quietly, as has been decreed . . .

1 For details of the history of this foundation see **[19]**, note 5.
2 The archbishop of Bulgaria was Adrian Comnenus (John in religion) and the great *drungarios* was Constantine Comnenus; both were emperor's cousins of the previous generation, sons of the *sebastocrator* Isaac, brother of Alexius I.
3 For the career and family associations of this man see Angold *Church and Society*, p. 293.

NIPHON IS CONDEMNED FOR BOGOMILISM

Decree, in which judgement was given on the false monk, the utterly foul Niphon, who confessed that he belonged to the Bogomil heresy, on Tuesday 22 February, seventh indiction. Under the presidency of our most holy lord and ecumenical patriarch *kyr* Michael in the right catechumenate of St Alexius; associated with his holiness in synod the great and most noble *protoasecretis kyr* Leo Icanatus and the most holy archbishops of Tyana, Laodicea, Dyrrachium, Thebes, Amastria, Colonea, Madyti, Lacedaemonia, Leucas, Parias and Gothia, and in the presence of noble lords.

Again concerning the monk Niphon . . . we received information about him from Thomas, priest of the great church, and the inhabitants of Pantychene, that as concerns the holy communion of the life-giving mysteries of Christ he introduced something irregular, alien to pious faith; from the most pious abbot of the venerated and royal monastery of the Pantocrator that he clearly said what was alien to piety. The evidence of the most holy metropolitan of Dyrrachium was also introduced, even though he simply denied it all flatly. So, then, what he has said this very day in the hearing of all left no doubt in our minds about him for the future, nor could we dispute what his opinions were. From the fact that he described the two bishops of the metropolitan of Tyana,[4] whom we recently deposed in synod because they were heterodox, as pious men with orthodox views, and simply through this put himself in opposition not merely to the synod, but to all the teaching Church which rejects their teaching as impious and wrong; in the presence of all of us today he repeated and said 'Anathema to the God of the Hebrews'[5] – from this we drew the conclusion without any ambiguity that his opinions were not orthodox; nor was his doctrine. So since we have had ample confirmation from this of his error and his completely godless teaching and thinking, it was determined that he should be banished to some place of retirement where no one should visit him, lest his plague infect others. In every way he was most clearly in opposition to the Catholic Church, and although he thought that he was orthodox and that others were otherwise, it was darkness and not light that he shared with those who frequented his company. Whoever then in future should dare to make common cause with him, whether in meeting or in manner of life or in anything else at all, openly or in secret, shall be deemed to share his views and be punished likewise.

---

4 See **[30]**.
5 Bogomils rejected the God of the Old Testament as the evil creator.

32. THE PATRIARCH COSMAS (1146–47) IS DEPOSED FOR FAVOURING BOGOMILS

The trial and condemnation of the patriarch Cosmas Atticus is presented by the records of the synod as a purely theological decision based on his support for the monk Niphon (see [31]), though the chronicle material ((b) below) gives evidence of a tradition more favourable to him, as does the letter of the scholar John Tzetzes (c). There is some evidence that he had, or was suspected of having, supported the emperor Manuel's elder brother Isaac as a claimant for the throne on the death of their father John Comnenus, which puts the trial in a different light.[1] The judges at the trial represent the imperial family and senior nobles.

(a) The text is translated from the version printed in Mansi, vol. 21, cols 701–5, that of

(b) from Nicetas Choniates' *Historia*, ed. Niebuhr, Bk.II, pp. 106–7, that of

(c) from John Tzetzes' *Epistulae*, ed. Leone, pp. 65–7 (letter 46), addressed to the emperor Manuel.

(a) Decree of deposition of the patriarch of Constantinople, Cosmas Atticus, who was shown to share the views of the Bogomil Niphon. These were extracted and confirmed in the usual way and published in the year 6652, in the month and indiction of the heading.

On Wednesday 26 February, the tenth indiction, under the presidency in the palace of Blachernae of our most potent God-crowned holy emperor *kyr* Manuel Comnenus, in the presence of the most fortunate *kyr* John, of the *panhypersebastos kyr* Stephen Contostephanus, of the *sebastohypertatos kyr* Constantine Angelus, of the cousins of our most potent lord the emperor *kyr* Alexius son of the purple-born Caesarissa *kyria* Anna, *kyr* Alexius and *kyr* Andronicus, sons of the purple-born *kyria* Maria and of her sister,[2] of the *pansebastos sebastos* and great drungarios *kyr* Constantine Comnenus[3], of the *pansebastos sebastos* Dicaeodotus and the eparch *kyr* John Turonites, of the great and most noble quaestor and judge of the *belos kyr* Basil Peculus, of the judge of the *belos* John Aloppas and many others from the senate, the judges of the people and in the presence of ecclesiastical leaders.

---

1 See (b) below.
2 John was the husband of the emperor Manuel's sister Maria; Stephen the husband of the emperor's sister Anna; Constantine Angelus had married the sister of John II (and so was the emperor's uncle); Alexius Comnenus was the son of Anna, and so the emperor's cousin; Alexius and Andronicus Euphorbenus were the sons of the emperor's sister Maria.
3 For this man and his relationship to the emperor see [31], note 2.

If his own lips are a strong snare for a man, and each man is caught by the words of his own mouth, he who was on the tribunal (and that a royal one) in the presence of the senate and also of the holy and divine synod, and not only in their presence, but in that of a great multitude besides, himself admitted what had been alleged against him by others and agreed that the truth was as those who had denounced him to our most powerful and holy emperor had described in the charges against him; how is he not justly fettered by his own lips and bound by their words, as if, in chains, he cannot escape? Such a thing happened today in the case of Cosmas, patriarch of the queen of cities. Some of the most holy archbishops were no little scandalized at his behaviour. They saw that a man who had earlier been condemned in synod as heterodox and as teaching and giving instruction otherwise than does the holy Catholic Church (as the sentence passed on him in the synod had made clear), that this accursed pseudo-monk named Niphon (of whom that numerous and holy synod had declared that he should be unapproachable and share nothing with anyone, even bare words and greetings – it is unnecessary to mention his food and drink and the other things which we habitually share with others) – how scandalized they were, then, as we said, to see the patriarch defending this man with clenched teeth, not only talking to him or dining with him in private, but when many other people were present. They went to our most powerful and holy emperor and, greatly upset by what was happening in his kingdom, they told him everything. So in his fiery zeal for piety he could not bear that such a scandal should exist in the Church. He summoned the patriarch and all those of us who were in the city to meet today. The patriarch began at once to speak of the charges against him and to set them out. The God of truth saw (as is evident) with what dejection of spirit and prayers to himself our God-crowned emperor had embarked on the present inquiry, as he began the interrogation with skill and the wisdom that is given to kings. The charges against him were revealed, and the emperor exposed how he had acted independently. So when he was asked by the emperor himself what sort of man Niphon was, unblushingly and (as the saying goes) bare-faced, he replied that he did not think he was a heretic, but orthodox. So then this second synod was convened and made its declaration by the synodic decree in the presence of the patriarch. It is superfluous for us as judges and for the most potent and holy emperor sitting in judgement with us together with the senate to make a great business of this, since he treated the decisions of the synod as worthless, and clung to and held fast his own opinions, just as today in the hearing of us all he called himself Lot among the inhabitants of Sodom. We all condemned him as sharing the opinions of the excommunicate Bogomil Niphon, and in accordance with this decree we have declared that he is expelled and unworthy of the patriarchate.

These extracts have been confirmed by the signatures below and were given in the month and indiction aforesaid in the year 1147.

(b) The *sebastocrator* Isaac,[4] the brother of the emperor Manuel, almost sacrificed to him [Cosmas] as to a god, taking everything that the patriarch recommended as pleasing to God and to be acted on, everything that he forbade as hateful to God and to be avoided. The company of those bishops who were hostile to virtue and opposed to this holy man accused him to the emperor, claiming that he was intriguing to obtain the empire for Isaac, and that his visits to the palace (which were not concealed) were secret approaches, that his conversations, which were not hole-and-corner affairs but held in daylight, were covert plots. So then Manuel, who was young and headstrong and had been induced by other means to suspect his brother of desire for power by the patriarch's accusers, sought to remove [Cosmas] from his throne . . . He hit upon the accusation that he shared the heresy of Niphon.

(c) My holy lord, your divine majesty did not appoint an elected patriarch independently . . . although you certainly might have done so had you wished, but shared the deliberation with the synod and with the senate, and made this holy appointment by the shared and careful decision of all after such scrutiny. Recently however [there have been] some malicious and factious elements who take pleasure in changes of power and habitually deceive the common run of people. One because he has not received a monastery in *charistike*,[5] another stubbornly set on some minor office, one aggrieved because one of the properties which formerly belonged to the Church has not been given to him, others because in their view the council of the *chartophylax* became a source of malice and schism and the fount of envy, another again, crazy and maddened (even though he is a professed monk), dreaming of the office of the patriarch, another of something else – all these, I know not how or with what motives have, as it appears to me, whispered in the royal ear, demanding the removal of a patriarch of this calibre in a way inconsistent with piety, when really, as I think, they are discontented for

---

4 Brother of Manuel. When John II died as a result of a riding accident on campaign in 1143 Manuel was with him, while Isaac, who had expected to inherit, was in Constantinople.
5 The custom by which the revenues of a monastery might be made over to a layman.

the reasons I have given . . . What is most extraordinary of all, those who deserve deposition for more than one reason demand the expulsion of a man like this, without a trial . . . So I beseech your philanthropic power not to allow this affair to proceed as the disaffected intend, but by your own verdict show them face to face what sort of judgement it is that the Comneni deliver . . . Teach all those in authority to act likewise, for if the ears of the emperor are open to those who are spiteful and go astray and wish to denounce their own superiors through enmity, soon heads will become feet and feet turn into heads. I have made this petition, greatly daring, I your unworthy servant, for love of a just defence; I do not only know the man by sight . . . for I am one of his household.

33. ST HILARION OF MOGLENA (1134–64) CONVERTS BOGOMILS IN HIS DIOCESE

St Hilarion was bishop of Moglena (Meglen) from 1134–64. His *Life*, described by Obolensky as 'one of the principal sources for a study of Bogomilism'[1] was written in Old Slavonic by Euthymius, last Bulgarian Patriarch of Trnovo (1375–93, died *c.* 1402). Although the date of the writing leaves the historical content of parts of the life open to debate, what is said of Bogomilism in the text cited here is consonant with the evidence of other sources from Manuel I's reign.

The Bulgarian text of the life was edited by E. Kaluzhniacki. This translation is based on that of Sharenkoff *A study of Manichaeism in Bulgaria*, appendix 3, pp. 79–80, but has been collated with the Old Slavonic text by Yuri Stoyanov, who has restored the original syntax and corrected the translation where necessary.

After a short time, while the saint was assiduously preaching and teaching to the believers, he discovered that a considerable part of them were Manichaeans,[2] Armenians[3] and Bogomils, who were reviling him and plotting against him; they were trying in the dark to shoot the righteous of heart, despoiling and leading astray the orthodox flock, like beasts of prey. Having seen that they were daily increasing in number, he suffered great sorrow and prayed earnestly from his heart to almighty God to stop their inveterate tongues. He often preached to his people, teaching and strengthening them in the orthodox faith. On hearing these ser-

---

1 Obolensky, *The Bogomils*, p. 164, note 1.
2 i.e. Paulicians.
3 For the presence of Armenians in Philippopolis see AC **[22(d)]** and note 10; cf. also Gouillard, 'Gagik II'.

CHRISTIAN DUALIST HERESIES

mons, the heretics were enraged in their hearts and gnashed their teeth like wild beasts, besides causing him various troubles. They were fond of disputing and wrangling with him, but Hilarion, the good shepherd of the sheep of Christ, having made God his stronghold, easily tore their intrigues and idle tales like a spider's web, and at this all the believers rejoiced.

Once the champions of the filthy Manichaean heresy, just like wolves in sheep's clothing, approached him timidly and tempted him, as the Pharisees did the Lord. They wanted to catch him in some word, but their iniquity proved its own censure. They fell into the traps which had been secretly laid by them and the lie was exposed by truth. They asked him, 'When we teach that the good God created the heavens and say that earth and all that is on it is a production of another, an evil creator, why do you philosophize, and do not submit, but contradict the truth?'[4]

Saint Hilarion answered, 'Listen to Christ, who says in the Gospels, "I have not spoken of myself, but the Father who sent me" [John 12.49]. I am not talking to you from myself, but from the Gospels of Christ which you claim to follow, and also from the apostles; therefore if you wish to pay any heed to my words, give up your pride. How is it that you affirm that the good God alone is himself the creator of the heavens but there is another creator of the earth and earthly beings?[5] There are even some of you who say that the sky itself and everything that is found there is an enemy's creation. If then the heavens, according to your opinion, are the production of the Evil One, how is it possible that the good God may abide there? How did our Saviour give us that wonderful and awesome prayer and teach us to pray in this manner, 'Our Father, which art in heaven, Thy will be done, as in heaven, so on earth'. And, 'If ye forgive men their trespasses, your heavenly Father will also forgive you.' And, 'Whosoever shall do the will of my Father which is in heaven, he is my brother and sister and mother.' Who dare say anything against the fact that the Saviour revealed to us the Heavenly Father, which is in heaven? Is there anything clearer than the words in which it is said: 'I confess before thee, O Father, Lord of the heavens and earth.' Not only the Lord of the heavens is worshipped, but also the Lord of the earth. Do you see how the words of the Gospel, on which you found your doctrine,

---

4 The rest of this passage against the Bogomils is based on EZ against the Paulicians; see **[23]**. Absolute dualism is a Paulician tenet, but it was also the belief of Bogomils belonging to the *ordo* of Dragovitia in St Hilarion's day, see our Introduction, p. 44. This form of Bogomilism would seem to have persisted at Thessalonica until the fifteenth century; see **[50]**.
5 Compare Bogomil teaching in EP **[19]**, EZ **[25]**, c. 7.

refute you? Why, the Saviour said unto Peter: 'I will give unto thee the keys of the Kingdom of heaven"' [Matt. 16.19].

34. AN ANTI-BOGOMIL WORK, POSSIBLY BY NICHOLAS OF METHONE

(a) *A TREATISE ON DEMONS* FALSELY ATTRIBUTED TO MICHAEL PSELLUS

The date and authorship of this work have been disputed, together with the question of whether the author is describing a real heretical group of which he has experience. We have followed the arguments of the most recent editor, Paul Gautier, who bases himself on the manuscript history of the work, which does not appear in the tradition representing the best text of the major works indisputably attributed to Psellus (1018–78), but is found with other minor dialogues attributed to Nicholas of Methone (d. *c.* 1166). Since the identification of the author is speculative, the date of the document remains uncertain. The letter of Nicolas of Methone included as (b) supports the view that he had an interest in the suppression of Bogomils. The evidence given by the dialogue of the beliefs of a heretical group is not very complete; it is more interesting as evidence of the thought-world about demons in which Bogomil theories of demonology found ready acceptance; see our Introduction, p. 43.

The following extracts have been translated from Gautier's edition, referred to above.

THRAX . . . I have encountered . . . impious men. Most people call them Enthusiasts and Euchites . . .[1] This deadly doctrine took its origin from Manes the mad . . . [who] supposed that there were two principles of the universe . . . These accursed Euchites added [a] third power; for them the father and two sons, the elder and the younger, are the rulers; of these they assign to the father only what is above the heavens, what is in the heavens to the younger son, and to the other, elder, son, power over what is on earth . . . Some of them give veneration to both the sons, and say that . . . they should both be worshipped because they come from one father and will be reconciled in the future. Others idolize the younger, because he rules the more important and superior part; they do not fail to honour the elder, but are on their guard against him because he has the power to harm. Some . . . distance themselves completely

---

1 'Euchites' was the Greek equivalent of the transliterated Syrian word 'Messalians', for whom see **[25]**, note 4; the later revised version of the Greek text adds here: 'whom the common herd call Bogomils', see J. Bidez *Psellos* p. 126,ll.22–3.

from the heavenly son and only embrace Satanael, the earthly son. They ... call [him] ... 'First-born,[2] creator of plants and animals and everything that is composite.' They [say that] ... the heavenly son ... envies his brother ... who takes good care of the earth and that ... he causes earthquakes and hailstorms and epidemics. That is why they curse him in other ways, including the abominable anathema.

TIMOTHEUS With what arguments, Thrax, have they persuaded themselves to ... call Satanael the son of God? ...

THRAX From ... the father of lies himself ... who boasted, 'I have put my throne above the clouds', and, 'I shall be like the most High'. ... He it is who made a revelation to such people, proclaiming himself the firstborn son of God, the creator of everything on the earth, that he leads and controls everything in the universe ...

TIMOTHEUS Do they gain anything when they forswear the traditional divine cult? ...

THRAX ... I think not. Even if the demons promise them gold and possessions ... they cannot deliver them, as they have no power, but they make varied exotic things appear to their initiates, which [they] call divine visions. For those of them who want to become spectators, alas, how many are their shameful initiations ... they reject everything which is lawful among us ... even the laws of nature ... Has anyone ever heard of a man ... tasting excrement?[3] ... Yet this is the first stage of initiation for these wretches. Such is the end part of their folly, which is shared not only by the leaders of the sect, whom they label apostles, but also by Euchites and Gnostics; as for their mystic sacrifice ... In the evening ... they assemble at a prearranged house the girls they have trained and putting out the lights ... they have sexual relations with the girls, each with whomever chance offers, whether it happens to be his sister or his daughter ... They wait for ... nine months, when it is time for the unhallowed offspring of this unhallowed seed to be born, and then meet again in the same place. On the third day after their birth they remove the unfortunate infants from their mothers, slash them all over with a razor and catch the blood which flows in bowls. They throw the babies on the fire and burn them, still breathing. Then they mix their ashes with the blood in the bowls and make an abominable mixture, which they secretly add to their food and drink[4] ... They believe that in

2 Cf. EZ [25], c. 6 and note 13.
3 This allegation is not found elsewhere.
4 Similar allegations of incest can be found in abjuration formulae [11(b) and (c)] and in PH [8], c. 24.

this way the marks of divinity in their soul are expunged... While they remain in their souls... the tribe of demons is fearful and keeps its distance...

TIMOTHEUS... Do [the demons] appear visibly to these evil wretches?

THRAX... This is the object of their endeavours, their meetings and sacrifices and ceremonies and everything... they do...

TIMOTHEUS But how, as they are bodiless, can they be seen with external eyes?

THRAX The demonic tribe is not bodiless... the divine Basil,[5] who saw the invisible realms which are hidden from us, maintained that not merely devils have bodies, but the sinless angels do too...

I met a man who was a monk in the Chersonese which borders on Greece. His name was Mark,[6] and he traced his family to Mesopotamia... He was an initiated spectator of demonic apparitions, but he... abjured them... He... revealed to me much that was extraordinary and demoniac. Once when I asked him if any demons have emotions, he said, 'Yes indeed, so that some emit sperm, and in their sperm are born tiny worms... They take nourishment... some through inhalation... some through moisture... they suck in the surrounding moisture and then, when it has reached a spermatic consistency, emit it. It is not all kinds which do this, but only... the watery and the subterranean kind.'

'Are there many kinds of demons, Mark?', I asked.

'Many,' he said, '... so that the air above us and around us is full of them, as is the earth and sea and the deepest and most hidden places'...

He said that in all there are six kinds... the first in the local language he barbarously called Leliouria[7]... which means 'fiery'. This flies around in the air above us; every kind of demon is expelled from the spaces round the moon, as something foul kept far from a holy place. The second roams through the air nearest to us, and many people call it especially 'aery'. Third... comes the earthy sort, fourth that which inhabits fresh and salt water, fifth that which lives underground. Finally

---

5 See Basil of Caesarea in *PG* 30, cols 532c–533a, 32, col.137a.
6 One MS has a marginal note here: 'This Mark came from Thebes. At first he was a teacher of Bogomils, later he became orthodox. He encountered Thrax, who had been sent against Bogomils, and who learnt from him what is said.' See our Introduction, p. 42.
7 This otherwise unknown word may be based on the Hebrew words for 'night' (*lel*) and 'fire' (*our*).

there is the kind which hates light, and is insensible. All these kinds of demons hate God and are hostile to man . . . The watery and the subterranean and also the light-hating are extremely harmful and destructive. He said that they did not harm souls by apparitions or arguments, but pouncing like the fiercest wild beast, they plan the destruction of men. The watery kind drowns all those who travel by water; the subterranean and light-hating, if given way to, creep into the entrails, and whoever they happen to have seized, they hold fast and make them epileptic or mad. The aerial and earthy . . . deceive men's minds and induce them to perverse and exotic passions[8] . . .

If the attacker is one of the subterranean kind, it agitates and partly destroys what it grasps, and . . . [uses] the speech of the sufferer as if it were its own voice. But if any of those called light-haters creeps in unseen, it produces paralysis, hinders speech and in general makes the person affected like a corpse . . .'.

'But Mark,' said I, 'doctors . . . say that these conditions are not the product of demons, but of humours . . .'.

'[Doctors] . . .', said Mark, 'only pay attention to bodies . . .'.

TIMOTHEUS . . . Do you agree with Mark when he says this?

THRAX Certainly, Timotheus . . . remembering the accounts given of those possessed by demons in the holy gospels . . . as well as what I myself saw and heard at Elason.[9]

There was a man possessed by a demon who behaved like an oracle . . . and foretold many things about me as well. When a crowd of initiates gathered, he said, '. . . a man is going to attack us: by him our cult will be persecuted and our worship dismissed. I shall be taken captive by him, with many others, though when he wants to take me as a prisoner to Byzantium, after much effort he will not be able to . . .'. He described my appearance, my clothes, even my habits . . . When at last I arrived, I asked how the spirit of prophecy had come to him. He did not wish to reveal his secret, but when he endured Spartan persuasion[10] he told the truth: 'I was initiated', he said, 'into the works of demons by a Libyan vagabond who took me up a mountain and told me to eat some herb or other. Then he spat in my mouth and put ointment on my eyes, so that I could see a host of demons. After that I perceived something

8 For the association of demons with darkness, water and underground places compare EZ [25], c. 7.
9 A town in Thessaly.
10 i.e. a beating.

like a crow flying towards me and swooping inside my mouth.[11] From that time until now the moving force has made me able to prophesy . . . Around the time of the crucifixion and resurrection it does not wish to make any revelation, no matter how much I would like it to.' . . . When one of my escort struck him on the face, he said, 'You will receive many blows in return for one; and you' – here he turned to me – 'will suffer much in your body; the demons are very angry with you for hindering their worship . . .'. Everything happened . . . I nearly died, overwhelmed by many dangers from which the Saviour rescued me against all expectation . . .

TIMOTHEUS I used to think like [doctors do] myself, until I happened to see something absolutely monstrous and extraordinary . . . [My] elder brother's wife . . . once when about to give birth . . . was . . . seriously deranged; she tore her garment and rattled off some barbarian language at the top of her voice . . . Some women brought in a . . . stranger [who] was bald, very elderly, with skin wrinkled and burnt almost black. He drew a naked sword, approached the bed . . . and in his native language – he came from Armenia – scolded her severely. At first she became bold, and rising from the bed, began to quarrel with him; as the barbarian used even more abuse and . . . made as if to strike her, all at once the woman, falling back and starting to tremble, said some humble words and fell asleep . . . Once she came to her senses, I asked her what had happened . . . She answered, 'The vision of a demon, shadowy, like a woman with her hair floating, appeared, attacking me. I was terrified and fell flat on the bed. Of what happened afterwards I know nothing.' . . . [She] was freed from her sickness . . .

TIMOTHEUS . . . What happened to make it fear the threats and the sword? . . .

THRAX . . . Mark . . . said that all the species of demons are very bold, but also very cowardly . . . The aerial kinds, which have the greatest understanding, if threatened, know how to evaluate the person who threatened them, and are only expelled from those they have attacked if he is holy in the sight of God and uses the dread name of God with divine power . . . the material kind, which is afraid of being sent to the abysses and to places underground, and also of the angels who dispatch there, whenever anyone . . . summons the angels who are in charge of this, are afraid and very agitated . . . Whether it is an old woman or a

---

11 The demon blasphemously parodies inspiration by the Holy Spirit in the form of a dove.

loud-mouthed old man who utters these threats, fear seizes them and often drives them away ... So they are easily tamed by the foul race of sorcerers, with the use of secretions, I mean saliva, nails, hair; once bound by lead or wax or fine thread through unhallowed invocations, they endure awful torments.'

'Why, if they are like this, do you and many others venerate them,' said I, 'instead of despising their weakness?'

'I did not,' said Mark, 'nor, I think, did anyone else who has even a little sense pray to these accursed creatures, but sorcerers and outcasts pay cult to them. All those of us who abstained from unhallowed actions were devoted particularly to the demons of the air, and by our sacrifices to them we prayed to them to ward off some underground demon ... If ... such a demon should slide in to terrify us, he would also throw stones:[12] this is a characteristic of underground demons ....'.

'What gain', said I, 'did you get from the worship of aerial demons?'

'None,' he said ... 'because their boasting and vanity is an ... empty fantasy. Fiery rays come from them upon their followers ... which the deluded think should be called divine visions, but which contain nothing true ... they are tricks, like those performed by conjurors to deceive the spectators ....'.

TIMOTHEUS Did he tell you whether demons have foreknowledge?

THRAX He said that they have foreknowledge, but that it is not ... based ... on knowledge, but only on the recognition of signs, so that it often fails, and especially that demons involved in matter have weak foreknowledge, so that they are seldom or never in the right.

(b) A LETTER OF NICHOLAS OF METHONE TO THE EMPEROR MANUEL (1143–80)

This letter is inserted as evidence that the emperor Manuel continued his grandfather's policy of persecution of Bogomils, most clearly shown in the trial of the Patriarch Cosmas, [32] See also our Introduction, p. 41.

The text is taken from the edition of Demetrakopoulos, p. 266.

[Just as your virtues shine out, so too do] all your great deeds and acts of valour performed in peace and in war, not only those which are evident and known to everyone, but also those which are concealed and

---

12 Compare the account of the imprisonment of the Bogomil Basil in Anna Comnena [24].

known only to a few of those who surround you, that is, those who are closest to you, like the triumph you recently celebrated against the godless heresy of the Bogomils, skilfully seizing its champions and with great force attacking the might of the devil, whom they worship, and so destroying his weapons, his equipment, the first fruits of the heresy.

35. POPULAR BELIEFS ABOUT BOGOMILISM RECOUNTED BY GEORGE TORNICES (1154)

This material provides an example of the way in which accusations of Bogomil sympathies were used as propaganda in ecclesiastical disputes. The author of these letters, George Tornices, was born between 1110 and 1120, and died in about 1157. He taught in the patriarchal school, where he was regularly promoted; in his speech acknowledging his promotion to the position of Gospel exegete he praises the patriarch Theodotus II (1151–4), whose austerity was renowned. This speech was delivered in November 1152. It is clear that after the death of Theodotus there was a war of pamphlets; the underlying issue was that of the orthodoxy of the Eucharistic doctrines of the newly appointed patriarch of Antioch, Soterichus Panteugenus, who was suspected of being pro-Latin in his views, at a time when this was particularly controversial. Because Antioch was in Frankish hands at the time, Panteugenus was in Constantinople, attached to St Sophia.

The text translated is from Darrouzès's edition, p. 209.

LETTER 7: TO A METROPOLITAN OF ATHENS

Why are you so anxious for me to tell you my news, which concerns you too? Take care lest you are not more seasick than when the Ionian sea was angry and raised its waves against you, when I tell you about the shameless attack on us of the base crowd of Hagiosophites,[1] when they nearly came to blows and laid hands on us. The reason was that, after the departure to God of the late patriarch,[2] like market hagglers they were unwilling to provide the rites for the dead. I spoke out quite boldly to the most shameless speaker ... To leave on one side the accusation which is no longer hidden in the soul of the most ignoble Panteugenus,[3] he added this to his earlier blasphemies; the right hand of the late

---

1 i.e. the clergy of St Sophia.
2 Theodotus II (see above).
3 This paragraph contains a number of wordplays on the name Panteugenus, whose literal meaning is 'All-noble'.

patriarch had become blackened during his illness. This occurred either because the hand, which was an extremity, was the first to mortify, or (which is my own opinion) because when he moved his body he supported himself by this hand on a hanging rope which compressed it, and from this compression in the normal way there was an influx of matter to the part compressed, which caused the blackening. The patient did not hide the symptoms because, as it seemed to me, his conscience did not reproach him about them. When Panteugenus came to know of this from those who had been present ... he said that this was a sign of bad ordinations, adding with a sigh, 'See what the ordinations have done.' The 'all-noble' ranted gratuitously that this was a characteristic symptom of Bogomils. He knew this from having opened many tombs of followers of this heresy and having always found them like this. What senselessness, if not insanity, that he did not hesistate to incur the reputation of a tomb-robber to bring a slur on someone else.

36. HUGH ETERIANO (A PISAN) WRITES A TREATISE AGAINST THE BOGOMILS OF CONSTANTINOPLE (c. 1165-80)

Hugh Eteriano, together with his brother Leo the Tuscan,[1] were employed by the emperor Manuel in his relations with the Italian states and the Roman Church. Hugh is best known as the author of a lengthy treatise issued simultaneously in Greek and Latin versions on the *filioque* clause, which was the main theological bone of contention between Constantinople and Rome. This minor pamphlet by him has not previously been printed; for knowledge of its existence we are indebted to Dondaine, 'Hugues Éthérien et Léon Toscan': for the manuscripts see below. The information this pamphlet contains about Bogomils in twelfth-century Constantinople is not remarkable in itself; the charges that are made against the heretics are the usual ones, though the emphasis on Bogomil refusal to swear oaths should be seen in the light of contemporary friction between Latins and Greeks on this as on many other matters.[2] For this reason scholars have not paid it the attention which it merits; for a discussion see our Introduction, p. 46. Although written in Latin, the edifying stories which bolster the argument for orthodoxy are all chosen from the Greek repertory, and the text is explicitly responding to requests from local opinion in Constantinople, with an emphasis on the role of the emperor Manuel and the unanimity in confronting heresy of both Greek and Latin Churches.

1 For a translation of the Greek Eucharistic liturgy made by Leo for a western reader, see Hussey, *The Orthodox Church*, p. 178.
2 See our Introduction, p. 46.

The translation has been made from the two extant MSS known to us, Seville, Colombina Cod. 5.1.24, fos 67r.–75v. (referred to as S) and Bodley MS Canon. Pat. Lat. 1 fos. 1–31 (referred to as B). The Seville text has been followed for the most part, because it is earlier, more complete and generally more accurate. Significant variants in the Bodley text are recorded in the footnotes.

For some time I have been asked by some men worthy of note, noble men whose intellect is strong and [——][3] whether an imperial decree should be allowed to become a dead letter, and whether the perfidious sect of the Patarenes[4] should be eliminated not merely from the districts around the Hellespont, but from the whole city.[5] I have written a pamphlet to give them a clear reply. In every way they deserve a capital sentence, hanging and burning, as being teachers of error, seducers, hypocrites, deceivers, who turn people from the Christian faith. John the apostle in his epistle says: 'If any man comes to you and does not have Christ's teaching, do not receive him into your house or give him greeting; for whoever gives him greeting agrees with the deeds of that evildoer' [2 John 10–11]. But the men of whom we are speaking have abandoned the teaching of the Church, which is Christ's teaching, that is, His words and commandments, that is: 'What I say to you in the darkness, proclaim in the light; what you hear whispered, proclaim on the housetops' [Matt. 10.27]. This means: 'What I have said to you alone and in one place (that is, in the dark and whispered), proclaim publicly and openly in the streets.' But these evil men, who are full of cunning, avoid the light and preach secretly in corners. For this reason they do not observe Christ's doctrine or His precept and commandment. Moreover, it is a commandment of God that no one should preach, as these evil men preach, unless sent by God. They are sent by Satan, which is manifest from the fact that they do not have any grace of the Holy Spirit. The apostle Paul says [1 Cor. 12.8–10] that to every preacher is given a word of wisdom[6] (as to John, Paul, Augustine,[7] Chrysostom and many others). To another, a word of knowledge from the same spirit, so that he may teach whoever he likes openly, and answer particular points. To another, faith in the same spirit, so that he can perform miracles and

---

3 Word illegible in both MSS, beginning 'ampli —; perhaps meaning 'men of substance'.
4 The name 'Patarene' (variously spelt) was commonly applied in Italy to the heretics known in France as Cathars, Wakefield and Evans, *Heresies of the High Middle Ages*, esp. p. 701, note 3.
5 B has 'whole world'.
6 This sentence is a free adaptation of 1 Cor. 12.8–10. B adds: 'for profit. That is, a grace through which is revealed what element of the Holy Spirit is in him. To another, he says, is given a word of wisdom in the Holy Spirit.'
7 S adds 'Jerome'.

move mountains.[8] To another, the grace of healing in the same spirit, so that he can heal all kinds of weakness and sickness. To another, the grace of power, so that he can punish unbelievers (as Paul blinded Elymas [Acts 13.11] and Peter killed Ananias [Acts 5.5]). To one, prophecy, to another, discernment of spirits, so that he may recognize which man is spiritual and which is carnal, who is a prophet and who is a deceiver. To one, the kinds of tongues, to another, the interpretation of tongues, but the aforesaid most wicked preachers have neither knowledge of tongues nor the interpretation of tongues; they are not prophets, but they are hidden deceivers, thieves and bandits, carnal men who do not perceive the things which belong to God. They are fools and ignorant, who can do no more harm than other men, since they cannot blind anyone, as Paul blinded Elymas, nor kill, as Peter killed Ananias by word alone; they themselves will admit it. Can they expel fevers, cure lepers, remove bodily weakness? They can do absolutely none of these. They dare not teach anyone openly, but only in secret, but Christ said nothing in secret, and ordered his disciples to do the same. Since then they lack the sevenfold grace of the Holy Spirit – true preachers have always embraced one of these graces – and preach in secret, breaking the commandment of God, it is clear that they have been sent to preach by Leviathan, that coiling serpent, and are forerunners of antichrist, contradicting the commandments of God by transforming themselves into angels of light, when in reality they are angels of Satan. Again there is another way in which it can be known that they are led by the spirit of the devil and are antichrists – that is, the opposite of Christ. Christ spoke to the crowds and to his disciples in these words: 'The scribes and Pharisees have taken their seat on the throne of Moses. Keep whatever they say to you, and do it, but do not act in accordance with their deeds' [Matt. 23.2]. He is teaching that we ought not to despise priests and condemn the tradition of the Church which they show us. What they say is ours, and for our benefit; what they do, on the other hand, is theirs, and concerns them. Their teaching gives us life, but if their life is evil and corrupt, it brings them death but does us no harm. Let us take what is ours and leave what is not ours. When you go before a judge, if he says what is right, his evildoing does not pervert justice; what he judges is valid and just. Although he may be perjured, a fornicator or a murderer, and godless, still his judgement is not tainted for that reason. So the evil behaviour of a priest does not taint his power and office. The false apostles for whom prison is waiting on account of their evil conduct

---

8 B adds 'that is, demons'.

claim that if a priest is a sinner, he is no priest, his mass is invalid, his service is useless and his power to bind and loose,[9] like his own person, is void and corrupt. They lie, and are full of the spirit of Satan, for Christ destroyed this view of theirs through Matthew, in his gospel: 'Many', he said, 'will say on that day, "Lord, did we not prophesy in Your name and cast out demons in Your name and do many mighty works in Your name?" Then will I declare to them, "I never knew you. Depart from me, you evildoers"' [Matt. 7.21–3]. At first many preachers used to cast out demons, although they were unworthy, since the demons flee because of the name of Jesus. For grace came even through the unworthy, like Judas, who worked miracles, or the detestable sons of Sceva. So it began from the earliest days of the Church, and will last to the end. For just as demons were cast out through the name of Jesus by Judas and those like him, so it happens now, and will till the end of time. Even bad priests put demons to flight in the name of Jesus Christ, from penitents and those who are to be baptized, and the people are sanctified by those who have already been rejected and condemned by God, but who in this instance are ministers of the grace of the Holy Spirit, and to be honoured for that reason. Grace has been given through them, and the Lord has opened their mouth, as he opened the mouth of Balaam's ass.[10]

Again they are clearly and obviously speaking against Christ and truth itself when they take away oaths from the Church. They do not realize what the Saviour told us in the gospel, and James in his epistle, in imitation of his master. He never forbade us to swear by God, but [did forbid us to swear] casually by his creatures, saying, 'Do not swear at all, either by heaven, which is the throne of God, or by the earth, which is his footstool, or by any other created thing' [Matt. 5.34–5], and this for the reason that there should be no room for idolatry. For they used to deify heaven and earth and the other created things by which they swore. God alone swears by Himself, He who is subject to no one. But we have no power of ourselves by which to swear, even by our own head, for that belongs to another – if your head is your own, change, if you can, the natural colour of one hair. The swearing of oaths is not to be forbidden, but nor is it to be desired as a good thing. To take an oath without need, or to swear falsely, is a great sin, but to take an oath from necessity, for instance, to confirm our innocence, or to ratify a peace agreement, or to convince hearers of what is useful for them, is a good and necessary act. For that reason all the Church of the Greek and Latin

---

9 i.e. his power to absolve sins which have been confessed to him.
10 Num. 22.30.

saints which the wicked and evil men contradict (and for this reason alone deserve death) holds and teaches that an oath should be taken when need arises, when men are reluctant to believe what is good and useful, for an oath is not against the commandment of God. The Lord and his disciple James should be understood to have forbidden oaths in this sense, that anyone should refrain from swearing as far as he can, since from the evil one comes not the oath, but the incredulity of the one who compels him to swear; yet it is not wrong, because it is necessary. However, to swear from greed, or the pleasure of swearing, as many do who have oaths on their lips like something great and pleasurable, is a great sin. If it were a sin to swear at all, as the most wicked men affirm, God himself would certainly not have done so: 'By myself have I sworn', said the Lord to Abraham, 'that because you have done this and have not spared your only son, I will bless you and multiply your seed like the stars of heaven' [Gen. 22.16–17]. God swore and did not repent. Abraham was an old man 'of many days', and God blessed him in all things. [The following is a free version of Gen. 24.1–10.] He said to the oldest servant of his house, 'Put your hand under my thigh, so that I may adjure you by the God of heaven and earth that you will not accept a wife for my son from the daughters of Canaan. The Lord God of heaven who took me from my father's house spoke to me and swore, "I will give your seed this land."' And so the servant placed his hand under Abraham's thigh and swore to him, in accordance with what he had said. Abraham himself swore too, for it is written, 'Abimelech and Ochozath his son-in-law and Phicol the leader of his army said to Abraham, "God is with you. Swear then by the Lord that you will not harm me or my posterity." And Abraham swore. For that reason that place is called Bersabee, because they both swore there' [Gen. 21.22–3].[11] Likewise Joseph was bound by an oath to Jacob his father: 'If', he said, 'I have found any favour in your sight, place your hand under my thigh, and swear to me that you will not bury me in Egypt, So swearing, Israel adored the Lord' [Gen. 47.29]. Moses too, that friend of God, swore to Raguel the priest of Madian [Reuel, Midian, RSV]. For so it is written: 'Moses swore that he would dwell with him.' Why should I quote more? Without oaths the world could not and cannot remain firmly based. We are forbidden to take the name of God in vain, but to swear by the name of God in case of necessity is not forbidden in the Old Testament or in the New. If swearing were a sin, John the evangelist would not have introduced an angel swearing, for he says: 'The angel

11 S adds: 'Jacob too swore to Laban, his father-in-law'.

whom I saw standing on the sea and on the sky lifted up his hand to heaven, and swore by Him who lives to the ages of ages that time should be no more' [Rev. 10.6]. The apostle knew the Lord's command, and yet he swore, saying, 'As God is my witness' – that is the same as saying, 'By God it is so-and-so'; this is more than to swear by the gospels, for the scriptures are holy on God's account, not God on account of the scriptures. So too, created things are hallowed by God. Indeed at the present time by an ordinance of the Church oaths take place when necessity demands, by touching the gospels. To swear by God means to cite God as a witness. To swear is to give God the legal power of truth and not of falsehood. An oath in necessary matters removes lasting enmities from the Church, and within the Church it makes peace between princes who are at odds. The Church has no other constraint by which it can bind them and bring them back to peace and unity. Those who completely remove oaths break the law of the Church, which it had from the beginning. For this reason alone, to say nothing of others, their most evil deeds should be 'uprooted and removed, like trees in autumn which do not bear good fruit, twice dead and uprooted, to be cut off from truth and cast into the fire, wise in their own eyes, but contrary to the apostles' precepts, they are wandering stars[12] for whom a storm of darkness is kept for ever' [Jude 12–13].

Moreover, the most pious emperor Constantine, Justinian and all the most Christian emperors promulgated this law to believers and unbelievers in the whole world. In the absence of proof, a lawsuit is decided by an oath; sometimes in favour of the plaintiff, sometimes of the accused. Again a judge swears that he will give judgement in every case in accordance with truth and by observing the laws, as seems just. We should believe the emperors, who are most dear to Christ, and those who do not obey them but obstinately gainsay them will be condemned to death. Greater than all these is the commandment of God, saying in Exodus through Moses that oaths ought to exist. 'If anyone delivers to his neighbour an ass, an ox or a sheep or any beast to keep, and it dies or is hurt or is driven away without anyone seeing it, an oath by the Lord shall be between them both to see whether he has not put his hand to his neighbour's property' [Exod. 22.10–11]. Although then God himself and the holy Church of God of the Latins and the Greeks has from the beginning allowed the swearing of oaths when necessity demands, and the holy and Christian emperors have ratified this, the Patarenes abolish it completely. Although Christ ordered us to preach openly, the

12 B has 'hedera' ('ivy').

Patarenes preach in secret against the commandment of Christ. Although Christ bade us observe everything which priests say in their capacity as priests, the Patarenes say that this should not be done, and abolish oath-taking. So it is clear that they are false apostles, heretics, antichrists, excommunicate from holy Church, cut off and separated. Nothing remains except that the most Christian emperor Manuel[13] should devoutly intervene and should have them and their followers sent to the fiery furnace, so that they may begin to burn here before they burn in the eternal fire.

If by any chance these miserable and deluded men say that the scriptural examples cited above should not be accepted because they are taken from the Old Law, the mouths of the speakers shall be closed and stopped. In the first place we must tell them that the Old Testament is the foundation of the New; anyone who rejects the Old is evilly disposed to the New. Just as Christ, that rock cleft from the mountain without hands, was born in accordance with the patriarchs and prophets and without sexual union, so his New Testament depends on the Old and is derived from it. Matthew begins like this: 'The book of the genealogy of the son of David, the son of Abraham', and so on [Matt. 1.1]. Luke too confirms this saying: 'Jesus himself, when he began his ministry, was about thirty years of age, being the son, as it was supposed, of Joseph, the son of Heli, the son of Nathan,[14] the son of Levi' [Luke 3.23], and what follows. Mark too adds his witness, towards the beginning of his gospel, proclaiming: 'Behold, I send my messenger before thy face, who shall prepare thy way' [Mark 1.2]. John too is in agreement with them, for he says: 'The law was given through Moses; grace and truth came through Jesus Christ' [John 1.17]. This is why when our Saviour defeated the devil he quoted evidence from the Old Testament, that is, 'Man shall not live by bread alone, but by every word that proceeds from the mouth of God' [Matt. 4.4, quoting Deut. 8.3]. Again, 'You shall not tempt the Lord your God' [Matt. 4.7, quoting Deut. 6.16]. In many other places in the gospels he acts in the same way. Again the apostle Peter calls wives to chaste living by the example of Sarah, when he bids them: 'Wives, be submissive to your husbands as Sarah obeyed Abraham, calling him Lord. And you are her children if you do right and let nothing terrify you' [1 Peter 3.1, 6]. The apostle Jude does the same,[15] saying: 'Abraham believed in God, and it was counted to him for righteousness, and he was called the friend of God' [actually Rom. 4.3].

13 B has 'The most Christian emperors'.
14 B: 'Matham'; RSV: 'Matthat'.
15 B adds: 'and so does the apostle James'.

Listen to what Paul, that chosen vessel, the doctor of the Gentiles, thinks of the Old Law. He says: 'The law is holy, and the commandment is holy and just and good' [Rom. 7.12] and therefore 'I delight in the law in my innermost soul' [Rom. 7.22]. Manichaeans and Patarenes[16] who criticize the Old Testament are confounded by the fourth universal council, which anathematized all those who made such claims, rightly, for it is written that it is like the sin of Ariolandus[17] to oppose the tradition held by the Church, and to refuse to abide by it is like the crime of idolatry. Since the aforesaid Patarenes have thrown out the tradition held by the holy Church of God, both Greek and Latin, the Lord has thrown them out of His kingdom as hypocrites and pretenders.

Their falsehood is apparent not only in what has already been said, but in the service of the Lord's body,[18] as they claim that even after the blessing the bread[19] remains as it was before.*[20] Moreover, they also hold a most wicked view about the sacrament of marriage, and say that all marriage should be repudiated. And in the veneration of the holy icons, which they say are deaf and dumb images, they have gone astray. They are guilty on all these counts. The sacrament of marriage condemns them in many ways. For if there were no marriage, the flower of virginity would not be found – that flower of virginity which can be picked here and nowhere else. So lawful marriage is thought to excel all earthly honour, its root is virginity and its blessing that of the world of reproduction, the foundation of mankind, the painter of the image of God, with the Lord's blessing. For He who begged to be incarnate presides over it, and He can assuredly be said to be present. God is the originator of marriage. He it was who decreed that woman should be a helper for man in the propagation of the human race. Adam recognized this purpose in the spirit when he said, 'This is bone of my bones and flesh of my flesh. For this reason a man leaves his father and mother and cleaves to his wife, and they become one flesh' [Gen. 2.23–4]. If their conjugal union had not been without sin, the Lord would not have ordered them to be united after the flood, saying, 'Be fruitful and multiply' [Gen. 8.17]. Multiplication cannot take place without physical desire. The apostle Paul provides a defence from all charge of sin when he says, 'So he who marries does well. Let a man give his wife her due, and a wife her husband. If the marriage is lawful, there is no sin' [1 Cor.

16 B adds 'simoniacs'.
17 Perhaps Arius is meant?
18 B adds 'and blood'.
19 B adds 'and wine'.
20 The passage between asterisks is omitted in B.

7.38]. Again at Cana of Galilee, did not the physical presence of the Lord and the miracle He worked consecrate marriage? Did he not say in the gospel that 'Anyone who divorces his wife except on the grounds of unchastity makes her an adulteress, and whoever marries a divorced woman commits adultery?' [Matt. 5.22]. One of the disciples said, 'If such is the case of a man with his wife, it is not expedient to marry.' But He said to him, 'Not all men can receive this saying, but only those to whom is it given. For there are eunuchs who have been made eunuchs by men, and there are eunuchs who have made themselves eunuchs for the sake of the kingdom of heaven. He who is able to receive this, let him receive it' [Matt. 19.10–12]. So He does not compel anyone to remain a virgin, nor does He deny the good of marriage, but rather tells us not to put aside a woman who has been married to a man. For this reason it is plain that marriage is from God and is good, and that it is approved by the Old Testament and the New. They are heretics and seducers who endeavour to abolish completely so great a good.

These most evil men attack the sacrament* of the Lord's body and blood, in which not wine nor only water should be offered, but both together, as both flowed from his side. The unseen priest changes this sacrament into the substance of His body and blood by hidden power, saying, 'Take, eat, this is my body', and when the consecration is repeated, 'Take and drink, this is my blood.' When these words are spoken without ambiguity, they change bread into flesh and wine into blood, and the rest truly to the praise of God, because He himself says, 'My blood is real drink and my flesh is real food.' This miracle instructs you, Patarene, and still you say, 'How is this real blood, how is this real flesh? I do not see anything like flesh or blood as I observe it.' Do you not believe Christ when he says, 'This is my body, this is my blood. Unless you eat the flesh of the Son of man and drink His blood, you have no life in you'? The word of Christ is performative, the word of Christ changes what is instituted by nature. Why are you surprised if at the Saviour's words bread becomes flesh and wine blood, when at the charmer's voice a snake is forced out and drawn from its cave? So the asp blocks her ears so that she may not hear the voice of the skilful charmer. If a spell can catch a snake, can a blessing not change bread and wine? You fool, while you are not looking, bread is changed into flesh in your stomach, and wine into blood.[21] The power of a blessing is greater than that of nature, and yet nature makes soft plants below the waves harden into

---

21 An argument also used by an Italian theologian of the previous generation; see Guitmund of Aversa, *De corporis et sanguinis domini veritate* 3, in *PL* 149.1444.

what is called coral when it reaches the air.[22] Moses held a rod, threw it down, and it became a snake [Exod. 7.9]. Again he seized the snake's tail, and it became a rod again. At Moses' voice the nature of rod and snake altered. The currents of the Nile were pure, and then suddenly from its spring real blood began to flow [Exod. 7.20]. Again at the prayer of Moses the blood ceased and the nature of water returned. Again, Moses lifted up his staff and the water of the Red Sea gave way; a footpath appeared between the waves [Exod. 14.21]. In defiance of nature the Jordan flowed backwards, and at Mara, by contact with wood, sweet water was provided in place of that which had been most bitter to the thirsty people [Exod. 15.23–5]. The words of Elijah called fire from heaven [1 Kings 18.38]. Then can not the words of Christ change bread into another substance, the words of Him who made everything out of nothing? Your mind refuses to admit the truth of a change which you do not see happen with your physical sight. But tell me, does not fire cook bread and other foods which are eaten? It enters these foods without itself being changed or corrupted, and alters them. So when the alteration is complete, the cooking finished and done, unless prevented it goes forth unchanged and unadulterated. Indeed, as it leaves a very fine air like smoke appears, but in fact it is a very delicate fire which is called heat. For it is one thing in substance, but another in appearance. The nature of fire is without doubt what is considered to be air on account of its airy heat alone (although it is indeed revolved in the air). Thus indeed it is flesh, which you wrongly affirm to be bread, on account of its outward appearance. For no classification should be sought in respect of the body of Christ, which the Virgin conceived and bore outside the natural order. Believe therefore Him who says, 'This is my body'; certainly it is no less consecrated by a bad priest than by a good one, since the consecration is not effected by the merit of the consecrator, but by the words of the Saviour and the power of the Holy Spirit.

Listen, Patarene, to what happened at Constantinople, and believe what the Catholic Church of God venerates and worships. In the time of the emperor Arcadius,[23] when John Chrysostom was bishop of the Church of Constantinople, a man of the heretical sect of Macedonius[24] approached him together with his wife, and having listened to his teaching, promised to abide by his instructions. He communicated this to his wife,

---

22 A simile based on Ovid, *Metamorphoses* 15.416–17.
23 B: 'Heraclius'.
24 The legend of the communion of Macedonius is first recorded in Sozomen, *Ecc. Hist.* 8.5.

who lived with him, as Easter was approaching, and she agreed to do the same. She came into church with her maid, bringing with her the communion [bread] consecrated by Macedonius. When she received communion from the hands of the bishop, she passed it over to her maid and then, with some sleight of hand, took back what she had given to her maid and gave the girl what she had taken from the bishop. The moment the communion of Macedonius touched the woman's lips, it turned to stone. As soon as what had happened became obvious, the aforesaid woman fell at the bishop's feet, begging forgiveness with tears and confessing what she had dared to do, while the stone was kept in a safe place. I would like to tell you also the similar events which occurred when Justin was emperor at Constantinople.[25] In that town there was a Jewish glass-maker who had one son and sent him to the Great Church to be educated. One day when the sacristan who looked after the church plate had many fragments left over from the holy table, he called the boys who were being taught, so that they might eat what was left. The Jewish boy was with them and also ate. When he went home his father asked him why he was so late. He answered, 'I went into the Great Church with the Christian boys and together with them I ate what was left on the altar, which they call the table. That was what delayed me.' The wretched father, raging inwardly like a wild beast, said nothing, and when the meal was over he took his son to the place where the glass was melted. There he threw him into the burning furnace, shut the door and went away. His wife realized her husband's anger against the boy. She ran hurriedly to the melting-shop and as she bent down by the opening in the door, she heard the boy's voice from the inside of the furnace. Immediately she broke open the door, rushed in and dragged her son from the furnace, unhurt. When his mother asked the boy who had thrown him into the fire and how the flame had not burnt him up, he replied in these words: 'My father threw me into the furnace. A venerable lady clothed in purple put out the flame, saying, '"Do not be frightened, child."' When she heard this, his mother was astonished. Immediately she hurried to the patriarch, together with her son. She told him what had happened, in order, and begged of him the faith of the Catholic Church. Then the patriarch took them both, that is, mother and son, to the emperor's majesty. The emperor ordered the boy's father to be brought. When he came, the prince tried most mercifully to persuade him with pious words and induce him with arguments

25 The legend of the son of the Jewish glass-maker and his miraculous preservation is also found in a collection of stories attached to the *Spiritual Meadow* of John Moschus; see Mioni, 'Il *Pratum spirituale* di Giovanni Mosco', pp. 79, 93–4.

and presents to become a Christian, together with his wife and son, but he refused. For that reason he ordered him to be hanged by imperial verdict, as the murderer of his son. His wife became a nun and the son a reader in the Great Church.

As for the adoration, cult and honour of icons, we have authority which surpasses all the impiety of the Patarenes, and for that reason I shall omit the miracles which God continually works by means of holy icons. Sometimes holy icons when struck by the wicked have shed blood which has prevented thieves from their crime; by touching some, health has been restored to the sick, and many have been freed from demons. Remember, Patarene, you who attack all these things, that the company of Christians does not adore icons because they are coloured and made of rich materials, nor does it commit idolatry because they do not see or speak or smell, like the Israelites who adored the golden calf [Exod. 32.8]; we pay them honour and reverence because of what they signify through the figure on them. This is the sense in which we honour and reverence the altar, the chalice and the gospel books, not because they are made of kid- or sheepskin, with ink marks, but because they bring to our attention the sayings and opinions of Christ. Listen then to a reason which you cannot deny for the devotion with which the faithful honour icons. Rouse yourself from sleep, and join us in paying honour and reverence to the human figure of the redeemer and of His saints. The woman who, according to Luke, was healed from a flow of blood by touching the fringe of the Saviour's garment [Luke 8.43–4] created in front of the portico of her house the bronze figure of a woman on bended knees, her hands stretched out as if begging, while opposite it, on a higher place, she set up a figure of the Saviour of the same material, wearing a cloak and stretching His hand out to the woman. By His feet there always grew a strange plant of some kind, which reached as far as the fringe of the cloak, while about the time of the Passion it reached the height of the figure of Christ. The power of the plant which grew at Caesarea Philippi lasted until the reign of the emperor Maximin.[26] He was an enemy of the Christian faith, superstitious and idolatrous. As he was journeying through those regions, he heard that the name of Christ flourished because of that statue and the plant, and ordered the statue of Christ the Saviour to be broken. At once the plant vanished. There is

---

26 The legend of the statue and the wonder-working plant is found in Eusebius. The account of the wonder-working statue is found in *Ecc. Hist.* 7.18; of its destruction by the emperor Maximin in *Comm. Lk.* 8.43 (*PG* 24.541). B has 'the emperor Maximian' for 'Maximin'.

another wonder I shall tell, one that is well known throughout the world. At about the same time there was a prince of Edessa named Abgar,[27] who suffered from a serious illness, an inflexible contraction of his limbs and leprosy black with ulcers. He heard of the miracles of Christ and sent messengers to Him many times, begging Christ to come to him and offering Him dominion over his kingdom or presents worthy of so great a deed. Jesus then, about the time of his Passion, while He spent the night in prayer and when His holy sweat was, as Luke writes, 'like drops of blood falling to the ground' [Luke 22.44], asked one of his disciples for a cloth with which to wipe his face. The ineffable provision of our perfect Saviour preserved His image impressed on the cloth. This He gave to Thomas the apostle, and told him to send it to Prince Abgar after His ascension, by Thaddeus.[28] Abgar received the messenger and the gift with great thanks and affection, and at the touch of Christ was freed from all the sickness which had tormented him. I must not omit what was even more astonishing; I will give a short account of how the aforesaid image on the cloth marked a tile with all the features of Christ. At the gateposts of that city there was placed a statue of one of the gods whom the pagans worshipped, and this all those who entered Edessa honoured as a god. By the order of Prince Abgar this was removed, and in its place was set up the revered image of the Saviour. He ordered reverence and honour to be paid to it by all those who entered the city, as they had done to the statue that had been removed. After some time there arose a prince of that city who was hostile to the Christian religion, a destroyer of holy figures, who threatened to destroy the holy portrait already mentioned with fire – in vain, for the bishop of the city hastily and with diligence arose at night with the equipment the affair required, and having dug a hole, he put in the figure and put in front of the image a lamp filled with oil, with a brilliant light. He blocked in the rest and covered the face of the Saviour with a tile. Outside he made the whole thing into a dome and whitewashed it. When many years had passed, age destroyed memory of all these things, so that there was no knowledge of the description of where the holy face had been hidden. Now when the Persians brought about a war against the people of Edessa, intending to destroy the city, the bishop of the city of Edessa, whose name was Eulalius, dreamt that he saw a woman of reverend appear-

27 The legends associated with Edessa, its prince, the letter written by Christ and the portrait of Christ were extremely popular. The version here closely resembles the account in Constantine Porphyrogenitus (*PG* 113, 421–54). See Cameron, 'The history of the image of Edessa'.
28 B: 'Matthew'.

ance who told him to take the Saviour's image. She showed him where it was hidden, and told him to go round the entire city with it, and said that in this way he might avert destruction. So the astonished bishop, anxious to carry out all the woman had commanded, hurried to the place she had indicated. He found the most holy image and the lamp still alight. Despite the time which had elapsed, it was still burning. On the tile, which had been placed as a cover for the Saviour's face, to keep it safe, the face was portrayed just as it was on the cloth. The pontiff took all the things mentioned, went round the city, as he had been told to, and wherever he sprinkled the oil from the lamp he had found on the Persians immediately he turned them all to flight, and the city remained unharmed. So the people of Edessa kept the sacred image as an inviolable treasure, inexhaustible wealth, their defence from evil, their cure for calamity and an invincible protection from danger and destruction. Then at length when it seemed to the Creator of all things that the magnificence of these images should become well known to the whole world, He moved the heart of the emperor Romanus to send legates, including Abraham, bishop of Samosata, with magnificent gifts to the people of Edessa, who sought with prayers what he had asked for. They brought the sacred portraits often mentioned above to Constantinople, that is, to the palace at Blachernae, on the fifteenth of August. On the sixteenth day of the same month the emperor, the patriarch, all the clergy and the entire people with lighted lamps, hymns and spiritual anthems brought the most holy image with the greatest honour and outstanding reverence to the Great Palace, while a great multitude of the sick followed. There they were placed with fitting honour and cult and are preserved until the present day. Every year the people of Constantinople keep a feast on 16 August, since they believe that it is by means of the great image of the Redeemer that they are kept free from pestilence, famine and pillage, and that the city has been preserved from capture through all the centuries.

It is not necessary to speak at length about the honour and reverence due to the life-giving cross, and how it should be used to protect the foreheads of the faithful, since this is abundantly clear from what has been said already, and can be plainly understood from both the Old Testament and the New. But perhaps the Patarene will say (like the Manichaean he is), 'As we do not honour a donkey just because Christ sat on one, so we should not honour the cross because Christ was nailed to it.' And again, 'Just as the faithful do not sign themselves with the image of the spear, or reed, or thorn or nails, although they too are holy, so to be signed with the sign of the cross is superstitious.' Listen to the answer to these points, Patarene, to which my distinguished brother Leo Toscanus,[29] the most skilful translator of the imperial letters, has given his assent. It was not on the donkey but on the cross that Christ achieved the salvation of the world, conquered the devil and made his kingdom deserted. That is why demons are not afraid of a donkey, but often flee the presence of the cross. So the assembly of the faithful do not pay to a donkey, but only to the cross, the honour that is its due. Moses' rod signified the cross, through which the world is defeated and the prince of this world, with his princes and powers, is triumphed over. For the rod when thrown on to the ground became a snake, the symbol of wisdom. After the cross came bringing faith and belief to men it consumed all the wisdom of the Egyptians, that is, of this world. Assuredly the wisdom of this world became foolishness, when it was apparent that Christ crucified is the strength and the wisdom of God. So the sign of the cross, not that of reed or thorn or nail or sponge or spear, is impressed on the foreheads of the faithful, because, as Paul says, 'Christ fixed the bond of the decree against us to the cross' [Col. 3.14], and not to any of the other things named. The bond and its demand is what God said to Adam: 'On the day that you eat of it, you shall die' [Gen. 2.17]. The devil had possession of it, and through it he was our enemy and our opponent. Christ removed it from the midst, striking it not with a spear or reed or any of the other things, but with the cross. When the innocent was killed, sin was crucified and the bond was cancelled. That is why we protect ourselves with the sign of the cross, not that of the other things, and sign ourselves, because we are always mindful of the bond that was nailed to it. From now on we shall not return to the old order. The cross is fixed on the forehead, which is the seat of bashfulness, so that like Paul, we may take pride in, it, saying, 'Far be it from me to glory, except in the cross of our Lord Jesus Christ' [Gal. 6.14]. The cross should be something in which all the faithful take pride, since it showed the love Christ has for us. What greater joy is there for a servant than to realize his master's love for him? However, others say that the cross was made up of two pieces of wood joined, which have been divided among the faithful. They claim that we show reverence to the pieces, as pieces of wood, when the shape of the cross has been destroyed. We must affirm that it is not the wood, but the image of the cross, that the faithful people honour and venerate. None of this applies in the case of the reed or

---

29 For the office and career of this man see Dondaine, 'Hugues Éthérien et le concile de Constantinople'.

sponge or the rest. That is why it is appropriate that we should sign our faces with the cross, rather than with anything else that has been mentioned, as a precaution against the snares of demons. Certainly it is this that John proclaimed in a loud voice in the Apocalypse, when he said, 'Lo, I, John, saw another angel ascending from the rising of the sun with the seal of the living God' [Rev. 7.2] – that is, the sign of the life-giving cross. The servants of our God are signed with this sign on their foreheads against the bitter and fearful day of the last judgement. But why would I ask the apostles, when I find our Lord Jesus Christ teaching this? For Luke writes, 'As Christ was about to ascend into heaven, our Redeemer led His disciples to Bethany, and lifting up His hands, He blessed them, and while He blessed them, He parted from them and was carried up into heaven' [Luke 24.50]. He blessed the disciples, giving them strength and protection in the hope of His coming. By doing this the Saviour clearly taught that even after His departure, priests and prelates in their blessings should make a sign and protect [the faithful] with their hands raised in the sign of the cross. That is why the holy Church of God, both of the Latins and of the Greeks, keeps this form of blessing to this day. Moreover, every Christian constantly defends and guards himself with this sign night and day, lest Leviathan, his old enemy, should entice him away from the body of the faithful, this sign by which the deacon Laurence gave sight to the blind.

You Patarene, unless you are protected by the aforesaid sign and show your unsullied faith, you will be struck on the forehead with stones wet from the river, and be cast into Avernus as food for the furies of hell, inasmuch as it has been demonstrated to you that we should obey priests even if they are wicked, on the authority of the Saviour, who told us, 'Observe whatever they tell you, but not what they do' [Matt. 23.2]. Again, if you lay aside your obstinacy of heart, you would realize that if the holy universal Church of God and the most pious emperor utterly forbade oath-taking, they would not allow court cases to be decided by an oath. If marriage were not allowed, as your wicked opinion holds, Christ would not have been a guest at a wedding and made the water into good wine. What else do you doubt? On the altar bread becomes flesh, and wine blood, as He Himself is witness, in whose mouth there is no guile. He said, 'My flesh is real food, and my blood is real drink,' So restrain your tongue from these shameless denials and from insulting the holy icons. If paying honour and worship to the life-giving cross and the holy icons were a sin, Christ would never have left His face to the world in picture form, nor would the Church honour it with the riches and plenty it brought.

In this pamphlet authorities are summarized, so that industrious men might have authorities to hand. Relying on these, they should easily persuade the most intelligent emperor Manuel to order that on the foreheads of this most perfidious sect a black *theta*[30] should be fixed.

37. THE MISSION OF *PAPA* NICETAS OF CONSTANTINOPLE TO THE WEST (*c.* 1170)

Western sources record the visit made to the Cathar communities of Italy and France by a Bogomil leader called *papa* Nicetas from Constantinople. His purpose was to convert the Cathars from the Bulgarian form of moderate dualism which they had all previously received to the absolute dualism of the Church of Drugonthia to which he belonged. 'Drugonthia' appears to be an attempt to render in Latin the name Dragovitia, the area south of Philippopolis where this new form of Bogomilism had originated. Nicetas considered that the spiritual baptism, or *consolamentum*, which the Cathars had received, was not valid, and persuaded them that all the initiated Cathars, known as the perfect, needed to be reconsoled, and their bishops reconsecrated. He began his work among the Cathars of Lombardy[1] and then travelled to southern France, where he presided over a council of the French and Italian Cathars at Saint-Félix. For a time the Cathars of the West were united in the new faith, but an embassy from the Bogomil moderate dualists, led by Petracius, impugned the validity of Nicetas' consolings. As a result the Italian Cathars became divided into three main groups, some of whom remained true to Nicetas' teaching and in communion with the Church of Dragovitia, while others returned to the moderate dualist Church of Bulgaria, and a third group received new consolings from the Bogomil Church of Bosnia. The southern French Cathars for the most part remained absolute dualists. Nicetas' mission took place between 1165 and 1177.

These sources are important because they are the earliest evidence for the existence of a schism among the Bogomils between moderate and absolute dualists; for the adoption of episcopal government by the Bogomils and for the existence of a Bogomil church in Bosnia. See our Introduction, pp. 44–5.

(a) THE CATHAR COUNCIL OF SAINT-FÉLIX

The Saint-Félix document is known only in a seventeenth-century printed text of a copy made in 1223. Although its authenticity has been questioned I (B.H.) have defended it in 'The Cathar Council of Saint-Félix reconsidered', and this

---

30 *Theta* is the first letter of the Greek word *Thanatos*, meaning 'Death'.
1 Here referring to the area of northern Italy now known by this name.

THE MISSION OF *PAPA* NICETAS TO THE WEST

has met with quite wide approval, e.g. by Obolensky, in his 'Papa Nicetas'. This translation has been made from G. Besse, *Histoire des ducs, marquis et comtes de Narbonne* (Paris, 1660), pp. 483–6.

In the month of May in the year of the Lord's incarnation 1167:[2] at that time the Church of Toulouse brought *papa* Niquinta[3] to the castle of Saint-Félix, and a great multitude of the men and women of the Church of Toulouse and of the other neighbouring Churches gathered there to receive the *consolamentum*[4] which the lord *papa* Niquinta began to administer. Afterwards Robert of Spernone, Bishop of the Church of the French,[5] came with his council; and also Mark of Lombardy came with his council; and Sicard Cellarier, Bishop of the Church of Albi, came with his council; and B[ernard] the Catalan came with the council of the Church of Carcassonne; and the council of the Church of Agen[6] was also present. And since they were all gathered there in such numbers, the men of the Church of Toulouse wished to have a bishop, and chose Bernard Raymond; and likewise Bernard the Catalan and the Church of Carcassonne, being requested and required to do so by the Church of Toulouse, and on the advice and with the agreement and permission of the lord S[icard] Cellarier, chose Gerald Mercier; and the men of Agen chose Raymond de Casals. After that Robert d' Espernone received the *consolamentum* and was consecrated bishop by the lord *papa* Niquinta, so that he might be Bishop of the Church of the French; likewise Sicard Cellarier received the *consolamentum* and was consecrated bishop, so that he might be Bishop of the Church of Albi. In the same way Mark received the *consolamentum* and was consecrated bishop, so that he might be Bishop of the Church of Lombardy; likewise Bernard Raymond received the *consolamentum* and was consecrated bishop, so that he might be Bishop of the Church of Toulouse; and likewise Gerald Mercier received the *consolamentum* and was consecrated bishop, so that he might

---

2 It is possible that the date of this document has been wrongly transcribed. Other evidence about southern French Cathars would suggest a slightly later date, *c.* 1175.
3 Niquinta may be a faulty transcription, or an attempt to render the unfamiliar name Nicetas phonetically.
4 This is the Latin term used for the Cathar sacrament of initiation by the laying on of hands, identical to that described as in use among the Bogomils by EZ **[25]**, c. 16.
5 At this period the *ecclesia Franciae* was the term used to describe the Cathar Church of northern France.
6 The document reads '*ecclesia Aranensis*' (the Church of the Val d'Aran), but there is general agreement among scholars that this is a wrong transcription of '*ecclesia Agenensis*' (the Church of Agen), where the presence of a Cathar bishopric is well attested in later sources.

be Bishop of the Church of Carcassonne; likewise Raymond de Casals received the *consolamentum* and was consecrated bishop, so that he might be Bishop of the Church of Agen.

After this *papa* Niquinta addressed the Church of Toulouse: 'You have asked me to tell you whether the customs of the primitive Churches were burdensome or light, and so let me tell you that the seven Churches of Asia were separated from each other by boundaries, and as a result none of them did anything to the detriment of any of the others.[7] And the Churches of Rome and Dragometia and Melenguia and Bulgaria and Dalmatia[8] are separated by boundaries from each other and none of them does anything to the detriment of any of the others, and so they are at peace with each other. You should do the same' [The rest of the document is concerned with the definition of diocesan boundaries].

(b) DE HERESI CATHARORUM IN LOMBARDIA

The *De heresi Catharorum in Lombardia* was written before 1214, perhaps by an Italian perfect converted to Catholicism. This translation has been made from Dondaine, 'La Hiérarchie cathare en Italie', I, p. 306.

In the earliest days, when the heresy of the Cathars began to spread in Lombardy, they had a certain bishop called Mark, under whose rule all the Lombards and Tuscans and people of the Marches were governed. And this Mark had been received into the *ordo*[9] of Bulgaria. A certain man called *papa* Nicetas came to Lombardy from the region of Constantinople, and began to impugn the Bulgarian *ordo* to which Mark belonged. For that reason Bishop Mark and his flock began to have doubts, and abandoning the *ordo* of Bulgaria, they were received by Nicetas into that of Drugonthia. And in that *ordo* of Drugonthia he remained for some time, with all his associates. Meanwhile, on another occasion there came from the regions beyond the seas a man called Petracius, together with his companions,[10] and brought some news about a certain Bishop Simon of Drugonthia, from whom the *ordo* into which they had been received by Nicetas took its origin. And this Petracius said that Simon

---

7 This may refer to Revelation 1.4–3.22, or to the seven Paulician churches of Asia Minor in the ninth century; see our Introduction, p. 11.
8 For a discussion of the location of these Churches see our Introduction, pp. 44–5.
9 The term *ordo* is used by western writers about the Cathars to designate the succession of consolings which linked the local Cathar Church to the apostles.
10 Petracius is not otherwise known. This delegation represented the moderate dualist Bogomil *ordo* deriving ultimately from Bulgaria.

THE *SECRET BOOK* BROUGHT FROM BULGARIA

had been found locked in a room with a certain woman,[11] and that he had done other things that were not right. But by the time this Petracius arrived Mark was already dead, and another man, called John the Jew, had succeeded him as bishop, and he had been consecrated by that same Mark. And because of the story told by this Petracius there were some who had doubts about the *ordo* deriving from that Simon, and there were others who did not; and for that reason a disturbance arose among them and they became split into two parties. [The source goes on to relate how the subsequent schism was never healed, but how different groups of Italian Cathars sent their bishops-elect to Drugonthia, Bulgaria and Bosnia to be consecrated.]

38. THE *SECRET BOOK* BROUGHT FROM BULGARIA (*c.* 1190)

The Italian Cathar Church of Concorezzo near Milan returned to the moderate dualist *ordo* of the Bogomil Church of Bulgaria after the death of Bishop Mark.[1] Nazarius, the fourth Bishop of Concorezzo, had, as the following passages show, visited Bulgaria in *c.* 1190 and brought back with him a *Secret Book*. He lived to be very old, and died some time before 1254.[2]

(a) RAYNERIUS SACCONI, *SUMMA DE CATHARIS*

Raynerius was a Cathar perfect for seventeen years and became a Cathar minister, although his rank is not known. In *c.* 1245 he was converted to Catholicism by St Peter Martyr and joined the Dominican Order. In 1252 he was appointed chief Inquisitor in Lombardy, a post he held until his death in *c.* 1262. His *Summa* was written in *c.* 1250 as a guide to other inquisitors about the beliefs of the various schools of Cathars.

This translation has been made from Sanjek, 'Raynerius Sacconi, *Summa de Catharis*', p. 58.

The errors of Nazarius, Bishop [of Concorezzo]. Nazarius, one of their former bishops and a very old man, said in my presence and that of many others that the Blessed Virgin was an angel, and that Christ did not take on

---

11 Simon is the first Bogomil bishop known by name. According to western writers fornication, or any other failure to observe the Cathar rule of life, led to the invalidation of all consolings conferred by a Cathar minister. To judge from this passage, the Bogomils held a similar belief.
1 See Glossary explaining the meaning of the term *ordo*.
2 Dondaine, La Hiérarchie cathare en Italie, III', p. 291.

human nature, but an angelic nature and a celestial body. And he said that he learned this error from the Bishop and the Elder Son of the Church of Bulgaria, now almost sixty years ago.[3]

(b) *THE SECRET BOOK*

The *Secret Book* appears to have been composed by the Bogomils and not merely adapted by them from some earlier Gnostic work. It is attributed to St John the Divine and set in the context of the Last Supper, in which John is represented as being told by Christ about the mysteries of the universe. It is known only in two Latin translations: an incomplete text preserved in a single manuscript in Vienna and a lost manuscript, which once belonged to the Inquisition of Carcassonne, of which multiple copies survive. It is not known what authority the Bulgarian Bogomils accorded to this work, though Edina Bozóky has pointed out how closely the doctrines it contains resemble those of the moderate dualists of Constantinople recorded by Euthymius Zigabenus[4] (Bozóky, ed., *Le Livre Secret des Cathares*). There is an easily accessible English translation in Wakefield and Evans, *Heresies of the High Middle Ages* (no. 56 B), so we have only translated the colophon here.

[The colophon of the Carcassone manuscript was added by an inquisitor and reads] Here endeth the *Secret [Book]* of the heretics of Concorezzo, brought from Bulgaria by Nazarius, their bishop. It is full of errors.[5]

39. POPE INNOCENT III AND THE BOGOMILS OF BOSNIA (1198–1203)

Among the Bogomil Churches listed by *papa* Nicetas at the Council of Saint-Félix in *c.* 1170 was that of Dalmatia.[1] More information about this Church is contained in western sources. The History of Split, written by Thomas, archdeacon of that city, in *c.* 1260, records how in the the late twelfth century Archbishop Bernard of Split had discovered heretics there and brought their leaders to trial. Thomas does not specify what their heresy was, but tells us that they had close links with Bosnia ((a) below). This situation is clarified by the correspondence of Pope Innocent III (1198–1216).

---

3 i.e. in *c.* 1190. This is the earliest reference to the office of Elder Son in the Bogomil hierarchy. See our Introduction, p. 44.
4 See **[25]**.
5 Bozóky *Le livre Secret des Cathares*, p. 86.
1 **[37]** above.

In 1199 King Vukan of Zeta[2] sent the Pope an alarmist report about the conversion of Ban Kulin of Bosnia[3] with thousands of his subjects to heresy ((b) below). Bosnia, like much of the Dalmatian coast, was Catholic in religion and subject to the Pope. Bosnia had only one bishop, who was a suffragan of the archbishop of Dubrovnik, and the Ban of Bosnia was in theory a vassal of the king of Hungary, though in practice he was an independent ruler. Innocent III made enquiries and discovered that the heretics of Bosnia were Paterenes (the Italian name for Cathars and Bogomils), who had taken refuge there after being expelled from the coastal cities, and he invoked the help of the king of Hungary to suppress this heresy ((c) below). In order to avoid Hungarian intervention, Ban Kulin sent an embassy to Rome asking the pope himself to examine the alleged Bosnian heretics ((d) below), and Innocent appointed legates who in 1203 reconciled the leaders of the Bosnian Bogomils to the Catholic Church at Bolino-Polje. Although J.V.A. Fine has argued that these heretics were not dualists,[4] his view has received little support and we are not convinced by it.

The translation of (a) has been made from Racki's edition of Thomas of Spalato, pp. 79–80 §30, of (b) from Innocent III, *Regesta*, II, no. clxxvi (*PL* 214, 725–6) and of (c–d) from *CICO*, ser. III, vol.1, nos. 19, 28, 36 (pp. 209, 224–5, 235–7).

NB In the papal registers, which contain copies of important papal correspondence, proper names are customarily omitted or are indicated only by initials.

(a) THOMAS, ARCHDEACON OF SPLIT, RECORDS THE PRESENCE OF HERETICS IN DALMATIA AND BOSNIA

Archbishop Bernard[5] . . . was a most industrious investigator of heretics. For at that time there were two brother, sons of Zorobabel, one of whom was named Matthew and the other Aristodius.[6] Although they had originated from Apulia, they had been citizens of Jadera[7] from boyhood. They spent most of their time in Bosnia, since they were excellent painters, skilful goldsmiths and adequately literate both in Latin and Slavonic. By the deceits of the devil they had been plunged into the depths of heresy, so that not merely did they believe the impious heresy

---

2 Vukan, the son of Stephen Nemanja, ruler of Serbia, was made prince of the province of Zeta in *c.* 1190. He later styled himself king. He abdicated in 1208. His kingdom comprised the modern provinces of Zeta and Montenegro, but his Latin title was King of Dioclea and Dalmatia.
3 Ruled *c.* 1180 – *c.* 1204.
4 Fine, *The Bosnian Church*, pp. 123–34. See our Introduction, pp. 47–8.
5 Ruled 1196–1217; also referred to in (c) and (d) below.
6 Nothing else is known of these two men; see Sanjek, *Les Chrétiens bosniaques*, pp. 38–9.
7 Now Zadar.

in the blindness of their hearts, but preached it with their wicked lips. Bernard discovered that they were resident at Split, and that many had been infected by them with their pestiferous doctrine. He undertook to entice them little by little to the Catholic faith with gentle words; he frequently summoned and exhorted them. They twisted and turned with the cunning of heretics, and falsely claimed to be converted. Immediately the archbishop had all their goods confiscated, fettered them in the chains of anathema and expelled them from the city in great disgrace. Then the aforesaid brothers, seeing that they had incurred great losses and opprobrium, returned to the obedience of the Church. The archbishop made them swear to abjure their heresy on the holy gospels; he freed them from the bonds of excommunication with due solemnity and had their property restored to them. All those whom they had deceived were likewise cleansed from the infection of heresy.

(b) KING VUKAN OF ZETA WRITES TO THE POPE ABOUT HERESY IN BOSNIA, 1199

To the most blessed and holy father and lord Innocent, by the grace of God supreme pontiff of the holy Church of Rome and universal pope, Vukan, by the grace of God King of Dioclea and Dalmatia, [sends] greetings and [his] deepest respect . . . we wish your Paternity to know that an uncontrolled heresy seems to be spreading in the lands of the King of Hungary – that is, in Bosnia – so that . . . Ban Kulin himself, led astray together with his wife and sister, the widow of Miroslav of Hum,[8] and many of his kinsfolk, has introduced more than 10,000 Christians to this heresy. The King of Hungary was concerned at this, and obliged them to go to your presence, but they returned with forged documents, claiming that you had given them permission. For this reason we beg that you would put pressure on the King of Hungary to expel them from his kingdom like tares from the wheat.

(c) INNOCENT III URGES KING IMRE OF HUNGARY TO TAKE ACTION AGAINST THE HERETICS OF BOSNIA, 11 OCTOBER 1200

To our most dear son in Christ H,[9] the noble king of Hungary . . . Now we have heard that recently our venerable brother . . . Archbishop of

8 Hum is now Hercegovina. Miroslav had died in 1198.
9 King Imre of Hungary (1196–1204). The Latin form of his name was Emerichus or Hemerichus. In (d) it has been wrongly transcribed as Henricus.

Split has expelled a large number of Paterenes from the cities of Split and of Trogir, but the noble Kulin, the Ban of Bosnia, has provided for them not merely a safe hiding-place, but an open shelter, and laying both his country and himself open to their perversity, has honoured them as if they were Catholics, indeed as if they were super-Catholics, calling them authentic Christians. So, then, lest this kind of disease should spread to the surrounding area, if not prevented in the beginning, and its infection overflow into the kingdom of Hungary . . . we exhort your majesty . . . to avenge such an injury done to Christ and to Christians . . . Unless the Ban aforesaid excludes all heretics from the land which is subject to his authority and confiscates all their property, you should exclude him and the heretics not merely from his territory, but from the entire realm of Hungary, and confiscate the goods of such people wherever they may be found throughout your land. Do not . . . overlook the Ban [himself], since you should exercise temporal authority over him, if there is no other way to summon him back to the path of righteousness . . .

(d) THE ACCORD OF BOLINO-POLJE BETWEEN THE LEADERS OF THE BOSNIAN BOGOMILS AND THE PAPAL LEGATES, 30 APRIL 1203[10]

In the name of God eternal, the creator and redeemer of the human race, in the year of His incarnation 1203 . . . We, the superiors of those who up until now have been uniquely privileged to be called Christians in the land of Bosnia, as representatives of all who are members of our society of brotherhood, in the presence of lord John de Casamaris, papal chaplain and legate of the Roman Church in Bosnia in this matter, in the presence of our patron Ban Kulin, lord of Bosnia, promise in the presence of God and of his saints to abide by the ordinances and commands of the holy Roman Church, as far as concerns our life and institutions, and to remain in its obedience and live in accordance with its laws. On behalf of all those who belong to our community we pledge ourselves, our houses and our possessions and property, if ever henceforward we shall have been followers of wicked heresy.

First we renounce the schism of which we are accused, and acknowledge the Roman Church as our mother, the head of the whole Church. In every place where a community of brethen is based we shall have a chapel where we shall assemble the brethren to say matins at night and

10 The provisions of this document are discussed in our Introduction, pp. 47–8.

the hours by day, publicly and together. In every church we shall have an altar and a cross, and we shall read the books of the New and Old Testament as the Roman Church does. In every place we shall have a priest whose duty it is to celebrate mass at least on Sundays and saints' days, in accordance with the Church's rule, to hear confessions and to impose penances. We shall have cemeteries near the chapels where the brethren shall be buried, and strangers who happen to die there. We shall receive the body of Christ at the priest's hands at least seven times a year, that is, at Christmas, Easter, Pentecost, St Peter and St Paul, the Assumption of our Lady, her Nativity, and the commemoration of All Saints, which is kept on 1 November.[11] We shall observe the fasts appointed by the Church and keep those which our predecessors in their wisdom enjoined. Women who are members of our community shall sleep in separate dormitories and eat in separate refectories; no brother shall have private conversations with a sister which might give rise to unfavourable suspicion. Nor, on the other hand, will we accept any married man or woman, unless both are converted together by mutual consent and the promise of continence. We shall celebrate the feasts of the saints ordained by the holy fathers and will not accept anyone who is reliably identified as a Manichaean[12] or any other heretic to live among us. Just as we are distinguished from others who are lay people by life and conduct, so we shall be separated by style of clothing. We shall wear a black tunic, reaching to the ankles. In addition we shall no longer call ourselves Christians, but Brethren, lest the distinction of name insult other Christians. For the future and in perpetuity, at the death of a Master, the priors and a council of God-fearing Brethren shall choose a leader, subject to ratification by the Roman pontiff. If there is anything which the Church of Rome desires to add or remove we shall devoutly accept and observe it.

We confirm this with our signatures so that it may remain in force for ever.

Enacted at Bosnia, beside the river, at the place called Bolino-Polje, on 8 April.

We, Dragite, Lubin, Drageta, Pribis, Luben, Rados, Bladosius, Ban Kulin and Marinus, archdeacon of Ragusa, have signed.

We, Lubin and Tregeta, at the desire of all our Brethren in Bosnia and

---

11 Sts Peter and Paul, 29 June; the Assumption, 15 August; the Nativity of the Virgin, 8 September.
12 In western European sources Manichaean means a Cathar or Bogomil.

of Ban Kulin himself, together with the same lord John the chaplain, having gone to H., the noble and most Christian King of Hungary, and in the presence of the king and of the reverend Archbishop... of Kolocsa,[13] of the Bishop of *Quinque Ecclesiae*[14] and of many others, have sworn to observe these statutes and any others which the Church of Rome may decide to determine in our case, and to abide by the Catholic faith. Enacted on the Royal Island[15] on 30 April.

40. THE FOURTH CRUSADE AND THE PAULICIANS OF PHILIPPOPOLIS (1205)

In 1204 the Fourth Crusade sacked Constantinople and set up a Latin empire under Baldwin I of Flanders. Baldwin appointed Renier de Trit[1] Duke of Philippopolis in the winter of 1204–5, and he was initially welcomed there by the Greek population. But a few months later a revolt broke out among the Byzantines of Thrace and Macedonia against the Latins, and the rebels were aided by Tsar Ioannitsa of Bulgaria.[2] Most of the Latin garrison of Philippopolis fled when this news reached them, leaving Renier de Trit with only fifteen knights. On 14 April 1205 the Tsar inflicted a severe defeat on the Latin forces at Adrianople, taking the emperor Baldwin prisoner,[3] and followed this up by capturing Serres. When this news became known in Philippopolis, the Paulician community offered to betray the city to the Tsar, as this passage relates. It is evidence that a century after Alexius I had sought to convert them to orthodoxy[4] the Paulicians of Philippopolis retained their identity and were as politically active as they had been in the time of the Comneni.

Geoffrey de Villehardouin was one of the leaders of the Fourth Crusade, and was made Marshal of the Latin empire by Baldwin I. His History was completed some time between 1207 (when his account ends) and his death, which occurred between 1212 and 1218.

This translation has been made from Geoffroi de Villehardouin, *La Conquête de Constantinople*, c. 399, ed. E. Faral, II, p. 210.

13 The primate of the Hungarian Church.
14 Now Pécs.
15 An island in the Danube at Budapest.
1 For Renier de Trit see Longnon, *Les Compagnons de Villehardouin*, pp. 150–2.
2 Ioannitsa, sometimes called Kalojan, Tsar of Bulgaria 1197–1207.
3 Baldwin IX, Count of Flanders (1194–1205), Latin emperor of Constantinople (1204–5), was taken prisoner by Tsar Ioannitsa at Adrianople in 1205 and died in prison later that year. His death was known in Philippopolis, but not in the capital until 1206.
4 See [22] above.

And the people of Philippopolis, which belonged to Renier de Trit, to whom the emperor Baldwin had given it, had heard that the emperor Baldwin had been killed and many of his barons, and that the marquis[5] had lost Serres, and saw that the kinsmen of Renier de Trit, including his son and nephew, had deserted him, and that there were only a few men [remaining with him], and they supposed that the French would never regain power. A large part of the population, who were Paulicians,[6] went to Ioannitsa and did homage to him, and said: 'Sire, ride to Philippopolis, or send your army there, and we will surrender the whole city to you.'

When Renier de Trit, who was still in the city, came to know of this... he made a sortie with all the men at his disposal as day was breaking, and came to one of the quarters of the city where the Paulicians lived who had gone to see Ioannitsa. He set fire to the quarter and burned down a great part of it. [Renier then withdrew to the castle of Stenimaka, knowing that he did not have enough troops to defend the city, and Ioannitsa captured it and killed the Greek population.]

41. THE *SYNODIKON* OF TSAR BORIL AGAINST THE BOGOMILS (1211)

The Bogomil heresy was condemned at the Council of Trnovo on 11 February 1211, at which Tsar Boril of Bulgaria (1207–18) presided.[1] As Gouillard has shown, the legislation of this council is based on the anathemas in the letter of the Patriarch Cosmas I (1075–81).[2] The anathemas have been arranged in a different order, and additional material has been incorporated in Boril's *Synodikon*.

The *Synodikon* is preserved in two manuscripts, the older of which dates from the late fourteenth century. The text has been edited by Popruzhenko in his 'Sinodik carja Borila', pp. 42–82. We have used the French translation made by Puech and Vaillant *Le traité contre les Bogomiles*, pp. 343–6, incorporating emendations made by Yuri Stoyanov, who has collated this translation with the Old Slavonic text.

Because our guileful Enemy has sown the Manichaean heresy through-

---

5 Boniface II, Marquis of Montferrat (1192–1207).
6 Villehardouin uses the Old French word *Popelican*, which western writers had used to describe Paulicians since the First Crusade. See our Introduction, p. 23.

1 See our Introduction, p. 48.
2 **[22]**.

out all the Bulgarian land and mixed it with Messalianism, to the leaders of this heresy anathema.[3]

1. To *pop* Bogomil who during the reign of the Bulgarian Tsar Peter adopted this Manichean heresy and spread it in the land of Bulgaria and also added to it that Christ our God was borne by the holy Mother of God and ever-virgin Mary [only] in appearance, that He was crucified in appearance and that He ascended in His divinized body and left it in the air; to his past and present disciples, known as apostles,[4] anathema.

2. To all those who are members of this heresy, their customs, meetings at night, mysteries and their pernicious teachings, and to their fellow-travellers, anathema.[5]

3. To those united with them in affection, who knowingly eat and drink with them and accept gifts from them because they sympathize with them, anathema.

4. To those who on 24 June, the birthday of St John the Baptist, practise magic and gather fruits and perform foul mysteries that night like pagan rites, anathema.[6]

5. To those who call Satan the creator of all visible things and call him the steward of rain and hail and of everything that comes from the earth, anathema.

6. To those who say that Satan created Adam and Eve, anathema.

7. To those who reject Moses, who saw God, and Elias the Tishbite, and the other holy prophets and patriarchs and that their writings are from God, and say that they are from Satan and that they wrote as they did impelled by him and that what they said of Christ was said against their will and under compulsion; to the Bogomils who for that reason reject the books of the Old Testament and the holy prophets who illuminate it, anathema.

8. To those who say that a woman conceives in her womb through the

---

3 For the historical Messalians see note 4 to EZ [25]; for the use of the term to describe Bogomils, see Rigo, 'Messalianismo = Bogomilismo'.
4 The corresponding anathemas in Cosmas [21] say nothing about the docetic Christology of the Bogomils.
5 'Mysteries' is loosely used to describe Bogomil initiation ceremonies, since the text continues to condemn the heretics for refusing to accept the validity of Christian sacraments.
6 Similar ceremonies for midsummer are recorded in the Greek material. This anathema, which does not relate to the Bogomils, may be interpolated.

agency of Satan[7], that Satan staunchly remains there, even until the birth of her child and that he may not be driven out by Holy Baptism, but only by prayer and fasting, anathema.

9. To those who blaspheme John the Baptist and say that he, together with his baptism with water, are from Satan and for this reason abjure baptism with water and baptize without water, reciting only the 'Our Father', anathema.

10. To those who abjure all the holy and divine chants in church, and the house of God itself . . . and speak of reciting the Our Father in whatever place they happen to be, anathema.

11. To those who reject and abuse the sacred Holy Liturgy and the whole order of priesthood, saying that these are the invention of Satan, anathema.

12. To those who reject and abuse the communion of the precious body of Our Lord Christ and reject the whole mystery accomplished by our Lord Jesus Christ for our salvation, anathema.

13. To those who reject the adoration of the precious and life-giving cross, and the sacred and holy icons, anathema.

14. To those those who admit such heretics into the Church of God before they have made confession and anathematized the whole heresy. . . . anathema.

15. To Basil the physician, who spread this thrice-acccursed heresy in Constantinople during the reign of the Orthodox emperor Alexius Comnenus, anathema.

16. To Alexander the blacksmith, Avdin and Photin, Aphrigij and Moses the Bogomil, anathema.

17. To Peter of Cappadocia, *dedec* of Sredec[8], Luke and Mandelej of Radobol, anathema.

18. To the thrice-accursed Bogomil, to his disciple Michael, to Theodore, Dobri, Stephen, Basil, Peter and all his disciples and adherents who ridiculously claimed that the Incarnation of Christ was only in appearance and He did not take flesh of our holy and most pure Lady, Mother of God, to all of them, anathema.

---

7 Compare Cosmas [15]. This is a Messalian belief with which the Bogomils were credited.
8 Sredec is Sofia. See our Introduction, p. 48.

42. POPE HONORIUS III AND THE BALKAN POPE OF THE HERETICS (1221–23)

The Agreement of Bolino-Polje did not mark the end of Bogomilism in Bosnia.[1] In 1221 Pope Honorius III ordered his legate in Hungary to exhort King Andrew II (1205–35) to suppress the heretics there.[2] No action was taken, but two years later Cardinal Conrad of Porto, the pope's legate in southern France,[3] found evidence of Bosnian intervention in the affairs of the Cathars of Languedoc.

It is known from thirteenth-century Italian sources that the Bogomil Church of Bosnia, like that of Bulgaria, adhered to moderate dualism.[4] The Cathar Churches of southern France had remained faithful to the absolute dualist teaching introduced by *papa* Nicetas,[5] but as Conrad's letter states, the Bogomil bishop of Bosnia was attempting to restore the southern French Cathars to the moderate dualist faith. His representative was Bartholomew of Carcassonne, who briefly obtained control of the Cathar bishopric of Agen.[6] In the long term this initiative proved unsuccessful, but Cardinal Conrad reacted intemperately to the report of this Bogomil *pop* in the Balkans, whom he supposed to be an antipope of the heretics,[7] and placed this matter on the agenda of a Church council which met at Sens in 1223. The document is of interest because it shows that the Balkan Bogomils preserved links with the Cathar Churches of the West well into the thirteenth century.

Two texts are known of the letter of Cardinal Conrad; one made by the Archbishop of Rouen, the other by Gervase, the Abbot of Prémontré. Our translation has been made from Mansi, who prints the Rouen text with the Prémontré variants (Mansi, vol. 22, cols 1203–4).

---

1 See **[39 (d)]** above.
2 CICO ser. III, vol. II, no. 83, p. 111.
3 Conrad of Porto had been Abbot of Cîteaux before his appointment as cardinal in 1219.
4 Sanjek, *Les Chrétiens bosniaques*, pp. 133–40.
5 See **[37]** above.
6 Y. Dossat has collected information from the Inquisition records about Vigouroux de la Bacone (the Vigorosus de Bathona of this source) and Bartholomew of Carcassonne, but does not think that there is any substance in Conrad of Porto's report about Bosnian intervention (see his 'Un Évêque cathare originaire de l'Agenais'). B.H. has argued that in the light of the southern French evidence Conrad's letter is worthy of credence (Hamilton, 'The Cathar council of Saint-Félix reconsidered', pp. 44–9).
7 See our Introduction, p. 48. For other western sources about a 'pope of the heretics', see Borst, *Die Katharer*, p. 210, note 38.

CARDINAL CONRAD OF PORTO INFORMS THE FRENCH CLERGY OF THE PRESENCE OF A HERETICAL ANTIPOPE IN BOSNIA, 2 JULY 1223

... Who is unmoved when Dagon stands upright and overturns and tramples on the ark? [1 Sam. 51.5; Isa. 42.19]. See what we have observed in the districts of Bosnia, Croatia and Dalmatia near to Hungary; because of the antipope[8] it cannot be doubted that the delay in the coming of antichrist will be shortened, as the new Lucifer, swollen with the poison of fresh arrogance, endeavours to establish his seat in the parts of the north [Isa. 14.13], not merely that he may be like the most lofty successor to the prince of the apostles, but also in order that he may damage and destroy him and the universal Church.[9] ... The Albigensians[10] flock to him so that he may answer their enquiries; they are eager for instruction and embrace the opinions of his damnable sect. This Satan appointed a man named Bartholomew of Carcassonne from his perverse sect to the bishopric of Agen. He came from Carcassonne, and was the antipope's deputy in making those corrupt regions drink the serpent's poison more deeply from the cup of Babylon [Rev. 14.8]. Vigorosus de Bathona, bishop of the heretics, has shown this Bartholomew baneful honour and granted him his own see and place in the town called Pujols, transferring himself to the area of Toulouse.[11] This Bartholomew sends letters everywhere, each of them beginning in this form: 'Bartholomew, the servant of the servants of the hospice of the true faith to so-and-so, greeting.'[12] Moreover (a thing detestable to say, and horrible to hear), he himself creates bishops and endeavours to establish churches of the perfidious sect[13].

---

8 Conrad was presumably misled by references to the Bosnian Bishop of the Bogomils as *papa*, a title reserved in the western Church for the Pope.
9 i.e. the pope of the heretics will take the place of the Catholic pope, the successor of St Peter.
10 A general name for southern French Cathars who established their first congregation in the Albigeois.
11 Vigouroux de la Bacone had been Cathar bishop of Agen in 1222. Pujols is in the Agenais (it is now in the département of Lot et Garonne) and may have been the see of the Cathar bishop (Hamilton, 'The Cathar Council of Saint-Félix reconsidered', pp. 45–8).
12 This is a parody of the opening words of papal letters. There is no other evidence that Cathar bishops ever used this form.
13 This suggests that the Bishop of Bosnia did not accept the consecrations of the southern French Cathars, stemming from *papa* Nicetas, and that new moderate dualist bishops like Bartholomew of Carcassonne had to be consecrated in the Bosnian *ordo*.

43. POPE GREGORY IX (1227–41) URGES THE KING OF HUNGARY TO CRUSADE AGAINST THE BOGOMILS

Gregory IX, who instituted the papal Inquisition to deal with the Cathar heresy, was concerned to stamp out Balkan Bogomilism as well. He deposed the Catholic bishop of Bosnia for failing to take any action against the heretics (see (a) below), and replaced him by a German Dominican. But there is no evidence that the latter was able to take up his office, for in 1234, because Bogomilism continued to thrive there, Gregory declared a crusade against Bosnia which was led by the Duke of Croatia and lasted until 1240.[1] In practice this was a Hungarian war against Bosnia which was given crusade status. Papal influence in Bulgaria[2] ended in *c.* 1232, when Boril's successor as Tsar, John Asen II (1218–41), restored the Bulgarian Church to the communion of the Orthodox patriarch of Constantinople. Receiving reports that Bogomilism was flourishing there, the pope in 1238 incited King Bela IV of Hungary (1235–70) to crusade against Bulgaria (see (b) below). Nothing came of this because of the Mongol invasion of Hungary in 1241–2, which also brought to an end the crusade against Bosnia.[3]

(a) and (b) are copies of papal letters in the Registers of Gregory IX, translated from the edition of CICO, ser. III., vol. III, nos.177, 229 (pp. 233–4, 308–10).

(a) GREGORY IX'S INDICTMENT OF THE CATHOLIC BISHOP OF BOSNIA, 5 JUNE 1232

To Ugrin, archbishop of Kalocsa,[4] and [Stephen] bishop of Zagreb and . . . provost of St Laurence in the diocese of Kalocsa.

We cannot overlook the serious and great faults of our brother . . . bishop of Bosnia, which have been recently brought to our apostolic notice, lest we should appear to make his failings our own, and risk our soul for him by encouraging him in his evil. As we learn, he has been quite unable to acknowledge his imperfections, that is, that he is illiterate, a public defender of heretics, and that he arranged for himself to be appointed bishop by the vice of simony,[5] through the agency of a known heretic. Since what begins from an evil origin can scarcely attain a good end, he who should appear to be a skilful cultivator of the vineyard of the Lord of Hosts, one who profits his subjects both by word

---

1 On the Bosnian Crusade see Fine, *The Bosnian Church*, pp. 137–45.
2 See **[41]** above.
3 On the Bulgarian Crusade see Fine, *The late medieval Balkans*, pp. 131–3.
4 Archbishop Ugrin of Kolocsa, Primate of Hungary (d. 1241).
5 Simony, i.e. the sin of buying holy things, particularly Church offices.

and by example, never celebrates the divine office in the Church, nor administers the sacraments of the Church, and, it is said, he is so much a stranger to the offices of the Church that he is wholly ignorant of the baptismal formula. That is not surprising if, as is claimed, he used to stay with a heretic on a certain country estate, and his blood brother is a known heretical leader – one whom he ought from the start to have recalled to the path of truth, whereas . . . he damnably encourages and defends him in his error . . . Make an accurate account of your findings, and send it under your seal to our presence, so that with adequate information from your report we may proceed forthwith as it is God's will that we should proceed, having first arranged a suitable time within which he should present himself before us to receive what he deserves[6].

(b) GREGORY IX'S ATTEMPT TO LAUNCH A CRUSADE AGAINST HERESY IN BULGARIA, 27 JANUARY 1238

To the noble king of Hungary.

Such indeed are the heretics and schismatics who refuse to be fed by so great a shepherd and pay no heed to his Vicar; more treacherous than the Jews, and more cruel than the pagans . . . Jews, though blinded by sin, believe that God the Father created everything, seen and unseen, while the heretics believe that what is visible was founded and created by the prince of darkness.[7] The pagans raged to butcher and punish the bodies of Christians, but the heretics covertly extract and steal souls from Christ, destroying men twice over. The traitor Asen[8] is one of their number. He has withdrawn from the unity of the Church and refused to be one of the sheep of Peter, saying that he will not be fed on the word of his teaching or the example of his words or the food of holy communion. He receives heretics in his territory and protects those by whom (it is said) that whole land has been filled and contaminated. Since, then, it is fitting that their blood should be upon them, to fulfil their iniquity, we send letters to our venerable brethren the archbishops of Strigonum[9] and Kolocsa, to the bishop of Palestrina, the legate of the

---

6 The Bishop of Bosnia was found guilty of the charges and deposed in 1233.
7 This shows that the heretics in question were moderate dualists, who believed that the devil had made the visible world.
8 Tsar John Asen II.
9 Robert, archbishop of Strigonum died late in that same year. For Ugrin of Kolocsa see note 4 above.

Apostolic see[10] and to all the bishops of Hungary, instructing them to preach a crusade against the aforesaid Asen and his country, granting the same indulgence to those crusaders who labour to this end, either in person or with their financial support, as is given to those who cross the sea to the aid of the Holy Land.[11]

44. THE PATRIARCH GERMANUS II (1222–40) WRITES AND PREACHES AGAINST BOGOMILS

Germanus II was Patriarch of Constantinople from 1222 to 1240, and was appointed by John III Ducas Vatatzes, who reigned from Nicaea. At the time of Germanus' appointment there was something of a power vacuum in the Latin empire. Yolanda, the widow of Peter of Courtenay, had ruled alone until her death in 1219 when her son Robert succeeded, but he was not successful in his attempts to defend his empire against the Greek claimant based in Epirus. Although the Pope had commanded that the Greek clergy after the conquest should take an oath of loyalty to the holy see, very few of the bishops had done so. The sermons and encyclical letter of Germanus should be read against this background; he is otherwise best known for his anti-Latin theological writings and for his attempts to impose his authority as patriarch against the rival claimant based in Epirus. The identity and location of the heretics he attacks can only be determined from internal evidence, which suggests, though it does not prove, that the chief target of the author was Bogomilism among the monastic clergy or those most closely influenced by them.

The translations have been made from extracts from three sermons which Germanus describes as his three-stranded scourge to chastise the Bogomils, and from an encyclical letter written to the orthodox in Constantinople.

(a) is from *PG* 140, 659–76; (b) from *PG* 140, 621–44; (c) from *Germanos ho B*, ed. Lagopates, pp. 234–43; (d) from Ficker, *Die Phundagiagiten*, pp. 115–25.

---

10 James, Cardinal Bishop of Palestrina.
11 A crusade to the Holy Land was being organized at this time in France by Theobald of Navarre and in England by Richard of Cornwall.

(a) EXTRACTS FROM A SERMON PREACHED ON THE SUNDAY OF ORTHODOXY, THE FIRST SUNDAY IN LENT[1]

But because there are still some remnants of the filth of Copronymus,[2] and these mad dogs, these swine that love the mire dare to hurl dung at the venerable and holy images of Christ and of all the saints (this is what I call the blasphemies of those who are now called Bogomils, the true disciples of antichrist, fellow-disciples of the traitor Judas), it is to them I turn the direction of my speech. I have often withstood them face to face and have shamed their impudent faces by the help of Christ, whom they insult . . . There are many of them going about now; they skulk in the dark and enter houses and sweep away many with them by their semblance of piety. In reality they are dark devils, but they pass themselves off as angels of light.

One of these diabolic Bogomils asked me, 'Why do you worship walls and panels and plaster and different colours?' When he said this he was muttering about the holy icons. I replied, 'When did you ever see anyone from our churches going to the kiln for plaster or to the quarry, where there are heaps of stones, or to the shops which sell pigments, and honour and venerate them? . . . We pay honour not just to the material, but to the form which appears on the material, and not just to any form, but to that of Christ, of the all-holy mother of God and of all the saints. The honour paid to the image passes over to the prototype . . . So again I ask you, and again, answer me. Do you say that the book of the Gospels is holy, and do you revere it as a treasury of eternal benefits, or do you reject it and class it among things which are not honoured?' 'No, no,' he says, 'It is not dishonoured, it is worthy of great honour; I venerate and kiss it.' 'You are right to say so, for it is truly most worthy of honour and holy, truly the book of eternal life.

See then, Bogomil, you are condemned out of your own mouth. Tell me now, is not this book made of boards, of parchment and of cords which join the parchments, of ink and often of colours as well? So then, when you venerate and kiss the book of the Gospels, do you venerate and kiss the boards and the ink and the parchment, or the words of Christ which are written in the book?' 'Yes,' he says, 'the words written in the book.' 'Can you write these words or read them without ink and paper?' 'No', says he. What conclusions do we come to? That to write the words of the

---

1 On this Sunday the restoration of the icons was celebrated; see also **[16]**.
2 Constantine V (741–75).

Gospel parchment and ink and the rest are taken, but what is honoured are the Lord's words written in the book...

Heretic, you are not just an opponent of the icons, but an opponent of Christ; that is why you attack his holy icon, driven mad by the devil that dwells within you. They say that panthers are hostile to men's faces and rush madly at them; even if they see a painting of a human face, they are furious with it and leap on it viciously, tearing it with their claws. The sons of destruction are like this, the forerunners of antichrist, the Bogomils who in truth are diabolic, who hate Christ extravagantly and cannot endure to see his venerable face, but call it an idol...

A Bogomil is far more impious than a Jew. For a Jew, even if evil in other ways, yet still confesses that God is the maker of creation, but the Bogomil makes creation over to the devil...

Again I ask you, 'Who is it who says, "The idols of the Gentiles are silver and gold",[3] and so on?' You will say, 'David'. What was the law of which David was a disciple and worshipper? The old law, the darkened law, or the new and enlightened law? Obviously the old. How can you, Bogomil, identify the old law as spurious, and say that the law in it belongs to the devil, not to the Good God, condemning all of this to silence and extracting only this little fragment from the verses which you now hold out to us?... Every man who is ruled by mind and reason confesses that the God whom he reveres is the same one who made heaven and earth and all that is on the earth, and that it is true that the creator of all this is one and the same. Bogomils ascribe the creation of the world to the devil, and so it follows that they think he is God, and worship him. The God of the Bogomils is a demon, and every one of these Bogomils refers the idols to their prototype, openly. They are darkened in shape and ugly; to put it in a word, they have the faces of demons. Let all those who honour and accept their blasphemy be like them, and may all such incur everlasting anathema.

(b) AGAINST THE BOGOMILS

Once more it is the feast of the Holy Cross, and again my people, the mystic chorus, is gathered together rejoicing; they are assembled in great numbers and surround me in a great circle... What then, noble soldiers of Christ... let me clothe you in the arms of faith, and let me make your mind so full of the arrows of faith that you may be able to shoot down

---

3 Ps. 135.15.

those foul men whom God hates, whom the majority barbarously calls Bogomils. There are many enemies of the cross – Jews, Agarenoi[4] and others, but Bogomils like these are more abominable and impious than all the others, obviously the mouthpiece of the devil, the forerunners of antichrist, the evident heralds that his appearing is almost here, the unambiguous signs of the end of the world. What I say is supported by evidence; I have Paul to support me, who wrote thus [1 Tim. 4.1–4]... The same apostle wrote this: 'Let no one deceive you in any way, for that day will not come unless the rebellion comes first and the man of lawlessness is revealed, the son of perdition, who opposes and exalts himself above every so-called god or object of worship, so that he takes his seat in the temple of God, proclaiming himself to be God' [2 Thess. 2.3–4]. What does he mean when he says, 'unless the rebellion comes first'? I think he is speaking about the Bogomils, about whom he writes to Timothy... that they, the truly diabolic Bogomils, forbid legal marriage and condemn all foods as impure and preach that the devil is God and confer on him the creation of the visible universe, you may hear as they speak.

What, then, is this nonsense which they utter against the venerable cross? They say that one ought not to adore or kiss the cross, but dishonour and reject it, because it removed Christ and put Him to death. Perhaps they have put you in a quandary in their argument, saying, 'If anyone hanged your father on a gallows and killed him, would you honour and worship that gallows? Of course not. You would oppose it and hate it and avoid it if you saw it from a distance, because it was an enemy, inasmuch as it had killed your dear father.'...

To sum up, whatever in some way provides mankind with benefit and pleasure, men praise and love, in proportion to their advantage. Again, conversely, anything which has been responsible for some harm, the cause of something hurtful, we both hate and reject, whether instruments or places or occasions... So who ought to love the cross? Those who have been freed from the tyranny of the devil by the power of the cross, those who have returned to heaven from Hades, who have been made worthy of the glory of the angels? or the devil, who has fallen from his original power because of the cross, and is liable to be made sport of and trodden pitiably under foot by mankind? [John 12.31–2]. All men have gained many benefits through the cross and have found eternal life, so they ought rightly to venerate and love the cross... but the devil

---

4 The children of Hagar, hence Arabs.

must hate the cross ... So all those who hate the cross and avoid it give clear proof of their good will towards the devil ... In harmony and agreement with their affection for the devil and their unbroken loyalty, the Bogomils say that the wood on which someone's father or friend was put to death is not the right thing for his children or friends to venerate. See, their friend the devil has suffered grievously because of the cross, as we have shown; that is why they hate the cross, because it has ruined and destroyed their father ...

(c) THIRD SERMON ABOUT THE GOOD ORDER OF THE CHURCH AND AGAINST THE BOGOMILS

... Now that my sermon has progressed so far, there have come to my mind the heretics ... those whom the common tongue calls Bogomils ... These Bogomils, forerunners of antichrist ... attack the Church of God, quoting the words of the Lord who said, 'Go into your room and shut the door and pray to your Father, who is in secret' [Matt. 6.6]. 'But you,' they say, 'build huge churches and gather people of all ages and races together, and stand there bawling, shouting in shrill voices and using many words. Do you think that your prayers and praises are heard, when Christ said, "for they [the Gentiles] think that they will be heard for their many words" [Matt. 6.7]?' ... There are three problems which the godless pose for us. Why do we erect churches? Rooms (they say) are sufficient. Why do we assemble openly and pray together in a group, disregarding the commandment to do this in secret? Thirdly, they criticize what they see as our verbosity, since the prayer entrusted to us verbally by Christ[5] is all that is needed.

Anyone who debates with them must attack their foolish ideas from the evidence verbally transmitted in the New Testament, that is, in the holy gospels and the apostles' letters, for they will not allow you to cite the Old Testament, saying blasphemously that this was not inspired by God, except where it is expressly quoted in the New Testament ... What then does the Bogomil say? 'Why did Christ's disciples and apostles say that God does not dwell in temples made with hands?' [Acts 7.48;17.24] [Germanus then gives the orthodox interpretation of this text] ... See, this is the third sermon which I have preached to you, plaiting three sermons together like a three-stranded whip ...

---

5 i.e. the Lord's prayer.

(d) LETTER OF THE PATRIARCH GERMANUS TO THOSE IN CONSTANTINOPLE AND AGAINST THE BOGOMILS

... Inspired by the Holy Spirit, [Paul] has given us a written tradition of teaching against the tares of the Bogomil heresy which sprout in these latter days, that is, securing beforehand with prophylactic assistance the limbs of the Church of Christ, so that this destructive and soul-destroying sickness may not overwhelm them, the sickness which sends those who suffer from it into the eternal fire [He cites 1 Tim. 4.1–4].

So in these words the apostle openly and clearly revealed the preaching of the devil, which is active now among the ... Bogomils, which this apostle calls the teaching of the demons and apostasy from faith in Christ, as you have already heard. That he was saying this in advance about this heresy is clear from the identifying marks and signs, that is, that they teach abstinence from foods and the rejection of legal marriage with a wife. Whose else is this teaching than that of the often-exposed demon-possessed and demon-inspired Messalians, that is, Bogomils? They denounce the impurity of all foods, and when they hear Paul speaking of foods which God established for the faithful to share, people like this, in their folly, say blasphemously that it was the devil who established this. These are people who blame wine because of drunkenness, when they should rather blame the drunkards ... The very lustful prevent marriage, because, being initiates, they know the rites of darkness, even though in this they are opposed to Christ and the teaching of the holy apostles. Christ at his first coming hallowed the marriage at Cana, and began to work his divine miracles at the wedding ...

The Bogomils, who are truly diabolic, not only oppose the teachings of Christ on these subjects, but on thousands more which I have not time to enumerate ... They say all that they teach to the honour and glory of their father the devil; they choose this created thing which has no grace but has exalted itself over its maker as the maker of all the visible creation, and its king. Then they name him the son of God, and brother of Christ, and do not learn from the gospels that Christ is called the only-begotten Son of God, as the evangelist says, 'The only Son, who is in the bosom of the Father, He has made Him known' [John 1.18]. For the only-begotten has no brother. O, your forbearance, Christ, our king ... The godless Bogomils blasphemously claim that [the devil's] power and authority is equal to yours. Indeed it is said in all ways that in addition to the honour that they pay him, they invite the devil to his own inheritance, him whom they have chosen as their king. For where the king is, thither his army makes its way. They dwell in darkness with the lord of darkness, and together with the many souls which he has destroyed and daily destroys, they have been sent to Tartarus. It would have been better for them if they had not been born, because without persecution or torture or punishment they denied the ancient faith inherited from the fathers. If anyone who has been swept away by this heresy wants to turn back, though caught in the devil's snares, and to return again to truth . . . such a one ought to utter anathema in church and say this distinctly in the presence of a large Christian audience.[6]

If anyone ascribes the making of this perceptible universe, and power over it, to the Lord of darkness, and asserts that the universe is governed by the disorderly and shameless one, anathema . . .

If anyone says that God made only human souls, but the devil made bodies, and combines God and the devil as collaborators in the shaping of men . . . if he does not rather confess that God alone is the maker and shaper of souls and bodies in accordance with the teaching of holy scripture, anathema.

If anyone insults and despises the Old Testament, whose lawgiver is God and law-establisher Moses, but blasphemously calls it the tradition of the devil . . . anathema. We know that one and the same God speaks in the Old Testament and in the New, even though He adapted His precepts to suit the times and the customs of men . . .

If anyone blasphemes against the venerable and life-giving cross and calls it a gallows, anathema. . .

The holy and life-giving mysteries [of the Eucharist], which our Lord and God Jesus Christ gave to His holy disciples and apostles . . . if then anyone says that these most holy mysteries are ordinary bread and ordinary wine, and teaches that in these we partake simply of corruptible foodstuffs, anathema.

We who preach and believe in Christ as true God believe that His words are true . . . He did not say, 'The bread which I shall give you is my word' as the Bogomils, who are enemies of Christ, misinterpret it, but called this bread His flesh . . .

To those who call the holy and august icons idols, like the shapes of demons . . . anathema . . .

---

6 For an anathema formula designed to be used by Bogomils see **[26]**.

There are many other headings also of the Bogomil heresy which should be anathematized. For this heresy is a many-headed hydra, and nothing right or sound can be found in all their words . . . to summarize it all in one word, we ought to catch hold of them and say, 'If anyone does not accept the seven holy councils of our divine and inspired fathers, and does not honour and love the canons and dogmas which they declared, but instead insults and tries to overthrow them, anathema.'

Let the final anathema be said in these words. If anyone anathematizes the Bogomil heresy only with his lips, but preserves and reverences and loves it in his heart, if in public he pretends to be orthodox, but in secret he venerates and preaches the dark mysteries of the Bogomils, may he inherit the everlasting fire, together with the traitor Judas. Whoever is accused of this Bogomil heresy, but turns and asks for forgiveness and reconciliation, must say the aforesaid anathema in church, in public, and so join the congregation of the faith.

Our Mediocrity exhorts you in the faith, you orthodox Christians in the city of Constantinople, to distribute to all the churches the present letter of our Mediocrity, and to enjoin this commandment on you that it should be read on all Sundays and at the services of the other feasts to rouse up the orthodox people and to destroy the satanic heresies of the Bogomils. For I know that this heresy creeps along everywhere like a snake, biting and injuring the flock of Christ. Like an ulcer it eats away at the body of the Church and feeds on it, because the coming of antichrist is already near at hand and the Bogomils advance as his forerunners, who preach that he is king and master of the universe . . . May you, Christ-loving and orthodox people of Christ, be guarded by the grace of the Holy Spirit and strengthened to fulfil the commandments of Christ, so that you may become sharers of His kingdom and gain eternal benefits by the intercession of our most holy lady, the ever-virgin mother of God and of the saints. Amen.

45. AN ITALIAN INQUISITOR'S VIEW OF BOGOMILISM (*c.* 1250)

For an account of the author, Raynerius Sacconi see [**38**]. This translation has been made from Sanjek, 'Raynerius Sacconi', pp. 50, 59.

[Information given by Sacconi about Cathar Churches 'beyond the seas'] The Church of Sclavonia, the Church of the Latins of Constantinople, the Church of the Greeks of the same place, the Church of Philadelphia *in Romania*, the Church of Bulgaria, the Church of Duguuithia.[1] And they all trace their origin to the last two.[2]

The Church of the Latins in Constantinople has almost 50 members. The total membership of the Churches of Sclavonia and Philadelphia and of the Greeks [of Constantinople] and of Bulgaria and of Duguuithia is some 500. Reader, you may rest assured that in the whole world there are no more than 4,000 Cathars of both sexes, and that reckoning has been made many times by them in the past.[3]

[...]

Finally it should be noted that the Cathar Churches of Toulouse, Albi and Carcassonne hold the erroneous teaching of Belesmanza and the Old Albanenses, and so do almost all the Churches of the Cathars overseas which I have described.[4]

---

1 This yet another variant western attempt to spell Dragovitia.
2 For the location of these Churches see our Introduction, pp. 45–50.
3 These figures relate only to the fully initiated members of the movement. Sacconi's total of 4,000 does not tally with the other figures he gives. For a discussion of the statistics see our Introduction, p. 51.
4 Belesmanza and the Old Albanenses were the Italian Cathars, who like the southern French Cathars remained true to the absolute dualism introduced by *papa* Nicetas (see. [**37**]).

46. EVIDENCE OF BOGOMILISM IN A LITURGICAL COMMENTARY (date unknown)

This anti-Bogomil passage is to be found in a commentary on the Eucharist attributed in the MSS to an otherwise unknown bishop, Theodore of Andida (named Nicolaos in some MSS).[1] The edition of his work by A. Mai on which the *PG* text is based attributes one of the MS to the eleventh century, but more recently this has been redated to the fourteenth (see Rigo, 'Messalianismo = Bogomilismo', p. 73). A twelfth-century date seems generally plausible.

The translation has been made from the text in *PG* 140, cols 418–67.

34. The Our Father ought to be said at this point for many compelling reasons which are known only to those who can reveal the mysteries of God; as I think because it fits with the most important part of the liturgy, because it sums it all up, and so that no one might have the opportunity of saying that this is the only prayer which Christ ordered us to say, and nothing else, as the heretics now called Euchites claim, those who are also called Messalians and Phoundaitai. They claim that even if you say it a thousand times, it ought to be repeated again and nothing ought to be added, and absurdly call other hymns and prayers vain repetitions. As in other things, so in this, Christ our God revealed in this prayer a type and pattern for prayers, teaching us how and for whom we ought to pray . . .

35. But these accursed Euchites, who attribute the power and government of this whole world to the evil one – absurdly, what foolishness – say that all the prayers of everyone who prays should be in these words only . . .

47. POPE JOHN XXII ALLEGES THAT CATHARS ARE FLEEING TO BOSNIA (1325)

When the Mongol threat to eastern Europe receded, Pope Innocent IV (1243–54) attempted to make the Church of Bosnia subject to the Church of Hungary, but it seceded from papal obedience in 1252. Scholars agree that there was a Bogomil Church in Bosnia after that time, but whereas the general view is that it became the established religion of the country, J.V.A. Fine has argued that the Bosnian Church remained Catholic while severing its links with Rome, and that

---

1 Krumbacher, *Geschichte der byzantinischen Literatur*, p.157.

the Bogomils there were merely a small dissenting group.[1] Thirteenth-century western sources do not help to address this problem, simply speaking of the presence of heresy in Bosnia. But in the early fourteenth century Bosnia was considered in the West to be the Balkan territory which was most congenial to dualist heretics. By the reign of John XXII (1316–32) the Catholic Church had won its century-long battle against Catharism, which was in a state of terminal collapse. In 1325 the Pope wrote to Stephen Kotromanić, Ban of Bosnia (c. 1314–53), informing him that heretics were converging there from all the surrounding regions. The Pope sent an inquisitor to the region and expressed a hope that the Ban would co-operate with him, but there is no evidence that this request had any effect. Since all trace of organized Catharism virtually disappeared from western Europe after that date, it is possible that the remaining Cathar perfect did withdraw to the one principality where they could be assured of toleration.

The text is taken from the Registers of Pope John XXII, ed. CICO, ser. III, vol. VII (ii), no. 78, p. 160.

JOHN XXII TO PRINCE STEPHEN OF BOSNIA, 5 MAY 1325

A credible account, often repeated by many, has reached our ears in the Apostolic see that – under the inspiration of the prince of darkness, who is jealous of man's salvation and greedy to cause him harm – a great company of heretics has come together from many different places to the principality of Bosnia, in the confident hope of disseminating their foul error and of remaining there in safety. These heretics, imbued with the cunning of the ancient enemy and armed with the poison of his falsehood, corrupt the souls of Catholics with the deceptive tricks of a feigned simplicity and a false claim to the name of Christians, while their talk creeps sideways like a crab. They sidle in humbly, but kill in secret; though inwardly they are ravening wolves, they appear externally in the clothing of sheep, since they can only deceive the true innocent sheep of Christ by hiding their bestial insanity under the name of Christian.[2] . . . we ask your nobility . . . to offer support to the elimination and removal of the aforesaid heretics forthwith . . . at the request of our beloved son Fabian, OFM, delegated with apostolic authority as inquisitor of heretical depravity in those parts, and of the other inquisitors deputed with the authority aforesaid . . . In this way you will render yourself more acceptable in God's sight, since this labour of faith finds

1 Fine, *The Bosnian Church*.
2 This is the same charge which had been made against the Bosnian Bogomils in Innocent III's reign. See **[39(d)]**.

more favour in the eyes of divine majesty than any other work of piety[3] ...

48. ST GREGORY PALAMAS (1296–1359) AND THE BOGOMILS

The passages in this section are all concerned with the allegation that among the monks of Mount Athos in the years 1335–50 there were Bogomils, or Bogomil sympathizers, and that the great theologian and spiritual writer Gregory Palamas, who practised and advocated a meditation technique known as Hesychasm, was tainted with their views.[1] The period was a turbulent one politically and theologically. In 1341 a synod presided over by the emperor Andronicus III declared that the views of Palamas, then in conflict with the south Italian theologian Barlaam, were orthodox. Within a week the emperor was dead, the heir (John V) was only nine, and the regency was disputed between the young emperor's mother, Anne of Savoy, supported by the patriarch John Calecas, and the former emperor's personal friend and military commander, John Cantacuzenus. In the six years of civil war which followed, the question of the orthodoxy of Palamas, who was a personal friend of Cantacuzenus, and of his supporters, became a political issue. (a) below is an extract from a life of Gregory Palamas written by his closest disciple, (b) and (c) come from the writings of a bitter opponent, Nicephorus Gregoras.

The text of (a) has been taken from the edition in *PG* 151, cols 562d4–565d3, (b) and (c) from the Bonn edition, ed. Schopen and Bekker, vol. II, pp. 717–20, 876.

(a) [After the death of his father, Gregory Palamas, together with his brothers, left Constantinople to join the monks of Mount Athos. They spent the winter of 1316/17 on Mount Patikion, 'between Thrace and Macedonia'.][2] The inhabitants of the mountains nearby, who had inherited the disease of Marcianism or Massalianism[3] from their ancestors, became a noble trophy of Gregory's wondrous tongue. When they learnt that he was on the mountain among the cells of the monks, they came to him, first in twos and threes, to meet him and test him, but when they realized they could not argue against him even from a distance, they withdrew to their own place again, saying that they themselves were not strong in argument and the discussion of salvation, but that their leaders were skilful and powerful in the things of God, and correct

---

3 The Pope presumably had in mind Luke 15.7.
1 For Hesychasm see our Introduction, pp. 53–4.
2 See map.
3 For the use of these terms to describe Bogomils, see above, **[25]**, note 4.

in matters of dogma. They said, 'You will not be able to confront them and argue with them even for a little.' But Gregory, filled with the Holy Spirit, enthusiastically put together a counter-argument about God. He did not reply to what they had said, but taking one of the brethren with him, went to them in haste. How many arguments he used in discussion with the leaders and teachers of the heresy and what sort they were, how easily, in union with the Holy Spirit, he brushed aside their problems and defences like so many cobwebs, and turned their position round, revealing that nothing of what they said was sound at all, and that they were babbling lies which they had invented against the Church to no effect – to write all this in detail is not appropriate at the present time or argument, since it demands a longer narrative. Nevertheless, one part deserves recording, to show, as the proverb has it, the whole from a part.

The leaders and teachers of these Messalians thought that the only prayer appropriate to Christians is that which Christ long ago spoke to the listening disciples, and they say that every other prayer and hymn which we have composed is useless, containing nothing supernatural or pertaining to the law of God. They have imposed this on the Church which obeys them and reject all other prayers. This, then, they set before Gregory (and others of our Church beside) as something serious and central, and said that to act otherwise was completely transgressing the law and revelation, which should not be flouted unnecessarily. Gregory responded like a friend and champion of holy prayer, saying, 'Even if, as you say in your attack, we despise what concerns that holy prayer of the Lord, what about those holy disciples of the Lord who were the first to be told about it, and that by Christ Himself? Do you say that they transgressed His teaching and instruction? What do you say about them?'

They replied at once in unison, 'The first disciples and apostles were the guardians and fulfillers of the commandments of Christ. They preserved the prayer themselves and transmitted it to their successors through the gospel. You despise the tradition and introduce inventions of your own.' Gregory, the inspired, said, 'Then why, after Christ's ascension into heaven and the descent of the Paraclete upon them in visible form, when they were being hounded by the god-slaying Jews in Jerusalem on account of the gospel and the preaching, did they lift up their voices with one accord to God, in their own words, as Luke the inspired tells in his Acts?[4] They did not pray using the words of the prayer, but others more

---

4 Acts 2.4.

appropriate to the occasion and their need. That is why their prayers and requests were successful, as God immediately showed from on high by an earthquake which shook the place where they were praying, and by the presence of the Holy Spirit to confirm their prayer.[5] Why did the tax-collector, in Christ's account, go home more justified than the Pharisee, although he did not pray that same prayer, but used different words? So anyone who has sense should reason and conclude from Christ's teaching that He did not include the whole of prayer in these words, but rather gave the faithful a model of prayer in it. He gave them this spiritual instruction, that they should pray and sing, make requests, and always have His praises on their lips, as David the inspired says, and everywhere remember the intention and purpose of these inspired words, and never deviate from that. Examine the teaching closely; he did not say, as he taught the apostles the prayer, 'Pray in these words, and in these words only' – but what did He say? He said, 'You should pray in this way, that is, with this intention and model which I am now showing you.' He made a rule and a pattern of how one should approach God in prayer, which is what they had asked Him for . . . We too follow them and act as they did in private and together, referring everything we say in prayer or hymn to the model, this original prayer. In this way we always pray and sing hymns in obedience to His word and teaching, for He said, 'Pray like this.'

Next he discussed what concerns the cross of Christ and our salvation and reformation through it with these enemies of the cross. He said that the image of the cross was at work earlier in the fathers and the prophets, and that by the very facts the mystery of the divine plan was revealed later. Even now we can hear that wise and theological voice most clearly and loftily in what he said of those who had written about the venerable cross. With these words and one like them he greatly astounded them and, as it were, sewed up their mouths, putting an end to their verbosity. So he departed from them like the best of victors and generals. The leader of the heresy took Gregory's words to heart. He realized their truth and inspiration immediately, and soon afterwards he went himself with many of his followers to Constantinople, approached the Great Church[6] of the faithful, abjured their ancestral error and became part of our holy council . . .

When Gregory returned, he caused no little astonishment to the monks who lived on the mountain, because he had successfully escaped from

5 Acts 4.31.
6 St Sophia.

the hands and plots of those wild beasts, who were so numerous and dangerous. Not merely had he single-handedly withstood the arguments and nonsense of the heresy, but, empowered by the grace of Christ, he had clearly defeated and overturned those who had often attacked those who argued against them, both secretly and in the open. Indeed, they made a secret attack on him and his brother . . . While they were still among those barbarians, and Gregory was arguing as I have already described, after the discussion finished they were going to their house. Then those blood-stained heretics decided to send some food to Gregory's party for their meal. Gregory realized that death was hidden in what they offered, but . . . he accepted it. He ordered none of them to touch any of it. All turned out as he expected. One of those present threw that bread to the dogs outside the door, as a test. One of the puppies ate it and died instantly. Immediately all the rest recognized Gregory's discernment, and that he had been right to forbid the others to share the food full of deadly poison which the murderers had given them.

(b) So from the beginning nature has made Mount Athos a workshop of virtue . . . and without a break it has made famous those who lived there in the past and up until now, all those who persevered to the end, to gather the harvest of virtue pure and free from every weed, while it drives far from there . . . the company of hypocrites and the corrupt . . . I will describe what happened recently; I mean what concerned Joseph the Cretan, George of Larissa and all those who joined the revelry round their foul table, led by their teachers to follow their abominable heresy; then what concerns Moses the painter and Isaac and David and Job, all those who, although they have hands and tongues and teachings which are totally foul, have the name of excellent men, with a reputation for virtue.[7] . . . Evidence that their opinions are corrupt and foul is contained in the tome written to the holy synod of Byzantium by holy men on Mt Athos, containing among other things . . . that they rub down and later burn holy icons, that in reverence for their teacher's urine they sprinkle it on their meals, that they do not accept the divine incarnation, and other things that I have left unsaid.

When they were found out, some were subjected to the appropriate punishments, while others were driven away as far as possible by all

---

7 Compare a longer list of alleged followers of 'the Cretan' who 'interpreted the Gospel in a spiritual sense and did not accept the reality of the Incarnation' in Rigo, *Monaci esicasti*, pp. 174–5.

available means. There were some who escaped secretly before their wickedness was completely revealed. They drifted to Thessalonica and to Berrhoea and to the city which has the chief power of all. I think that they considered that when they were there, as it is the general refuge of people from all parts of the world, where many languages and habits of speech and opinion are to be found, their iniquity would be hidden.

(c) [This passage follows the account of the election of the Patriarch Callistus in 1350. He was a supporter of Gregory Palamas and of John Cantacuzenus.] But before three whole months had elapsed since his election, the majority of the bishops broke fellowship with the patriarch, all swearing on oath that he was clearly a Messalian, and evidently one of those who had been arrested not many years earlier on Mt Athos, about whom I have spoken earlier in my history. He resisted, took an oath in opposition, and laid charges against each of them, accusing one of tomb-robbery, another of adultery, another of the Bogomil heresy, another that he offered the priesthood for sale and sold it to the worst of men, and others of other things, so that a schism developed for quite some time until the emperor intervened, persuading both sides to abandon their accusations, both the charges they had secretly laid against one another and the insults they had made openly, so that this should not be an addition to the objections they had made to us about the faith.

49. ST THEODOSIUS OF TRNOVO (*c.* 1350) LEGISLATES AGAINST BOGOMILS

St Theodosius of Trnovo was the most important Bulgarian disciple of the Hesychast teacher St Gregory of Sinai (d. 1346). After a peripatetic early life, Theodosius founded the monastery of Kilifarevski near Trnovo, under the patronage of Tsar John Alexander (1331–71). Theodosius was a strong advocate of Hesychasm and also of the rights of the Oecumenical Patriarch of Constantinople, which the Patriarch Theodosius of Bulgaria was seeking to attenuate. St Theodosius died when visiting Constantinople in 1363.

His life was written in Greek by the Patriarch Callistus I of Constantinople (1350–3, 1355–63), who was also a Hesychast, but the only version now known is in Old Slavonic. Kiselkov argued that this was an expanded version of Callistus' text made in the fifteenth century by an anonymous reviser, and his view has gained a cautious acceptance by later scholars.[1]

1 Kiselkov, *Zitieto na Sv. Teodosii T'rnoviski kato istoriceski pametnik.*

The *Life* is an important source for the history of Bogomilism in fourteenth-century Bulgaria. St Theodosius is represented as the leading force in the fight against heresy. Kiselkov speculated that this role might in fact have been taken by the Patriarch Theodosius, and have been attributed to St Theodosius as a result of confusion on the part of the fifteenth-century reviser, but it is equally possible that the Patriarch Callistus wished to play down the role of the Bulgarian Patriarch who challenged his prerogatives, and that St Theodosius was acclaimed as the champion of orthodoxy in the original text. See our Introduction, pp. 54-5, for an account of the context of the following passages.

This translation has been made by Yuri Stoyanov from the edition of V.I. Zlatarski, pp. 452-5, 458.

(a) HERESY IN THESSALONICA AND IN THE HOLY MOUNTAIN OF ATHOS; THE EXPULSION OF THE HERETICS FROM ATHOS, THEIR ARRIVAL AND ACTIVITIES IN BULGARIA (TRNOVO)

A certain nun in Thessalonica, named Irene, was committing wicked deeds. Residing in Thessalonica, she passed herself off as if living in purity, but furtively and secretly she was a perpetrator of all kinds of impurity and vileness. When the monks discovered what kind of woman she was, many of them began to meet together where she was living. She, the totally unclean one, had mastered the entire Messalian heresy,[2] which she taught in secret to all those who visited her for the sake of impiety. Because the heresy became widespread, many monks were affected by the error, and when they went, in separate groups, to the holy mountain of Athos, they offended the monasteries there with poverty and begging. If it happened anywhere that they were left without sufficient bread or drink, they used to cut down the olive trees which were outside the monasteries, and often also the vineyards and the like, and committed everything that was injurious. This heresy spread for three years, or even longer. The fathers at this holy mountain could no longer tolerate this impious heresy, as well as the many very pernicious and shameless actions, so they convened a council and exposed their error and insidiousness. They expelled them altogether and consigned them to eternal damnation. From these heretics two went to Trnovo. The first of these was named Lazarus, the other Cyril, also known as Bosota [the barefooted]. After they had spent a short time there, they could not conceal their error for long. Lazarus began to behave like a madman; bare to the skin, he went about all over the town, wearing a

---

2 In this text Messalianism is equated with Bogomilism, as section (d) makes explicit.

gourd on his private parts to conceal them – a weird and hideous sight for all those who saw him, and offensive for the genital parts given to people by God to generate children. And Cyril (the aforementioned Bosota) began gradually to reveal his heresy. On some occasions he reviled the holy icons, and at other times he vilified the holy and life-giving cross, and besides that he organized gatherings at the houses for drinking and eating unclean foods. He taught that dreams are divine revelations and that men and women should abandon legitimate marriage, and many other impieties and profanities. He had a disciple, the impious priest Stefan, who was like him in his evil nature and equal to him in his demonic wickedness, and a rigorous custodian of his unholy heresy.

(b) ST THEODOSIUS' ORATION CONCERNING THE HERETICS DURING THE FIRST ANTI-HERETICAL COUNCIL (*c.* 1350), CONVENED IN THE REIGN OF TSAR IVAN ALEXANDER (1331–71)

'How dare you speak about two principles, the first good, and the second evil, and [say] that God presides over the good which is on earth, whereas his adversary rules over the heavenly realm? If this is true, why and how were we taught to recite the prayer 'Our Father... in heaven... thy will be done on earth as in heaven'? So then, God is a creator and maker of heaven, earth and all creatures. Which demon taught you to revile the holy icons, the life-giving cross and the other holy vessels, and also to accept the holy communion received during the holy sacraments only as simple bread, insolently and without fear, and to desecrate Christian bread and wine? When you are found out, you swear, without shame and fear, with all kinds of oaths. Because of this you are really and truly enemies against the law, offenders against the gospel, violators of the faith, deceivers and seducers, lying transgressors and perjurers. You swear shamelessly with oaths and vows, while God says, "But what I tell you is this, you are not to swear at all" [Matt. 5.34]. And when you are exposed as heretics, then you renounce the Messalian faith and curse it as evil and justify yourselves with terrible oaths. And you think, because of the fear hanging over you, that you have not committed a sin. When you find yourselves somewhat calmed, you return to your loathsome faith, "like a dog returning to its vomit"' [Prov. 23.11].'

When the blessed Theodosius said these and other things they stood dumbstruck. On seeing them entirely disgraced, the Tsar rejoiced greatly, together with the entire pious council and, as scripture says, 'David growing steadily stronger, while the house of Saul became weaker and weaker' [2 Sam. 3.1]. Because the deceit was exposed by the truth and those who held false teaching were overcome by shame, Lazarus, who understood his error, spent all his days in penance, even to his end. The impious Bosota and his like-minded adherent Stefan remained petrified. For this reason, seeing their false wisdom, the Tsar ordered that their faces should be branded with red-hot iron, and expelled them for ever from the confines of his land.

(c) CONDEMNATION OF BOGOMILISM DURING THE SECOND ANTI-HERETICAL COUNCIL (AGAINST JUDAIZERS AND HERETICS, *c.* 1360), DURING THE REIGN OF IVAN ALEXANDER[3]

Not only this, but cursed be the Bogomil, that is to say, Messalian, heresy, impious and hateful to God, and also the other newly appeared heresy of Balaam and Acyndinus, and let their adherents and leaders be expelled from the confines of the realm, so that the Bulgarian land may be cleansed from these unclean weeds, and so that the pious faith may shine in purity, even more than the rays of the sun . . .

(d) LAST WORDS OF ST THEODOSIUS CONCERNING HERESY

First he ordered them to keep strictly and staunchly to the pious faith of the conciliar and apostolic Church and its orthodox dogmas, and to flee as they ought to from the Bogomil, that is to say the Messalian, heresy.

---

3 This extract contains no detailed information about Bogomilism. It is included as evidence that the measures taken in 1350 against the Bogomils had not proved completely effective.

50. SYMEON, ARCHBISHOP OF THESSALONICA, PREACHES AGAINST BOGOMILS (BEFORE 1429)

Symeon was the last metropolitan of Thessalonica to hold office before its siege and capture by the Turks in the spring of 1330. His writings should be set against the turbulent history of his city. Between 1387 and 1403 Thessalonica had been under Turkish control. After the defeat of the Sultan Bayezid at Ankara in 1402 it was restored to the Byzantine empire, but from 1411 to 1421 frequent Turkish attacks resumed, which caused considerable internal dissension. In 1423 the city was ceded by the Byzantine emperor to the control of the Venetians, who were able to import provisions for a town which no longer had command of its agricultural hinterland. In his theological writings Symeon attacks the doctrines and practices of the Latins; rather more surprisingly he claims that in the earlier Turkish occupation some of the citizens had converted to Islam. He uses similar language about them – 'despising the holy and venerable icons . . . insulting the precious cross . . . making mock of the saints'[1] – to his invectives against Bogomils here. Besides the treatise against heresy from which this extract has been taken, he wrote expositions of the sacraments and rituals of the Orthodox Church, suggesting that he felt a need to educate and to encourage his clergy.

This translation has been made from the text printed in *PG* 155, 65.

DIALOGUE AGAINST HERESIES

11. Next in sequence after these . . . were many others who are enemies of truth, who falsely taught that there are two principles. The present Bogomils are of their number, a profane group who are also called Koudougeri.[2] So you must learn about them, since they exist near where you live.

With great hypocrisy they pretend to pray and to love the Gospel and the Acts and Epistles of the Apostles. The other scriptures they reject summarily. The atheists do not act on anything that is contained in the gospels or apostles . . . Rather they completely enact the intentions and deeds of the party of antichrist, performing frenzies in secret and filthy spells [*epodes*][3] and other impious, abominable and accursed acts. To-

---

1 Cf. Balfour, *Politico-historical writings of Symeon*, pp. 43, 84.
2 Also spelt 'Kudugeri'. Obolensky, in *The Bogomils*, p. 167 says that the word survives in the names of two Macedonian villages, but that the meaning has not been satisfactorily explained. Loos, in *Dualist heresy in the Middle Ages*, p. 333 suggests that the word is a corruption of the Byzantine term *kalogeros* ('good old man'); cf. the vernacular term 'bonshommes' for the Cathars of the Languedoc.
3 For the use of *epode* to describe Bogomil rites see also EP **[19]**.

gether with the faith, they reject the mysteries of Christ and blaspheme against them, most particularly the holy icons, the venerable churches, the inspired scripture of the Law and the Prophets, all the just men and martyrs, priests and saints, in short everything holy, following Satan the apostate and the demons. By his inducement these filthy people blaspheme against the one God in Trinity, the incarnation of the Word and everything that is God's . . .

Moreover, He did not enjoin only the Our Father but other prayers as well, with which He himself made prayer to the Father, and the acceptance of the law and the prophets which were proclaimed on His account, and reverence for holy shrines, as He showed with that ancient temple, when He chased out those who were selling there with a whip, and called it a house of prayer . . . They have some visions of demons, since they are overpowered by demoniac reasoning so that they may see something, the chief leader of evil, the wicked devil, whom in their barbarian language they call Topax,[4] that is, inhabitant, or master, who rules sins and darkness, and the wretches worship him like pagans. Led astray by him, they become difficult to cleanse, as they are enslaved to error. Even if they name Christ, but act as do the impious, they are perhaps even worse, because they serve the devil, and involve not only themselves but others as well in some monstrous pollution, as we have learnt.

Especially at the end of life they lead many of the pious astray and sever them from Christ,[5] for at the time of their end they summon them to denial. You should avoid them with all your might and spurn their pretences, which are full of the craft of the evil one. This impiety is a mixture of all vice, and it is for this reason that I have set out what concerns it at more length, so that all the faithful may be preserved and not share fellowship with them, for they are keen to do this, to corrupt the pious.

---

4 This name for a demon is not otherwise recorded. Perhaps a reminiscence of the term *toparchos* for a local official.
5 This is the only description in the eastern material of the reception of Bogomils at death: the custom was established among Cathars; see our Introduction, p. 55.

APPENDIX 1
THE *RITUAL* OF RADOSLAV THE CHRISTIAN

It is known from the accounts of Euthymius of the Periblepton and Euthymius Zigabenus that by the eleventh century the Bogomils had a liturgy, but no text of it has survived.[1] All the Cathars in western Europe used essentially the same form of liturgy, which is first attested in 1163 and thus predated the schisms which developed in the last quarter of the twelfth century.[2] Because the forms of worship contained in the two surviving exemplars of the Cathar *Ritual* correspond very closely to the descriptions of Bogomil worship in Byzantine sources, it seems reasonable to assume that the Cathar *Ritual* is derived from a lost Bogomil exemplar.[3] Christine Thouzellier tried to demonstrate a western provenance for it, but as Duvernoy has shown, she could only prove her case in regard to the gloss on the Lord's prayer, which is the only part of the *Ritual* which the officiant was able to extemporize.[4]

Part of a Slavonic ritual is preserved in a manuscript which is now in the Vatican Library. It was written by Radoslav the Christian for Goisak the Christian in the reign of King Stephen Thomas of Bosnia (1443–61).[5] Some experts in Old Slavonic palaeography have argued that this *Ritual* may have been copied from a twelfth-century exemplar.[6] The text resembles very closely that of the opening section of the Cathar *Ritual* of Lyons, and there is no doubt that it was intended for use in worship by the fifteenth-century Bosnian dualists. Because of its late date and because Bosnia had been heavily influenced by western Cathars it is possible, though not in our view very likely, that this text was translated from a western original.[7] But because it may not be an authentic Bogomil text we have placed it in an appendix.

The text is that of the Vatican Library, MS Borgiano Illyrico 12, fos. 56–8, and this translation has been made by Yori Stoyanov from Thouzellier's *Rituel cathare*, pp. 287–9, where it is printed alongside the text of the Cathar *Ritual* of Lyons. We have supplied the rubrics.

[The Lord's Prayer]

Our Father, who art in heaven, hallowed be Thy name; Thy kingdom come, Thy will be done in earth as in heaven. Give us this day our daily

---

1 See above, **[19]**, **[25]**.
2 Egbert of Schonau, *Sermones contra Catharos* 8.2 (*PL* 195, 51).
3 Hamilton, 'Wisdom from the East', pp. 46–9.
4 Thouzellier, *Rituel cathare*, pp. 182–4; Duvernoy, *Le Catharisme*, unnumbered final pages, 'Addition à la conclusion'.
5 Fine, *The Bosnian Church*, p. 304.
6 Thouzellier, *Rituel cathare*, pp. 64–5.
7 Fine, *The Bosnian Church*, p. 83.

CHRISTIAN DUALIST HERESIES

bread[8] and forgive us our debts, as we forgive our debtors, and lead us not into temptation, [but] deliver us from evil. For Thine are the kingdom and the power and the glory for ever. Amen.[9]

[Litany]

Let us adore the Father and the Son and the Holy Spirit.

It is right and worthy [to do so].[10]

Let us adore the Father and the Son and the Holy Spirit.

Let us adore the Father and the Son and the Holy Spirit.

The grace of our Lord Jesus Christ be with [us] all evermore. Amen.

Bless us, forgive us. Amen.

Be it unto us, O Lord, according to Thy word.

May the Father, the Son and the Holy Spirit deliver you, may they forgive you all your sins.

[The opening words of St John's gospel]

In the beginning was the Word and the Word was of God and the Word was God. All things were made by Him, and without Him there was nothing which exists.[11] In Him was life, and the life was the light of men. And the light shone in the darkness and the darkness did not master it. There was a man sent from God whose name was John. He came as a witness to bear witness to the light so that all might believe through him. He was not the light, [but] the witness of the light. The true light was in

---

8 'Daily bread' in the Slavonic and RSV versions of the Lord's Prayer is a translation of the Greek *epiousion arton*. In the Latin Vulgate the rare first word of this phrase was translated to give *panem supersubstantialem* (which might be translated either as 'bread which is more than sufficient' or 'more than physical') in Matt. 6.11, and *panem cotidianum* ('daily bread') in Luke 11.3. Both versions were orthodox, but the Cathars found *supersubstantialem* more attractive.

9 Euthymius of the Periblepton accuses the Byzantine Bogomils of leaving out the doxology of the Lord's Prayer; see **[19]**. The Cathars always said it, and the Bosnian Bogomils may have adopted it under Cathar influence.

10 The Cathar *Ritual* does not contain this phrase, but its use by the Byzantine Bogomils of the mid-eleventh century is attested by Euthymius of the Periblepton **[19]**. That is probably not very significant. This is one of the most ancient Christian liturgical phrases, attested by St Hippolytus as being in use in Rome during the third century and subsequently used by almost all the churches of East and West; see *The Apostolic tradition of St Hippolytus*, ed. Dix, p. 7.

11 St Augustine described this form of punctuation of John 1.3 as Manichaean, but it had been used by earlier Christian writers who were orthodox. This punctuation is therefore simply a textual variant, but one which was preferred by dualists as more consonant with their beliefs; that the material world is 'nothing' and that God has not made it. See Thouzellier, *Catharisme et Valdéisme*, pp. 404–5.

being which gives light to everyone entering the world. He was in the world and the world was made by Him and the world knew Him not. He came unto his own and His own received Him not. To those who received Him he gave the power to become the children of God, to those who believe in His name, those who were born not of blood nor of the lust of the flesh nor of the lust of man but of God. And the Word became flesh and dwelt among us, and we beheld his glory, like that of the only son of the Father, full of grace and truth. John bore witness to Him and proclaimed [Him] saying: here is He of whom I said, 'He who comes after me takes precedence over me, because He was before me.' Of his fulness we have all received grace upon grace. For the law was given from Moses, [but] grace and truth are given us through Jesus Christ.

[St Paul's Epistle to Titus, 2.12, 13]

And the Apostle Paul speaks in his Epistle to Titus of renouncing the godlessness and lusts of the flesh in order to live a life of chastity and godliness in this present age, awaiting the blessed hope and the manifestation of the glory of our great God.[12]

---

12 This passage is not found in the Cathar *Ritual* of Lyons.

APPENDIX 2
ARMENIAN SOURCES AND THE PAULICIANS

The interpretation of Paulician history which we have given is substantially that of Paul Lemerle, and is based on the Greek sources. Dr N.G. Garsoian has argued that the Armenian sources present a different picture:

> There were two traditions. The older form of Paulicianism exhibited an Adoptionist doctrine with an emphasis on the importance of baptism and a rejection of extreme asceticism, to which was joined an inflexible iconoclasm. This was the main current of the doctrine and it remained substantially unchanged in Armenia throughout the history of the sect. In Byzantium, however, a variant form appeared, probably in the ninth century ... characterised by a docetic Christology and a mitigated dualism.[1]

In other words she is claiming that the Armenian Paulicians were followers of Paul of Samosata, Bishop of Antioch (deposed in 268), whose Trinitarian speculations are sometimes loosely described as Adoptionism, the belief that Jesus Christ was fully human by birth and nature, and owed His divinity to adoption by the Divine Word. Her thesis has not met with any wide acceptance, and we do not find the evidence she adduces convincing. She has firstly to prove that there were Paulicians in Armenia before the seventh century. The chief sources she cites are these. Firstly the Council of Sahapivan in 447 decreed that heretics called *Mcłne* should be branded with the mark of a fox.[2] This name was used in fifth-century Armenia to describe the Messalians, who were then a living movement.[3] That the Paulicians were described as *Mcłne* in the eighth century and that the Tondrakians were punished in the same way in the eleventh century as the *Mcłne* were in 447 does not appear to us very strong grounds for supposing that all three groups professed the same faith.[4] The Greek sources commonly call Bogomils Messalians, because they share some characteristics with that heresy, but that does not prove that they are identical. The second piece of evidence which Garsoian adduces is the *Call to Repentance* of the Catholicus John I (478–90), which contains a phrase about penances to be imposed on the *Polikean*, which would mean Paulicians; but the manuscript dates from 1268, and Bartikyan has argued, with some plausibility, that this phrase may be interpolated. Thirdly, the Oath of Union of the Council of Dvin of 555 condemns those who receive communion at the hands of the

---

1 *The Paulician heresy*, p. 232.
2 *Ibid.*, pp. 82–3.
3 Nersessian, *The Tondrakian movement*, pp. 8–9.
4 Garsoian, *The Paulician heresy*, pp. 94–5, 144.

Paulicians, but Bartikyan again has argued that this is almost certainly a scribal error made in the only manuscript of this text, written in 1298, and that it should read Paulianists (i.e. Adoptionists). This argument is persuasive, because the Paulicians did not celebrate the Eucharist, and the prohibition would have been pointless in relation to them.[5]

So we see no reason to doubt that the earliest secure evidence that we have about the Paulicians in Armenia comes from the reign of the Catholicus Nerses III (641–61) and correlates well with the evidence of Peter of Sicily.[6]

THE TONDRAKIANS[7]

That there were Paulicians in Armenia in the age of the *didaskaloi* is not in dispute. But after the fall of Tefrice Armenian sources do not speak of them, but begin to refer to the dualist heresy of the Tondrakians. They are first mentioned in a treatise of Ananias of Narek (943–65),[8] and more detailed information about them is given in the correspondence of Gregory Magister, the Armenian Dux of the Mesopotamian theme in the reign of the Byzantine Emperor Constantine IX (1042–55). The latter tells us that the sect was founded by a certain Smbat 'the wolf', from Tondrak near Manzikert, who lived 'in the days of the Lord John and of Smbat Bagratuni'. This may refer to the Catholicus John V (899–931) and to King Smbat I (890–914), and fall in the period 899–914, although that would not synchronize with Gregory's precise statement that the sect had been anathematized for 170 years, which, as he was writing in the mid-1050s, would place its foundation in the mid-880s. Nevertheless, both statements indicate that the movement was in existence by the first decade of the tenth century. Gregory Magister names seven leaders between Smbat the founder and 'the light-haired hound', Lazarus the Blind, who headed the sect in his own day.[9]

---

5 *Ibid.*, pp. 80–94 and Appendices I, II, pp. 234–8; Bartikyan, 'Concerning the evaluation of certain sources on the Paulician movement', pp. 85–97 (in Armenian). We owe our knowledge of this work entirely to Garsoian's citations from it, but unfortunately we find these more convincing than her arguments.
6 See our Introduction, pp. 10–13.
7 We have not included material about the Tondrakians in this collection because the chief sources about them are already available in English in the appendices to Conybeare's edition of *The Key of Truth*.
8 This is known only through citations from later authors, notably in a letter of Ananias' nephew, Gregory of Narek.
9 The relevant parts of Gregory's letters are translated in Appendix III of Conybeare, *The Key of Truth*, pp. 142, 144; Nersessian, *The Tondrakian movement*, pp. 38–9, would prefer a foundation date in the first half of the ninth century.

That there was a connection between the Tondrakians and the Paulicians seems beyond doubt. Gregory Magister considered that both groups were Manichaeans, but that the Paulicians were found in the land of the Greeks, while the Tondrakians were Armenian.[10] Paul of Taron (d. 1123) confirms this. Writing to a Byzantine correspondent, he says: '[the Tondrakians] whom you call Poplikianosk ... are disciples of the evil Smbat ... who got his poison from the sect of the Paulicians.'[11] Moreover, the two movements held many beliefs in common. The Tondrakians rejected Orthodox baptism as 'mere bath-water', together with the sacrifice of the Mass, Holy Orders, the sacrament of marriage and the sign of the cross.[12] On the other hand, they appear, if correctly reported, to have been moderate dualists rather than absolute dualists like the Paulicians,[13] and some of them were world-renouncing, which was alien to the ethos of the Paulicians.[14]

So although it is tempting to see in the Tondrakians the survivors of Armenian Paulicianism, perhaps even the descendants of those who followed Vahan, better known as Baanes the Foul,[15] there is no evidence to support this. A new religious movement founded by Smbat of Tondrak appears to have developed in Armenia in the generation after the fall of Tefrice, one which had much in common with the Paulician movement and no doubt recruited some of its adherents from the Paulicians of Armenia, but which remained distinct from it. Vrej Nersessian expresses this neatly: '[The Tondrakians] clearly had views similar to the Paulicians, but the fact that they split and presented themselves under two different names implies that there were two different sects, whose connections must be proved rather than assumed.'[16]

In the reign of Constantine IX (1042–55) Gregory Magister persecuted members of this sect throughout the theme of Mesopotamia, and made a special expedition to Tondrak, their place of origin, to destroy the cult there. He did not invoke the death penalty against them, although he could have done so under Byzantine law, but contented himself with outlawing the members of the movement and destroying their homes.[17]

10 *Ibid.*, p. 50.
11 *Ibid.*, p. 65.
12 Gregory of Narek in Conybeare, *The Key of Truth*, p. 127.
13 Gregory Magister reports that they believed that Satan created the world (Conybeare, *The Key of Truth*, p. 148).
14 Gregory Magister claims to have dissolved a Tondrakian monastery (*ibid.*, p. 148).
15 See our Introduction, p. 21.
16 Nersessian, *The Tondrakian movement*, p. 71.
17 Conybeare, *The Key of Truth*, pp. 143, 146–7.

This did not mark the end of the sect, which is recorded as still active in twelfth-century sources,[18] but all scholars agree that there is no mention of the Tondrakians after the fourteenth century.[19]

THE *KEY OF TRUTH*

Then in 1791 the Catholicus Luke informed the Armenian Patriarch of Constantinople that he had imprisoned a certain John who had associated himself with the evil sect of the Tondrakians.[20] In 1837 members of this sect from the village of Ark'weli were involved in a heresy trial mounted by the Armenian Orthodox Church, and a copy of their service book, *The Key of Truth*, was impounded and placed in the library of the Catholicus at Ejmiacin. It was written by Yovhannes Vahaguni, and the opening words read: 'The book called *The Key of Truth*. It was written in the era of the Saviour 1782, but that of the Armenians 1230; and in the province of Taron.'[21]

As Nersessian has pointed out, if there is indeed a continuity between the medieval sect founded by Smbat of Tondrak and these late-eighteenth-century Tondrakians, their beliefs had changed a great deal over the centuries. For *The Key of Truth* is not a dualist work: it belonged to a sect which accepted adult baptism with water, celebrated the Eucharist, and held an Adoptionist, not a docetic Christology: that is to say, they believed that Jesus was a man who at his baptism was adopted by God as His son, not that He was a spiritual being who only had the appearance of a human body. All this is a far cry from the group described by Gregory of Narek and Gregory Magister.

It is difficult to explain how the name Tondrakian persisted, unless the sect had a continuous history from the Middle Ages to the late eighteenth century, but as Nersessian observes, that is not incompatible with a considerable shift in their belief-system.[22] There is no evidence that *The Key of Truth* was inherited from the medieval Tondrakians, let alone from the Paulicians, and the chief reason for supposing that it might be is that it is written in an archaic form of Armenian. But the scribe of the 1782 manuscript, Yohvannes Vahaguni, may also be the author of the work. He had been to the Armenian monastery at Venice, where he could

18 Paul of Taron in Conybeare, *The Key of Truth*, pp. 173–7.
19 Garsoian, *The Paulician heresy*, p. 145.
20 Nersessian, *The Tondrakian movement*, p. 89.
21 Conybeare, *The Key of Truth*, p. 71.
22 Nersessian, *The Tondrakian movement*, p. 47.

have learned classical Armenian, and as Runciman has justly observed, liturgical writers tend to have 'a strange love . . . for archaisms in grammar, vocabulary and style'.[23] The Armenian scholar Ter Mkrttschian believed that Yohvannes had been influenced while living in Venice by western Baptists.[24] It is therefore possible that he composed *The Key of Truth* in archaic, liturgical Armenian as a vehicle for Protestant reforming ideals, and introduced it on his return home to the ancient dissenting sect of the Tondrakians. If in the late eighteenth century the sectaries underwent a reform of the kind suggested, this might explain why, after centuries of silence, they began to attract the attention of the Armenian Orthodox authorities once again.

It is our view that The *Key of Truth* has nothing to do with the history of Christian dualism, and we should not need to discuss it at all if it were not for the views of its editor and translator. F.C. Conybeare was a distinguished Armenian scholar, who found the manuscript of this work in the library of Ejmiacin and published it in 1898. He was convinced, as his subtitle made plain, that this was 'A Manual of the Paulician Church of Armenia', and that it had been the service book of the medieval Paulicians. Conybeare was a nineteenth-century rationalist,[25] and was attracted to the theory that the original form of Christianity had been Adoptionism, the belief that Jesus of Nazareth was just an ordinary man who had been uniquely well-pleasing to God and adopted by Him at his baptism. In his very long introduction to *The Key of Truth* he sets out his reasons for thinking this, and describes how '[as a result of the European reformation] under the form of Anabaptist and Unitarian opinion, this leaven of the Apostolic Church [i.e. Adoptionism] is found modifying other forms of faith. In engendering this great religious movement, we feel sure that the Bogomiles . . . played a most important part. They were the chief purveyors to Europe of Adoptionist tenets, partly imbibed from Paulician missionaries.'[26] Conybeare considered *The Key of Truth* a very important piece of evidence, because he believed that it linked his own century with the Adoptionism which he supposed had been the most primitive form of Christianity.

This thesis has been revived in a modified form by Nina Garsoian. The main thrust of her argument is as follows: *The Key of Truth*, even though it

23 Runciman, *The medieval Manichee*, p. 56; Nersessian, *The Tondrakian movement*, appendix III, pp. 89–96.
24 Ter Mkrttschian, 'Die Thondrakier in unseren Tagen'. I owe this reference to Nersessian, *The Tondrakian movement*, p. 91.
25 Mariès, 'Frederick Cornwallis Conybeare'.
26 Conybeare, *The Key of Truth*, p. cxcvi.

only survives in a manuscript of 1782, is indeed a manual of the medieval Armenian Tondrakians who were themselves the continuing Church of the Paulicians. It portrays a community with an Adoptionist Christology and simple forms of sacramental worship, but one which is anti-sacerdotal and hostile to ceremonial and to representational art. It therefore follows that the early medieval Paulicians were Christians of that kind, and were followers of Paul of Samosata. Garsoian sets great store by this text, because she argues that it was written by the Paulicians themselves and that it should therefore be believed in preference to the hostile evidence of their religious opponents. Thus the detailed descriptions of the Paulicians given by Byzantine writers can at best be considered only as evidence of the beliefs of those Paulicians who settled in Byzantine territory, which were very different from those of the Armenian Paulicians. Garsoian, of course, adduces many more arguments than I have considered here, but the fact remains that if the 'Conybeare' thesis is rejected, then the rest of her arguments become either untenable or irrelevant.

But the acceptance of such arguments is only possible if one is prepared to dismiss as sectarian prejudice a large body of contemporary evidence which claims that the Paulicians and the Tondrakians were Christian dualists. The difficulty of setting aside a concordant body of contemporary evidence written by Greek, Armenian and Arabic authors, widely separated in space and time, many of whom were extremely hostile to each other's traditions and most of whom were unaware of each other's work, is considerable. Such a course of action could only be justified by accepting a conspiracy theory of vast dimensions, involving the Byzantine, Orthodox Armenian and Islamic establishments over a period of 700 years in a plot to conceal the truth about the Paulicians. The candid reader might feel justly sceptical if the sole evidence for believing in such a conspiracy was a liturgical book written in 1782, which does not even claim to be a copy of a medieval work.

We do not find the Conybeare/Garsoian thesis convincing. It does not appear to us consonant with the main body of historical evidence, and in any case the very simple teachings of *The Key of Truth* are not in the least like the subtle Christological distinctions of Paul of Samosata. Those who are interested must form their own opinions by reading the work of Conybeare and Garsoian, and we would also draw attention to Paul Lemerle's critique, with which we are in broad agreement.[27]

27 Lemerle, *T & M* 5 (1973), pp. 12–15.

GLOSSARY

Allegorical interpretation of Scripture. The explanation of the symbolic meaning which Biblical texts have in addition to their literal meaning (e.g. the gifts of gold, frankincense and myrrh which the Magi gave to the Christ child are allegories of his kingship, priesthood and sacrificial death). See also **Type**.

Anathema. Separation from the community of Christian believers. **Kat(an)athema** is an alternative form of this word found in Rev. 22.3.

Antichrist. In the New Testament named as the Great Opponent of Christ. In the Middle Ages he was expected to appear on earth and initiate the final persecution of the Church before the Second Coming of Christ.

Antitype. See **Type**.

Apocalypse. The name given in the Middle Ages to the New Testament Book of Revelation.

Apocryphal writings. Writings which are ascribed to Biblical characters or which deal with Biblical themes but which do not form part of the **Canonical Scriptures** (q.v.). Some apocryphal writings were adjudged heretical by the Church (e.g. the Ascension of Isaiah), while others were considered to be merely works of pious fiction (e.g. the Protevangelium which describes the family life of the Infant Jesus).

Archon, evil. Literally 'ruler'. The evil archon was the devil, whom Jesus had described as the archon of this cosmos (John 12.31); or, in the view of some Christian dualists, the evil creator of the material universe.

Archons. In the Byzantine Empire this title was given to a wide range of local government officials.

Ascesis. Literally 'exercise'. The practice of religious exercises designed to gain mastery over the body in order to lead the life of Christian perfection (e.g. voluntary poverty, fasting, keeping vigil).

Autocrator. 'Sole ruler', the title of the senior Byzantine Emperor.

Basilissa. The title of the Byzantine Empress-consort.

Canonical Scriptures. The books of the Bible accepted as authentic by the Church. In the Middle Ages the Orthodox Church accepted the New Testament, and the Old Testament in the Greek translation known as the Septuagint. This included books which are known only in Greek texts and for which no Hebrew version exists (e.g. I, II Maccabees): in Protestant Bibles these are either omitted or printed as Apocryphal books. These should not be confused with **Apocryphal writings** (q.v.).

Catepan. From the late tenth century the title of the governor of the Byzantine provinces of south Italy.

GLOSSARY

Catechumenate (**architectural**). The narthex of a Byzantine church. An area separated by rails or columns from the entrance to the nave and set aside for the use of those who have not yet been baptised.

Catechumens. Those under instruction in the Christian faith who have not yet been baptised. **Oil of Catechumens**: holy oil used to anoint catechumens before their baptism.

Catholicus. The title of the chief bishops of the Armenian and Georgian Churches (and in the early Middle Ages also that of the head of the Church of Caspian Albania).

Chalcedonian Christians. Those who accept the decisions of the Fourth General Council of Chalcedon of 451, which the **Monophysites** (q.v.) rejected.

Christopolites. A fellow citizen with Christ (of the Kingdom of Heaven).

Chrysobull. A Byzantine imperial diploma sealed with a golden seal.

Colophon. The passage at the end of some manuscripts which gives information about their contents and the circumstances in which they were written.

Comes. The commander of a division in the Byzantine army in the ninth and tenth centuries.

Consolamentum. The rite of initiation of the Western Cathars.

Cosmocrator. This word, which literally means 'world-ruler', is used in the Greek New Testament to desribe the powers of evil (Eph. 6.12), and was therefore sometimes used by Byzantine theologians as a synonym for the devil.

Court of the belos/velos. The court held in the covered hippodrome at Constantinople at which the **Great Drungarius** (q.v.) presided.

Demiurge. The English form of a Greek word meaning 'craftsman'. This term was used by some Gnostics to describe the creator of the physical universe, whom they considered distinct from and inferior to the Godhead.

Docetic Christology. The belief that Jesus Christ was a spiritual being who did not become human but only took the appearance of a man.

Domestic of the Schools. In the ninth century the senior of the four commanders of cavalry divisions stationed in Constantinople.

Doux. Before the eleventh century the governor of a small district in the Byzantine Empire. In the Comnenian period (1081–1185) this title was given to provincial governors.

Elect Manichaeans. Fully initiated members of the Manichaean faith.

Elias the Tishbite. The Greek name for the prophet Elijah.

Encyclical letter. A letter written, normally by a pope or patriarch, intended to be read aloud in all the churches subject to his authority.

Eparch. The city prefect of Constantinople.

GLOSSARY

Epode. A charm which is sung; in a pejorative sense a black magic spell.

Eschatology. The Church's teaching about the Last Things: death, judgment, Heaven and Hell. In general usage the term refers to Christian beliefs about the end of the world.

Exarch (ecclesiastical). An official appointed by the Patriarch of Constantinople to oversee monasteries in a specified area.

Filioque clause. The words 'and from the Son' added by the Western Church to the section of the Nicene Creed relating to the Holy Spirit: 'I believe in the Holy Spirit the Lord, the giver of life, who proceeds from the Father and the Son (*Filioque*)'. The Orthodox Church refused to accept this addition, which became a major cause of division between the Churches of East and West.

General Councils of the Church, also called Oecumenical Councils. Coucils attended by representatives of the five patriarchates of Rome, Constantinople, Alexandria, Antioch and Jerusalem, empowered to make decisions about matters of belief and practice binding on the entire Christian Church. The Orthodox Church recognizes seven General Councils: Nicaea I (325), Constantinople I (381), Ephesus (431), Chalcedon (451), Constantinople II (553), Constantinople III (680–1), Nicaea II (787).

Grand Domestic of the Schools. Commander-in-chief of the Byzantine army under the Comneni (1081–1185).

Great Church. The cathedral of Hagia Sophia (the Holy Wisdom) in Constantinople.

Great Drungarius. Under Manuel I (1143–80) this official became one of the principal judges of Constantinople, responsible for the **Court of the belos** (q.v.).

Higoumenos. The Greek word for abbot.

Holy City. If used without any qualification this term refers to Jerusalem.

Holy Synod. The standing committee which advised the Patriarch of Constantinople and from the tenth century came to possess important legislative, administrative and judicial powers.

Iconoclast. Literally 'a destroyer of images'. The term is generally applied to those opposed to the veneration of religious images in Orthodox churches, and when written with a capital 'I' relates to those Byzantine Emperors in the eighth and ninth centuries who sought to enforce this belief.

Iconodule. Literally 'an image-worshipper'. A term used to describe those who accept the veneration of religious images in Orthodox churches in accordance with the rulings of the Second General Council of Nicaea (787).

John Chrysostom, St, (d. 407). Patriarch of Constantinople and one of the four Greek Doctors of the Universal Church. Chrysostom occupied a particular place of honour in the Orthodox Church of Constantinople because the liturgy in daily use there was attributed to him.

GLOSSARY

John the Theologian, St. The normal way of referring in the Orthodox Church to St John the Apostle and Evangelist.

Kastron. A fortified settlement.

Krites. A Byzantine judge.

Kyr. Literally 'lord'. A polite form of address, which, like modern Italian 'signore', could be used of any man, including the emperor, and was also sometimes applied to the saints.

Legate, papal. The pope's personal representative charged with a specific mission; often, though not necessarily, a cardinal.

Libellum. Literally 'little book'. The written form of recantation which convicted heretics were required to present to the bishop when they were reconciled to the Orthodox Church.

Mediocrity (title). When spelt with a capital 'M', a title used by some Orthodox prelates as a token of their humility.

Metropolitan. In the Orthodox Church this was originally the title of a bishop who exercized authority over other bishops in a church province, but in the Middle Ages it was sometimes given as an honorary title to a diocesan bishop.

Monophysites. Literally 'those who believe in the one nature' (in Christ). The name given to those Christians who would not accept the teaching of the Fourth General Council of Chalcedon about the divine and human natures of Christ, and who for that reason are sometimes called 'non-Chalcedonian Christians'.

Mother of God. A literal translation of *Theotokos*, a title given to the Blessed Virgin Mary by the General Council of Ephesus in 431, and by which she is usually known in the Orthodox world.

Mysteries, sacred. The New Testament uses the term 'mystery' to describe truths revealed only to fully initiated Christians. In the Middle Ages the term was applied to the sacraments, particularly to the Eucharist.

Nicene Creed. A more elaborate version of the Creed endorsed by the First General Council of Nicaea in 325. It is accepted as a common profession of faith by all the traditional Churches of East and West.

Oecumenical Council. See **General Councils of the Church**.

Oecumenical Patriarch. The Orthodox Patriarch of Constantinople.

Ordo. The term used by the Cathars to describe the chain of spiritual baptisms which, they claimed, linked them to the Apostles.

Orthodox Church. This consisted of Christians who accepted the teaching of the Seven General Councils of the Church and who were in communion with the five chief Patriarchs, those of Rome, Constantinople, Antioch, Alexandria and Jerusalem. Since the thirteenth century the four Eastern Patriarchs have not been in communion with the Patriarch/Pope of Rome and the Catholic Church of the West.

GLOSSARY

Panhypersebastos. A title created by Alexius I (1081–1118) for his brother-in-law, Michael Taronites, and conferred more generally as a mark of honour by later emperors.

Pansebastos. A title devised by Alexius I (1081–1118) for his brother Adrian and later granted to other members of the imperial kin.

Papa. See **Pop**.

Paraclete. Another name for the Holy Spirit.

Patarene. A word of uncertain origin used by medieval Italian Catholic writers to describe Christian dualists, both Cathars and Bogomils.

Patriarch. A title originally given to the five chief leaders of the Christian Church: the Bishops of Rome, Constantinople, Antioch, Alexandria and Jerusalem. The Bishop of Rome came to be known as the Pope, while the title of patriarch was later also conferred on other bishops (e.g. the heads of the Bulgarian and Serbian Churches).

Patrician. A title of honour given to some Byzantine officials.

Pentateuch. The first five books of the Bible: Genesis, Exodus, Leviticus, Numbers and Deuteronomy.

Phenomenal universe. The visible universe; that is, the material universe, as opposed to the spiritual universe (Heaven and Hell) which, the Church teaches, is not located in space and time.

Pop. Literally 'father'. A title given to Orthodox parish priests in Slav-speaking lands. It was used by Bogomil, the founder of Bogomilism, and by some of the leaders of the sect in later centuries. In Greek-speaking lands it became *papa*.

Proedros. A title conferred on some members of the Byzantine Senate.

Protoasecretis. Originally the head of the imperial chancery of Byzantium; by the reign of Manuel I (1143–80) he had become a judge.

Protomandator. The title of a ninth-century Byzantine provincial official.

Protos of Mount Athos. The monastic superior charged with the supervision of all the monasteries on the Mountain.

Protospatharius. A high-ranking official of the Byzantine court.

Quaestor. An important judicial official in twelfth-century Byzantium.

Rite, Slavonic, Greek, Latin, Armenian, etc. The forms of liturgy and ceremonial used in public worship, categorized by the languages in which they are celebrated.

Ritual. A service book containing standard liturgical forms for prayer and the celebration of the sacraments.

Sacellarius (ecclesiastical). The bursar of the Patriarch's court.

Scholion. A marginal note in a manuscript.

Sebastocrator. A title invented by Alexius I (1081–1118) for his brother

Isaac, to give him a rank superior to any other save that of Emperor. It was later more widely used.

Sebastohypertatos. An honorific invented for members of the imperial family by John II (1118–43).

Semeioma. An authenticated record, normally of judicial proceedings.

Synodikon. The official record of the acts of a provincial church council.

Theme. The name used from the seventh century to describe Byzantine provinces.

Tome. An official letter, normally an ecclesiastical record.

Type. Literally 'figure' or 'example'. Medieval churchmen interpreted the Old Testament as a prophecy of the Christian revelation, e.g. they considered that the sacrifice of Isaac was a type, or prophetic example, of the death of Christ on Calvary. An antitype is the person or event to which the type refers, i.e. Christ's death is the antitype of the sacrifice of Isaac.

BIBLIOGRAPHY

SOURCES

Manuscripts

Latin

Hugh Eteriano, *Contra Patarenos*, Seville, Colombina Cod. 5.1.24, fos 67r.–75v., Bodley MS. Canon Pat. Lat. 1, fos. 1–31

Printed sources

Greek

Amorion. V. Vasilevskii and P. Nikitin, 'The forty-two martyrs of Amorion' [Greek with Russian commentary], *Zapiski Imper. Akad. Nauk (serie 8, classe hist-phil.)*, vol. 8, 2 (1905), pp. 22–36

Anna Comnena, *Alexiad*, ed. B. Leib (Paris, Budé 3 vols., 1937–45)

Apocrypha. *New Testament Apocrypha*, ed. E. Hennecke, re-ed. W. Schneemelcher, tr. R. McL.Wilson (London, Lutterworth Press, vol. 1, 1963, vol. 2, 1965)

Auxentius, St. Joannou, P.-P., *Démonologie populaire – démonologie critique au XIe siècle: la vie inédite de S. Auxence par M. Psellos* (Wiesbaden, Otto Harrassowitz, 1971)

Balsamon, Theodore, *Scholia in Nomocanon Photii Patriarchae* (*PG* 104, 975–1218)

Basil of Caesarea, *Opera* (*PG* 30)

Cedrenus, George, *Historiarum Compendium*, ed. I Bekker (*CSHB*, Bonn, Weber, 1839)

Cerularius, Michael, *Edictum Synodale* (*PG* 120, 743–4)

Constantine Chrysomallus. J. Gouillard, 'Quatre procès de mystiques à Byzance' *REB* (1978), 5–81

Constantine Porphyrogenitus, *De administrando imperio*, ed. G. Moravcsik, tr. R.J.H. Jenkins (Dumbarton Oaks texts 1, Dumbarton Oaks, 1967)

——*Narratio de imagine Edessena* (*PG* 113, 421–54)

Councils. G.D. Mansi, *Sacrorum conciliorum nova et amplissima collectio* Florence and Venice, 1758–98, repr. Paris, Welter, 1901–27; and Graz, Akademische Druck und Verlagsanstalt, 1960–1)

Cyril of Jerusalem, *Cyrilli Hierosolymarum Archiepiscopi Opera quae supersunt omnia* 1, ed. G.C. Reischl (Munich, Leutner, 1898, repr. Hildesheim, Olms, 1967)

Ecloga. A manual of Roman law: the Ecloga, ed. and tr., E.H. Freshfield (Cambridge, Cambridge University Press, 1926)

Eleuteri, P. and A. Rigo, *Eretici, dissidenti, musulmani ed ebrei a Bisanzio: una raccolta eresiologica del xii secolo* (Venice, Il Cardo, 1993)

Eusebius, *Ecclesiastical History* (London, Heinemann, 1949–57 (Loeb Classical Library))

—— *In Lucam* (*PG* 24, 529–606)

Euthymius of the Periblepton. In G. Ficker, *Die Phundagiagiten: ein Beitrag zur Ketzergeschichte des byzantinischen Mittelalters* (Leipzig, Verlag von J.A. Barth, 1908), 3–86; *PG* 131, 47–58

Euthymius Zigabenus, *Dogmatic Panoply* (*PG* 130, 19–1362)

——*Narratio*, in Ficker *Die Phundagiagiten*, 87–125

Genesius, *Regum*, ed. C. Lachmann (*CHSB*, Bonn, Weber, 1834)

Germanus II, Patriarch, *Germanos ho B', Patriarchos Konstantinopoleos–Nikaias 1212–40: bios, sungramata kai didaskalia autou*, ed. S.N. Lagopates (Tripoli, 1913)

—— *Orationes* (*PG* 140, 621–44, 659–76)

Hippolytus of Rome, *The Apostolic tradition of St Hippolytus*, ed. G. Dix (rev. edn) (London, SPCK, 1968)

——*Refutatio omnium haeresium*, in his *Werke*, ed. P. Wendland (Berlin, Societas Regia Scientarum: Kirchen-vater Commission, 1916) (Die griechischen christlichen Schriftsteller der ersten drei Jahrhunderts, 26)

John of Damascus, St, *De haeresibus* (*PG* 94, 677–780)

Justin Martyr, *Die Apologien Justins des Martyrers*, ed. C. Kruger (Tübingen, Mohr, 1915, repr. Frankfurt, Minerva, 1968)

Justinian. *Justinian. I: Corpus Iuris Civilis; 2: Codex Iustinianus*, ed. P. Krueger (Berlin, Weidemann, 1929)

Lazarus the wonder-worker, St, *Acta Sanctorum; Nov. iii: Vita S. Lazari auctore Gregori monacho*, vol. 3 (1910), pp. 508–88

Macarius, St, H. Delehaye, 'S. Macarii Monasterii Pelecetes Higoumeni: Acta Graeca', *Analecta Bollandiana* 16 (1897), pp. 140–3

Morea, Chronicle of the. *Crusaders as conquerors: the chronicle of Morea*, tr. H.E. Lurier (New York and London, Columbia University Press, 1964)

Moschus, John. E. Mioni, 'Il *pratum spirituale* de Giovanni Mosco', *OCP* 17 (1951), pp. 61–94

Nicephorus Bryennius. *Nicéphore Bryennius: introduction, texte, traduction et notes*, ed. P. Gautier, *Corpus Fontium Historiae Byzantinae* vol. ix, Brussels, Byzantion, 1975

Nicephorus Gregoras, *Byzantina Historia*, ed. L. Schopen and I. Bekker, 3 vols (*CHSB*, Bonn, Weber, 1829–55)

BIBLIOGRAPHY

Nicephorus the Patriarch, *Antirrheticus I adversus Constantinum Copronymum* (*PG* 100, 205–328)

——*Breviarium*, ed. C. de Boor (Leipzig, Teubner, 1880)

Nicetas Choniates, *Historia*, ed. B.C. Niebuhr (*CHSB*, Bonn, Weber, 1835)

Nicholas of Methone. A. Demetrakopoulos, *Bibliotheca ecclesiastica* (Leipzig, Otto Bigand, 1866, repr. Hildesheim, 1965)

Paul the Younger, St, H. Delehaye, 'Vita S. Pauli Iunioris', *Analecta Bollandiana* 11 (1892), pp. 136–82

Peter the Higoumenos, *Précis*, ed. C. Astruc, W. Conus-Wolska, J. Gouillard, P. Lemerle, D. Papachryssanthou and J. Paramelle, *T & M* 4 (1970), pp. 69–97

Peter of Sicily, *Historia*, ed. C. Astruc, W. Conus-Wolska, J. Gouillard, P. Lemerle, D. Papachryssanthou and J. Paramelle, *T & M* 4 (1970), pp. 3–67

——*Sermons* (*PG* 104,1305–1350)

Philotheus, *Encomium of Gregory Palamas* (*PG* 151, 551–656)

Photius, *Diegesis*, ed. C. Astruc, W. Conus-Wolska, J. Gouillard, P. Lemerle, D. Papachryssanthou and J. Paramelle *T & M* 4 (1970), pp. 99–183

——*Sermons*, in C. Mango, *The homilies of Photius, patriarch of Constantinople* (Cambridge, Mass., Harvard University Press, 1958)

Physiologus, tr. M.J. Curley (Austin and London, University of Texas Press, 1979)

Psellus. P. Gautier, 'Le *De demonibus* du Pseudo-Psellos', *REB* 38 (1980), pp. 105–94

Scylitzes, John, *Synopsis historiarum*, ed. H. Thurn (*CSHB*, Berlin and New York, 1973)

Shepherd of Hermas. Die apostolischen Vater, I: das Hirt des Hermas, ed. M. Whittaker (Berlin, Akademie-Verlag, 1956) (Die griechischen Schriftsteller der ersten Jahrhunderts, 48)

Sozomen, *Church history*, ed. G.C. Hansen (Berlin, Akademie-Verlag 1960)

Symeon of Thessalonica, *Dialogus contra Haereses* (*PG* 155, 33–176)

——*Politico–historical works of Symeon, Archbishop of Thessalonica (1416/17–1429)*, ed. D. Balfour (Vienna, Österreichen Akademie der Wissenschaften, 1979 (Wiener Byzantinische Studien, 13))

Synodikon. Synodikon of Orthodoxy. J. Gouillard, 'Le Synodikon d'orthodoxie', *T & M* 2 (1967), pp. 1–313

——*Synodikon of Tsar Boril.* J. Gouillard, 'Une Source grecque du synodik de Boril', *T & M* 4 (1970), pp. 361–74

Theodore of Andida, *Commentatio liturgica* (*PG* 140, 418–67)

Theodore Lector, *Ecclesiastical History* (*PG* 86 pt. 1, 165–228)

Theodore of Nicaea, *Epistoliers Byzantines du Xe siècle* ed. J. Darrouzès (Paris, Institut Français d'Études Byzantines, 1960) (Archives de l'orient chrétien, 6)

Theodore the Studite, *Epistulae* (*PG* 99, 1481)

Theophanes, *Chronographia*, ed. C. de Boor (Leipzig, Teubner 1883, repr. Hildesheim, Olms, 1963)

Theophanes Continuatus, *Chronographia*, ed. I. Bekker (*CHSB*, Bonn, Weber, 1838)

Theophylact Lecapenus. I. Dujčev. 'L'epistola sui Bogomili del patriarca constantinopolitano Teofilatto', *Mélanges E. Tisserant II*; Vatican City, 1964 (*Studi e Testi 232*), pp. 88–91

Timotheos of Constantinople, *De receptione haereticorum* (*PG* 86, 11–74)

Tornikes, G. and D. J. Darrouzès, ed., *Georges et Démétrios Tornikès: lettres et discours* (Paris, editions du Centre National de la Recherche Scientifique, 1970)

Tzetzes, John, *Epistulae*, ed, P. Leone (Leipzig, Teubner, 1972)

Xiphilinos, John, *Sermons* (*PG* 120, 1289–92)

Zonaras, *Epitome historiarum*, ed. L. Dindorf (Leipzig, Teubner 1875)

—— *Epitome historiarum*, ed. M. Pinder and T. Bultner-Wobst; 3 vols (*CSHB*, Bonn, Weber, 1841–97)

Latin

Alberic of Trois Fontaines, *Chronicon*, ed. P. Scheffer-Boichorst, *MGH SS* 23, 631–950

Annales Barenses, ed. G.H. Pertz, *MGH SS* 5, 51–6

Bernard, St, *Letters* (*PL* 182)

Clementine Homilies, tr. A. Roberts and J. Donaldson (Edinburgh, T.& T. Clark, 1870) (Ante-Nicene Christian library, vol.17)

Clementine Recognitions, tr. T. Smith (Edinburgh, T. & T. Clark, 1867) (Ante-Nicene Christian Library, vol. 3)

De heresi Catharorum. ed. A. Dondaine, 'La Hiérarchie cathare en Italie, I: Le *De heresi catharorum*', *AFP* 19 (1949), pp. 280–312

Egbert of Schonau, *Sermones contra Catharos* (*PL* 195, 67-716)

Gregory IX, Pope, *see* papal collections

Guitmund of Aversa, *De corporis et sanguinis domini veritate* (*PL* 149, 1444)

Honorius III, Pope, *see* papal collections

Innocent III, Pope, *Regesta* (*PL* 214) *see also* papal collections

Interrogatio Iohannis. Le Livre secret des Cathares: Interrogatio Iohannis; apocryphe d'origine bogomile, ed. and French tr. E. Bozóky (Paris, Beauchesne, 1980)

John XXII, Pope, *see* papal collections

BIBLIOGRAPHY

Ovid, *Metamorphoses*, ed. and tr. F.J. Miller (London, Heinemann; New York, Harvard University Press, 1916) (Loeb Classical Libray)

Papal collections. *Acta Honorii III et Gregorii IX*, ed. A.L. Tautu, CICO III (iii) (Vatican City, 1950)

—— *Acta Innocenti III*, ed. T. Haluscynski, CICO III (ii) (Vatican City, 1944)

—— *Acta Iohannis XXII*, ed. A.L. Tautu, CICO III (vii, 2) (Vatican City, 1952)

—— *Acta Romanorum Pontificum ab Innocentio V ad Benedictum XI*, ed. F. M. Delorme and A.L. Tautu, CICO III (v, 2) (Vatican City, 1954)

—— *Acta Urbani IV, Clementis IV, Gregorii X*, ed. A.L. Tautu, CICO III (v, 1) (Vatican City, 1953)

Ritual, Cathar. *Rituel cathare*, ed. C. Thouzellier (Paris, Éditions du Cerf, 1976) (Sources chrétiennes, 236)

Sacconi, Raynerius. F. Sanjek, 'Raynerius Sacconi, OP, *Summa de Catharis*', *AFP* 44 (1974), pp. 31–60

Tertullian. *Tertulliani contra Marcionem*, ed. and tr. E. Evans (Oxford, Clarendon Press, 1972)

Thomas, archdeacon of Spalato, *Historia Salonitanorum pontificum . . . usque ad Rogerium*, ed. F. Racki, *Monumenta spectantia Historiam Slavorum meridionalium* 26 (Zagreb, 1894)

Wakefield, W.L. and A.P. Evans, *Heresies of the High Middle Ages* (New York, Columbia University Press, 1969)

William of Apulia, *Gesta Wiscardi* (*MGH* SS 9, 239)

—— Guillaume de Pouille, *La Geste de Robert Guiscard*, ed. M. Mathias, Instituto Siciliano dei studi bizantini e neo-ellenici, 4 (Palermo, 1961)

Old Slavonic

Cosmas the Priest, *Against the Bogomils*, intr. M.G. Popruzhenko (Sofia, 1936)

—— *Against the Bogomils*, tr. into modern Bulgarian with a preface by V. Sl. Kiselkov (Sofia, 1934)

—— *Le Traité contre les Bogomiles de Cosmas le Prêtre*, ed. and tr. H.C. Puech and A. Vaillant (Travaux publiés par l'Institut d'Études Slaves) (Paris, 1945)

—— *Kosma presviter v slavjanski literarturach*, Ju. K. Begunov, ed. and intr. (Sofia, 1973)

Dushan. *Dushan's code: the fourteenth-century code of Serbian Tsar Stephan Dushan. The Bistritza transcript*, intr. and trs. Đurica Krstić (Beograd, Vajat, 1989)

Euthymius the Patriarch. *Werke des Patriarchen von Bulgarien Euthymius nach den besten Handschiften*, II: *Leben Hilarions Bischofs von Moglen*, ed. K. Kaluzhniacki (Vienna, C. Gerold's Sohn 1901, repr. London, Variorum, 1971)

Ivanov, J., *Livres et légendes bogomiles: aux sources de catharisme*, trans. M. Ribeyrot (Paris, Maisonneuve et Larose, 1976)

Synodikon of Boril. M. Popruzhenko, 'Sinodik carja Borila' (Sofia, Academy of Sofia, 1928) (Bulgarski Starini, 8)

Theodosius of Trnovo, *Life*, ed. V.I. Zlatarski, *Sbornik za narodni umotvorenija nauka i knizhnina* 20, pp. 1–44 (Sofia, 1904)

Hebrew

Jerahmeel. *The chronicles of Jerahmeel*, ed. M. Gaster (London, Oriental Translation Fund, n.s. 4, 1899; repr. New York, Ktav Publishing House Inc., 1971)

Targum. *Targum du Pentateuque*, ed. R. le Déaut and J Robert (Paris, Editions du Cerf, 1978) (Sources chrétiennes, 245)

Armenian

The Key of Truth. F.C. Conybeare, ed. and tr., *The Key of Truth: a manual of the Paulician church of Armenia* (Oxford, Clarendon Press, 1898) (this work contains translated extracts from the works of Gregory of Narek, Aristaces of Lastivert, Gregory Magistros, John of Otzun and Paul of Taron)

French and Provençal

Besse, G., *Histoire des ducs, marquis et comtes de Narbonne* (Paris, A. de Sommauille, 1660)

New Testament. *Le Nouveau Testament traduit au xiii siècle en langue provençale suivi d'un rituel cathare publié par L. Clédat* (Paris, 1887, repr. Geneva, Slatkine Reprints, 1968)

Ritual, Cathar. *Rituel cathare*, ed. C. Thouzellier (Paris, Éditions du Cerf, 1976) (Sources chrétiennes, 236)

Villehardouin, Geoffroi de, *La Conquête de Constantinople*, ed. E. Faral 2 vols, Paris, Les Belles Lettres, 1938–9 (Classiques de l'histoire de France au Moyen Âge)

Coptic

Nag Hammadi. The Nag Hammadi Library in English, J.M. Robinson gen. ed. (3rd edn, Leiden, E.J. Brill, 1988)

SECONDARY WORKS

Ahrweiler, H., 'L'Histoire et la géographie de la région de Smyrne entre les deux occupations turques (1081–1317), particulièrement au xiiie siècle', *T & M* 1 (1965), pp. 1–204; repr. in *Byzance: les pays et les territoires* (London, Variorum 1976)

―― *Byzance et la mer: la marine de guerre, la politique et les institutions maritimes de Byzance au vii–xii siècles* (Paris Presses Universitaires de France, (1966) (Bibliothèque byzantine, 5)

BIBLIOGRAPHY

Alexander, P.J., *The Patriarch Nicephorus of Constantinople: ecclesiastical policy and image-worship in the Byzantine empire* (Oxford, Clarendon Press, 1958)

—— 'Religious persecution and resistance in the Byzantine empire of the eighth and ninth centuries: methods and justification', *Speculum* 52 (1977), pp. 238–64

—— 'Historiens byzantins et croyances eschatologiques', *Actes du xii congrès international des études byzantines* II, pp. 1–8, repr. in his *Religious and political thought in the Byzantine empire* (London, Variorum, 1978)

Anastos, M.V., 'Iconoclasm and imperial rule, 717–842', in J. Hussey, ed., *CMH* IV (1), pp. 61–104

Angélou, A., 'Nicholas of Methone: the life and times of a Byzantine bishop', in *Byzantium and the classical tradition* (University of Birmingham Spring Symposium of Byzantine Studies, 1979), ed. M. Mullett and R. Scott (Birmingham, Centre for Byzantine Studies, 1981), pp. 143–9

Angold, M., *The Byzantine empire 1025–1204: a political history* (London, Longman, 1984)

—— 'Greeks and Latins after 1204: the perspective of exile', in B. Arbel, B. Hamilton and D. Jacoby, ed., *Latins and Greeks in the eastern Mediterranean after 1204* (London, Frank Cass, 1989), pp. 63–86

—— *Church and society in Byzantium under the Comneni, 1081–1261* (Cambridge, Cambridge University Press, 1995)

Anguélov, D., *Le Bogomilisme en Bulgarie*, tr. I Pétrova-Boinay (Toulouse, Privat, 1972)

Athos. *Le Millénaire du Mont Athos 963–1963: études et mélanges*, 2 vols ([n.p.], Éditions de Chevetogne, 1963–4)

Bareille, G., 'Euchites', *DTC* V(ii), pp. 1454–65

Barnard, L., 'The Paulicians and Iconoclasm', in *Iconoclasm: papers given at the spring symposium of Byzantine studies, March 1975*, ed. A. Bryer and J. Herrin (Birmingham, University of Birmingham Centre for Byzantine studies, 1977)

Bartikyan, H., 'Concerning the evaluation of certain sources on the Paulician movement' Erivan, *Izvestia Akademii Nauk Armianskoi SSR*, 1957 (in Armenian)

Beaton, R. and C. Rouaché, *The making of Byzantine history* (Aldershot, Variorum, 1993)

Beck, H.G., *Kirche und theologische Literatur im byzantinische Reich* (Munich, C.H. Beck, 1959) (Handbuch der Altertumswissenschaft, 12, 2, 1)

—— *Das byzantinische Jahrtausend* (Munich, C.H. Beck, 1978)

Biller, P. and A. Hudson, ed., *Heresy and Literacy, 1000–1530* (Cambridge, Cambridge University Press, 1994)

Borst, A., *Die Katharer* (Stuttgart, Hiersemann, 1953) (*Schriften der MGH*, 12)

BIBLIOGRAPHY

Brand, C.M., *Byzantium confronts the West, 1180–1204* (Cambridge, Mass., Harvard University Press, 1968)

Browning, R., 'The speeches and letters of Georgios Tornikes, metropolitan of Ephesus, XIIth century' *Actes du XIIe Congrès des Études Byzantines* (Belgrade, 1964)

——*Byzantium and Bulgaria: a comparative study across the early medieval frontier* (London, Temple Smith 1975)

——*Studies on Byzantine history, literature and education* (London, Variorum, 1977)

Bryer, A., 'Excursus on Mananalis, Samosata of Armenia and Paulician geography', in *Iconoclasm: papers given at the spring symposium of Byzantine studies, University of Birmingham, March 1975* (Birmingham, University of Birmingham Centre for Byzantine studies, 1977), pp. 83–4

Bryer, A. and J. Herrin, ed., *Iconoclasm: papers given at the spring symposium of Byzantine studies, University of Birmingham, March, 1975* (Birmingham, University of Birmingham Centre for Byzantine studies, 1977)

Buckler, G., *Anna Comnena: a study* (London, Oxford University Press, 1929)

Cameron, A., 'The sceptic and the shroud' (London, King's College, 1980)

——'The history of the image of Edessa: the telling of a story', in *Okeanos: essays presented to Ihor Sevčenko on his sixtieth birthday, Harvard Ukrainian Studies* 7 (1983), pp. 80–95

Cavarnos, C., *The holy mountain* (Belmont, Mass, 1973)

Charanis, P., 'The Slavic elements in Byzantine Asia Minor', *Byzantion* 18 (1946), pp. 69–83

——'Ethnic changes in the Byzantine empire in the seventh century', *DOP* 13 (1959), pp. 25–44

Cheynet, J.C., *Pouvoir et contestations à Byzance (963–1210)* (Paris, Byzantina Sorbonnensia 9, 1990)

Coüasnon, C., *The church of the Holy Sepulchre in Jerusalem* (London, Oxford University Press, 1974) (*The Schweich Lectures for 1972*)

Crow, J., 'Alexios I and Kastamon', in *Alexios I Komnenos*, I, ed. M. Mullett and D. Smythe (Belfast, Belfast, Byzantine Enterprises, 1996) (Belfast, Byzantine texts and translations, 4, 1)

Dando, M. 'Satanael' *Cahiers d'études cathares* (autumn 1979) series 2, no.83, pp. 3–21

——'Peut-on avancer de 240 ans la date de composition du traité de Cosmas le prêtre contre les Bogomiles?' *Cahiers d'études cathares* 34 (2nd series, no. 100, winter 1983), pp. 3–25

Darrouzès, J., 'Des notes marginales du Vindobonensis historicus graecus 70', *REB* 45 (1987), pp. 59–75

Dédéyan, G., 'L'Immigration arménienne en Cappadocie au XIe siècle', *Byzantion* 45 (1975), pp. 41–116

BIBLIOGRAPHY

Delehaye, H., 'Cyprian d'Antioche et Cyprian de Carthage', *Analecta Bollandiana* 39 (1921), pp. 14–32

Dondaine, A., 'La Hiérarchie cathare en Italie, III: catalogue de la hiérarchie cathare en Italie', *AFP*, XX (1950), pp. 278–305

—— 'Hugues Éthérien et Léon Toscan', *Archives d'histoire doctrinale et littéraire du Moyen Âge* 19 (1952), pp. 67–134

—— 'Hugues Éthérien et le concile de Constantinople de 1166,', *Historisches Jahrbuch* 17 (1958), pp. 473–83

Dossat, Y. 'À propos du concile cathare de Saint-Félix: les Milingues', *Cahiers de Fanjeaux* 3 (1968), 209–14

—— 'Un Évêque cathare originaire de l'Agenais, Vigouroux de la Bacone', *Bulletin philologique et historique (jusqu'à 1610)* année 1965 (1968), 623–39, repr. in his *Église et hérésie en France au XIII*ᵉ *siècle* (London, Variorum, 1982)

Drijvers, J. W., *Helena Augusta: the mother of Constantine the Great and the legend of her finding of the True Cross* (Leiden, E.J. Brill, 1992)

Dujčev, J., 'Dravitsa-Dragovitia', *REB* 22 (1964), pp. 218–19

—— 'Quelques observations à propos des courants dualistes', *Studi Veneziani* 12 (1970), pp. 107–25

Duvernoy, J., *Le Catharisme: la religion des Cathares* (Toulouse, Privat, 1976)

Dvornik, F., *The Photian schism: history and legend* (Cambridge, Cambridge University Press, 1948)

Every, George, *The Byzantine patriarchate, 451-1204* (London, SPCK, 1947, repr. New York, AMS Press, 1980)

Fedalto, G., *La chiesa latina in Oriente*, vol. I (2nd end, Verona, Casa editrice Mazziana, 1981)

Filoramo, G., *A history of Gnosticism*, tr. A. Alcock (Oxford, Blackwell, 1990)

Fine, J.V.A., *The Bosnian Church, a new interpretation: a study of the Bosnian church and its place in state and society from the thirteenth to the fifteenth centuries* (New York and London, East European Quarterly, 1975)

—— *The early medieval Balkans: a critical survey from the sixth to the late twelfth century* (Ann Arbor, University of Michigan Press, 1983)

—— *The late medieval Balkans: a critical survey from the late twelfth century to the Ottoman conquest* (Ann Arbor, University of Michigan Press, 1987)

Garsoian, N., *The Paulician heresy* (The Hague, Mouton and Co., 1967)

—— 'Byzantine heresy: a re-interpretation', *DOP* 25 (1971), pp. 87–113

Gay, J., *L'Italie méridionale et l'empire byzantine* (Paris, Bibliothèque des Écoles Françaises d'Athènes et de Rome, 1904, repr. New York, Franklin, n.d.)

Gill, J., *Byzantium and the Papacy, 1198–1400* (New Brunswick, NJ, Rutgers University Press, 1979)

Gouillard, J., 'Deux figures mal connues du second iconoclasme', *Byzantion* 31, 1961, pp. 371–87

—— 'L'Hérésie dans l'empire byzantin jusqu'au xiie siècle' *T & M* 1 (1965), pp. 299–324

—— 'Constantin Chrysomalle sous le masque de Syméon le nouveau théologien', *T & M* 5 (1973), pp. 313–27

—— 'Gagik II, defenseur de la foi arménienne', *T & M* 7 (1979), pp. 399–418

—— *La Vie religieuse à Byzance* (London, Variorum, 1981)

Graef, H., *Mary: a history of doctrine and devotion*, 2 vols (London and New York, Sheed and Ward, 1963, 1965)

Greenfield, R.P.H., *Traditions of belief in late Byzantine demonology* (Amsterdam, Adolf M. Hakkert, 1988)

Grégoire, H., 'The Amorians and Macedonians, 842–1025', in J. Hussey, ed., *CMH* IV (1), pp. 105–92

Gress-White, D., 'Bogomilism in Constantinople', *Byzantion* 47 (1977), pp. 163–86

Guiraud, J., *Histoire de l'Inquisition au Moyen Âge*, 2 vols (Paris, Picard, 1935, 1938)

Hagman, Y., 'Le Rite d'initiation chrétienne chez les Cathares et les Bogomiles', *Haeresis* 20 (1993), pp. 13–31

Hamilton, B., 'The origins of the dualist church of Drugunthia', *Eastern Churches Review* 6 (1974), pp. 115–24

—— 'The Cathar council of Saint-Félix reconsidered', *AFP* 48 (1978), pp. 23–53

—— 'The Cathars and the Seven Churches of Asia', in J. Howard-Johnston, ed., *Byzantium and the West c. 850–c. 1200* (Amsterdam, Adolf M. Hakkert, 1988), 269–295

—— 'Wisdom from the East', in P. Biller and A. Hudson, ed., *Heresy and literacy* (Cambridge, Cambridge University Press, 1994), pp. 38–60

Hanson, R., *The search for the Christian doctrine of God: the Arian controversy 318–81* (Edinburgh, T. & T. Clark, 1988)

Head, C., *Justinian II of Byzantium* (Madison, University of Wisconsin Press, 1972)

Hirschfeld, Y., *The Judean desert monasteries in the Byzantine period* (New Haven and London, Yale University Press, 1992)

Hussey, J., *The Orthodox Church in the Byzantine empire* (Oxford, Clarendon Press, 1986)

Janin, R., *La Géographie ecclésiastique de l'empire byzantine, première partie: la siège de Constantinople et le patriarcat oecuménique*, vol. III: *Les Églises et les monastères* (Paris, Institut Français d'Études Byzantines, 1969)

—— *Les Églises et monastères des grands centres byzantins: Bithynie, Hellespont, Latros,*

Galésios, Trebizond, Athènes, Thessalonique, (Paris, Institut Français d'Études Byzantines, 1975)

Jarry, J., 'Hérésies et factions à Constantinople du Ve au VIe siècle' *Syria* 37 (1960), pp. 348–71

Kelly, J.N.D., *Early Christian Creeds*, 2nd edn (London, Longman, 1962)

Kennedy, H., *The early Abbasid Caliphate: a political history* (London, Croom Helm, 1981)

Kiselkov, V.S., *Zitieto na Sv. Teodosii T'rnovski kato istoriceski pametnik* (Sofia, 1926)

Klimkeit, H.J., *Manichaean art and calligraphy* (Leiden, Brill, 1982)

Krumbacher, K., *Geschichte der byzantinischen Literatur von Justinian bis zum Ende des oströmischen Reiches, 527-1453* (Munich, Beck, 1897)

Lambert, M., *Medieval heresy*, 2nd edn (London, Blackwell, 1992)

Laurent, J., *L'Arménie entre Byzance et l'Islam depuis la conquête arabe jusqu' en 886* (Paris, Fontemoing, 1919) (Bibliothèque des Écoles Françaises d'Athènes et de Rome, vol. 117)

Lemerle, P. 'Invasions et migrations dans les Balkans depuis le fin de l'époque romaine jusqu'au VIIIe siècle', *Revue historique* 211 (1954), pp. 265–308

—— 'Thomas le Slave', *T & M* 1 (1965), pp. 255–99

—— 'L'Histoire des Pauliciens d'Asie Mineure d'après les sources grecques', *T & M* 5 (1973), pp. 1–137

Leroy-Molinghen, A., 'Médecins, malades et remèdes dans les lettres de Théophylacte de Bulgarie', *Byzantion* 55 (1985), pp. 483–9

Lewis, B., *The Assassins* (London, Weidenfeld and Nicolson, 1967)

Lieu, S.N.C. *Manichaeism in the later Roman Empire and medieval China: a historical survey* (Manchester, Manchester University Press, 1985)

Lock, P., *The Franks in the Aegean, 1204–1500* (London, Longman, 1995)

Longnon, J., *Les Compagnons de Villehardouin: recherches sur les croisés de la quatrième croisade* (Geneva, Droz, 1978)

Loos, M., 'Certain aspects du Bogomilisme byzantin du 11e et 12e siècles', *Byzantinoslavica* (1967), pp. 39–53

—— *Dualist heresy in the Middle Ages* (Prague, Academia, 1974)

Magdalino, P. *The empire of Manuel I Komnenos, 1143–80* (Cambridge, Cambridge University Press, 1993)

Mariès, L., 'Frederick Cornwallis Conybeare (1856–1924). Notice critique et bibliographie critique', *Revue des études arméniennes* 6 (1926), pp. 185–332

Marsenger, E., *Der Matthaus-Kommentar des Theophylactos von Achrida* (Schneidwitz, 1924)

Meyendorff, J., *A study of Gregory Palamas*, tr. G. Lawrence (London, Faith Press, 1964)

BIBLIOGRAPHY

―――*Byzantine Hesychasm: historical, theological and social problems* (London, Variorum, 1974)

Moore, R.I., *The origins of European dissent*, 2nd edn (Oxford, Blackwell, 1985)

Morris, R., *Monks and laymen in Byzantium, 843-1118* (Cambridge, Cambridge University Press, 1995)

Mullett, M., *Theophylact through his letters: the two worlds of an exile bishop* (Ph.D. thesis, University of Birmingham, 1981)

Nelli, R., *La Philosophie du catharisme: le dualisme radical au XIIIe siècle* (Paris, Payot, 1975)

Nelson, J. L., 'Religion in "histoire totale": some recent work on medieval heresy and popular religion' *Religion*, 10 (1980), pp. 67–70

Nersessian, V., *The Tondrakian movement* (Allison Park, Pennsylvania, Pickwick Publications, 1988) (Princeton Theological Monograph series)

Nicol, D.M., *The last centuries of Byzantium* (Cambridge, Cambridge University Press, 1993)

―――'The Fourth Crusade and the Greek and Latin empires', in J. Hussey, ed., *CMH* IV (1) (1966), pp. 275–330

Obolensky, D., *The Bogomils: a study in Balkan neo-manichaeism* (Cambridge, Cambridge University Press, 1948)

―――'Papa Nicetas: a Byzantine dualist in the land of the Cathars', in *Okeanos: essays presented to Ihor Ševčenko on his sixtieth birthday*, Harvard Ukrainian Studies 7 (1983), pp. 489–500

―――*Six Byzantine portraits* (Oxford, Clarendon Press, 1988)

Oikonomides, N., *Les Listes de préséance byzantines des IX et X siècles* (Paris Le Monde Byzantine, Ed. du Centre Nationale des Recherches Scientifiques, 1972)

Papachryssanthou, D., 'La Date de la mort du *sébastocrator* Isaac Comnène, frère d'Alexis Ier et de quelques évènements contemporains', *REB* 21 (1963), pp. 250–5

Puech, H.-C, *Le Manichéisme: son fondateur, sa doctrine* (Paris, SAEP, 1949) (Civilisations du Sud)

Ramsay, W.M., *Cities and bishoprics of Phrygia: being an essay on the local history of Phrygia from the earliest times to the Turkish conquest* (Oxford, Clarendon Press, 1895)

Rigo, A., *Monaci esicasti e monaci bogomili* (Florence, Leo S. Olschki, 1989) (*Orientalia Veneziana 2*)

―――'Messalianismo = Bogomilismo: un equazione dell'eresiologia medievale bizantina', *OCP* 56 (1990), pp. 53–82

―――'Il processo del Bogomilo Basilio (1099 ca.): una riconsiderazione', *OCP*, 58 (1992), pp. 185–211

——'Il patriarca Germano II (1223–1240) e i Bogomili', *REB* 51 (1993), pp. 91–110

Rudolph, K., *Gnosis: the nature and history of gnosticism*, tr. ed. R. M. Wilson (San Francisco, Harper and Row, 1987)

Runciman, S., *The emperor Romanus Lecapenus and his reign: a study of tenth-century Byzantium* (Cambridge, Cambridge University Press, 1929, repr. 1988)

——'Some remarks on the image of Edessa', *Cambridge Historical Journal* 3, 3 (1931), pp. 238–52

——*The medieval Manichee: a study of the Christian dualist heresy* (Cambridge, Cambridge University Press, 1947)

Sanjek, F., *Les Chrétiens bosniaques et le mouvement Cathare XII–XV siècles* (Paris, Vander-Oyez; Louvain, Nauwelaerts, 1976)

Segal, R., *Edessa, the blessed city* (Oxford, Clarendon Press, 1970)

Semkov, G., 'Der Einfluss der Bogomilen auf die Katharer', *Saeculum* 32, 4 (1981), pp. 349–73

Shaban, M.A., *The Abbasid revolution* (London, Cambridge University Press, 1970)

Sharenkoff, V., *A study of Manichaeism in Bulgaria with special reference to the Bogomils* (New York, Carranza, 1927)

Skoulatos, B., *Les Personnages byzantins de l'Alexiade: analyse prosopographique et synthèse* (Louvain, Université de Louvain, Recueil des Traraux d'Histoire et de Philologie, series 6, vol. 20, 1980)

Soden, H. von, *Die Schriften des Neuen Testaments* (Göttingen, Vandenhoeck & Ruprecht, 1911)

Söderberg, H., *La Religion des Cathares: études sur le Gnosticisme de la basse antiquité et du Moyen Âge* (Uppsala, Almqvist & Wiksell, 1949, repr. New York, AMB Press, 1978)

Soulis, G.C., 'The legacy of Cyril and Methodius to the Southern Slavs', *DOP* 19 (1965), pp. 21–43

Starr, J., 'An Eastern Christian sect: the Athinganoi', *Harvard Theological Review* 29 (1936), pp. 93–106

Stoyanov, Y., *The hidden tradition in Europe* (London, Arkana, Penguin Books, 1994)

Ter Mkrttschian, K., 'Die Thondrakier in unseren Tage', *Zeitschrift für Kirchengeschichte* 16 (1896), pp. 253–76

Thallóczy, L. von, 'Bruchstücken aus dem Geschichte der nordwestlichen Balkanlander, V: Beiträge zur kenntnis der Bogomilenlehre', *Wissenschaftliche Mitteilungen aus Bosnien und der Hercegovina, von Bosnisch-Hercegovinischen Landesmuseum in Sarajevo* 3 (Vienna, 1895), pp. 360–71

Thompson, S., *Motif-index of folk literature: a classification of narrative elements in folk-*

tales, ballads, myths, fables, medieval romances, exempla, fabliaux, jest books and local legends (Copenhagen, Rosenkilde and Bagger, 1955–8)

Thouzellier, C., *Catharisme et Valdéisme en Languedoc à la fin du XIIe et au début du XIIIe siècle* (Paris, Presses Universitaires de France, 1966)

Toumanoff, G., *Studies in Christian Caucasian history* (Washington, DC, Georgetown University Press, 1963)

Tournebize, Fr. *Histoire politique et religieuse de l'Arménie* ((Paris, Librairie Alphonse Picard et Fils, 1910)

Vlasto, A.P., *The entry of the Slavs into Christendom: an introduction to the medieval history of the Slavs* (Cambridge, Cambridge University Press, 1970)

Whittow, M., *The making of orthodox Byzantium, 600-1025* (Basingstoke, Macmillan, 1966)

Widengren, G., *Mani and Manichaeism*, tr. Ch. Kessler, revised by the author (London, Weidenfeld and Nicolson, 1965)

Yovkov, M., *The Pavlikians and the Pavlikian towns and villages in the Bulgarian lands in the fifteenth to eighteenth centuries* (Sofia, Kliment Ohridski University Press, 1991) Bulgarian with an English summary

Zaehner, R.C., *The dawn and twilight of Zoroastrianism* (London, Weidenfeld and Nicolson, 1961)

Zaehner, R.C., *Zurvan: a Zoroastrian dilemma* (Oxford, Clarendon Press, 1955)

INDEX

Abgar, king of Edessa (1st century) 162, 246
abjuration formulae
 Paulicians 6, 102–10
 Bogomils 142, 207–10
Acmonia 32, 142–3, 159–60
Adoptionists *see* Paulinians
Adrian Comnenus, Orthodox archbishop of Bulgaria 216–20
Alexander the blacksmith, heretic 262
Amorium, forty-two martyrs of 62–5
Ananias of Narek, Armenian theologian 293
Anna Comnena, historian 24, 37–8, 43, 166–71, 175–80, 232 n.12
Antichrist 28–9, 132, 143, 151
Aphrigij, heretic 262
Apocryphal writings, Old Slavonic translations of 31
Apulia 22–3
Argaoun, Paulician stronghold 20–1, 62, 90–1
Ark'weli, Tondrakian centre 295
Armenia 4, 5, 8, 10, 12, 13, 17, 155–7, 163–4, 292–7
Armenian church 4, 11, 35
 Catholicus John I 292
 Catholicus John IV of Ojun 14
 Catholicus John V 293
 Catholicus Luke 295
 Catholicus Nerses III 14, 293
Armenian rulers
 Smbat I 293
Armenians, in Thrace 57–8
Arsamosata 7, 10, 75–6
Artavasdus, Byzantine rebel leader 16

Astatoi, Paulician supporters 20, 90
Athingani, heretical Byzantine sect 59 and n.1, 60–1, 90 n.67
Avdin, heretic 262

Baldwin I, Latin emperor of Constantinople 259–60
Bartholomew of Carcassonne, vicar of the Bogomil bishop of Bosnia 48, 263–4
Basil, St, Doctor of the Church 121, 124, 155 n.53, 229
Basilides, Gnostic theologian 8, 77
Belyatovo, Paulician fortress 24, 168
Bernard, Archbishop of Split 47, 254–7
Berrhoea, Bogomils at 53, 282
Bogomil beliefs
 absolute dualism 44–5, 48–50, 54, 226–7, 263, 284
 alleged political radicalism 132
 angel Amen, the 135
 apocryphal writings used by 45
 Archangel Michael equated with Jesus 186, 206
 ascetic way of life 27–8, 30, 32–3, 100, 116, 128, 136–7, 158–9, 175, 193–4, 198, 211–12, 241–2, 270, 272
 baptism with water rejected 129–30, 138, 143, 160–1, 189–90, 214
 Biblical exegesis 194–5
  Commentary on St Matthew's gospel 195–203
  Pentateuch 187–8
 Blessed Virgin Mary 123–4, 143, 144 n.10, 192, 253–4, 261

319

INDEX

bodily resurrection rejected 52, 144–5, 192
canon of scripture 27–8, 38–9, 120, 123, 125, 153–4, 182, 191–2, 219, 221 n.5, 240–1, 261–2, 271, 273, 286–7
catechism 39, 194, 204–7, 211
church buildings redundant 138, 143, 176, 190–1, 262, 271, 287
confession of sins 28, 132–3
creation myths 109 and n.18, 152–3, 184–5, 204–7
Eucharist 27, 52, 119–20, 135, 139, 143, 161, 176, 190, 241–5, 262, 273, 284
Holy cross, aversion from 52, 117–19, 135, 138, 143, 161, 178, 189, 247–9, 262, 270–1, 273, 280, 284
Holy Trinity 182–3, 193, 206, 211, 287
icons rejected 52, 117, 124–5, 136, 188, 245–7, 262, 268–9, 273, 281, 284, 287
initiation of the dying 55, 287
initiation rite 33, 139, 147, 149, 208, 218, 286
Jesus Christ 28, 52, 125, 130, 135, 186–7, 206, 253–4, 261–2, 281, 287
life after death 153
liturgies, traditional, hostility to 120–1, 137–8
Lord's prayer, use of 28, 33, 40, 52, 130, 138, 151, 161–2, 191, 262, 276, 279–80, 287
moderate dualism 26–7, 42–5, 48–50, 118, 126–7, 135, 143, 151–2, 183–5, 211, 227–8, 254, 261, 263, 270, 272–3
ordained priesthood, rejection of 121–2, 161, 262
refusal to swear oaths 46, 234, 237–40, *contra* 284

relics, rejection of 117–18, 190–1
Ritual 33, 161, 289
St John the Baptist reviled 262
saints not honoured 155, 161, 188, 287, *contra* 188
sex equality 28, 133
willingness to conform to Orthodoxy 28, 34, 161, 208, 274
Bogomil churches
  Bosnia (Sclavonia) 47, 49–51, 250, 253–9, 263–6, 275–8
  Bulgaria 43–5, 50–1, 54, 250, 252–4, 266–7, 275
  Constantinople (Greek) 44–6, 49–51, 53, 175–80, 252, 275
  Constantinople (Latin) 49–50, 275
  Dalmatia 45, 47, 252, 254–6
  Dragovitia/Drugonthia 43–5, 50–1, 54, 226 n.4, 250, 252–3, 275
  Melenguia 45, 50, 252
  Philadelphia in Romania 49–51, 275
Bogomil hierarchy
  Apostles 37, 147, 175
  Bishops 44, 48, 250–3, 253 n.11, 254, 264 and n.13
  Elder sons 44, 254
  Younger sons 44
Bogomil leaders
  Aristodius of Jadera 255–6
  Basil the doctor 37–9, 43, 49, 135 n.2, 175–207 *passim*, 210, 262
  Bogomil, *pop* 27, 30, 36, 116, 135, 261–2
    Michael, his disciple 262
  Cyril Bosota 54, 283–5
    Stefan the priest, his disciple 284
  David the monk 281
  Dobri 262
  George of Larissa 53, 281
  Irene (Porine), nun of Thessalonica 53, 283

INDEX

Job the monk 281
John Tzurillas 32–3, 35, 47, 153 and n.43, 159–60
Joseph the Cretan 281
Luke 262
Mandelej of Radobol 262
Mark Mesopotamites 42, 229–32
Matthew of Jadera 255–6
Moses the Bogomil 262
Moses the painter 281
Nicetas (Niquinta), *papa* of Constantinople 43–5, 47, 49, 50, 250–2, 263
Peter of Cappadocia, *dedec* of Sofia 45, 146 n.16, 262
Petracius of Bulgaria 45, 250, 252–3
Priors of 'Christians' of Bosnia 257–9
Stephen 262
Symeon, Bishop of Dragovitia 44–5, 252, 253 and n.11
Theodore 262
Bogomils
  accused of licentiousness 54, 228, 286
  accused of Satanism 34, 42–3, 146–51, 153, 162–3, 191, 208, 227–32, 272–3, 287
  alleged blasphemous conduct of 35, 148–9, 209
  conversion to Islam controversial 55
  dressed like monks 144, 146, 175, 193, 211
  influenced by Paulicians 35, 38, 44, 163 n.16
  persecution of 27–8, 39, 99, 125, 175–80, 203, 215, 223, 285
  statistics 50–1, 275
Bolino-Polje, agreement of 47–8, 257–9
Bosnia, Catholic Church in 48, 51–2, 265–6, 276–7
  Rulers of
    Kulin 47, 255–9
    Stefan Kotromanić 51, 277–8

Stephen Thomas 289
Bukovič, Bogomils at 52
Bulgaria / Bulgars 17, 23–31 *passim*, 36, 49, 114–34 *passim*, 166
  Orthodox Church of 25, 27, 48–9, 265
  Pagan folklore in 261
  Paulician mission to 25, 31, 66
Bulgarian rulers
  Boril 48, 260–2
  Boris 25, 31, 66
  John Alexander 282, 284–5
  John Asen II 49, 265–7
  Kalojan/Ioannitsa 48, 259–60
  Krum 59–60
  Peter 26–7, 36, 98, 113–14, 116, 135
  Samuel 31, 37
  Symeon 26
Byzantine emperors
  Alexius I 23–4, 37–9, 50, 166–71, 175–81, 203, 211, 262
  Andronicus II 52
  Andronicus III 278
  Basil I 6, 22, 66, 92, 96–7
  Basil II 31, 36–7, 142, 159
  Constans II 1, 8, 10, 11 n.36, 12, 76 and n.28
  Constantine IV 12
  Constantine V 17, 38, 57–60, 188, 268
  Constantine VIII 142, 159
  Constantine IX 23, 145 n.14, 293–4
  Irene 19, 58, 60, 86
  John I Tzimisces 23, 31, 114, 169
  John II 40, 175, 219, 222
  John III Vatatzes 267
  John VI Cantacuzenus 278, 282
  Justinian I 2, 4, 13 n.42, 99 n.4, 239
  Justinian II 13, 79–80
  Leo III 5–17, 80–1, 104
  Leo V 19, 61, 90
  Leo VI 22, 92, 97
  Manuel I 24, 40–1, 46, 215, 222–5, 232–4, 240, 250

321

INDEX

Michael I 19, 59–61, 90
Michael II 21, 61
Michael III 22, 62, 65
Michael VIII 52
Nicephorus I 19, 59
Romanus I Lecapenus 26, 98, 247
Romanus III Argyrus 142, 145 n.14, 159
Theodora, Regent 21, 62–3
Theophilus 21, 62, 86
Byzantine themes
Anatolikon 21
Armeniakon 5, 169
Kibbyrrhaiot 32, 34, 113, 157
Mesopotamian 293–4
Opsikion 32, 34, 157, 159
Thrakesion 34

Callinice the Manichaean 7, 8, 14 n.44, 75–6, 93, 101
Callistus, governor of Colonea 22, 62–5
Cappadocian bishops, tried for heresy 40, 215–19, 221
Caspian Albania, Orthodox church of 14
Cathar council of Saint-Félix 43–4, 250–2
Cathar *Rituals* 33, 55, 289–91
Cathars 1, 43–6, 51 n.166, 55, 151 n. 35, 277, 287
  alleged migration to Bosnia 51, 276–8
  of Lombardy 250, 275
    Belesmanza, Bishop of absolute dualists 275
    Mark, first Bishop 251–3
    Nazarius, Bishop of Concorezzo 253–4
  of southern France 250–2, 263–4, 275
Cedolini, Peter, Apostolic Visitor 24
Church Councils
  Chalcedon (451) 4
  Dvin (555) 14, 292–3
  Constantinople, *in Trullo* (692) 5

Constantinople (1351) 54
Ephesus (431) 81 n.46
Nicaea I (325) 98, 115
Nicaea II (787) 19, 188 n.47
Sahapivan (447) 292
Trnovo (*c.* 1350, *c.* 1360) 54, 284–5
Clement of Ochrida, St 31
Colonea 11–13, 21, 62–3, 77–9, 87
Conrad of Porto, Cardinal 48, 263–4
Constantine Chrysomallus, alleged heretic 40, 148 n.20, 212–14
Constantine Comnenus, Great Drungarius 216–20, 222
Constantine of Mananalis *see* Paulician, *didaskaloi*
Constantinople 7, 19, 34, 57, 59–60
  Church of St Alexius 212
  Holy synod of 52, 166
  Holy Wisdom (Haghia Sophia), cathedral of 39, 233–4, 243–4, 280
  Latin empire of 46, 49, 52, 259–60, 267
    Bogomils in 272–4
  Orthodox patriarchs of
    Anastasius 15–16 and n.52, 80 and n.45, 81
    Callistus I 53–4, 282–5
    Cosmas I, of Jerusalem 36, 48, 165–6, 260
    Cosmas II, Atticus 41, 219, 222–5
    Germanus II 49–50, 267–74
    John Xiphilinus 36, 210
    Leo II Stypes 40, 212–14
    Methodius I 6, 21
    Michael I Cerularius 35 n.109
    Michael II 40, 215–21
    Nicephorus 19, 58, 61, 90 n. 67
    Nicholas III Grammaticus 175–6
    Photius 6, 21, 22 n.76, 65, 111 n.5, 171
    Theodotus II 233

INDEX

Theophylact Lecapenus 26, 98–102, 114
Paulicians in 60
Periblepton monastery 220
  Bogomils in 145–63 *passim*
Cosmas the priest, Bulgarian theologian 27–32, 38, 114–34, 158 n.64
Crusade
  Albigensian 48
  First 23
  Fourth 24, 46–7, 259
Crusades, against Bosnia and Bulgaria 48–9, 265–7
Cumans 168, 170
Cyril of Jerusalem, St, theologian 74 and n.20

Demonology, Byzantine 42–3, 146, 177, 185, 227–32
Diblatius, a Bogomil 178
Diocletian, Roman emperor, anti-Manichaean laws of 75 n.27
Dynamis, a Gnostic book 109 and n.19

Eclogues, The, law-code 15
Elasson, Bogomils at 42, 230–1
Eleutherius of Paphagonia, Byzantine heretic 32
Ephesus 22–3
Epirus, Despotate of 46, 49, 267
Epode see Bogomil beliefs, initiation rite
Episparis in Phanaroia, Paulician centre 7, 13, 14 n. 44, 16, 18, 75, 80–2, 93
Euchaita, Paulicians at 112
Euthymius, Bulgarian patriarch of Trnovo 225–7
Euthymius, monk of the Gerocomeion monastery 213
Euthymius of the Periblepton, Byzantine polemicist 23, 32–5, 38, 43, 142–64, 289–90
Euthymius Zigabenus, Byzantine theologian 37–9, 43–4, 65, 171–4, 177, 180–207, 210, 254, 289

Genesius, Byzantine historian 96
Geoffrey de Villehardouin, historian 259–60
George Maniakes, Byzantine general 23
George Pamphilus, *proedros* 213–14
George Tornikes, Byzantine theologian 233–4
Gnosticism 1–3, 228
Gnostic writings 34
Gregory Akindynus, Byzantine theologian 53
Gregory Magister, Byzantine official 293–5
Gregory of Sinai, St, Hesychast 282
Gregory Palamas, St, Hesychast 52–4, 278–82

Hesychasm 53–4, 278, 282
Hieron, monastery of St Nicholas at 212–14
Hilarion of Moglena, St 24, 225–7
Hugh Eteriano, Pisan theologian 46, 50, 234–50
Hungary 47, 51, 255, 265–7
  rulers
    Andrew II 48, 263
    Bela IV 49, 266–7
    Imre 256–7, 259

Iberia (Georgia), kingdom of 156–7
iconoclasm, iconoclasts 14, 15, 17, 19, 21 57–8, 134, 268 n.1
Inquisition, Papal 49, 253–4, 277–8
Isaac, *Sebastocrator*, brother of Alexius I 38, 175–6
Isaac, *Sebastocrator*, brother of Manuel I 41, 220, 222, 224

Jacobites, schismatic Eastern Christians 112, 140 n.8, 169
Jerusalem, pilgrimage to 145, 163
John, son of Callinice 7, 14 n.44, 63, 75–6, 93, 101, 106

323

INDEX

John Chrysostom, St, Doctor of the church 38, 121, 146, 155 n.53, 192 and n.64, 235, 243
John of Casamaris, papal legate 257–9
John of Damascus, St, Church Father 137 n.10, 157–8
John Scylitzes, Byzantine historian 97, 165
John Tzetzes 41, 222, 224–5
John the Exarch, Bulgarian scholar 26, 29

Kalocsa, Archbishops of, Primates of Hungary 259, 265–6
Kephalaia, Manichaean book 208
Keramidion (Holy tile) of Edessa 162 and n.87, 247
Key of Truth, The, Tondrakian service-book 295–7
   Protestant influence on 296
Kudugeroi 55, 286 n.2, 287

Larissa 36, 165
Lazarus of Trnovo, Adamite 54, 283–5
Lazarus the wonder-worker, St 141–2
Leo the Tuscan 234
Luke, Evangelist and icon-painter 162 and n.88
Lycopetrus (Peter the Wolf), heresiarch 19, 34–5, 136–7, 146, 154–8, 163, 209

Macarius of Pelecete, St 20, 61–2
Macedonia, Bogomils of 53
Macedonians, heretical sect 243–4
Mananalis, Paulician centre 10, 12, 16, 76, 81
Mandylion of Edessa 162 and n.87, 246–7
Mani, founder of Manichaeanism 1–2, 7, 68, 74, 77 and n.33, 93, 95, 101, 107, 148 n.21, 154, 158, 175 n.4, 227
Manichaean books 74, 77, 208

Manichaeism, Manichaeans 1–4, 7, 8, 12, 13 n.42, 15, 29, 75–6, 93
   in Byzantium identified with Paulicians 66
   in Middle Ages 29–30
Marcion, heresiarch 3
Marcionists 207
Melitene 57–8
   Emir of 20–2, 62, 90 and n.70, 91
Messalianism, fourth-century heresy 30, 174, 181 n.4, 189, 214 n.4, 292
   equated with Bogomilism 136 and n.6, 143 and n.8, 209
Michael Douceianus, Catepan of Bari 139–40
Michael Psellus 41, 227
Miletus, dualist heretics at 23, 113
Miroslav of Hum 256
Moglena, diocese of
   Armenians in 225
   Bogomils in 41, 225–7
   Paulicians in 225–7
Mongols 49, 265
Montanists, heretical sect 77, 88 n.63, 112
   Leo the Montanist 88–9
Montanus, heresiarch 154, 158
Mount Athos, Bogomil presence on 52–4, 278, 281–3
Mount Galesius, monastery of 141–2
   Paulicians at 141–2
Mount Papikion/Patikion, monastery of 52, 278–81
   Bogomils nearby 279–81

Nahum of Ochrida, St 31
Nicaea 22, 49
   Byzantine empire of 46, 49–50, 267
   Bogomils in 268–71
   Eustathius, Metropolitan of 170 and n.11
Nicephorus Bryennius, Caesar and historian 170, 175

Nicephorus Gregoras, historian 53, 281–2
Nicephorus Phocas the Elder, general 22, 97
Nicetas Choniates, historian 224
Nicholas of Methone, *Dialogue concerning demons* 41–3, 227–33
Niphon, monk, tried for heresy 40–1, 219–24
Niphon, *Protos* of Mount Athos 53
Nomocanon 215
Normans of Southern Italy 23–4, 36–7, 139–40, 167
Novatians, separated church of 11, 111

Panormus, Bogomils of 135
Patarenes/Paterenes, Italian name for Bogomils 46, 55, 234–50, 255
Patzinaks 23–4, 36–7, 165–6, 168–9
Paul, St, apostle 11–13, 24, 88, 158
Paul, son of Callinice 7, 14 n.44, 63, 75–6, 93, 101, 106–8
Paulician
 beliefs
  absolute dualism 6–7, 72, 94, 103, 106, 108–9, 172, 226–7
  angel, Amen 107, 135
  asceticism, lack of 10
  baptism 9, 10, 16, 24, 80, 95, 106, 108, 110
  Blessed Virgin Mary 9, 16, 69, 72, 80–1, 94, 103, 106, 108
  canon of scripture 8, 24, 68, 69 and n.10, 73–7, 93, 95–6, 104, 174
  Christ's church 9, 95, 106
  Eucharist 9, 16, 72, 80, 94–5, 103, 106–7
  exegesis 9, 68, 80–1, 84–5, 95, 172–3
  fasting 106, 108
  Holy Cross 9, 16, 24, 73, 80, 95, 104, 106, 108
  Holy Trinity 94, 103
  icons 24, 106, 108
  Jesus Christ 9, 69, 72, 107–9
  oath-taking 107
  saints and angels 9, 95
 churches
  Achaia-Mananalis 17, 88, 93, 105–6
  Colossae-Argaoun 20, 88, 94, 105–6
  Corinth 11, 88
  Ephesus-Mamistra 20, 88, 105–6
  Laodicea-Cynochorion 19, 20, 88, 90, 94, 105–6
  Macedonia-Cibossa 12–14, 77–80, 88, 93, 105–6
  Philippi-Antioch-in-Pisidia 18, 32, 88, 94, 105–6
 didaskaloi 9–10
  Baanes (*or* Vahan) the Foul 18–19, 21, 83, 89–90, 93, 101, 104–5, 294
  Constantine-Silvanus of Mananalis 1, 8–14, 24, 76–8, 88, 93, 101, 104–5, 109
  Genesius (Gegnesius)-Timothy 13–17, 57, 80–1, 88, 93, 101, 104–5, 109
  Joseph-Epaphroditus 17–18, 81–3, 88, 93, 101, 104–5, 109
  Sergius-Tychicus 5, 11, 17–22, 35, 83–91, 93, 101, 104–5, 109, 137, 154, 163–4
  Symeon-Titus 12–13, 78–80, 93, 101, 104–5
  Zacharias 17–18, 81–2, 93, 101, 104–5
 folklore
  Arzeberius the dog of Sergius-Tychicus 35, 164
 leaders
  Carbeas 21–2, 64, 91, 106
  Chrysocheir 6, 22 and n.76, 92, 96–7, 106
  Couleon 167, 170–1

INDEX

Cousinus 170–1
Diaconitzes 22, 97
Justus son of Constantine 13, 78–9
Lacas 165
Paul (*c.* 700) 7, 13–14, 80, 101
Pholos 170–1
Theodore, son of Paul 13–14, 80, 101
Traulos 24, 168
Xantas 167
notaries 10, 95, 105 and n.15
synekdemoi 9–10, 21, 95
  Basileius 22, 91–2, 104
  Canacharis 91, 104
  John Aoratus 91, 104
  Michael 91, 104
  Theodotus 21, 90–1, 104
  Zosimus 22, 91–2, 104
Paulicians
  accused of licentiousness 96, 107, 109
  alleged occasional conformity to Orthodoxy 94
  persecuted by Byzantines 12–13, 19–22, 61–5, 78–80, 90 n.67, 167–8, 170–1
  under Ottoman rule 24–5
Paulician warriors 19–24, 96–7, 139–40, 166–71
  converts from Byzantine army 58
  in Muslim armies 23
Paulician writings
  commentary on St Matthew's Gospel attributed to Sergius 137
  epistles of Sergius-Tychicus 73, 86–9, 104
Paulinians, Paulians (Adoptionists) 7, 26, 99, 292–3, 295–7
Paul of Latrus, St 113
Paul of Samosata (third century), heresiarch 7, 26, 68, 75, 108–9, 154, 158, 292, 297
Paul of Taron, Armenian scholar 294

Paylikeank, Armenian Paulicians 7, 14
Peter, abbot of St Athenagoras 213–14
Peter of Sicily, Byzantine theologian 5–22 *passim*, 25–6, 57, 63, 65–96, 102, 171, 293
Peter the Higoumenos *see* Peter of Sicily
Philippopolis
  Armenians at 169
  Bogomils at 169
  Paulician settlement at 23–4, 41, 114, 169–71, 175, 259–60
Philotheus, metropolitan of Euchaita 110–12
Photin, heretic 262
Phundagiagitae, a name for Bogomils 32, 143–64 *passim*
'Pope of the heretics' 48, 263–4
Popes
  Gregory IX 48–9, 265–7
  Honorius III 48, 263–4
  Innocent III 47–8, 254–9
  Innocent IV 51, 276
  John XXII 51, 276–8

Rainier Sacconi, papal inquisitor 49–51, 253–4, 275
Renier de Trit, Duke of Philippopolis 259–60
'Revelation of St Peter', allegedly read by Bogomils 34, 147 and n.17
Ritual of Radoslav the Christian 33, 289–91
Robert Guiscard, Duke of Apulia 167

St Sabas, Jerusalem, monastery of 142
Samael/Satanael, Bogomil names for the Devil 180 n.3
Secret Book of St John, Bogomil apocryphon 253–4
Simon Magus, heresiarch 34, 154

INDEX

Smyrna, Bogomils at 159
Socrates the Scholastic, church historian 74 and n.21
Soterichus Panteugenus, Orthodox Patriarch of Antioch 233–4
Split, Bogomils in 254–6
Stephen Dušan, Tsar of Serbia 53
Symeon, Archbishop of Thessalonica 55, 286–7
Symeon the New Theologian, St, mystic 40, 53, 212
Synodikon of Orthodoxy 21, 35 n.112, 39–40, 42, 134–9, 207, 209–10
Synodikon of Tsar Boril 48, 166, 260–2

Tavium 19, 83
Tefrice, Paulician headquarters 7, 19–23, 25, 65–6, 91–2, 97, 293
Thebes 42, 229 n.6
Theodore, Bishop of Andida, liturgical scholar 276
Theodore, Metropolitan of Nicaea 110–12
Theodore Balsamon, Byzantine canon lawyer 40, 45, 215
Theodore of Studium, St 20, 60–1
Theodore II, Orthodox Patriarch of Antioch 23, 114
Theodosiopolis 17, 57–8
Theodosius of Trnovo, Patriarch of Bulgaria 282–3
Theodosius of Trnovo, St 53–4, 282–5
Theophanes, Byzantine historian 57, 59–61, 90 n.67
Theophylact of Ochrida, Archbishop of Bulgaria 36–7

Thessalonica, Bogomils at 53, 55, 226 n.4, 282–3, 286–7
Thomas, Archbishop of Neocaesarea 20, 90
Thomas, Archdeacon of Split 47, 254–6
Thomas the Slav, Byzantine rebel leader 20
Thrace
  Bogomils in 53
  Paulicians in 17, 25, 57, 169
Tondrakian leaders
  Lazarus the blind 293
  Smbat the wolf 293–5
Tondrakians 292–7
Topax, Bogomil name for the Devil 287
Turks
  Ottoman 52, 55, 286
  Seljuks 36–7
Tyana, church province of 216–19
Tzanion of Nicopolis, assassin 91, 104

Vahagun, Yovhannes, writer of *The Key of Truth* 295–6
Valentinus, Gnostic theologian 8, 77
Venetian empire 46, 52, 286
Vidin, Bogomils in 54–5
Vision of Isaiah, Gnostic book read by Bogomils 39, 137
Vukan, King of Zeta 255–6

William of Apulia, historian 140

Zonaras, Byzantine historian 38, 62–3, 65, 114, 166 n.1
Zoroastrianism 1, 8
Zurvanism 29, 31